THE Jack Brabham Story

The Jack Brabham Story

SIR JACK BRABHAM OBE WITH DOUG NYE
FOREWORD BY SIR STIRLING MOSS OBE FIE

PAVILION

ADDITIONAL CAPTIONS

PAGE 1
Triple World Champion's crash helmet—1966.

PAGE 2
"…How could such a nice bloke out of a car grow such horns and a tail inside one…"—Sir Stirling Moss, 2004.

PAGE 3
The Model Repco Brabham BT19 commissioned by Esso in recognition of the team's double World Championship titles, 1966.

PAGE 4
The midget "speedcar" with which the winning began, owned and restored 2003 by Andrew Halliday.

PAGE 5
The favoured tinted goggles.

ENDPAPERS
The scary bridge, Longford, Tasmania, 1965—"Yes, you're right. We must have been nuts!"—Sir Jack Brabham, 2003.

First published in Great Britain in 2004 by
PAVILION BOOKS LIMITED

An imprint of Chrysalis Books Group plc

The Chrysalis Building, Bramley Road
London W10 6SP United Kingdom
www.chrysalisbooks.co.uk

Text © Salamander Books Limited
Design and layout © Salamander Books Limited
For picture acknowledgements see p.256

Project Editor: Antony Shaw
Assistant Editor: Katherine Edelston
Designers: John Heritage, Cara Hamilton
Production: Don Campaniello
Colour Reproduction: Mission Productions Limited

All rights reserved. No part of this book may be reproduced, stored in a retrieval system or transmitted in any form or by any means, electronic, mechanical, photocopying, recording or otherwise, without the prior permission of the copyright holder.

A CIP catalogue record for the book is available from the British Library

ISBN 1 86205 651 X

Printed in Singapore

This book can be ordered direct from the publisher.
Please contact the marketing Department. But try your bookshop first.

Note: Most of my life has been spent around racing cars, so nearly all of what follows revolves around them. But it's not intended to be the exhaustive listing of every single race I ever drove, though it covers every one I thought important. It is the story essentially of the factors which shaped my life in racing, and of the way my twenty-three year frontline driving career unfolded. I hope you enjoy reading it. Most of the time I certainly enjoyed living it—Sir Jack Brabham, 2004.

Contents

Foreword	6
Introduction	8
Part 1 The Early Years	**16**
Chapter 1 Schoolboy to Midget Racer	18
Chapter 2 Road Racing and the *Redex Special*	34
Part 2 An Australian in Europe	**46**
Chapter 3 First Steps, First Mistakes!	48
Chapter 4 Cooper Works Driver	58
Monaco 1957	62
Chapter 5 Tussle for the World Title	78
Chapter 6 Tasman Interlude	102
Chapter 7 Double World Champion	110
Sporty Cars in America	124
Chapter 8 Indy and All That	128
Chapter 9 Cooper On The Cliff	138
Part 3 Brabham Racing Organisation	**146**
Chapter 10 A Winning Partnership	148
Chapter 11 Championship Challengers	168
Chapter 12 Tasman Interlude II	184
Chapter 13 Champions of the World	190
Chapter 14 The Season of '67	206
Formula Two Was Fun 1964–1970	212
Chapter 15 Goodbye Repco	216
Chapter 16 Hello Ford	226
Sports–Racing Swansong	236
Chapter 17 Final Victory–Final Season	238
Chapter 18 Reflections and Later Life	248
Index	254
Acknowledgements	256

BP
START - FINISH
COR
PIT ENTRANCE
By courtesy of MELFORD MOTORS
COOPER

FOREWORD

OUR LATE FRIEND DENIS JENKINSON christened Jack Brabham "The Nut-Brown Australian". I first saw his Aussie tan glaring over the aero screen of a terrible old Cooper-Alta at Goodwood on Easter Monday, 1955. Through the following eight seasons—until my frontline career ended in the corresponding Goodwood meeting of 1962, he and I must have driven literally thousands of racing miles, many of them nose-to-tail or wheel-to-wheel, in events both major and minor, all over the world. Occasionally we co-drove the same car—as in 1958 when we won the Nürburgring 1,000kms together in a works Aston Martin sports car—and I came to value Jack highly as a fellow driver, sportsman, and friend.

On track he was always the toughest of tough competitors, tough sometimes to the point at which I'd wonder how could such a nice bloke out of a car grow such horns and a tail inside one! You'd always know when Jack was on a charge because he'd crouch down and almost disappear within the cockpit. Tail-out, broadsiding, showering me with gravel and tuffets from the verge—dear me, you could take the Aussie out of the dirt-tracks, but you couldn't take the dirt-tracks out of the Aussie.

But the greater side of Jack's character was always his natural sportsmanship.

I vividly recall the 1959 New Zealand Grand Prix when my Rob Walker Cooper broke a drive-shaft in the preliminary race and we had no replacement, so I'd have to miss the main event. Jack immediately offered us his spare, despite knowing darned well I was perhaps the only man capable of beating him there. He made the offer because he wanted that Grand Prix to be a real race, a real crowd-pleaser, and—perhaps—to measure himself again against me. He had a 2.2-litre Climax engine in his Cooper, I had a 2.1-litre unit in mine, and thanks to his sporting generosity pre-race, I won—and he finished second. I thanked him for the loan—and he responded that it had been pretty unsporting of me still to beat him. He laughed as he said it, and meant it, because in our day we still raced for fun.

Seriously, if you ever raced against Jack you'd really know you'd been in a race. He was everything we Poms have come to expect of a great Australian sportsman—play the game as if your life depends on it, no quarter asked, and absolutely none given. To his natural driving ability he added a deeper technical understanding of his cars than any of us could match, and he was absolutely expert in setting them up just as he wanted.

In the period we raced together, his combined armoury of talents was truly formidable and, as his career continued after my own enforced retirement, I really enjoyed his continued success in almost every kind of car—Formula 1, Formula 2, Tasman Formula, sports, and saloon alike. Even in his final frontline season, 1970, he could still win and lead Grands Prix at the age of 44. I could only think what battles we might have had together, because I'd been only 32 when I'd had to retire.

We've kept in regular touch ever since around both the contemporary and historic racing scenes, and it's a great pleasure now to pen this foreword to what I'm sure will be an enjoyable and illuminating book as "The Nut-Brown Australian" reveals some of his secrets....

Stirling Moss.

SIR STIRLING MOSS OBE FIE

LEFT
Warriors on the startline, Albert Park, Melbourne, 1958—Stirling Moss in pole position in Rob Walker's Cooper-Climax, studies his main rival, Jack Brabham, in the works-liveried sister car. They are poised to do battle...another one of so very many, captured in this wonderful shot from David Blanch's superb Autopics collection.

INTRODUCTION

I drove rear-engined Cooper cars from 1955 to 1961 and they certainly brought me great success. By far the best of them was the "Lowline", the 2½-litre Climax 4-cylinder engined car we hurriedly designed and built between the first two Grand Prix races of the 1960 season, and which then carried me to five consecutive race wins in the Dutch, Belgian, French, British, and Portuguese GPs, and my second consecutive title as World Champion Driver.

When Australian racing driver Sir Jack Brabham first really made his mark upon motor racing in Britain and Europe during the late 1950s, motor racing writer Denis Jenkinson—known to generations of *Motor Sport* magazine readers as that journal's Continental Correspondent—nicknamed him "The Nut-Brown Australian".

When he left the Cooper Car Company Team with two Drivers' World Championship titles under his belt at the end of 1961, and founded his own racing organisation, his mechanics there called him "The Guv'nor".

When he became the first racing driver ever to score World Championship points in a car bearing his own name, and then became the first not only to win Grand Prix races but also both the Formula 1 Drivers' and Constructors' World Championship titles, the French press named him *"Le Grand Champion"*.

When he won the 1970 South African Grand Prix, and also lost both that year's Monaco and British Grands Prix only by being passed on the very last corner of each race, he crowned an extraordinarily successful frontline motor racing career which saw him retire at the top...still capable, in his day, of confronting the motor racing world's finest on equal terms, and of beating every one of them fair and square.

Sir Jack Brabham was an intensely practical, thoughtful and wily driver-cum-engineer who—in his 16 seasons of International racing—drove in 126 Formula 1 World Championship-qualifying Grands Prix, won 14 of them, was three-times World Champion Driver and—with his

RIGHT
Dapper Jack? Hardly, but—as he recalls, "I had to wear the cardy, my wife had gone to the trouble of knitting it for me. "Here's the 1959 and 1960 World Champion Driver, seated in his "Lowline" Cooper-Climax in the pits at Reims-Gueux, before the 1960 French Grand Prix, which he won hands-down, humbling the more powerful works Ferraris… something he always particularly relished.

business partner and car designer Ron Tauranac—twice took the honours as World Champion Formula 1 Constructor. He was the first of the modern drivers to build his own racing cars, the first to win a *Grande Epreuve* in a car bearing his own name, and the first to take the Championship in his own car.

In the process, this outwardly tough, silent, apparently secretive man operated in what was portrayed as a rather guarded, relatively publicity-shy manner. But his taciturnity combined with success left few people in any doubt; *nobody* in modern motor racing has been a brighter operator than "Black Jack" Brabham.

Sir Jack Brabham was born as a second-generation Australian, whose grandfather came from Twickenham in south-west London. His father, Tom Brabham, ran a grocery store outside Sydney, and Jack was an only child with a typically outdoor Australian up-bringing. Father was a keen motorist who taught Jack to drive when he was tall enough, using the family Chrysler and the grocery business' trucks. He left school at 15 and went to work in a garage, while studying engineering in the evenings.

In 1944, aged 18, he joined the Royal Australian Air Force and served for two years as ground crew before becoming a one-man motor repair and engineering business's in 1946. He met an American living in Sydney named Johnny Schonberg who raced midget "speedcars", and for 1947 helped build him a new racing chassis and then hand-crafted a new engine to power it.

Brabham took over their midget speedcar when Schonberg's wife persuaded the American to stop racing. He made his racing debut at Sydney's Parramatta Park Speedway. After only three nights racing he had acclimatised so well to the rough-and-tumble, gritty, dangerous world of speedcar racing that he won the feature event.

In his first racing season he went on to win the New South Wales Championship at Sydney Showground—a success he would repeat—and he continued to shine in this lucrative, noisy, rugged racing arena until one bleak night in Adelaide, when he lost the South Australian title as the midget's special engine literally exploded and caught fire.

It was the end of Brabham's exculsive midget racing, but in the meantime he had also tried his hand driving in a few competitive hill-climbs and had met an enthusiastic young engineer named Ron Tauranac who was building hill-climb specials at home with his brother Austin. These dry, taciturn characters were entirely kindred spirits to the young Sir Jack. He had tackled hill-climbing alongside them in the speedcar. As an incomer entering a clubbie world of imported sports cars and home-built Australian road racing specials, however, he was regarded as a threat from the hurly-burly dirt-track world, a professional from the quarter-mile oval tracks. Far worse, he was driving a vulgar little dirt-track racing midget, absolutely "not a proper car...".

Overcoming such bitter opposition from the conservative road racing purists, he promptly stormed to victory in their Australian Hill-Climb Championship. Their reception for such a "tearaway" from the dirt tracks was frosty, and when he was disqualified from the results because his speedcar had no front brakes one can appreciate how a certain amount of needle surfaced in his subsequent decision to acquire a Cooper–JAP 1100 (a "proper car") to take the road racers on at their own game. Brabham proved sufficiently successful to gain backing from RedeX, the fuel additive company. They

ABOVE
Sir Jack whooping down through the gearbox in his works-entered Lowline Cooper, entering *La Source* hairpin at Spa-Francorchamps in the ill-starred 1960 Belgian Grand Prix meeting. During practice there, two drivers—Stirling Moss and Mike Taylor—were seriously injured in high-speed crashes. During the Grand Prix itself two more—Alan Stacey and Chris Bristow—were killed. Jack's victory at record speed was overshadowed...but such human cost was inseparable from motor racing throughout his front-line career.

12 | THE JACK BRABHAM STORY

RIGHT
As much the well-trained and hugely experienced practical engineer as gifted racing driver, Sir Jack adjusting the front anti-roll bar on his 1966 World Championship-winning Repco Brabham. In this case, running on Goodyear racing tyres similarly designed and developed with tremendous input from the man himself (and using Esso fuel and lubricants) he became the first driver ever to win a premier-level Grand Prix driving a car bearing his own name, and then the first ever to win the Drivers' World Championship in one. Victory was no fluke… his all-round input had been immense.

helped him purchase a British-built Cooper-Bristol single-seater racing car. The Australian sporting authority then objected violently to RedeX advertising he painted on the car, and so Jack took it to New Zealand where he was very welcome as reigning Queensland and New South Wales Road Racing Champion.

He finished sixth with the car in the 1954 New Zealand Grand Prix, and returned there the following season when he met Dick Jeffrey, manager of the British Dunlop racing tyre division, and Dean Delamont, another English visitor, who was competitions manager of the Royal Automobile Club in London. They persuaded the young Australian to try his driving skills in Europe.

He sailed to Britain, leaving his wife and young son in Australia in case things did not work out. Selling his ingeniously developed *RedeX Special* he put his faith in a Cooper-Alta which was diabolically unreliable, but his spectacular dirt-track style immediately endeared him to the crowds at British circuits like Goodwood and Ibsley. He met the Coopers, father and son, and with their blessing built himself a rear-engined 2-litre Cooper-Bristol in which he made his World Championship debut in the 1955 British Grand Prix at Aintree.

Jack invested in a Maserati 250F Grand Prix car for the 1956 Formula 1 season. This proved a major mistake. In recovery he joined the Cooper works team as a F2 driver, and through 1957–1958 he took part in several World Championship races, competing in the 1½-litre Formula 2 class when there was one, or with stopgap-sized-1.9- and 2.2-litre engines as a hybrid F1 contender. More significantly, he invested his engineering experience and invention into the Cooper programme, with Ron Tauranac back home acting as a technical pen-pal and advisor, and together with John Cooper, they progressively developed a world-beating proposition.

By 1959 the little rear-engined works Coopers were running full 2½-litre Coventry Climax-made engines, and Jack Brabham with his forceful, crouching style developed on the Australian dirt-tracks won both the Monaco and British Grand Prix races. He accumulated sufficient points elsewhere to win the Drivers' Championship in dramatic style by pushing his out-of fuel car across the line in the deciding United States Grand Prix at Sebring in Florida.

The following 1960 season witnessed complete Brabham triumph. While he had really clinched the 1959

LEFT
Cornering his 1966 World Championship-winning Repco Brabham BT19 in the Mediterranean sun at Monaco—even this far into his glittering career Sir Jack still displayed the "Brabham crouch" which he had developed in his earliest motor racing days on the Australian cinder-tracks in the late 1940s and early '50s, when he found a faceful of cinders really hurt!

RIGHT
Triumphant partnership—Sir Jack with his business partner, fellow engineer and equally committed "Racer" Ron Tauranac and the 1967 centre-exhaust Repco Brabham BT24. Ron had become a customer of Sir Jack's tiny one-man machine-shop in their early days in Australian racing. Later as a technically adept pen pal he played a crucial role in the moves which elevated the works Cooper-Climax cars to Formula 1 greatness. From 1961 he and Sir Jack were partners in Motor Racing Developments Ltd, producing "Brabham" racing cars. While certainly friends they by no means lived in each other's pockets, and had their differences. Towards the end of their MRD partnership a serious rift developed between Ron and Sir Jack's first wife, Betty. This friction adversely affected Sir Jack's business relationship with Ron. In retrospect Sir Jack now believes they could have gone further had Ron been more flexible and less intent upon customer car matters: "I used to read about my mates Bruce McLaren and Denny Hulme having so much fun racing CanAm sports cars in the 'States…and earning all those dollars there. I would have loved to join in but Ron was too busy doing our production cars and looking after customers. He was right, of course, but I always felt I was missing out…"

title by the skin of his teeth, in this new season he won no fewer than five consecutive *Grandes Epreuves* to leave nobody in any doubt about the combined effectiveness of Brabham and the rear-engined Cooper-Climax which he had done so much to co-develop.

When the Formula 1 regulations then changed from permitting full 2½-litre engines to a new limit of no more than 1½-litres in 1961, the British teams were handicapped by the slow introduction of competitive new-sized power units. It was Brabham who drove the first new Climax V8 in the German Grand Prix at the Nürburgring that August, and he smartly reversed it straight through a hedge on the opening lap…a rare error.

By the end of the season it had become obvious that Cooper—who had pioneered the rear-engined revolution in Grand Prix racing—had been left behind. Sir Jack had foreseen that possibility and he had backed a new production racing car venture named Motor Racing Developments Ltd (MRD), building Formula Junior cars which had been designed by Ron Tauranac, newly arrived in Britain, for customer sale.

At that time the Brabham garage empire was growing in Britain, and in mid-1962 the first MRD-made "Brabham" Formula 1 car made its debut. Fifth place for Jack in the United States Grand Prix yielded the first Championship points ever won by a driver in a car of his own manufacture.

For the remaining three seasons of that 1½-litre Formula, the Brabham Racing Organisation team was formed with Jack being joined by the lanky American ace Dan Gurney, ex-Ferrari, BRM, and Porsche. Their first Formula 1 victories came quickly, in the 1963 non-Championship events at Solitude in Germany and Zeltweg in Austria. But World Championship-qualifying success proved elusive until the French Grand Prix of 1964, which Gurney won with Jack a delighted third.

As pressure of business increased, so Jack Brabham then went into partial retirement during 1965, hoping for new driver Denny Hulme to take his place. But it was a largely luckless season and when Gurney went off to build his own Eagle cars for the new 3-litre Formula in 1966, Jack returned in full harness as a driver.

Formula 1 regulations changed again in 1966 and doubled engine capacity to a full 3-litres. Racing engines for such a Formula promised to be costly and complex. It took rare insight and understanding to spot an opportunity there. Jack Brabham had both. He opted for an ingenious, relatively inexpensive, and simple conversion of an American production V8 engine which was engineered by old friends at the Repco company in Australia. It would not offer great power but it would be both light in weight and strong on reliability. And so it proved in 1966 when he drove his modestly powerful, intensely practical Repco Brabham to win the French,

British, Dutch, and German Grands Prix, and became the first driver other than Fangio to become a Formula 1 triple World Champion. In this supreme season his Brabham-Honda Formula 2 car also tore its particular class apart, winning nine times to take the *Grands Prix de France* Championship. Brabham's teams won hundreds of bottles of Champagne...one or two of which he shared.

In 1967 Hulme then took the Formula 1 World title in revised Repco Brabhams. Jack was runner-up in the Drivers' competition and winner of the French and Canadian Grands Prix. For 1968 Austrian driver Jochen Rindt joined the team. They struggled with new and more complex Repco V8 engines and suffered a bad season.

That year saw Jack running at Indianapolis—where in 1961 he had pioneered the rear-engined revolution in American-style Speedway racing with a Cooper-Climax developed from his Champion Formula 1 machine. In 1964 there at Indy he experienced the narrowest escape of his racing life. He had driven one of his own cars, powered by an Offenhauser engine, through the second lap fireball which stopped the race and killed two drivers. It was hardly surprising he took four years to return.

But irrespective of whether or not the purse was big enough, Jack Brabham would always put his heart into a race. In 1969 Formula 1 he turned to the Cosworth-Ford V8 engine and drove hard and well in support of his new young Belgian team-mate Jacky Ickx. But Jack broke his left ankle in a mid-season testing accident at Silverstone, where he had won a rain-soaked International Trophy race earlier that year. That injury put him out of the game until the Italian Grand Prix.

In the face of increasing family pressures he had long been thinking of retirement, but the non-availability of top-line drivers had kept him behind the wheel. Now 1970 was to be his last season—his 23rd year in the game—and it started brilliantly with victory in South Africa, first time out in a new Ron Tauranac-designed monocoque car.

He should have won at least twice more, at Monaco and Brands Hatch. A wrong choice at the Mediterranean resort, however, put him into the straw bales on the last corner while leading. Then in the British Grand Prix he deprived Rindt's Lotus of the lead, stormed by and was pacing himself to victory when his car ran out of fuel halfway round the last lap! He placed second in both races, and after late-season troubles was fifth in his last World Championship. His final frontline race before retirement was that year's Mexican Grand Prix, and there he was running third when his engine failed.

Sir Jack Brabham's racing career was quite extraordinary. Throughout it he remained ferociously competitive, and he always knew when to race all out and when to conserve a car or a place. If a car failed him—if the stakes were high—he could always nurse it to the finish like a baby. Jack's early dirt track style moderated as he matured, but when the chips were down, he would hurl his cars around, showering pursuers with dust and stones. Numerous rivals who retired with holed radiators mumbled darkly of flying pebbles. Nobody else in major league motor racing was as hard as "Black Jack" on a black day.

Racing sports cars was an infrequent relaxation. After early drives for Aston Martin and in his Cooper Monacos, in his final season he enjoyed being one of the Matra endurance team's "hired men" without the responsibility of team ownership on his shoulders.

When Sir Jack Brabham retired at the end of 1970, many thousands attended the Brands Hatch farewell meeting held in his honour. This was a heart-warming and heart-felt tribute by the massed enthusiasts to motor racing's great elder statesman, the veteran triple-World Champion Driver and racing car constructor who had never passed his peak...what follows, in his own words, is his story.

ABOVE
Another Formula 1 era that Sir Jack survived—when several friends did not; the tall strutted wings emerged on Grand Prix cars during 1968 and were banned after several incidents culminating here in the 1969 Spanish Grand Prix at Barcelona. With his early air force background, Sir Jack was one of the most aerodynamically aware of all leading drivers. His interest was matched by Ron Tauranac's. Their Formula 1 cars had been wind-tunnel tested very early in MRD's history. They were leaders in adopting add-on aerodynamic fins and 'foils. Sir Jack recalls: "Those tall strutted wings were a damned sight more dangerous than what we'd done before…but as long as Colin Chapman of Lotus fitted bigger and taller wings we had to match him, just to keep competitive."

Part 1
THE EARLY YEARS

Here's the essence of Australian road racing in the early 1950s—pretty primitive circuit, imported European-built racing cars, prepared and developed with a bit of Aussie improvisation, care and skill —and driven immensely competitively, oh yes, we all earnestly wanted to win! That's me in my extensively modified Cooper-Bristol *RedeX Special*, flanked by two Ferraris—Dick Cobden in his 1951-type V12 on the centre of the front row, and beyond him Lex Davison in his sports-engined 1952–53 4-cylinder.

J.A. Brabham, "General Engineer", 1946–1947. This is the little workshop behind my grandfather's house. This superb Australian-made Nuttall lathe had a geared head instead of the old-fashioned belt drive. It's set-up here to machine semi-trailer hubs which I did in batches of 20–30 a time for Freighter Trailers. The circular plate to the right was a cone I made up mounted on a ball-race which I'd insert into the end of each hub to steady it during machining. This enabled me to run a deeper cut so I could machine each hub more quickly, increasing the rate of pay!

CHAPTER 1
SCHOOLBOY TO MIDGET RACER

How the only child from Hurstville and wartime Beaufighter flight mechanic, first found his feet in midget-car Speedway racing

Hurstville, about 10 miles (16 kilometres) south of Sydney city centre, has, like Australia itself, changed quite a lot since I was born there, on 2 April 1926. The main street is now one way, McQuarie Street where I grew up has now been merged into what used to be the nearby Queens Road, our old house has long gone together with those of our neighbours, and the entire area is now a car park. Surrounding districts have also changed: favourite fields and paddocks, where men would gamble on illicit games of "2-up" (and we kids would go and throw rocks at them) is now an area known as Beverley Hills. Thousands of acres of once open land are now covered with new houses, while many older ones were demolished for the Olympic-year freeway to be driven through to Sydney Airport.

Hurstville was a middle-class commuter town, growing up around the main Sydney to Cronulla railway line. My paternal grandfather, who was born in Twickenham in south-west London, got a job in the galley of a ship and sailed to Australia. He disembarked at Melbourne in 1885 when he was 16 and decided to stay. When my father was nine, Grandad had bought a grocery shop business in Adelaide, South Australia. After my father had married May, my mother, they moved to Sydney, settled in Hurstville and developed the greengrocery business there.

The houses in Hurstville were built on land divided up into 40–45 feet (12–13½ metre) wide blocks around 75–100 feet (23–30½ metre) deep. At the bottom of our garden was a peppercorn tree which was my favourite climbing place—and my refuge in which I'd hide from Mum whenever she was chasing me—until I slipped one day, fell out of it, and nearly broke my neck.

While modern Australia has changed from the kind of large, country town feel which I remember, some things are just the same. The weather was always on our side. My cousin Ken and his friends used to go off on their pushbikes with me tagging along on my "push and go" scooter. I wasn't allowed a bike! One day Ken towed me on that scooter all the way to Cronulla Beach for a swim—a good 12 miles (19 kilometres).

Later I graduated to a tricycle and, after another dangerous escapade on that, my parents removed the saddle and handlebars. I taught myself to ride it regardless, sitting on the crossbar and steering with the pedals. Mum and Dad relented and returned the saddle and handlebars, but I was so pleased with myself that I preferred to ride without them. We also built billy carts ("soapboxes") with a plank, four wheels, and rope steering. We used to race them down the hill on Patrick Street regardless of all its crossroads and the main road at its foot. It was in the billy cart, I suppose, that I had my first-ever races. They were great fun.

My first school was Hurstville Primary, which I entered at the age of four. My greatest interest at the time was steam trains—which were constantly thundering by on the nearby railway—plus cars, aeroplanes, and just making things in general. I was always pretty good with my hands. I had a great Meccano set and graduated at quite a young age to making flying model aeroplanes out of balsa wood and tissue paper. We did not start from kits back then, we just dreamed up a design, or copied someone else's, cut out the wood and paper, and used wound-up rubber bands to power the propeller.

I was always entranced by the sight of aircraft flying overhead and vividly recall the trimotor monoplanes operated by the famous aviator Charles Kingsford-Smith. They used to pass overhead on the daily service to Melbourne. One morning in 1931 I saw his Fokker *Southern Cloud* (actually an Avro 10 built in Britain under licence to a Fokker design) fly over our house, heading south, and remember all the dismay and drama the following day because it hadn't arrived in Melbourne and

BELOW
Young John Arthur—first birthday and probably third or fourth birthday. I loved my Mum and Dad, and I suppose they loved me too.

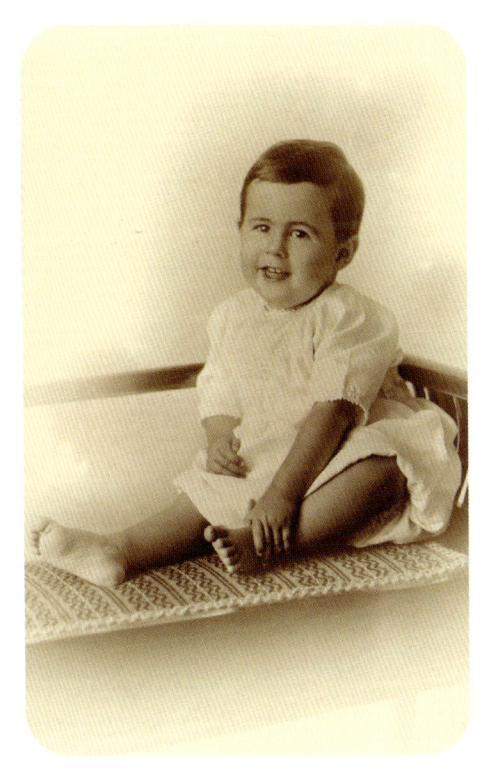

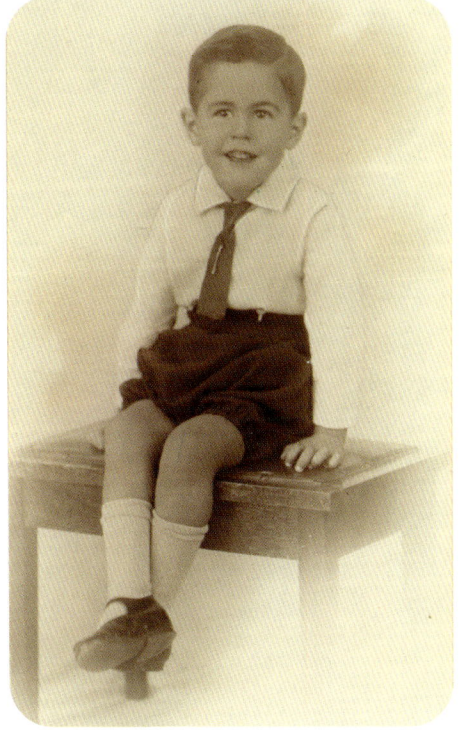

was declared overdue and missing. Its fate actually became a celebrated Australian mystery, until one day in November 1958, 27 years later, its wreckage was found hidden in the forests on the hills of the Toolong Range.

When I was 10 my father at last let me have a bicycle and every weekend a bunch of us would ride off to go swimming, usually in a river at National Park, our favourite swimming place. The park was about a 25-mile (40-kilometre) ride and we'd picnic and swim all day. I cycled everywhere through my early teens—it was great. Not far from our house there was a cycle track at the Hurstville Oval where I watched the cycle races until I was old enough to have a go myself one night. I finished fourth, in a field of four, and it made my legs ache. I was never an enthusiastic athlete.

My father, however, was a keen motorist. He took delivery of his first car—a 1926 Willys Knight open tourer with canvas top—the week I was born, and my parents were so thrilled at having both their first car and their first child in the same week they believed it helped shape my subsequent career.

They ran the Willys for the next 10 years. I don't recall the car that clearly, apart from sitting in it, in the garden one day, quite unable to reach the pedals, when somehow I managed to release the handbrake. The Willys rolled straight through a trellis before smashing into the garden fence. That was due cause for me to scoot straight up my trusty peppercorn tree until the initial excitement had settled down a little.

I have clearer memories of its replacement—a Chrysler 77—because my father began teaching me to drive it when I was about 12. For the greengrocery business, father also had Albion and Dodge trucks which he'd let me drive occasionally around the yard. I loved it. He paid me pocket-money for working in the shop each weekend and he'd let me drive down to the markets with him. Afterwards, I was allowed to drive home—all long before I had a licence.

The war broke out when I was 13. The day it began, I was actually on my first big trip away from home on a 500-mile (800-kilometre) train ride with my cousin Ken to stay with my grandfather in Melbourne. As fuel shortages struck Australia, Father converted two of the trucks to burn charcoal: the burner bolting onto the front of the Albion and generating gas which was fed to the carburettor. After we'd stoked it up it would run all week, and at weekends I'd have to "de-coke" the burner, clearing out the clinker and always ending up covered in soot from head to foot. However, the Army was short of transport and they arrived on the doorstep one day to requisition the Dodge. Later we received a lend-lease Chevrolet in its place, which we also had to convert to a charcoal burner.

Meanwhile I'd progressed to Technical College. At that time, in Australia, engineering and mechanics were really in their infancy and to get anywhere you had to do it yourself because you couldn't get spares for anything. Aussies were accustomed to having to improvise and make mechanical parts. I had always been happiest making things and my course taught basic metalwork, carpentry, and technical drawing. I liked them all and did pretty well in each, could handle maths, and just about scraped by in English and geography. But I was no historian—a subject I hated!

At the age of 15 I left school and started my first job in an engineering shop in Sydney. I imagined myself pitching in straight away, running machines, but instead found myself sweeping floors and running messages. It was difficult to see any future there. Three weeks was quite enough for me.

I then found a job at Ferguson's in Treacy Street, Hurstville. This was the garage which maintained my father's cars and trucks. While working at Ferguson's, I spent two or three nights a week at the Kogarah Technical College doing a course in mechanical engineering. While at Ferguson's I had my 16th birthday. Cousin Ken had already been a proud owner of a motorbike for six months—and now my father helped me buy my first bike, a 350cc Velocette. Before long I had taken it all apart and put it all back together again. It restarted and ran well, I sold it for a small profit and, thus encouraged, began my first "business venture"—buying clapped-out motorbikes, repairing them and selling them on. I quickly found the more effort I put in to rebuilding them the better price I seemed to achieve, and soon I was averaging £A15–20 a bike, with the occasional star deal fetching as much as £A50 a time. I concentrated on Velocettes and, every Saturday morning, I'd be up at 5am, eager to get my nose into the *Sydney Morning Herald* classifieds. If anybody had a Velocette for sale I'd be first on his doorstep.

FAR LEFT
Proud owner—I had a really tough time convincing my Dad I should have a push-bike, before he came up with my first, a "Master", seen here outside a friend's house in South Hurstville.

BELOW
Far more serious business—wartime service with the RAAF saw me working on these Australian-made Bristol Beaufighters of "B-Flight" seen here on the apron at Williamtown aerodrome, north of Newcastle in New South Wales. I thought these were terrific aircraft, and their air-cooled Hercules radial engines were really nicely made, I loved working on them.

RIGHT
Flight Mechanic J. A. Brabham—when I went through the engine instruction course in the RAAF there were two parallel classes under instruction with 20 young cadets in each. At the end of the course I emerged with the highest marks amongst both classes combined. It was a subject and work I really, really enjoyed.

Ken and I covered huge distances on our motorbikes. At 17 I got my driving licence at last and we started to drive further inland, often far into the bush, and navigating by compass, to shoot kangaroo and fox. I really enjoyed those trips.

At work, Harry Ferguson was a fine mechanic, running a well-equipped workshop and he took me under his wing for the next three years. Initially he paid me 18s 6d a week, rising to 25 shillings after two years. As he was also running his Dodge and Standard-Triumph spare parts business, he began leaving me to work alone. I rapidly gained experience of almost every kind possible with regards to a motor vehicle. In wartime Australia, parts availability was even worse and I had to improvise all the time. Burning charcoal in the greengrocery trucks did their engines no good at all, so I'd spend the weekends working on them when I wasn't stripping and overhauling my ever-changing stock of used motorbikes. My parents had moved from Hurstville to a bigger property in Penshurst. We didn't have a garage there, but the house had a particularly spacious back verandah which I adopted as my motorcycle workshop.

Meanwhile, the war raged on. My most vivid memory of this period, before I joined the Royal Australian Air

RIGHT
The tragic remains of Wing Commander Crombie's Beaufighter in the scrapyard at Williamtown after the accident in which he was killed, and in which I would almost certainly have perished too but for becoming fortuitously involved in a game of cards. Our tractor driver had flown in my place. He was much more powerfullybuilt, and was able to brace himself against the impact when the "Beau" stalled-in, and survived the crash, whereas I wouldn't have stood a chance…one of many strokes of sheer good luck during my life.

Force (RAAF), is of the Japanese raid on Sydney Harbour. There had been much talk of the Japanese mounting some kind of invasion after the air raids on Darwin. As I recall, we heard the noise of very high-flying aircraft earlier in the day and air-raid sirens sounded. At night all the lights were turned out. Then guns opened fire in Sydney Harbour and we heard the concussion of explosions. Midget submarines had penetrated the anchorage and sank some ships. It was frightening to hear the action going on and frankly everybody was scared, shouting, "They're here!" But the Japanese did not come in force, did not land, and Australia settled down again.

After two years of the three-year course at Kogarah Technical College I was finally called up and joined the RAAF. I was dead keen to fly and was profoundly disappointed when the recruitment sergeant said, "I'm sorry, we've got enough pilots thank you. What else would you like to do?"

My RAAF service began with a month's preliminary training in a tented camp at Cootamundra. The food was dreadful. I've always been fussy about what I eat, but I was particularly thin then and began to think I would die of starvation. I was sent to a RAAF stores unit at Dubbo to await posting but became delayed by crashing a motorcycle sidecar combination when its rusty frame snapped. The crash sent me off the road between a telegraph pole and a mail box—I banged my knee and ended up in hospital for a week, missing my first posting so that I had to stay in Dubbo driving a travelling crane until another posting came through.

I was sent to Adelaide for three months of initial training as a flight mechanic. It was followed by an aero engine course in Melbourne. Finally, I was posted to an operational training unit at Williamtown, about 130 miles (209 kilometres) north of Sydney, where I was to spend the next two years, mostly engaged in maintaining B-Flight's big twin-engined Bristol Beaufighters.

I was disappointed not to have been selected as aircrew but they had sufficient numbers and the real shortage was in trained flight mechanics. However, we quite often went up on test flights after jobs on the aircraft had been completed, and it was on one of these flights that tragedy intruded. Wing Commander Crombie was in charge of pilot training and conversion to the tricky Beaufighter. We all respected his ability and I always looked forward to flying with him. One day he came down to the flight hut where we'd hang out after completing some work on an aircraft, and said he was going to take it up on a test. I put my name down to fly with him but he had to go off to the Officers' Mess (for some reason that I can't remember) and didn't return for ages. While waiting I got involved in a card game in another hut. Unknown to me, Wing Commander Crombie had returned but, because he couldn't find me anywhere, took up our tow-tractor driver in my place and a rookie pilot.

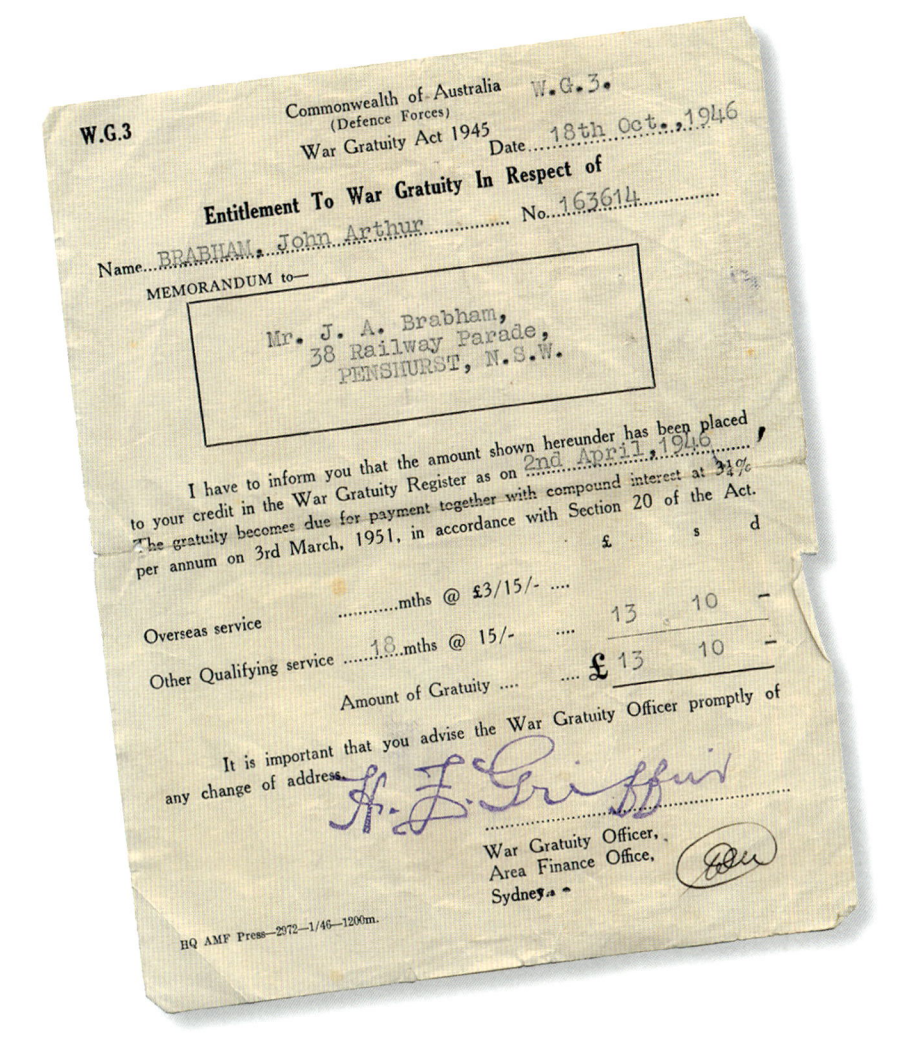

About a half-hour later their Beaufighter reappeared over the base on one engine with the other's propeller feathered. Wing Commander Crombie had just been demonstrating feathering when the battery exploded leaving him unable to unfeather the prop. He had always drummed it into his pilots that if they found themselves on one engine they should never drop the dead one in a Beaufighter, it could be un-recoverable. We watched him in the circuit, low and slow, with the flaps and undercarriage down. He had to wait while another aircraft landed. Then, to our horror, he turned the wrong way and dropped the dead engine. Unbelievable! The

ABOVE
The big pay-off from a grateful Government— £A13 10s gratuity for wartime service to King, Country, and Empire. It wasn't particularly special by the standards of the time, but I think we all regarded the War Gratuity as pretty reasonable in the circumstances. It was certainly better than we might have expected.

RIGHT
In my first workshop. My engineering experience from RAAF service and further instruction from Bill Armstrong equipped me with the knowledge to build our own midget racing car.

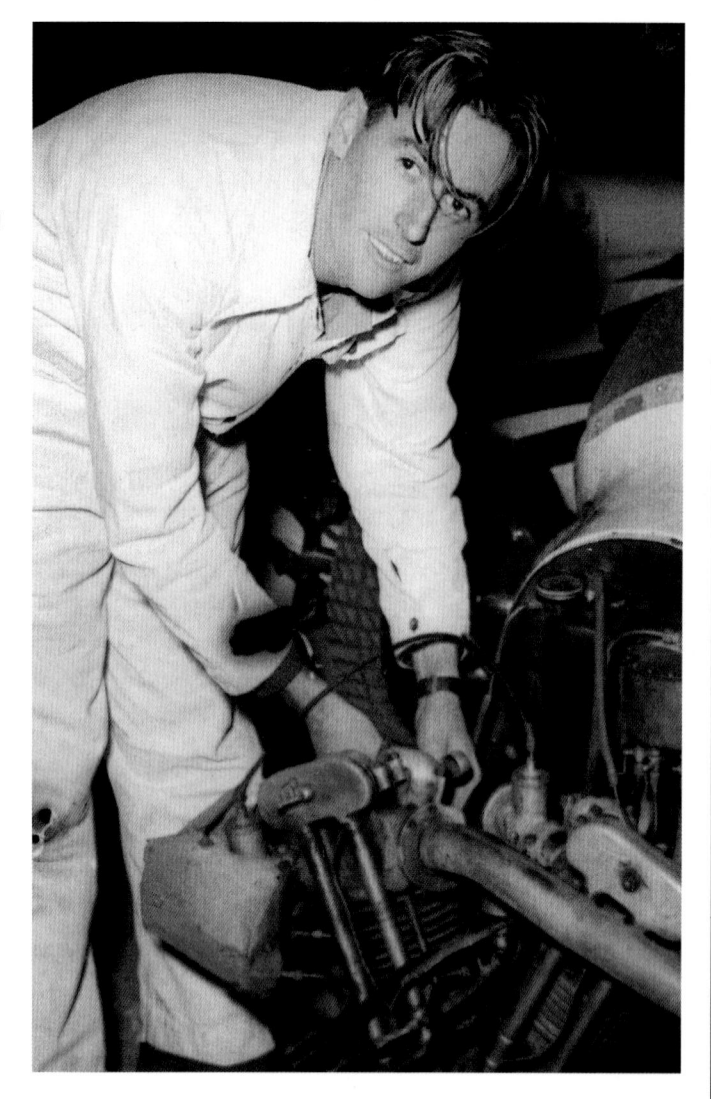

FAR RIGHT
Johnny Schonberg, the American midget car driver who introduced me to "speedcar" track racing in the brand-new car which we knew generally just as "28". I built it for him around an air-cooled twin-cylinder JAP "80" engine, and would soon take it over as regular driver. Why did I slope the nose forward like that? Just to be different, though inside it housed a forward sloping mesh stoneguard to deflect flying shale downwards, away from the engine.

Beau just smashed down into a rubbish tip just short of the runway.

Miraculously, it didn't burn. We all sprinted across to help the crew. We found the trainee pilot wandering about just battered and bruised, but Wing Commander Crombie was plainly dead. He had been thrown out and cracked his head on one of the engines that had broken away from the wing. As for the tractor driver who'd gone up in my place, he was trapped in the well where you climb up into the navigator's seat. It was crazy as we were all wading around in a large puddle of fuel that had spilled from ruptured tanks—one spark and we'd all have gone up. We smashed through the fuselage glass to get him out. The tractor driver explained that just before the impact he'd braced himself against the cannon bins immediately in front of the navigator's position. He was such a powerfully built chap he'd actually pushed the back out of his seat, and had fallen down into the well. That alone

SCHOOLBOY TO MIDGET RACER | 25

ABOVE
Front cover of the race programme for the Speedway Royale meeting on Saturday, 28 February 1948—written across the top is the note "Jack's first night at Speedway Royal— 3 starts, 3 firsts".

BELOW
Contemporary press cutting from 1949–1950 when I was established on the speedways and was always expected to do well.

SPEED STAR'S NEW CAR READY

Jack Brabham will drive a new car in the Australian 15-lap speed car championship at the Showground on Saturday night.

Brabham, holder of the title, has been working on a ne wcar for several months. Postponement of the race owing to rain last Saturday night enabled him to get his car ready for this week.

Frank Brewer, Ray Revell, Sel Payne, Andy McGavin, Brabham and other interstate star drivers will take part.

---

possibly saved him from being hurled forward and probably killed. I would never have had the strength to do that. If I had not got involved in that game of cards and had flown in his place I'd have had my chips for sure.

When I was demobbed from the RAAF in 1946, several happy coincidences helped me begin to earn a living. For starters there was a sizeable plot of land behind my grandfather's house, and my uncle was a builder. So I got him to build me a workshop there, and I began doing service and repair work on neighbours' cars. I thought that with my training and RAAF experience, I might be able to make a career out of it.

I'd befriended a retired engineer named Bill Armstrong. He'd kept a little hobby shop of his own in Blakehurst, where he spent a lot of time teaching me how to use a lathe and do general machine work. A daughter of a near neighbour had married an American named Johnny Schonberg, who had settled in Sydney after being discharged from the US Army. Occasionally Schonberg drove midget racing cars at the Sydney sports ground track. But what interested me more at that time was a disposal sale in Darwin that we heard about. Johnny's in-laws ran a produce distribution business so we decided to fly up there in view of chasing a bargain on some trucks or machine tools.

There was no direct Sydney-to-Darwin flight so we had to route via an overnight stop in Brisbane. It was a Monday, and we were kicking our heels in the hotel, when Johnny noticed in the local newspaper that the previous Saturday night's midget car racing event had been rained out "...and they're racing tonight!"

I'd never even seen a midget car and Johnny said I should take a look. Anything was better than hanging around the hotel, so we went off to the track that afternoon. Johnny introduced me to some of the drivers, we looked around their cars and returned that same night to watch them racing. I was more intrigued than impressed by these little machines. They ran on ¼ mile (400 metre) oval cinder tracks, and that's exactly how they looked—dirty and scarred, and shot-blasted by the flying dirt and cinders. I was pretty impressed by the night's racing but left the ground convinced that they were all lunatics. They bundled into the corners, all in a jostling pack, sliding sideways under full throttle, and clattering and barging against one another. This didn't give me any immediate desire to try it for myself.

Up at the sale in Darwin we bought three trucks and a utility, plus a load of machines, tools, and related goods. The biggest truck was a semi-trailer, so we roped one truck on top of it, put the utility on the back of the other, and the pair of us brought all four home to Sydney. I promptly attended a couple of midget races in which Johnny was driving. I was interested in the cars' technicalities, and we agreed we'd build a new one between us. We spent some time studying all the others, so we could build a better one.

We were not unaided. A fellow midget car owner named Ronnie Ward, who also built his own cars, and Bill Armstrong, both helped. After four or five months' work —and an expenditure of around £A400—there she stood, on her wheels, our first midget car.

We'd made a tubular chassis and fitted our own steering box, then cut a Morris Cowley gearbox in half to make it a two-speeder, and added a Harley-Davidson motorcycle clutch. We suspended a straight front axle beam on semi-elliptic leaf springs, and used hubs from a

LEFT
Nervous? Who's nervous? This shot was taken on the first night I drove "28", on the Cumberland Oval track at Parramatta Park. I'm belted in because, if you didn't strap in, the bumps on the track would throw you clean out of the cockpit! Under my feet are just two pedals—clutch and throttle—because in speedcar racing you never used the brakes anyway, broadsiding the car would slow it down. The outside handbrake operated the drum brakes (mounted only at the rear) simply to stop the car in the pits or in a real emergency. Those wire-spoked wheels could fly apart so Ron Tauranac drew replacements for me, cast in 226HT aluminium by Belshaw's Foundry, with separate bolt-on spun steel rims we could make any width we wanted. If you hit anything, a bent steel rim could be quickly removed and a fresh one bolted-on to Ron's cast centres, which never failed.

RIGHT
The name of the game—hold it in tight, balance throttle against steering and run flat-out from start to finish. Wearing the scarf to protect my face I'm holding my lightweight "28" down low on the Speedway Royale with Ray Ravell's heavier American Offenhauser-engined midget teetering round on the high line. We had some fantastic match races. On a slick track I'd usually beat him, his car was heavier, and he'd slide high, it was more powerful and would spin its wheels. With heavy clay-shale top dressing on the track his power would tell. In one match race I had Ravell beaten when, at the last gasp, my engine stripped its cam-gear teeth. The following week they'd top-dressed the track so I had no hope. I'd made "28"s front axle to carry Amilcar hubs (note no front brakes) and the back end was also Amilcar. Art Senior rebuilt the cams for me, and it absolutely flew!

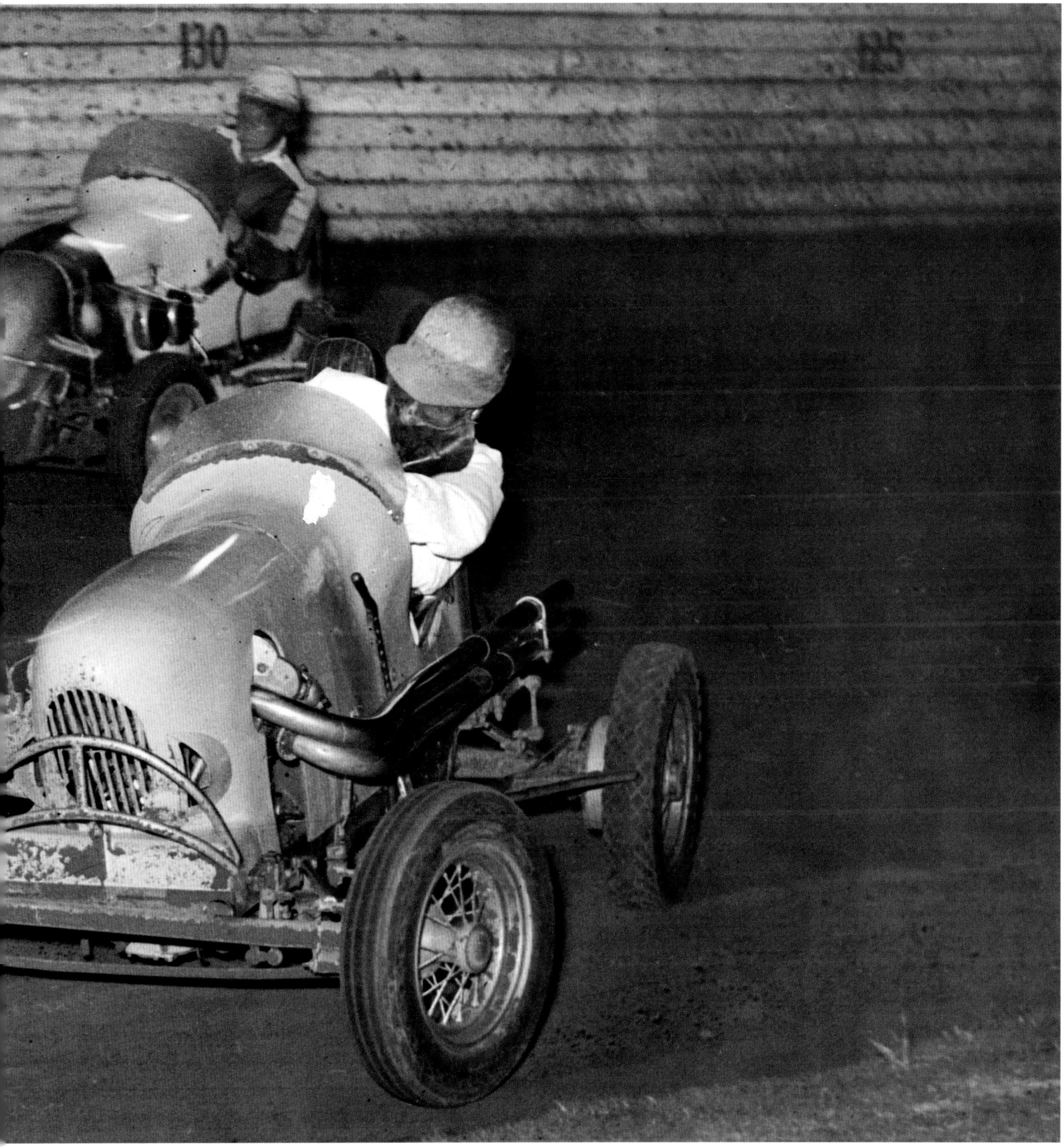
130
125

RIGHT

My speedcar, "28", still survives in Australia. This is its vee-twin air-cooled engine which I made to replace the original JAP "80" unit. It was enlarged from around 1,000cc to nearer 1,350 and the only components retained were the JAP rocker covers. With the larger-bore Harley-Davidson type cylinder barrels their use dictated narrower included angles between the inlet and exhaust valves. The engine was very successful but I never really understood why. Then in 1965–1966 Honda introduced narrower valve angles in our 1-litre Formula 2 engines which set new power output standards, benefiting the improved gas flow and combustion obtained. Sometimes the ignorant just get lucky.

RIGHT

Collecting the swag—I had some great nights racing at Adelaide's Kilburn Speedway in South Australia. There's always been tremendous sporting, political, and commercial rivalry between the various Australian States, and as I repeatedly carried the South Australians' trophies and prize money back home to New South Wales I wasn't perhaps their most popular visitor. It would have been worse if I'd been from neighbouring Victoria! Decades later I would become patron of South Australia's annual Adelaide Classic Rally, a fantastic event, so no hard feelings.

pre-war French Amilcar, carrying wire wheels. We got it going with a 1000cc JAP engine, but it gave us a great deal of trouble.

We then got to know Art Senior, one of Australia's real, old-time motorcycle aces, who ran his own machine shop in Sydney. He helped us modify the JAP engine and to bore it out to a full 1100cc. We raced that for the rest of the Australian summer season of 1946–1947. I was growing more confident in our ability—with our friends—to design and make parts, and we decided the JAP engine just wasn't up to the job...so made our own.

By this time my little backyard engineering shop was well enough equipped to produce crankcases, flywheels, con-rods, cylinders, and cylinder heads. I assembled a new

1350cc engine, the only remaining original JAP parts being the two rocker boxes for the valvegear. This engine would do us proud for several years.

Johnny drove for about half our first season, but in the second half—into 1948—his wife persuaded him to stop racing. This left us with a racing car but no driver, and Johnny said, "Why don't you drive it yourself?"

We took the midget car down to Tempe mud flats where Johnny gave me a few pointers on how to balance it round corners on the loose surface, and I just took to it like a duck to water. Then, at a smaller Wednesday night meeting on the Parramatta Speedway, I then entered my first-ever motor race. My initial impression, which I'd concluded from my previous sight of that race in Brisbane, was dead right. They were all lunatics. I just could not believe the amount of dirt and rocks that were flying around the track. It was like willingly sitting in front of a shotgun blast. Virtually within seconds, the flying dirt and cinders would obscure your goggles. Later, we used to go to the startline wearing five or six pairs of cellophane anti-gas goggles so that once they'd clouded-over you'd just pull off the top pair to use the next. Being a new boy I had to start right at the back. After two nights running dead last, however, I became accustomed to this cinder shower. On the third night I began to get a grip on what you had to do. In the feature race they'd start 12 cars with the fastest at the back. After my two nights starting at the back, I now lined up right at the front. And that night

BELOW
Drifting "28" with exhaust muffler fitted at the Speedway Royale. In the early 1950s we had to fit silencers like this, but you didn't really notice much difference.

FOLLOWING PAGE
What the truly safety conscious midget speedcar driver would wear? Not quite, but this was a publicity shot taken before my first appearance at the Speedway Royale.

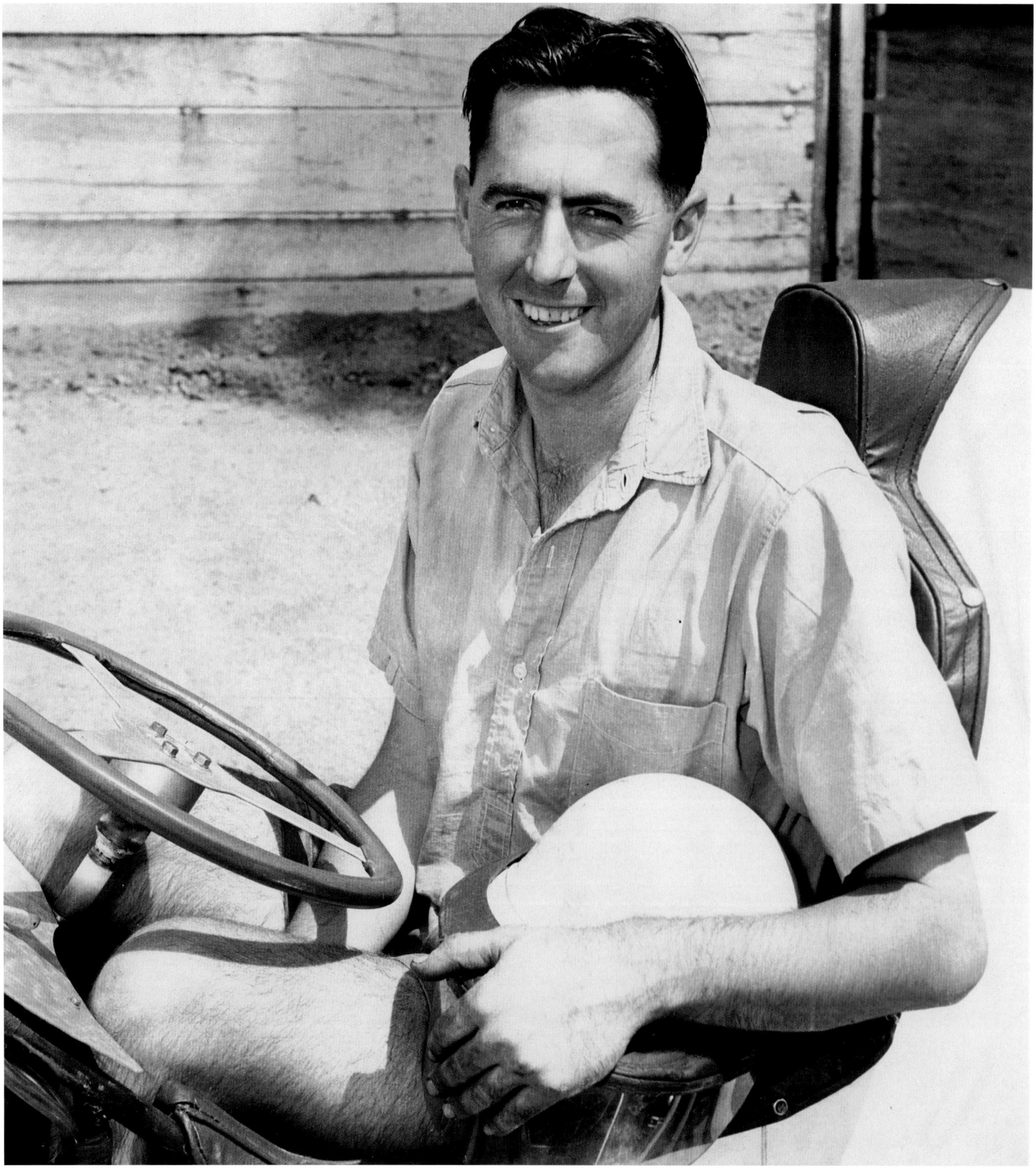

I was still there when the race ended. I had won and, quite frankly, I'm not sure who was more surprised at the result, my rivals, or me!

Winning like that on only my third night's racing really gave me confidence and thereafter I raced with ease against the best of them. After finding my feet like this at Parramatta, the next grade up was the big-time Royale Speedway at the Sydney Showground. I entered three races on my first night there and won all of them. Empire Speedways, who ran the races, really latched on to my winning streak resulting in a lot of promotion in the local newspaper which went down well. I was, after all, the "Youngest driver in midget racing".

At the Sydney Showground in my first season, I won the New South Wales Championship. I just seemed to have the knack of winning in midget cars on cinder tracks. It was terrific driver training. You had to have quick reactions: in effect you lived—or possibly died—on them. The car was only just on the very verge of control—all the time. Numerous people had the most terrifying accidents and it was genuinely dangerous, yet I was fortunate enough to survive nearly six years of it without ever once turning the car upside down. I must have been about the only driver of that period who hadn't ever rolled his car.

Midget racing was very popular in Australia, especially in Sydney. The promoters would bring over American drivers each year, to mix it with us for the season. This created a lot of interest because Aussies just love beating the world. Crowds of anything up to 40,000 would attend.

Interstate racing was very popular. You'd load up your midget and kit on a car and trailer, then motor off into the blue, jolting along for hours and hours from Sydney to Melbourne, or way down south to Adelaide, or up north to Brisbane. The Sydney Showground track scored points on two systems, one for handicap and one for feature events. Throughout my midget car career I was able to win one or both every year.

Ray Ravell was the established midget racing star of those times. In my first season the highest points scorer of the year would win a very nice gold watch. When I beat Ray Ravell to it by one point, he wasn't exactly delighted.

I was spending nearly all my time either working on the midget or making parts for it during the day, then racing it in the evenings. My father had rapidly become my number one supporter and biggest fan, and always used to come with me on these trips. One particular evening, during my fourth annual visit to Adelaide, and after I had won all four races including the South Australian Championship, I was left to coast to a halt on the infield with the midget ablaze. Our engine had virtually cut in half and it was at this point that I realised that I'd done everything worth doing in midget racing and that it really was time to move on.

My father still had his fruit and greengrocery shop. We were considering buying a big semi-trailer truck so we could buy fruit in South Australia and transport it to Sydney. With this in mind we'd gone to see a promising truck for sale on the Friday of that weekend in Adelaide, only to discover on Monday that someone had offered more money for it. If the vendor had accepted our offer for the semi, and stuck to it, I'm convinced my motor racing career could have finished there and then, but I was obviously not destined to be a wholesale greengrocer! Apart from dirt track racing, I had already competed in some hill climbs with the midget and I'd met another occasional hill-climber and road racer who had also designed and built his own car. And his name was Ron Tauranac.

ABOVE
Sel Payne was a fellow speedcar driver and best man at my wedding to first wife Betty. Here's Sel in a slightly more tricky position at the Speedway Royale, having already knocked off his car's right-front wheel.

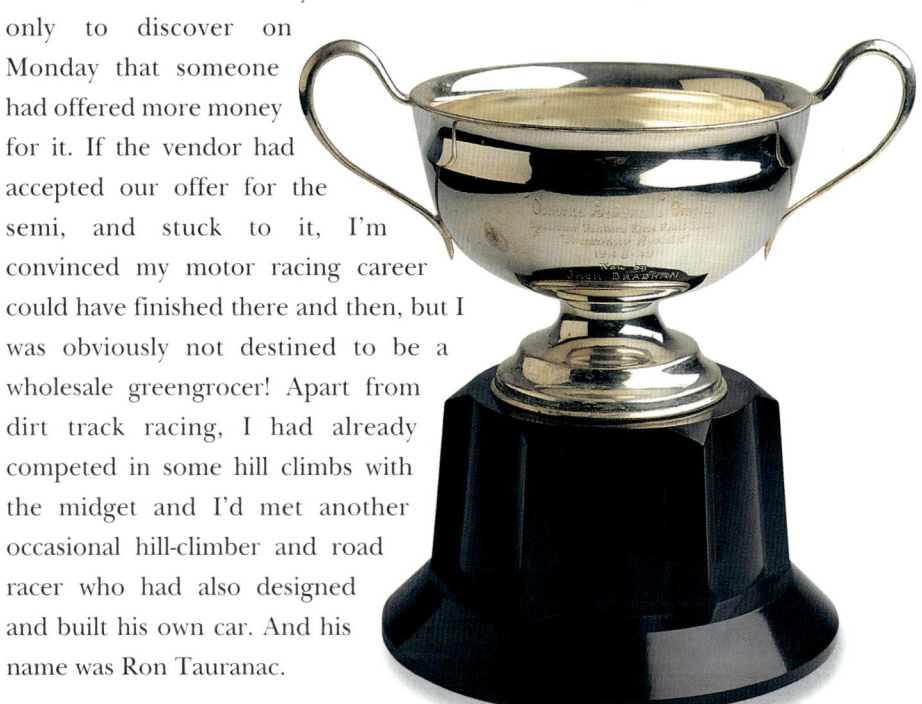

BELOW
Speedway Royale trophy for the 1948–1949 Season.

Straight out of the memorabilia box, this hand-coloured print of my *RedeX Special* Cooper-Bristol shows it at Southport, Queensland, before the 1954 Australian Grand Prix. While the *RedeX* was remarkably successful it always gave trouble at the Grand Prix meetings. Here the Bristol engine's front camshaft bearing turned in its housing which blanked-off the drilling for the lubricating oil—so it seized and left me sidelined.

CHAPTER 2

ROAD RACING AND THE *REDEX SPECIAL*

Developing the unfair advantage in Australasian road racing with the world's fastest Cooper-Bristol

Racing the midget Speedcar had become virtually a full-time job for me. At one stage we were racing three nights a week—at Parramatta Speedway every Wednesday, followed by the Sydney Sports Ground on Fridays, and then the Royal Showground on Saturdays. I almost had to give up my everyday business because it was virtually a full time job maintaining the car.

There were some compensations. Most significantly I could earn as much as £A50–75 a night. This was lot of money in those days when the Australian average weekly wage was probably around £A6 10s! I won consistently and didn't have expensive crashes, and so I earned my living doing that.

Speedcar racing became time-consuming because I did the engineering myself and made the parts. I also had some really good friends either helping me or charging me peanuts for work and parts. I used to go to the races with two of my father's truck drivers, Ken Sutton and Ernie Ball as helpers/mechanics, and two more friends, Bob Gibbins and Charlie Upton (ex-RAAF), also pitched-in occasionally.

After watching me race in Sydney, the promoter Aub Ramsey invited me down to Adelaide and offered good terms. There were no motorcycle engined Speedcars in Adelaide at the time—they all seemed to be water-cooled, from Model A Fords and suchlike—so we could go down and blow them all off the road.

From Sydney to Adelaide was about 1,100 miles (1,800 kilometres) over poor roads and it would take a day-and-a-half (stopping overnight) driving my 1938 straight-6 Dodge (a terrific vehicle), with a two-wheeled trailer on the back. The organisers paid me expenses to go and then I'd return with all their prize money too. I don't think I was very popular with my South Australian competitors!

Meanwhile, on the handful of hill-climbs I'd tackled with the midget, amongst the opposition had been two brothers: Ron and Austin Tauranac. I'd advertised a Velocette engine for sale and Ron came to see it. He also became interested in my engineering shop because he worked for Colonial Sugar Refining who needed some machining done. Ron got me to do it for them. I also carried out some machining for the brothers personally, and made parts for the early Ralt racing cars they were putting together.

Ron would become a wonderful technical "sounding board" for me. I developed great respect for Ron's abilities and he would later become my partner, designer, and the constructor of Brabham cars in Britain.

During the period in which I was hill-climbing in the midget, the Australian Sporting Car Club had invited me to their hill-climb at Hawkesbury in 1951. The little speedcar was simply in another class against all the regular runners. On my first practice climb, just finding out which way the road went, it took about 5–6 seconds off the record! The organisers promptly billed my appearance as a "demonstration run", and ruled that my Speedcar was not a proper motor car because it didn't have brakes on all four wheels. That irritated me so, to prevent this happening again, I then fitted front brakes in addition to the rears in time for the Light Car Club of Australia's Rob Roy hill-climb in Victoria.

The Rob Roy event was billed as the 1951 Australian Hill-Climb Championship. The favourites were Reg Hunt and John Crouch, the Australian importer of Cooper cars. Hunt had a Phil Irving HRD Supercharged Special. Crouch was running the latest chain-driven Mark V with a rear-mounted air-cooled 1100cc JAP engine. It was fresh out from Britain and the only one in Australia. However, my light and powerful little Speedcar won it. The Light Car Club people were pretty unhappy when they were beaten not only by a midget from the dirt tracks, but one fitted with four-wheel brakes. So it had now been transformed into "a proper motor car" and could no longer be dismissed. I went home with the trophy.

The experience was so enjoyable that I became interested in tackling serious road racing. That led me to buy a Mark IV Cooper chassis and BSA-based 500cc engine, but I found it pretty unexciting. So I put a 1000cc Vincent-HRD engine in that frame and ran that for a while, but alas, it wasn't very reliable. I replaced the Mark IV with a Mark V Cooper chassis with a big 1100cc JAP twin-cylinder engine which was much more fun.

To finance these road racing ambitions, I finally sold my midget Speedcar to speedway promoter and radio personality, Kim Binython. I would continue in midget racing, however, for another couple of years, driving a car owned and prepared by Spike Jennings. He'd modelled it upon my old car and used a Harley-Davidson vee-twin cylinder engine built by Eddie Dark, the Harley speedway engine expert of the time. I just drove it as an earner, splitting the prize money with Spike. When I bought my next road-racing Cooper it would take over my life and I

ABOVE
Young Geoffrey—my first son, later joined by Gary and David—in the *RedeX Special* at Katoomba circuit in the Blue Mountains of New South Wales. Everything about the Cooper-Bristol was quite light, quite simple, and pretty practical which of course I liked. Cooper's cast-alloy wheels were exceptional for the period in combining lightweight with strength and stiffness, the aluminium bodywork was the least complicated imaginable, and while the bonnet's centreline blister cleared my preferred Holden carburettors with their modified intake throats, the big offset blister made space for the Bristol engine's ignition magneto.

would finally bid the speedways farewell. It was in the Australian winter of 1953 that I was able to buy the car which really made my mark. This was a 2-litre, 6-cylinder, front-engined Cooper-Bristol Mark 2 which would become famous as the *RedeX Special*.

It was brand-new (the vendors, the Chambers Estate, said) and it cost £A4,250. There was no way I could have afforded it unaided but my father—always enthusiastic and very supportive—contributed some of the money. I committed as much as possible and the RedeX fuel additive company provided the rest. This was thanks to their racing manager Reg Shepheard who'd become a tremendous supporter. The car had actually been ordered by a chap named David Chambers, but he'd committed suicide before it arrived so John Crouch was left to sell it on behalf of the estate. It was a great day at Crouch's place in Sydney when we loaded that shiny new car on the trailer which I had quickly built for it.

I first took it up to the Mt Druitt circuit—an old wartime emergency landing strip just outside Sydney—to give it a run. After only a few miles its oil pressure dropped alarmingly and it was obvious the car wasn't brand new. The car had been out on the track somewhere so I pulled it all apart to investigate. It was horrific. Inside the engine I found its crankshaft was bent and the bearings were shot. I'd learn later that it had been Cooper's display car at the 1952 London Motor Show and had then been shipped to Buenos Aires for John Barber to drive in the 1953 Argentine Grand Prix. Upon its return to London they'd just washed it down and stuck it back on the boat to Sydney! Although I wrote to John Cooper I obviously couldn't expect much from them, over 12,000 miles (20,000 kilometres) away, in Britain. I got a local firm to straighten the crank and regrind it, we line-bored the block to get the bearings true again, reassembled it all and finally went racing.

I ran the car a couple of times without changes, but when I took it apart I'd been amazed by the immense weight of its flywheel and clutch. From my experience with the midget's compact little Harley-Davidson clutch, I made a similar one for the Cooper-Bristol and sidelined the original. We finished up with a tiny yet reliable clutch and machined-down flywheel. This weighed around 15–17lb (7–8kg) instead of the original's weighty 75–85lb (34–38kg)!

What I didn't know was that in Britain the Cooper-Bristols regularly cracked their long, thin crankshafts, thanks to the enormous mass of the standard flywheel and clutch hung on one end. I later learned that merely spinning a Cooper-Bristol could snap the end clean off the crank because of the monstrous flywheel/clutch assembly's gyroscopic effect. I had made adjustments, however, which eliminated this without even knowing that I was doing it, and the acceleration of the car was greatly improved.

My racing debut in the new car was made at Leyburn in August 1953 where we won the Queensland Road Racing Championship. I took it to the Gnoo Blas circuit at

Orange—a brilliant road course on which one section was known as "Mental Straight" after the adjacent psychiatric hospital. At Gnoo Blas I set the quickest time in the New South Wales Grand Prix. However, I had to non-start in that year's Australian Grand Prix at Albert Park, Melbourne, after the rear camshaft bearings ran again in practice due to excessive friction. With my experience of racing and developing the Speedcar I knew you couldn't stand still and merely race what you'd bought—you had to improve your machinery continuously to keep ahead of your opposition. If you stood still they would be past you like a shot.

One day, soon after I'd begun racing the *RedeX Special* I got a call from a pre-war Brooklands engineer and Alfa Romeo GP car owner/driver named Frank Ashby. He had just recently emigrated from Britain, and simply wanted to become involved in the Australian racing world. I went up to see him in a nice waterside house at Whale Beach, north of Sydney. Frank Ashby was plainly very experienced and competent. I later showed him the Bristol cylinder head.

I had already dumped the Bristol's original Solex carburettors in favour of Australian-made Holden Strombergs. Ashby advised that they, with their additional accelerator pumps, looked pretty good apart from their lousy air intake shape. He recommended I should fit the intakes with smoothly formed bell-mouths to ease air entry. So I machined some up which dropped into the top of each intake and nestled there virtually out of sight. When I next tested the car the difference these improvements made was instantly apparent. Ashby's recommendations on the most effective way to rework the engine's porting and gasflow had provided greater power and driveability.

Frank Ashby should take a lot of credit for opening my eyes to the wide and wonderful world of mechanical motor racing advantage. I already knew that the harder you looked at your machinery, the more benefit you could release from it, but Ashby's input really added to my racing education.

Just when everything seemed to be going so well, I fell foul of the Confederation of Australian Motor Sport (CAMS), the new racing governing body. The organisation was based in Melbourne, Victoria, so as proud New South Walians we weren't too well disposed from the start. CAMS officials were seeking to make their mark nationwide. They were super-conservative and took their cue from what was standard practice in Britain. Painting *RedeX Special* on my car to promote the company who'd helped me buy it in the first place was regarded by them as a criminal act! At that time the CAMS officials said no advertising was permitted on racing cars in Britain, so they wouldn't let any appear on racing cars in Australia—where the sport was stunted from the beginning by lack of funding. All our good cars had to be imported. This was immensely expensive so the only way Australian competitors could afford good state-of-the-art cars would have been to do what I'd done and get themselves a sponsor.

CAMS was anxious to flex its muscles and assert itself. I arrived for one race at Orange to be confronted by Don Thompson, the CAMS official, who told me "You can't race with this advertising on the side of your car, take it off or pack up and take it home." This was my first real brush with CAMS and I'd already been racing the car for about a year without problems—but it now became a big problem for me. Reg Shepheard of RedeX and the family had come a long way to watch me race so this was a bloody disaster. I've never forgiven the CAMS even though, when I asked Thompson if it would be OK for me to cover the sign writing with masking tape, he said that would be fine. So I taped it over lightly and went out to the start. On the first lap the masking tape all blew off in the airstream so I was racing the *RedeX Special* in front of them for all to see...and my sponsors were happy.

Unfortunately, the CAMS weren't so pleased. They banned me from appearing again with advertising on the car. It was around Christmas 1953 and as Queensland and New South Wales Road Racing title-holder I was invited to run in the New Zealand Grand Prix in January. So I loaded the Cooper-Bristol on the boat and made my first trip to race abroad, with *RedeX Special* lettering on the side and Redex in New Zealand providing great assistance to me.

The New Zealand GP was run on Ardmore aerodrome circuit outside Auckland. There I met some of the International racing circus members for the first time—drivers such as Tony Gaze, Peter Whitehead, Reg Parnell, and Ken Wharton. I finished sixth. During my time there I met and stayed with an Auckland garage-owner and keen

BELOW
Rob Roy Hill Climb trophy 1951.

RIGHT
Working on the *RedeX Special* in my workshop at Penshurst, the lathe's away to the left of this shot. One day here I found a crack in a chassis tube beneath the engine, so I jacked-up the car and lay under to repair it with a welding torch. Unfortunately some fuel had dripped onto the workshop floor which the torch flame ignited. Wouldn't you know it, my big fire extinguisher was in a big separate shed I'd built outside, and when I sprinted to it—I found the doors were locked. I yanked them so hard the bolt jerked clean out of the ground, enabling the doors to part sufficiently for me to reach inside, grab the extinguisher, and douse the blaze. That day I could have lost everything.

racer named McLaren, who had an even more enthusiastic young son and budding racing driver named Bruce—a young man I would come to know very well. Another overseas racer there was big and burly Horace Gould. He was a garage proprietor from Bristol who was running a similar Cooper-Bristol to mine.

Gould came over to Mt Druitt after the New Zealand Races of 1954, and a match-race was arranged between us. At the drop of the flag I'd reached the end of the straight before he'd really got off the line and he was staggered by my car's performance. When he asked me what revs I was using and I told him "six–five" he plainly didn't believe me and said, "Never in your life—everyone knows that anything above five–eight will break the crank." He even asked how many crankshafts I'd gone through. When I said, "None," Gould plainly thought I was having him on because he just did not believe me at all. At the time, I didn't pick-up on what he was saying—in Britain the *RedeX Special* could have been very special indeed! Alas, I was too stupid to recognise the fact.

John Medley was a spectator at Mt Druitt when Horace Gould challenged me in their "International" match race. He recalled:

"I was standing near the start line in the pits: for the first 50 yards the two Cooper Bristols were side-by-side. Brabham was crouched while Gould's beefy arms were turned outwards. Then Gould backed off for Castle Corner. Brabham didn't and was GONE, winning easily. It was not that Horace wasn't trying; it was that

BELOW
These are the outside shed doors I had to burst apart to grab that fire extinguisher the day I nearly lost the *RedeX Special*. Into 2003 every time I return to Goodwood in Britain for its historic Festival of Speed and Revival race meeting, it irritates the hell out of me that I sold this car in Australia and didn't take it to England with me in 1955. If I had I'm sure we'd have absolutely cleaned up.

ABOVE RIGHT
The 1954 Orange Redex trophy.

Brabham's car was at least as quick, and lap record holder Brabham was such a trier, and incredibly competitive. The thing about Brabham at that stage was his EARNESTNESS. You just knew that every time he was on the grid he was there to race—and Horace copped it in spades that day."

Back in the '50s and '60s rallying was like an endurance test, especially the round-Australia RedeX Trial. As my sponsor, Redex entered me in their 1954 Trial, driving a Holden for the Savell Brothers, the Penshurst GM dealership I already knew pretty well. The opening leg north to Darwin was on reasonably good roads. The route went west on dirt roads to Hall's Creek in the Western Australian desert. My co-driver Harry, a Penshurst GM mechanic, had travel sickness. He was no use to me so I navigated and drove effectively single-handed for some 30 hours. We improved on the minimum average speed, completing the stage without penalty.

Hall's Creek was remote and fly-blown—115-degrees in the shade—but provided about six hour's fitful rest. We

LEFT
Dashing turn out for J.A. Brabham and "the immaculate *RedeX Special*". Note the special "custom-made driving shoes"—regular lace-up leather, straight off the shelf.

had a brew-up and sat close to the fire to repel the flies. The route led on to Broome on the west coast, down to Port Hedland, then across to Marble Bar, a gold mining hamlet, and through to another remote outpost called Meekatharra.

Tommy Sulman, driving a big Humber, led us out of Marble Bar at night. We were supposed to be ahead of him, so I was keen to pass and pressed him pretty hard. After about 10–12 miles (15–20 kilometres) we dipped down to cross a dry creek bed. I think the diff beneath Tommy's Humber hit a big rock which it hooked and stood up on end, right in my path, and I hit it. The impact sounded like a bomb. Harry and I were slammed forward. The rock smashed the car's entire front suspension assembly right back, leaving the front wheels outside the front doors, jamming them shut on us!

We were blocking the whole Trial. Eventually enough cars were backed up to provide sufficient manpower to lift

RIGHT
Lining up for yet another match race at Mt Druitt—me in the *RedeX Special* on the left against Dick Cobden in the ex-Peter Whitehead V12 Ferrari on the right. Dick was a stock-broker, a good friend, and a regular competitor. We got on well and when he brought this car to Britain in 1955 it became the first Ferrari ever to appear—for example—at Brands Hatch circuit. With me in the white overalls are Keith Holland (left) and the invaluable Arthur Gray of Belshaw's Foundry (right).

the Holden bodily and dump it at the roadside. Everybody then rushed off and we were left alone. There was no sweeper vehicle nor back-up in those days. We just slept in the car 'til morning, then examined our problem. Basically we were stuffed.

I decided I'd better walk the 12 miles (20 kilometres) or so back into Marble Bar so I left Harry with the car and set off across the desert. That was a bad idea. Just as I was flagging a ball of dust appeared—the first car to come along in 12 hours. It was a retired Trial car and its disappointed four-man crew were simply driving it home. The Holden was miles back and they just seemed completely bemused to find me—where the hell had I come from?

They took pity and drove me into Marble Bar, where I found the tin-shed local garage deserted. At that moment a jeep drew up outside. Kennedy, the driver, worked for the Blue Speck goldmines and had come to "town" for supplies. I thought if I could get some oxygen bottles and welding gear, I might be able to get the Holden running again. Kennedy then drove me to the mine to get some oxy bottles but they were about 8 feet (2.4 metres) tall. There were piles of scrap metal around the site and I collected some pieces which might help us. We loaded the gigantic bottles and some welding rod into the jeep and drove back to Harry.

Our friendly miner said he'd give us a hand with the repairs and, for sure, we'd have the car running in an hour. When he saw it he just blanched and gasped, "Blimey mate! You are in trouble aren't you?" He made his excuses and left. Under Trial rules we had seven days food and water. Once again we were alone.

Next morning we began working. The front subframe was folded back and the radiator smashed around the front of the engine but we had a spare in the boot. We had to rebuild a frame to support the new radiator, and then remake a chassis subframe to locate the front wheels in approximately the right place. A real problem was a steering ball-joint which had been wrenched apart. We used some fencing wire to bind it up.

At about 4pm Harry announced a car was coming. I was under the car welding. It was another jeep driven by a local who had a station about 50–60 miles (80–100 kilometres) further on. The driver stopped and seemed riveted by our gigantic oxy bottles and how we got them. While he stood and watched, we restarted the Holden's engine but it made a terrible noise. The sump had been crushed in and the crank was hammering against it as it rotated. We had to remove the sump, hammer it straight, and then refit it. But it would not fit tight against the engine block. It was warped and created an oil leak that we couldn't fix. Still, we crept off at about 10–15mph (15–25km/h) following our "helpful" jeep driver. After 30–40 miles (50–65 kilometres) we reached a bar with a pump and refilled from our meagre spare supply. We

ABOVE
More RedeX sponsorship very apparent on the Holden I drove in our epic "RedeX Round-Australia Trial" episode in 1954. We set off for a regular rally, and ended up missing for days, marooned in the outback, rebuilding a Holden which any sensible insurance company would have long-since condemned as a total write-off.

bought all the oil that they had and limped on to our new friend's sheep station. He and his wife provided an enormous meal—our first in days.

That night, we set off again aiming for Perth, 1,000 miles (1,600 kilometres) from "The treacherous Rock"! Exactly halfway was Meekatharra. Before we reached it, our steering broke three or four times and we ran out of oil near to the town. We sat by the roadside for three or four hours, until someone drove by and we bought a quart of oil from him. We desperately needed a new sump, fan belt, and our new radiator was leaking because our rough support frame had twisted the bottom off it. We'd been pouring in Barr's Leaks and anything else we could think of to seal it.

Nobody involved with the RedeX Trial had a clue where we were. We'd been posted missing. Meekatharra, however, had telephones and we got a call through to Sydney. My father was on the other end and he nearly burst with relief! I told him we'd spend a couple of days in Meekatharra to do a better repair, then we'd drive the last 500 miles (800 kilometres) to Perth to meet him. But his last words were that he might try to get to Meekatharra to help us.

We rang the Perth dealership for parts. They arrived by plane that evening but one suspension wishbone was cracked and about to fail completely, so we had to ring Perth again. However, instead of waiting for another plane, I welded the cracked wishbone and we set off. But the engine wouldn't run on all six cylinders and we wasted so much time trying to clear this that the plane with the part became due.

We drove out to the airstrip and the plane taxied in...and out stepped my father. Three-up, we drove pretty happily on to Perth. After three days in the GM dealership workshops we replaced the Holden's entire front end and finally drove it the 2,500 miles (4,000 kilometres) across the Australian outback to Sydney. We finally returned to Sydney about two weeks after the RedeX Trial had actually finished!

I thought Savells would be furious with us, but instead they seemed thrilled to bits with all the publicity—proving the endurance of the mighty Holden! It had been a fantastic experience, but after the trip I decided to stick to circuit racing. It was generally more comfortable.

Throughout 1954 the *RedeX Special* continued to do well but CAMS would still not relent on their advertising ban and that rankled with me. I had some great battles with Dick Cobden's V12 Ferrari, Lex Davison's HWM-Jaguar, and Stan Jones's famous *Maybach Special*. But then it was approaching New Year, and I returned to New Zealand for the Grand Prix at Ardmore in January 1955.

I stayed with Leslie "Pop" McLaren and his son Bruce, and was the first Antipodean-based entry, finishing fourth in the *RedeX Special* behind the winner, the Etonian Prince "Bira" in his state-of-the-art Maserati 250F Formula 1 car. Two sister, big-engined 4-cylinder Ferraris were second and third ahead of me, driven by Reg Parnell from Britain and Tony Gaze, another Australian owner/driver but one who had for some time been based in Britain and was now racing in Europe. They were all very nice to me and pretty complimentary about the performance I'd been able to put up. But there were two even more important British visitors attending the event at Ardmore: Dick Jeffrey, who had just been appointed competitions manager of the Dunlop Tyre Company, and Dean Delamont, who was competitions manager of the Royal Automobile Club in London.

During that race meeting we all attended a party thrown at the house of Reg Greason, one of the organisers. I had borrowed a road car for use during that trip and I offered to drive Dean Delamont back to his hotel.

Both he and Dick Jeffrey had been telling me I should come to Britain and try my hand in a season of British and European racing. Now as we drove back to Dean's hotel the discussion continued. Dean was painting a very rosy picture. We pulled up outside his hotel and just sat in the car and continued talking. I would ask the questions and he would provide the very detailed and reasoned answers.

In my youthful enthusiasm I kept him up virtually all night, chattering about the possibilities of racing beyond Australia and New Zealand. When I sailed for home I'd already made up my mind. If just half of what Dick and Dean had told me was right then I'd be mad to dismiss the opportunity. I decided to make the trip to Britain for at least a season of racing there and in mainland Europe. Then I could measure whatever abilities I had against the world's best. With a bit of luck, and a following wind there might just be a real opportunity here. Little did I suspect how hard it would be—and how almost my first move would be to make a terrible mistake.

ABOVE
Right from my grounding in midget speedway racing I appreciated that race promotion could be good for commercial suppliers. Australia's CAMS governing body became bitterly opposed to any overt display of advertising on the cars, and while in later years Esso—for example—would be allowed to dress our area in the paddock, it was a different matter when we put advertising logos on the cars—as on the *RedeX Special*.

LEFT
In the overalls are my mates and mechanics, Keith Hillard (far left)—the Hurstville butcher who'd also helped me around the speedway tracks—and Arthur Gray (cigarette) my friendly Belshaw's Foundry man who cast so many components for me.

Part 2
AN AUSTRALIAN IN EUROPE

Oh yes, I recognise this bloody thing. This shot fills me with revulsion—it's the ex-Peter Whitehead Cooper-Alta with which I saddled myself for my British debut at Goodwood on Easter Monday, 1955. I'd been sold the idea on the basis I just had to have a modern twin-overhead camshaft engine, the *RedeX*'s old 6-cylinder Bristol was obsolete. Well, all they had done to this car was take a perfectly good Cooper-Bristol and destroy it. The Alta engine was a load of rubbish, those centre-lock wire wheels must have weighed twice as much as Cooper's cast-alloy standard ones, and as I floundered around with this heap, my good car was 12,000 miles away…and sold.

Leading an A-Type Connaught around the straw-baled aerodrome at Ibsley in the New Forest, 1955. I knew the Cooper-Alta was a bad mistake, and had made up my mind to buy a Bristol engine for it. In fact I couldn't wait to rid myself of that Alta unit.

CHAPTER 3

FIRST STEPS, FIRST MISTAKES!

Bitten by the badly chosen Cooper-Alta, saved by the self-built rear-engined Cooper-Bristol "Bobtail"

It was early in 1955 when I bade farewell to Betty, our son Geoffrey, and my parents. I boarded a Qantas Super Constellation bound for Europe. To finance the trip I had either sold, or was in the process of selling, virtually every piece of motor racing hardware I had. Later, I would come to regret selling my lathe and other workshop machinery but my immediate need, however, was the money.

Stan Jones, father of Alan who would become Formula 1 World Champion driving for Williams in 1980, had wrecked his *Maybach Special* during the 1954 Australian Grand Prix. On my return from New Zealand in 1955 I sold him the *RedeX Special*. I would later realise that this was a bad move—if I had only recognised its international potential instead of believing all the stories I'd been told about how sophisticated the British racing scene would be, I should have taken it with me. In retrospect, I'm absolutely confident the car would have cleaned up!

There was no way I could have known that at the time, though. I just assumed that everything in British racing would be streets ahead of anything we'd ever seen in Australia. At Ardmore, during the New Zealand Grand Prix meeting, I met British driver Peter Whitehead. He was quite a superstar at the time, having won Le Mans in a Jaguar, and was one of Ferrari's earliest private Formula 1 car customers. Whitehead had suggested I should buy his 2-litre Formula 2 Cooper-Alta. It had a similar chassis to the *RedeX's* but I understood that it was powered by a "state of the art" 4-cylinder racing engine made by Alta Engineering. I thought the twin overhead camshafts would make it light years ahead of the *RedeX's* (basically) pre-war BMW-derived 6-cylinder Bristol design. I'd taken in everything Whitehead told me and we agreed a price and I was to take delivery in his garage at Chalfont St Peter upon arrival in Britain. Meanwhile, Dean Delamont had arranged an entry for me in the first big race of the British season at Goodwood on Easter Monday.

I had the outline of a full season's racing mapped out and had contacted John Cooper in his works at Surbiton. I'd previously only corresponded with him through the

LEFT
Driving my ex-Whitehead Cooper in Bristol-engined form in the BRDC International Trophy race at May Silverstone, 1955. That's a Maserati 250F in the background—I really fell for its Italian lines and twin-overhead camshaft 6-cylinder engine. That had to be the way to go—I thought. Shortly the stage would be set for me to make my second big mistake…but first of all the Cooper Car Co. came to my temporary rescue.

RIGHT
Charles and John Cooper gave me free run of their little racing car factory in Hollyfield Road, Surbiton, to build this Bristol-powered, rear-engined "Bobtail" Formula 1 hybrid in time for the 1955 British Grand Prix. Their little 1100cc "Bobtail" sports cars used the same centre-seat chassis and wheel-enveloping aluminium bodywork made by in-house panel-bashers "The Beddings", Fred and son Pete. When at Le Mans as the works Bristol team's reserve driver, one of my new team-mates was Jim Mayers. He had a "Bobtail" Cooper sports built for him to race in the 1955 Tourist Trophy at Dundrod, and invited me to co-drive it with him. We tossed a coin there to decide who would take the first stint. He won, and was killed in a terrible fiery crash on the second lap. Dean Delamont thought I'd been driving and he arrived at our pits—grim-faced to break the news of my death to Betty…only to find me sitting there, worried about Jim Mayers.

LEFT
The 2-litre Bristol 6-cylinder engine installed in the back of my "Bobtail" Cooper which I completed just in time for the 1955 British Grand Prix at Aintree. The Cooper used their lightweight cast alloy wheels and of course the chassis frame used the curved-tube concept from which Charlie Cooper and perhaps more so his designer, Owen Maddock, simply would not be budged. The problem with this "Formula 1" Bristol engine was that it didn't benefit from the cylinder head and carburetion tweaks developed on the *RedeX Special* which I bitterly regretted having sold. The only bit I had brought from Australia was the Harley-Davidson clutch, and ironically that was the bit which let me down at Aintree.

mail. We hit it off straight away and had a great deal in common. He was faultlessly enthusiastic and we would remain firm friends.

I had run the Cooper-Alta in as many single-seater races as possible, while a group of better-heeled, Aussie owner-drivers were to campaign a team of Aston Martin DB3S sports cars in Europe—the "Kangaroo Stable". I was to drive alongside them. They were Tony Gaze, Dick Cobden, Les Cosh, Tommy Sulman, and David McKay.

The long trip in the growling Super Connie aircraft took three-and-a-half days from Sydney to Rome. With letters of introduction to visit Maserati, Ferrari, Abarth, and then Mercedes-Benz in Germany, I set off from Rome to Modena where the Maserati people were very friendly and then tried my luck with Ferrari—but my reception was very different: they turned me away. I thought "Fine" but couldn't forget it. Of course, nobody there had a clue who this strange visitor might be but they'd find out a few years later when they were having to chase my Cooper's tail. I caught the train up to Milan, then Turin to visit Abarth—

a trip that became a fair-sized drama. I was falling behind schedule so, upon arrival in Turin, quickly checked into a hotel just across the street from the railway station before taking a tram to the Abarth factory.

The people were very friendly and I spent the whole day there before catching a tram back. The trouble was that I had checked-in to the hotel so quickly that I couldn't remember its name! I tried to retrace my steps and, remembering where the tram had come from, tried to hop off at the same place. However, I alighted at the wrong station and there was no hotel in sight. It was my first time on "foreign soil", I couldn't speak a word of Italian, and could find nobody who spoke English. Finally I decided to follow the railway line so, tramping along beside the tracks, I was relieved when my plan worked like a charm and I was able finally to flop into bed that night.

My next journey was to Daimler-Benz in Stuttgart where their press officer gave me a guided tour of the Mercedes works. One of the staff was driving to Amsterdam the next day and he gave me a lift to Hanover

ABOVE
When I bought my replacement engine from Bristol to breathe some life into that terrible Cooper-Alta, the man I dealt with was Vivian Selby (right). He was also in charge of their works sports car team entered for Le Mans, and he offered me a run there as the Bristol team's reserve driver. Here during practice I'm just about to drive the minimum mileage necessary to qualify. My services were not required in the race.

Airport to catch the BEA Elizabethan for the final leg of my journey: to London's Heathrow Airport. Finally, I had arrived for my first season's racing in Britain and mainland Europe with no way of realising that I would remain, in effect, British-based for the next 16 years. My feelings were that I'd just launched myself into the great unknown so, before sending for my family, I had to make sure I was doing the right thing. I couldn't wait to see my new Cooper-Alta and rushed off to Whitehead's garage at Chalfont St Peter. It wasn't long before the realisation dawned—I'd made a dreadful choice.

I took the vehicle to Goodwood for the Easter Monday meeting where I met John Morgan, Secretary of the BARC (British Automobile Racing Club), to finalise my entry. I knew, of course, they'd pay some kind of start money but I struggled to keep a straight face when he offered double what I expected. I really appreciated his support because, at the time, he didn't know me at all.

I needed fuel. The Shell company in Australia had given me a letter of introduction which I took to Bryan Turle, their UK racing manager, in the paddock. But he said it was not possible to have any fuel without having a contract with them. I didn't want a contract—I just wanted some darned fuel! Nothing doing. That really fazed me, but John Cooper introduced me to Reg Tanner of Esso: "Certainly, no problem". Back in Australia, we didn't use methanol fuel because the engines running it were always thirstier, so I had no experinece of using it. I calculated how much fuel I'd need, based on the car's fuel

FIRST STEPS, FIRST MISTAKES! | 53

LEFT
Cornering the "Bobtail" Cooper-Bristol with its clutch already slipping in my debut World Championship-qualifying Formula 1 race—the 1955 British Grand Prix at Aintree. Following me are Leslie Marr's streamlined Connaught B-Type (38) and Harry Schell's early Vanwall (30), which used a chassis designed to order by Cooper. Tony Vandervell was having a replacement Vanwall frame designed for him by Colin Chapman of Lotus for 1956. It would win the Constructors' World Championship.

ABOVE
British Grand Prix—hard pressed into Tatts Corner on the Aintree circuit during the 1955 British Grand Prix. Following me are Karl Kling's third-placed Mercedes-Benz (14) and Roberto Mieres' works Maserati 250F (6). I was learning fast.

consumption quoted by Whitehead's mechanics. This information was way off so my maths let me down. I was about two gallons short and just before the finish line, the Alta engine spluttered and died. When I coasted into the pits out of gas the hot engine wouldn't restart.

For the duration of the race that the car had kept running for, I'd given it my best shot. A race report, the first naming me in Britain and written by the editor of the weekly *Autosport* magazine, read: "This Aussie is certainly a presser-onner, and possesses remarkable control over his car. More will be heard of this young gentleman." On my next outing, at Ibsley aerodrome in the New Forest, not much was heard from me. Just as I was running fourth in a race led by Roy Salvadori, that frail Alta engine broke.

I decided to ditch this engine and bought a Bristol instead. I moved the car out of Peter Whitehead's place at Chalfont St Peter where I'd been working on it and moved down to Bob Chase's garage at Saltdean, near Brighton (Bob had owned the Cooper-Bristol in which Mike Hawthorn had made his racing mark three years earlier). I fitted the Bristol engine and returned the Alta unit to its manufacturer, Geoffrey Taylor in Chessington, to rebuild and modify it to their latest spec (although by the time he returned it, my first European season was over and, later, I'd take it back home and sell it in Australia).

I drove the Alta with the Bristol engine installed at Silverstone for the first time in the BRDC (British Racing Drivers' Club) International Trophy race. It was my first time on a proper Grand Prix circuit and it was a real thrill to be in the same race with the likes of Moss, Hawthorn, Collins, Salvadori, and again with Prince "Bira" who had won the New Zealand GP back in January. I finished seventh and *Autosport* again commented on my cornering. You might take the boy out of the speedway, I guess, but you couldn't take the speedway out of the boy.

Meanwhile, I was always popping in and out of the Cooper Car Company works in Hollyfield Road, Surbiton, for parts and a natter. Dismayed and disappointed by the Cooper-Alta we dreamt-up a more modern replacement. John and his father Charlie Cooper (a tough old stick) agreed to my using their facilities to build an enveloping-bodied Formula 1 car. This would combine a lengthened version of their latest centre-seat "Bobtail" sports car chassis and bodywork, with a rear-mounted Bristol 6-cylinder engine. I pitched into this project during the late spring and early summer. One day, early on, John had asked me to try out the new Cooper "Bobtail". This as standard used a Coventry Climax fire pump engine mounted in the back, driving through what had been a Citroen front-drive gearbox unit. This was modified by a French company named ERSA and turned about-face to drive the Cooper's rear wheels. To have the engine behind the driver was quite unique at that time.

For some reason, when we took the car down to Goodwood for our test session, I had to drive the transporter. On the road south from Dorking I could have sworn I heard bells ringing. My first thoughts were, "I didn't know they had bell birds in England." Then I glanced in my rearview mirror to see a police car in hot pursuit—of me! I'd never seen a police car with bells on it, we didn't have them in Australia, but I was seeing one now all right. I'd been speeding. The coppers demanded my name and address and inspected my licence, and I gave my address as, "c/o Cooper Car Company, 243 Ewell Road, Surbiton." Before long the inevitable summons dropped onto the mat at Cooper's but John just picked it up and wrote on the envelope "Returned to Australia—forwarding address unknown." We heard no more about it. I thought then that this bloke was good news.

About halfway through that 1955 season I began working at Cooper's on a daily basis. I wasn't an employee, typically perhaps, they didn't pay actual *money*, but I just pitched in and became "part of the fittings" as John later put it. I was confident there was a future here and sent to Australia that Betty should join me. Geoffrey stayed with my parents. After a few weeks stay with one of Bob Chase's mechanics, Peter Morrice, we moved into a flat in Ewell Road, Surbiton, adjacent to Cooper's. Our landlady, Mrs Stott, had a small garage adjacent to the house where I worked on the racing car.

I'd already made my debut by this time with the "Kangaroo Stable" team in the 6-Hours race at Hyeres in France, where our three Astons finished second, third, and fourth. The winning Ferrari actually blew-up on its *tour d'honneur*–very frustrating because it meant that we'd been so close to a win. It was the first time I'd ever driven as part of a team instead of just an individual. Soon afterwards the sports-car calendar was shattered by the Le Mans 24-Hours disaster in which a Mercedes crashed into the crowd, killing its driver (Levegh) and over 80 spectators. I'd actually been present at Le Mans, as reserve driver for the works Bristol team—for whom of course I'd become a customer. During practice I'd just been left hanging around, awaiting my chance to drive. They finally seemed to remember me at dusk, just as dense mist settled along the Mulsanne Straight. I'd never driven on a race track at night before and didn't like either the experience or the car very much. I was relieved not to be required during that tragic race. Most of the later-season events which had been on the "Kangaroo

ABOVE
By the time of the big Snetterton meeting in August I had sorted out the "Bobtail"-Bristol to the point where I could lead on a damp but drying track. Here I am, doing my darndest to keep Stirling Moss at bay in his private Maserati 250F. As the track dried his power proved decisive, but my race that day convinced me to persevere and return to Britain the following year. Looking back from almost 50 years' range, this was a crucial turning point in my career.

BELOW
My wife Betty and I with the "Bobtail"-Bristol at the Crystal Palace circuit in 1955. We returned to Britain in 1956 by boat, bringing our son Geoffrey, tools and equipment, and a load of household stuff.

Stable's" schedule were cancelled, leaving me without my further expected drives.

During this time I was working feverishly on the rear-engined Cooper-Bristol "Bobtail", which was barely finished the night before the British Grand Prix at Aintree. This was my World Championship-qualifying Grand Prix debut, but on race morning the clutch was giving trouble. I finally retired with it slipping hopelessly but felt confident the car had potential. For darned sure it had better potential than the unlamented Cooper-Alta!

Initially, my optimism was unfounded. The clutch jumped out of gear at Crystal Palace which bent the valves as it over-revved, and at Brands Hatch it split its gearbox case—a Cooper habit which would become painfully familiar over the next few years. I towed it all the way up to Charterhall in Scotland where at last I crossed the finish line taking a couple of fourth places. Then we took it to a more important Formula 1 race at Snetterton which was dominated up front by the works Vanwalls of Harry Schell and Ken Wharton who ran away. But my "Bobtail"-Bristol went really well. I had a hell of a battle for third place with Stirling Moss in his private Maserati 250F. The press got pretty excited about it, Gregor Grant of *Autosport* described it as "a classic contest":

> "...the crowd even forgot to watch the Vanwalls, so engrossed were they with the struggle. Brabham threw the little rear-engined Cooper around at a fair rate of knots, with Moss ever on the lookout for a chance to pass. Brabham, to the huge delight of his friends in the Kangaroo Stable, stubbornly refused to be passed by the redoubtable Moss. For lap after lap they raced in close company, the Australian doing things with a car that were reminiscent of Pete Walker in his early 'Skid' Walker days—but no matter what he did, he managed to hold off Moss. Stirling did slip past into the Esses, only to be repassed in Coram's Curve. The Maserati went ahead again, but this time Brabham cheekily nipped in front at Riches Corner, sliding wildly on the rapidly drying track, but keeping the car on the tarmac. Then, with four laps to go, the Australian spun off at the hairpin, collecting a miniature haystack in his under-chassis air scoop. Undaunted, he set off in an attempt to catch Moss, but he had lost far too much ground, and the Maserati sailed home to an unchallenged third place..."

Apart from ultimately overcooking that corner, I certainly enjoyed that race, and so did Stirling—or at least, he said he did. It was a real landmark race for me. Until that time I hadn't really seen a glimmer of the kind of form and success to which I'd become accustomed in my years of racing at home. After all, I'd been racing on the speedways and then road circuits for seven years. I'd

FIRST STEPS, FIRST MISTAKES! | 57

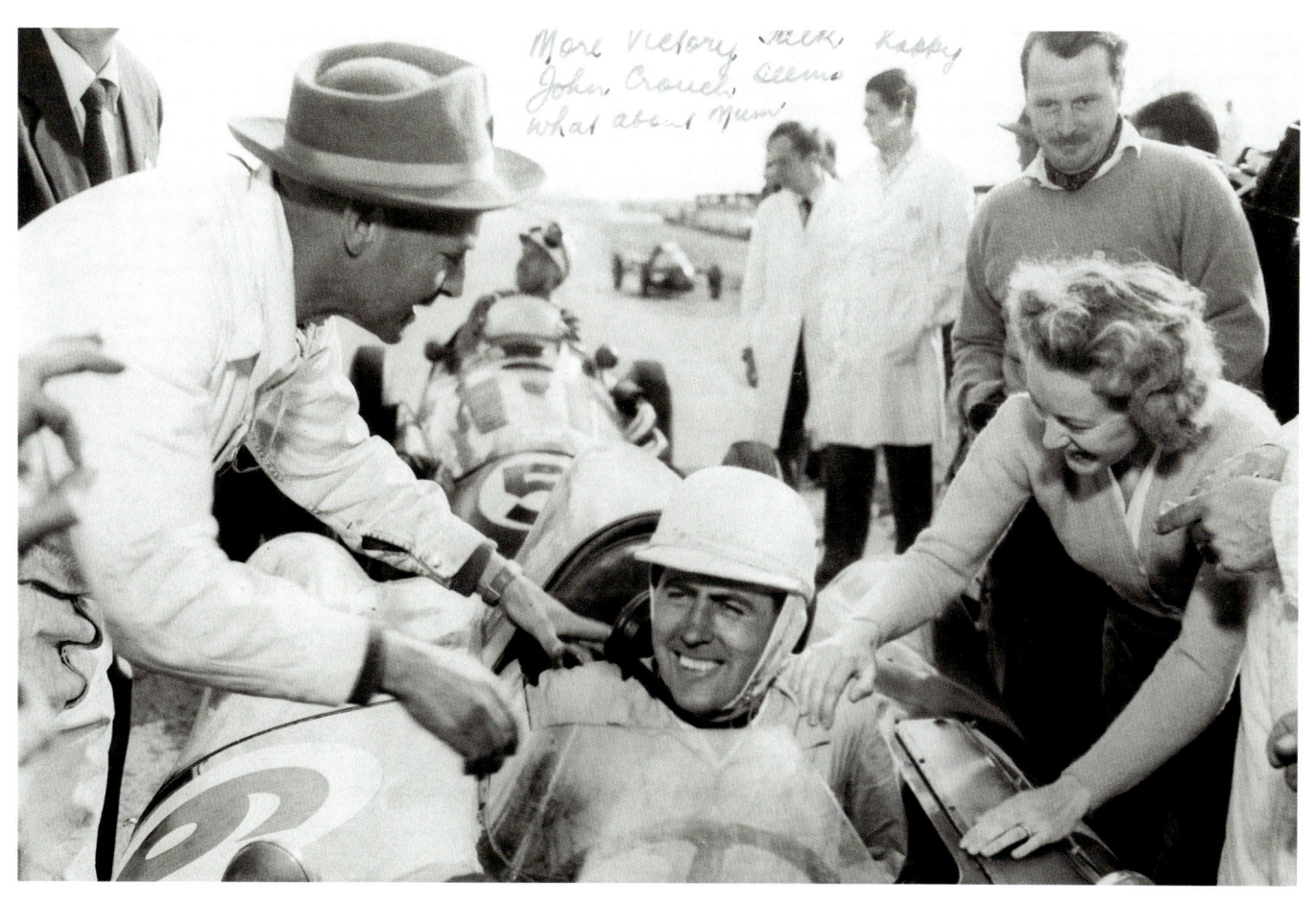

LEFT
It's an understatement to say I was pleased with my win in the Australian Grand Prix on the barren little artificial road circuit at Port Wakefield, South Australia, in November '55. Here I'm greeted by Reg Thompson of RedeX Melbourne (left) who later managed my racing in Australia, with Betty to the right and Cooper importer John Crouch beyond her.

experienced almost immediate success, and had come to Britain with high hopes and tremendous encouragement from Dean Delamont, John Cooper, and others. So far it had not really come off. If it hadn't been for that race I might have gone back to Australia for good. However, I'd been driving a car which drove really well and felt that I had performed pretty well too. So I laid plans to return home temporarily for the Australian summer/British winter, and to return to Britain the following year. The "Bobtail"-Bristol had won its spurs and I shipped it home to continue racing there.

At Bathurst in October 1955 it sheared its oil pump drive during practice. At Orange I coasted home second in a preliminary race after leading, and then lasted only one lap of the feature. My father helped me tow all the way down to Adelaide for the Australian GP in November, which was being run on a desolate little artificial circuit at Port Wakefield. I'd never any luck in my home Grand Prix but this time would be different. Reg Hunt's Maserati 250F took the lead from Stan Jones's rebuilt *Maybach Special* with myself third in the Cooper. Hunt's engine went onto five cylinders, Jonesie's clutch froze, and I began catching them both. On lap 11, I got by the *Maybach* into second place and was able to reel-in Reg Hunt before passing him too, just before half distance. At one point I went off on some spilled oil, stuffing the Cooper's intakes with vegetation, but retained my lead to the end. It was not only the first Australian GP I'd ever managed to finish, it was also my longest-ever race in that one-off stop-gap "Bobtail"-Bristol.

I raced the car several times during that Australian summer, winning once at Mt Druitt, but had to non-start in what should have been my third New Zealand GP in January 1956—the gearbox case split again. Never mind, the car was the Australian GP winner, and the profit I made from selling it helped finance my return trip to Britain. I had big plans: I was going to buy a proper Formula 1 car—a Maserati 250F. This was to be my second big mistake.

BELOW
The 1955 Australian Grand Prix trophy.

CHAPTER 4
COOPER WORKS DRIVER

How the good years began with Charlie Cooper saying, "Yeah, you can drive the transporter down to Imola"

I needed a thirst-quencher in the works *Bobtail*-Climax sports car on the Italian circuit at Imola where I finished second to Castellotti's OSCA. I'd spent all night repairing and rebuilding one of our three team cars and had only just managed to dive back to our hotel for a quick shower before reporting at the circuit just in time to race. Oh, and I drove the works transporter there and back as well.

In March 1957 I was more than ready to return to England to commence my third season of racing in Europe. Cooper customer Rob Walker had sent me a telegram suggesting I should meet him in Sicily where he would like me to drive his Formula 2 car in the season-opening Syracuse Grand Prix.

I jumped at the chance, flying from Sydney to Rome, where I found that the connecting flight to Syracuse had been cancelled. Fellow driver Harry Schell and newspaperman Alan Brinton were in the same boat. We shared a taxi to the Rome railway station and caught the overnight sleeper south. In the middle of the night I woke to find the train silent and motionless. It had stopped in a station. I nodded off to sleep again, and when I woke up, this time to sun streaming through the window, I looked out upon the self-same station. I couldn't believe it, we hadn't moved an inch.

This was a disaster. You cannot arrive late for a motor race. Nobody will wait for you. Harry Schell was out on the platform bawling, yelling, and waving his arms about. Apparently a derailment had blocked the line ahead. Practice would be starting that morning in Syracuse. We couldn't just hang about at the mercy of the Italian railway system. Alan and I left the multilingual Harry to fix-up something. Eventually Harry returned in triumph, announcing that he'd managed to hire a taxi. When it turned up, in a cloud of smoke, we thought it must have been Italy's first-ever. It was a cranky old museum piece, but we crammed into it, and staggered off south but not for long, it had a puncture.

We changed the wheel in almost modern Formula 1 pitstop time, before the driver had even put his coat on, and leapt back in, urging on the driver who plainly couldn't understand why we seemed to be in such a hurry. "Syracuse!" I bawled at him, "*Siracusa*", yelled Harry Schell, "*Forza!!!*".

At last we spluttered to a halt at the ferry port, rushed onto the boat and Harry went to work on the Captain to

LEFT
Another big Brabham mistake—the ex-Owen Racing Organisation (BRM team) Maserati 250F in which I'd invested every penny I had in the world for my return to British and European racing at the start of 1956. That's young Geoffrey at the wheel of the green-and-gold Australian-liveried car, with two mechanics helping from Cooper's (right) and Geoffrey Taylor's Alta works (left). The Maserati looked good but the bills it ran up did not. Purchase tax on BRM's 250F had been unpaid so when I bought it I had to re-import it via the Channel Islands and the Newhaven crane driver nearly dropped it on the dock! A third place at Aintree preceded costly engine trouble and return to Maserati for rebuild. I drove a VW 1500 Combi to Modena with Betty and Geoffrey to collect it, where Maserati cleaned me out. A huge shunt with a French truck was narrowly averted before our ferry rammed another in English Channel fog! I never raced the 250F again, and John Cooper rescued me with sports and Formula 2 drives. Ending 1956, John agreed I could drive in the team if I returned from the 1956–1957 "down-under" races...and that is what I did.

THE CLIMAX ENGINE

Cooper cars had always used off-the-shelf engines made by Coventry Climax of Widdrington Road, Coventry.

A Civil Defence contract meant they had effectively cornered the market in fire-pump engines. The specification demanded pumps which were light and portable by two men. Well, they might have had to be two particularly husky men, but the all-aluminium engine they developed, initially with a single overhead camshaft operating the valvegear, was light and respectably powerful. The contract also meant the pump was produced in sufficient numbers to make its unit price affordable. The result was an ideal power unit for a production racing car, available to private owner/drivers.

This single-cam Climax engine was known as the type FWA for Featherweight series A, and was adopted by Cooper, Lotus, Kieft, Elva, and numerous other racing constructors of the mid 1950s. It was used mainly in 1100cc form but for 1956 an enlarged single-cam FWB version was developed, of 1500cc. This single-cam was regarded as a stop-gap until a new twin-overhead camshaft engine could be developed. This new twin-cam Climax engine finally emerged for 1957 and became the backbone of the new 1500cc F2 racing category, powering fleets of privately-owned as well as works-entered Cooper and Lotus cars.

The dry-sumped twin-cam 1475cc Climax FPF engine (designed and developed under the direction of Wally Hassan) was the first genuine production racing engine ever built in Britain. It would subsequently be enlarged to 2-litres to provide us with a tentative toe-in-the-water of F1. Ultimately, with a new larger cylinder block and head, it would grow to a full 2½-litre Formula 1 capacity for the 1959 World Championship season. We could not have achieved what we did without Coventry Climax Engines Ltd.

---

fix us some transport on the other side. Landing at Catania we found a brand-new Fiat 1100 awaiting us. Harry filled-in the rental company paperwork with the proprietor emphasising how the little car had completed delivery mileage only, and begging us to take care and run it in carefully. He'd just finished this little speech when Harry dropped the clutch and we screamed off in a cloud of tyre smoke.

That drive to Syracuse was something else. I'd dived straight into the back when I realised Harry was intent on driving, which left Alan transfixed for the duration in the front passenger seat. I braced one foot on each side and found some straps to hang onto in the middle. It helped not to have a vivid imagination.

Rob was his usual unflappable self when we finally fell out of the steaming, smoking, worn-out wreck of a Fiat in the Syracuse paddock. Amongst full 2½-litre Formula 1 company which included the works Ferraris, Maseratis, Vanwalls, and Connaughts, I finally finished sixth in his 1500cc Cooper. Sixth out of seven finishers.

The Easter Monday Goodwood took place the following weekend in Britain. I drove a works Cooper in the Formula 1 Glover Trophy race and finished fourth. Meanwhile Rob had been very impressed by the little single-seater Cooper's potential, and during a previous test session at Goodwood Roy Salvadori had suggested that enlargement of the Climax engine could make it a competitive proposition around a really tight Formula 1 circuit, such as Monte Carlo, for the Monaco Grand Prix.

Rob was a great enthusiast, and he immediately offered to underwrite such a project, paying for Coventry Climax to enlarge an engine from its standard 1498cc to 1960cc—just under 2-litres. Roy couldn't drive it, he had signed to drive BRM works Formula 1 cars that season, though he would still be running the Coopers in Formula 2. Rob decided to take his car to Monaco as a 1500 Formula 2 entry, while I was entrusted with the Cooper works' 2-litre "interim" Formula 1 car there.

This makeshift "Formula 1" Cooper-Climax had been fitted with larger fuel tanks as well as the bigger engine. But I was late getting to Monaco (to Charlie Cooper's disgust) and when I took it out in the second practice session I found its brakes had not been properly bedded-in and the front-to-rear brake balance was way out.

We had to set a time amongst the top 16 to qualify for a start in the Monaco GP, so I had to press on because it might rain during final practice, which would have wasted all the effort we had put in. I'd been juggling the braking ratio but now with time running out it was do or die. I went for a time, whistled over the top of the hill into the adverse-camber left-hander at the Casino and the rear brakes locked-up on me.

I slithered straight off into the right-side barrier, which in those days comprised sandbags and telegraph poles. The little car punched-in beneath one pole, threw it up high into the air, and shot underneath it before the pole came down like a guillotine blade, "crunch" on to the engine cowl, just behind my head. Our special car was quite beyond immediate repair.

This was acutely embarrassing, but Rob's 1500cc Formula 2 Cooper had also been taken down for Les Leston to drive only for its engine to fail during first practice. So here we had one wrecked 2-litre "F1" car with a perfectly healthy engine, and one perfectly healthy F2 car with a wrecked 1500cc engine. So overnight we dropped the special 2-litre engine into Rob's F2 chassis, which I then drove in the Grand Prix...to poor Les Leston's discomfort.

The race then went really rather well and I started 13th fastest on the grid. And after benefiting from faster cars' failures up ahead and with the car proving so quick and nimble around the houses, I found myself running third with only three laps to go when, climbing the hill towards the scene of my Friday crash, the engine coughed, stammered, and was plainly running out of fuel.

The engine picked-up and ran as I dived down around the Station and out on to the seafront, but then it cut dead in the tunnel. The fuel pump mount had broken and it had fallen from its drive. I was able to coast down through the chicane onto the quayside, and then rolled to a stop on the little rise at Tabac Corner. I was pumped up and dismayed. It was about 800 yards (75 metres) to the finish line. In those days I really hated to be beaten, so I threw myself at the car and began to push. I was soaked in sweat but at last reached Louis Chiron who was waving the chequered flag—and we had finished sixth.

I received the biggest ovation I'd ever had up 'til then, and our performance really hit the headlines. The little Cooper had amply demonstrated what nimble handling and light weight could do in Formula 1 company with just

ABOVE
Our team: John Cooper (left), myself, and Harry Spiers who was in charge of engine dyno testing and also the customer liaison engineer with Coventry Climax engines. Cooper cars with Coventry Climax engines mounted behind the cockpit would revolutionise the face of motor racing and racing car design with a bit of help from myself, and from Ron Tauranac, the Australian engineer and my pen pal.

MONACO 1957

ABOVE
The original uprated 1.96-litre Cooper-Climax, which Rob Walker had funded to compete in the 1957 Monaco Grand Prix, ready to go before practice in the Monte Carlo pits.

ABOVE RIGHT
And I'm afraid this is what I did to our bright and shiny brand-new car, although the fact that the front and rear brake circuit master cylinders had ben piped up the wrong way round certainly contributed.

RIGHT
With my head sunk down into my shoulders (thoroughly cheesed off and embarrassed) I feel I've just wrecked all our hopes as I clamber from the wreck. That telegraph pole has rolled off the engine cover onto the roadway. We have a lot of work ahead of us before the race.

MONACO 1957

LEFT
The lightweight little rear-engined Cooper's good handling and acceleration with just 1.96-litres and about 180-horsepower embarrassed many big front-engined cars.

ABOVE
Practice shot showing me trying out Rob Walker's spare Formula 2 car into which we fitted the enlarged 1.96-litre Climax engine from my Casino wreck for the race.

BELOW
Giorgio Scarlatti in the traditional front-engined Maserati 250F clips the apex at the Station Hairpin as I turn in tightly with the new-generation rear-engined Cooper-Climax.

a little more power than was standard in Formula 2. That Monaco GP was a real landmark in motor racing history, for it signposted the way ahead—the truly-competitive rear-engined Formula 1 car was on its way—even though, plainly, it was not there yet. There had been numerous retirements of faster cars, yet because of the small fuel tanks I'd had to make a mid-race refuelling stop, yet we had still got up into third place overall.

Gregor Grant again provided great support, reporting in *Autosport:* "Brabham's effort in pushing his crippled car nearly a mile to the finish was warmly applauded. The little hill at the tobacconist's kiosk nearly defeated him, and when he finally reached the finish line, the Australian was so exhausted that he could not hear what was being said to him, nor could he utter a word". The truth of it is that I didn't want to talk, not that I couldn't—that fuel pump mounting failure was pretty disappointing.

Over the Whit weekend we had Formula 2 races at Brands Hatch on Sunday and Crystal Palace on Monday. At Brands I won both parts of the Formula 2 race, beating Roy—and next day he and I had a tremendous tussle on his favourite circuit. He really was "The King of the Palace" and he won the first F2 race there while in the second I beat him to win the London Trophy overall, setting a new lap record along the way.

Now I was racing full-time for Cooper, and the following weekend found us at Montlhéry in France for the *Prix de Paris*, where I beat Mike MacDowel. After the race journalist-cum-Lotus owner/driver "Jabby" Crombac took me to the ERSA factory where our special 4-speed gear sets were made. The idea was to see if ERSA would make a special gearbox for us. They said "Yes" but it would take 11 or 12 months.

This was bad news, but as I was there I asked if it was possible to see their foundry. I could hardly believe my eyes! We came across hundreds of Citroen gearbox cases fresh from casting. It suddenly hit me; it would be dead easy to modify some cores before they were cast. Luckily, the foundry foreman was a bit of a racer, and he agreed to the modifications if I did the job myself. So I spent the rest of the day putting in ribs with plasticine and adding metal in all the places where we'd had trouble.

The guys at ERSA finally agreed to cast about 25 special gearbox casings for us. This was a big step forward for Cooper, and within two weeks they were on our workshop floor in Surbiton.

BELOW
Seeing this picture made me cringe. I was holding a sure third place in only my second World Championship-qualifying Grand Prix (at Monaco in 1957) when the machined bracket broke which was holding a special high-capacity aircraft fuel pump that I'd brought with me specially from Australia. That large-capacity pump had promised to be far more reliable than the rather nasty SU pumps Cooper used as standard. Cooper had a lot of machining done by Jack Knight's specialised shop in London. But when I arrived in Britain I discovered two things Poms couldn't do: one was lay smooth concrete, the other was to machine parts reliably. The sharp angle machined on the pump bracket provided a stress raiser which caused fatigue failure of the bracket. If the angle had been gently raised there would have been no stress raiser and it would not have failed.

We had a busy schedule. I even co-drove with Ian Raby at Le Mans that year—our Cooper "Bobtail" sports car finishing 13th overall and third in class, which we had won the year before. The French Grand Prix followed on the demanding Les Essarts circuit around a densely wooded valley just outside Rouen. I had driven occasionally in the same race as Juan Fangio, but it was here at Rouen that I fully appreciated his true greatness. After the pit area, the road dived downhill through a series of fast and deceptive curves. Fangio drifted his works Maserati *Lightweight* down through this series of bends at simply fantastic speed, just flicking it from lock to lock, left, right, left. His control in that car was perfectly magnificent, and it was a privilege to see—as he hurtled past me.

He won, and I finished seventh. On that course, particularly on the climbing back section where power really told, our little makeshift 2-litre Cooper just wasn't man enough for the job. We did the best we could, but another sight which impressed me that year was Ron Flockhart's violent shunt in the BRM. I liked Ron a lot. He was a Scot from Edinburgh, and a private flyer who rekindled my interest in aviation. I was behind him when he went off on oil, dived into a ditch, and then somersaulted off the roadside bank. He got away without serious injury, which was perhaps the weekend's most surprising news.

We ran the Cooper in the British Grand Prix at Aintree where Moss and Brooks shared home victory in the big green Vanwall, and my clutch failed when I was seventh. At Nürburgring, the German Grand Prix proved to be a real classic, with Fangio up-front eating Hawthorn and Collins alive in their Ferraris, to win after a long delay in the pits. He clinched his fifth and final World Championship title with that win. Roy and I ran 1500cc Coopers in the race's Formula 2 section. Roy knew the circuit really well and qualified fastest in Formula 2 and on row four amongst the Formula 1 cars, while I lined-up on row five. But the bumpy course beat us both; Roy's car broke its suspension and my gearbox failed...again. I found myself spectating in the pits, and I recall that race as one of the finest I ever saw from the sidelines. The drama was fantastic as Fangio repeatedly smashed the lap record during his come-back drive, caught the two English boys in their Ferraris and then passed them both to win the race and the World Championship. I could only dream. One day....

LEFT
I'd been interested in aeroplanes since my childhood. The double Le Mans-winning Jaguar driver Ron Flockhart (right) was a great private flyer and firm friend who often flew down from Edinburgh to see us in Surrey. I flew with him to a few Continental races in 1958 and by 1959 I was learning to fly here at Fairoaks aerodrome, near Woking, instructed by Wing Commander Arthur. I bought my first plane, a Cessna 180, and did the last 10 of my required 40 hours training in that. The day after I passed my general flying test I took off in the Cessna with Betty and Dean Delamont of the RAC...bound for Oporto.

ABOVE
The 1957 Pescara Grand Prix programme.

RIGHT
Out for a sun-soaked drive in the countryside. The Pescara circuit on Italy's Adriatic coast was a fantastic place to run a World Championship Grand Prix. Here I am, leaning on it in the 1½-litre-engined Cooper between tall concrete kerbs, straw bales, banks, trees, and ditches. It was pretty similar to some of the road courses and weather I'd grown up with back home in Australia. But what I didn't expect to find when I ran out of fuel was a trackside filling station. It was open, ready, and willing to do business! I finished 7th, lapped three times by Stirling Moss's winning 1-litre larger Vanwall.

Our next Grand Prix date was at Pescara, the first of two World Championship rounds to be held in August and Sepember of 1954 in Italy. The course was a genuine country road circuit, 17 miles (27 kilometres) round with an enormously long seaside straight parallel to the Adriatic beaches. Roy was out of luck, bending his Cooper against one of the many roadside marker stones. There were plenty of retirements in the thin field and with only seven survivors still running after half distance I had a lonely drive in the sun. At one point I came past the pits to see Roy standing there holding my pit signal board. It read simply "I'm going swimming".

I started my last lap fifth or sixth, and was going pretty well when I ran out of fuel. Unbelievable. I was coasting along, hearing only the clatter of grit and gravel being thrown up by the tyres, when there came into sight, on the right-hand side of the road, a filling station! There were a few spectators standing there, and I coasted into the forecourt, and pulled up at the pumps. The pump attendant just about burst with excitement. Cometh the hour, cometh the man. He was brilliant, he grabbed the pump hose, fired in just a few litres, enough to get me home, and I restarted and rejoined the race. I finished seventh (again), three times lapped.

Next morning Roy, John Cooper, and I were driving back to Britain with Tony Brooks and his Italian girlfriend, Pina. I was late out of the hotel, and when I got to our Hillman Minx (yes, we certainly used to travel in style) there was only one seat left, the driver's. So it was down to me.

We hadn't been going long when we came up behind a local on a motor scooter who was attempting to overtake a big semi-trailer truck. I hesitated, giving him room, which triggered a barrage of criticism and/or encouragement from my passengers. Roy was particularly noisy, "Come ON Jack, get ON with it—PASS him for heavens' sake". I finally did as requested, but the chap on the scooter was alongside the truck at almost zero passing speed, and as we drew abreast of them both Roy suddenly leaned over, grabbed my steering wheel, and gave it a tweak which nearly punted the poor chap straight under the lorry's wheels. Roy obviously found this amazingly funny but that Italian scootercrat was understandably upset. In fact that's an immense understatement. He was utterly enraged!

I drove on with one eye on my rearview mirror. Sure enough he was laid flat on his scooter's tank, head down, absolutely going for gold, intent upon squeezing the last ounce of performance out of his 50cc and catching me. I drove as quickly as I could and lost him.

I'd just relaxed when we came round a bend to be faced by roadworks and a traffic jam. Oh my. Sure enough, here in my mirror appeared this incensed little mosquito of a scooter and there wasn't a thing I could now do to prevent its rider drawing up alongside. He slithered to a stop beside the Hillman's left-front door. But the car was right-hand drive. He was absolutely boiling with rage, too far gone to recognise that Pina sitting there was only a front-seat passenger, not the driver. The window was open and he reached in, grabbed her arm, and began screaming at her in Italian. Pina understood every word, including many that such a well brought-up lady might have preferred not to hear. Then the jam cleared ahead and I could drive off, leaving the chap behind.

The traffic soon forced another stop, and he caught us up again. This time he was absolutely fit to burst, he pulled his scooter round in front of us and began to write down our car's number. As the traffic moved off I was able to go again. This time he took in a huge breath and spat through the open passenger window, all over the innocent Pina!

Roy meanwhile had been chortling away, enjoying every moment, but after a few clear miles we came up behind an enormous slow-moving queue of traffic backed-up behind a convoy of trucks, carrying the weekend's police detachment home from Pescara. Roy and Tony were at it again, urging me to pass the lot. They wouldn't take "No" for an answer. Then a movement in the rearview mirror caught my eye. It was the bloke on the scooter catching us up again.

I couldn't take any more and shot down the outside. But I ended up behind a truck packed with police and escorted by police motorcycle outriders. I wasn't going to risk us all ending up in jail, and said so. Tony finally snapped. "Right!" he said, "Only one thing to do. Pass me my gloves! I will drive!" So we swopped over on the move to keep our place in the queue and did he go for it. It had begun to rain but Tony just sliced through the speed cops. He shot round the outside of all the trucks, we tore along, looking out the back of the car at the cops on their motorbikes, lights flashing, sirens wailing, giving furious chase, but falling further and further behind.

Today it's customary for Grand Prix drivers to be delivered to their private jets by courtesy cars, before wafting effortlessly home in pressurised-cabin luxury. This is just another example of how times have changed.

Roy was always a terrifying public road driver though. He particularly favoured VW Beetle hire cars, and on a particular trip we took together after leaving the Nürburgring, we found out why. John Cooper was sitting beside him and I was in the back, Roy was overtaking a huge articulated truck when another appeared, coming in the opposite direction on the narrow road. Just as I thought we were goners for sure, Roy tucked the right-side of the Beetle underneath the trailer of the truck we were overtaking, making just enough room for the oncoming driver to miss us. The Beetle was just the right length to slot between the truck's axles! John had

ABOVE
Pescara's road circuit had a lap length of almost 16 miles (25.75 kilometres). At various points around the Abruzzi countryside it shot through villages and down an immense seaside straight before skirting through the suburbs of Pescara itself. I'm amazed today to look at pictures like this and think back to the days of racing when such trackside hazards were accepted absolutely without question. We weren't exceptionally brave, we certainly weren't paid to take undue risks, so I guess we really were pretty stupid.

vanished—he'd dived straight down into the footwell and boy was he mad!

Another time I felt Roy had really stretched the elastic too far, overtaking on a blind brow, and I told him as much. "How can you possibly know there's nothing coming?" I demanded. He was totally unfazed. "Boy," he replied, "there's all the footpath not being used yet."

Back home—miraculously—in Britain we passed on the Italian Grand Prix at Monza because the historic old autodrome was a real power circuit on which our small-engined Coopers would have been a liability. But the International Trophy race of 1957 was run at Silverstone that September—having been postponed from its traditional May date by the Suez Crisis.

BRM finished 1-2-3, and I was fifth, and then at Goodwood in a F2 race I managed to set a new lap record. The Oulton Park Gold Cup race followed—again for Formula 2—and there I took the race from Cliff Allison's factory Lotus. First prize was £1,000 and the gold cup was real! It was my biggest win to date, and the money really cheered me up.

A non-Championship Formula 1 race followed, at Casablanca in Morocco, in which John Cooper entered a works car for Roy while Rob Walker sent his car down for me. Midway through the race my car's gearbox broke. We pushed the car behind the pits, and race control took this as indicating our retirement. But as the race developed more and more cars retired. They were dropping like flies. And we thought, "If we can fix the gearbox, we could pick up a decent place here". We actually replaced the broken gearbox with a spare, and I hopped back into the car and shot back out onto the circuit. Nobody seemed to object, so off I went.

Clerk of the Course was "Toto" Roche, an excitable little blob of a Frenchman who ran the racing at Reims and regularly made a spectacle of himself at the French Grand Prix. He suddenly realised I was back out on circuit, and sent a message down to Rob in our pits saying that I was to be black-flagged and disqualified unless he brought me in voluntarily. Rob objected and said nothing in the rules gave just cause for me to be disqualified. Roche had to get out his black flag and wave me off next

RIGHT
Works driver for Aston Martin at the 1958 ADAC 1,000 Kilometres classic on the North Circuit of the Nürburgring in Germany. I'm trying the 3-litre 6-cylinder Aston Martin DBR1 for size with my co-driver and team leader Stirling Moss holding forth on what does what.

LEFT

Humble little rental cars often cried themselves to sleep after being used and abused by itinerant Formula 1 drivers. Here in Casablanca before the 1957 Moroccan Grand Prix the rent-a-car Renault's knees were probably knocking as I posed for the camera beside it with (left to right) Tony Brooks, my great Cooper team-mate and lifelong friend Roy Salvadori, and the immensely likeable, so unlucky, Stuart Lewis-Evans. Back at Casablanca the following year, Stuart would crash when his Vanwall's engine seized at high speed, and sustain fatal burns.

BELOW

The 1st Australasian Driver, 1958 New Zealand Grand Prix trophy.

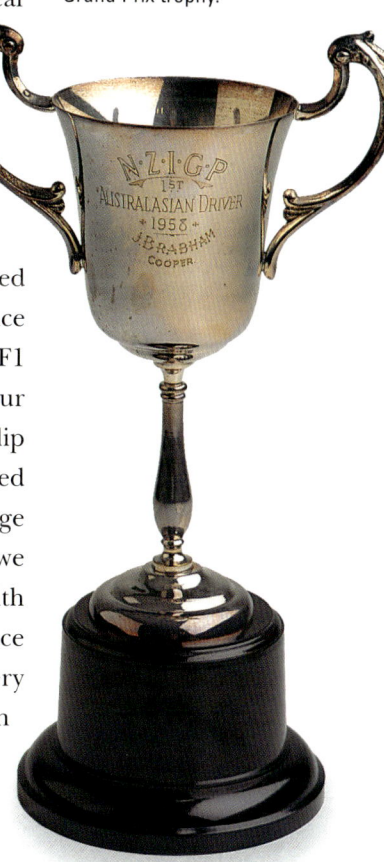

time past the pits. But it was late in the day and looking back up the circuit from the pits was straight into the glare of the setting sun. Every time I came round Rob would tap him on the shoulder and start remonstrating with him, and every time Roche looked back he'd see nothing even resembling our little Cooper. This went on for two or three laps until Roche almost literally had steam hissing from his ears. After Rob distracted him yet again he suddenly broke away, spun round, and waggled his black flag violently at the next car by. It happened to be Fangio, the new World Champion, in his Maserati.

Poor old Fangio dutifully pulled into the pits next time round, thoroughly confused over the reason for the black flag, though he had spun earlier on and received some assistance to rejoin. So he concluded there was, perhaps, just cause. However, the Maserati mechanics didn't see it that way and were going mad, waving him back into the race, and bawling at Roche. The crowd were giving Roche the bird, and he was purple in the face. Finally he threatened Rob that unless he called me in he—Roche—would report him to the FIA (*Federation Internationale de L'Automobile*) and have his entrant's licence pulled. Rob called me in, but we could have scored a profitable finish.

The year ended with me staying in Britain for Christmas and racing on Boxing Day at Brands Hatch, where I won in Rob's 2-litre engined Cooper-Climax. I then flew down to win the New Zealand GP at my fifth attempt, while the car was flown out to Buenos Aires for the hastily-organised opening round of the 1958 World Championship series—the Argentine Grand Prix. There it was driven for Rob by Stirling Moss, and the combination became the first rear-engined winner of a Formula 1 World Championship Grand Prix. The Cooper-Climax had scored its first victory in the pinnacle class. Now we knew the unthinkable was possible. And of course our ambitions grew to match.

The new year began with the New Zealand GP Association launching their "Driver to Europe" scheme, under which they sent the most promising Kiwi driver of their season to Britain. The driver was expected to build his racing career. Young Bruce McLaren was one of the first candidates and while I was in New Zealand in January and February I was actually on the judging committee.

As a fan of Bruce, I naturally recommended him, and he was selected. The scheme rules stipulated that whichever youngster was chosen should not only show driving ability on track, but must also be a suitable "ambassador" for New Zealand. On both counts 20-year old Bruce was just perfect.

Back in Britain, Betty, Geoffrey, and I had settled into a house in Dorking. This was rented from Rob Walker. We were making Britain our permanent home for the time being—and what's more the country really began to feel like home for us.

During this time the latest Cooper chassis had emerged for both Formula 1 and 2 racing—the only difference being in engine and fuel tank capacities (2½-litres for F1 and 1½-litres for F2 respectively). It featured our improved transmission with the German ZF limited-slip differential and a pair of quick-change spur gears inserted between the clutch and gearbox, enabling us to change final-drive ratios easily to match each circuit on which we were racing. The front suspension was also new, with adjustable Armstrong coil-spring/damper units in place of the preceding transverse leaf springs. Every modification we made was viewed with intense suspicion by Charles Cooper. Change equaled expenditure, and he would bleat continually, "Why change it when we're winnin?". It became his theme tune.

RIGHT
Far away and long ago…a mixed touring party of British and Australian drivers larking about with an advert for the Anthony Steele/James Robertson Justice movie *Checkpoint* which was based on the Mille Miglia 1,000-mile round-Italy race. We were all in New Zealand for the free-Formula races opening the 1958 racing season. Left to right are little Archie Scott-Brown (a fantastic bloke and a brilliant driver despite having been born with only one proper hand and stunted legs), tall Salvadori, Stuart Lewis-Evans, Bib Stillwell, Lex Davison, yours truly, and Arnold "Trinkets" Glass (foreground), the Sydney motor trader/racer.

Fortunately John was more realistic, recognizing that if we stood still we'd inevitably be left behind. I was the one who visited ZF in Germany to arrange supply of limited-slip diffs—John covered for me and hid the expense from his father. This was not the first time we had conspired to press ahead with improvement, nor would it be the last. Once he saw such improvements perform on track, old Charlie would be content, indeed he'd probably enjoy the credit for having rung the changes. Persuading him to change anything, absolutely anything, in the first place would have been almost impossible.

The Easter Goodwood meeting was memorable for me thanks to a fantastic wheel-to-wheel duel I had with Graham Hill's Lotus in the Formula 2 race, and for my spinning on oil dropped by Moss's blown-up Walker Cooper in the Formula 1 Glover Trophy. Graham and I had a real bar-room brawl of a race. We passed and repassed until he retook the lead and held it until the last lap. I'd tried everything, and eventually decided there was only one way to get by and that was across the infield grass at Woodcote to enter the chicane first, then I could hold him off to the finish line! I managed it…just!

At the Aintree "200", Stirling was leading comfortably when his Walker Cooper's clutch began to slip. I had already lost nearly a minute in the pits refilling my car's radiator but into the finishing stages I was able to close the gap, and into the last lap I was sure I could pass him. Finally I managed it at the top of the back straight on the last lap, and was confident of holding him off through Melling Crossing and then the tight last corner at Tatts, but I had misjudged him.

Stirling Moss always had talent in reserve, and when he forced alongside me in Tatts Corner, I had to lift momentarily. Stirling had the impetus to push his car's nose ahead of me—just as we reached the flag. He won by 0.2 of a second.

After their sometimes encouraging outings with the 1,960cc "stretched" versions of the twin-cam Climax FPF engine during 1957, both John Cooper and Colin Chapman of Lotus had pleaded with Wally Hassan, the Chief Engineer of Coventry Climax, and his boss Leonard Lee, to go further. Hassan didn't want to push his luck but Lee authorised an initial next step in which four special 2.2-litre FPF engines would be built to enable Cooper Cars Ltd and Team Lotus to compete in Formula 1, with two engines each. They actually displaced 2207cc, with the biggest cylinder bores possible in the standard FPF block casting, and an extra long stroke which demanded longer cylinder liners. They protruded above the standard block's top deck, and the only way to accommodate them was to insert a packing plate, about a quarter-inch thick, between block and head. Hassan disliked this kind of fudgery but Lee said "do it", and he did.

All of us at Cooper and Cliff Allison, and Graham Hill at Lotus had both 1960cc and 2.2-litre FPF engines to run against the full 2½-litre "proper" Formula 1 cars but we were in with a better chance than ever before. Rob Walker's Cooper, meanwhile, was powered by a 2015cc engine of their own, put together by "Alf Francis" (who was then chief mechanic to RRC Walker Racing Ltd, Rob

LEFT
The best of times… We raced like the dickens once the starter's flag fell, but got on famously in between times, even here on the starting grid at Brands Hatch in 1958, with Stirling Moss telling some unlikely story, much to my amusement in my red-nosed bottle-green Cooper with its scuttle-top gold flash. Stirling's mechanic, "Alf Francis", sees the joke (he must have had a sense of humour to wear that tea-cosy hat) while at the left stands Mike Hawthorn, typically deep in thought, who sat out this race after hurting himself in an earlier one.

Balancing the works Aston Martin through the curve leading on to Adenau Bridge during the 1958 Nürburgring 1,000 Kilometres. It was my job when co-driving with Stirling just to keep the car safely in contention without losing too much ground while he had a regulation rest between pit-stops, ready to take back a still-healthy car. It was more important I did nothing to compromise his lead than go for gold. And this, I'm happy to recall, I managed to do. We won. It was my only big win in a Sports Car World Championship-qualifying race.

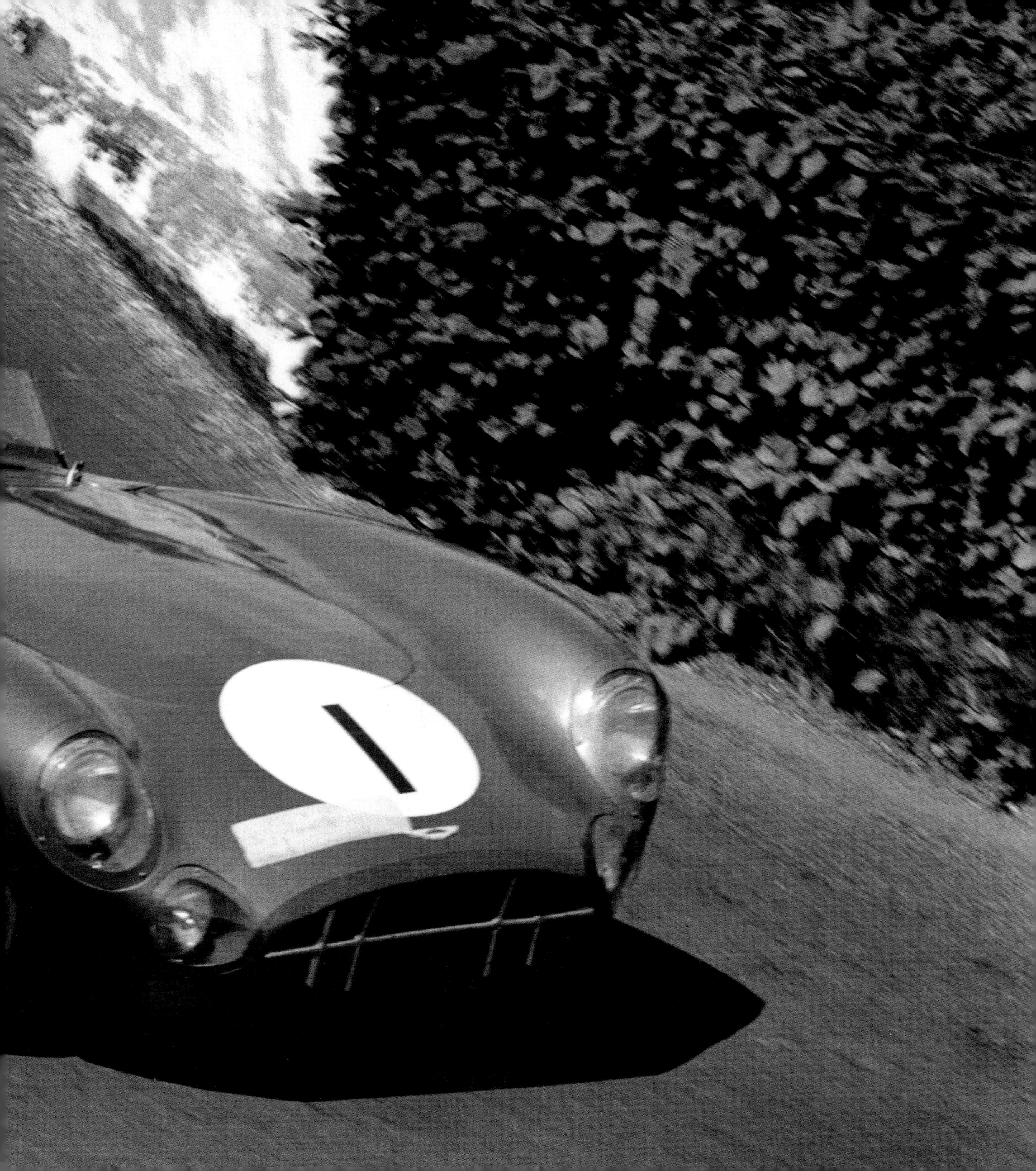

Walker's private team) along similar lines to Climax's "specials" for us.

During the winter the FIA had also changed Formula 1 Grand Prix regulations, slashing race distance from a minimum 310 miles (500 kilometres) to only 186 miles (300 kilometres), and banning alcohol fuel "brews" in favour of maximum 130-octane AvGas aviation gasoline. These twin changes meant the cars now needed less fuel to run race distance, and in any case burned less fuel because engines tuned to run on AvGas had inherently better fuel economy than those tuned to burn methanol mixes. Formula 1 cars from 1958 forward could therefore be smaller and lighter. Much more, in fact, like a Cooper or even a Lotus.

At the start of the 1958 Monaco Grand Prix I found myself lining up for the start on the front row of the grid. I was a 10th of a second faster than Maurice "Trint" Trintignant in the Walker Cooper, and alongside Jean Behra's full-sized BRM and Tony Brooks's Vanwall. Ending the first lap, the local hero Behra led for BRM from Vanwall and then my Cooper. Unfortunately, I soon had to call at the pits with an anti-roll bar link adrift. It lost me a lap. Trint had begun racing pre-war, he was hugely experienced, and had already won this race for Ferrari in 1955. He was utterly consistent and he just paced his way round while the Ferraris and Vanwalls dropped out ahead. He just lapped metronomically to the finish, and, as a Frenchman, scored another tremendously popular victory. This was also the second consecutive Grand Prix victory for a Walker Cooper. I finished fourth.

In the Dutch Grand Prix, at Zandvoort, Roy was fourth, and I was eighth. The Belgian GP saw our small-engined cars overpowered by the big boys but the French GP at Reims—another power circuit—wasn't as bad as we'd feared, and I salvaged sixth place. I was a having a very

BELOW
A typical day in my office circa 1958. We all worked until we were ready to drop, building our Cooper-Climax cars, developing them, preparing them, setting-them up for optimum performance, and then on race days driving them against the best in the world. I'd always been brought up to believe that what you get out of life depends on how much you put in. It worked for me.

LEFT
In the small-engined works Coopers during the 1958 Formula 1 season we were really beating our heads against a brick wall, though it was all good experience. Here in the French Grand Prix at Reims I managed to salvage sixth place behind a pretty illustrious group. Mike Hawthorn won for Ferrari, from Moss's Vanwall, von Trips in a second Ferrari, Fangio (in his last race before retirement from driving) in the *Piccolo* Maserati, and Peter Collins in yet another Ferrari. We were learning a lot...if only that patience is a virtue.

successful season in Formula 2, but the F2 supporting race at Reims saw my engine throw a rod on the starting grid. Sadly, Luigi Musso of Ferrari was killed in the Grand Prix there when he lost control of his car in the flat-out right-hander after the pits.

The British Grand Prix at Silverstone was dominated by Musso's surviving British team-mates, Peter Collins and Mike Hawthorn, scoring a Ferrari 1-2. But Roy drove one of his best-ever races in the Cooper to finish third behind them. I managed sixth place...and all of us on the same lap.

Roy again excelled in the German Grand Prix at the Nürburgring, where he finished second behind Tony Brooks's winning Vanwall, but for all of us the race was bitterly overshadowed by Peter Collins' bad crash in his Ferrari. Whilst battling to keep pace with Tony Brooks's leading Vanwall, Collins lost control and slid off the circuit. He suffered severe head injuries and was flown by helicopter to a hospital in Bonn.

Trintignant was third in the Walker car (completing a Cooper-Climax 2-3) while young Bruce McLaren absolutely shone by winning the Formula 2 section in his car and taking fifth place overall. John Cooper had taken to doing a forward roll in the pits whenever one of his cars won, and he did one then in Bruce's honour.

My performance, however, didn't match up. I clipped the tail of Jo Bonnier's Maserati on the opening lap, knocking off its oil tank, then promptly skated off on the spilled oil doing further damage to my car. I limped my now short-wheelbase Cooper back to the pits feeling pretty foolish.

In those days the German GP was traditionally followed next day by the August Bank Holiday meeting at Brands Hatch in Britain. We'd move heaven and earth to

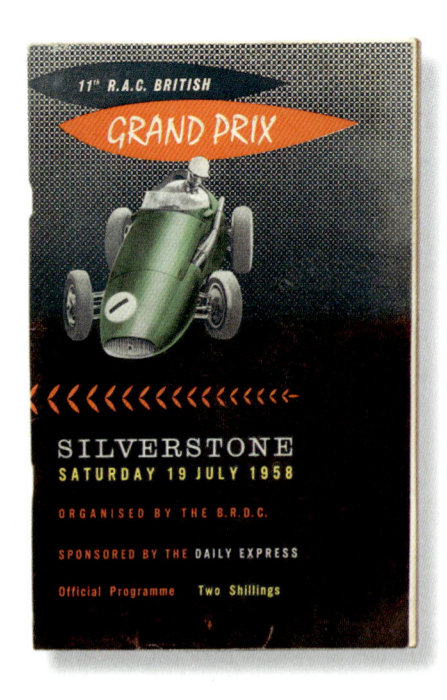

ABOVE
The programme from the British Grand Prix, Silverstone, July 1958.

RIGHT
Front engined Lotus (Graham Hill) versus rear-engined Cooper (mine) at Stowe Corner, Silverstone, during the 1958 British Grand Prix. While my teammate Salvadori finished third (first British car home and beaten only by the Ferraris of Peter Collins and Mike Hawthorn), I was sixth while Graham retired early on with overheating. Colin Chapman of Lotus at this time was still saying how wrong we were to ignore traditional front-engined configuration and mess about with the Climax engine in the back of our cars. We changed his mind eventually and he built his first rear-engined car, the Lotus 18, in 1960. It was a minor victory. In retrospect quite a satisfying one.

get back in time, often arriving in the small hours of Monday morning, then getting to Brands after only three or four hours sleep. In retrospect, it wasn't very sensible. Fortunately I could get by with very little sleep.

After my exceptionally short German Grand Prix, I managed to win both parts of the F2 race at Brands. But the news had come through that Peter Collins had died of his injuries in Germany. I couldn't believe it.

Peter's death really hit me hard. Two drivers who had been really helpful to me from the moment I had first arrived in Britain were Peter Collins and Ron Flockhart. Peter was a real gentleman, a very, very nice fellow as well as being a terrific driver. He had always offered me very sound advice and his death really upset me for quite some time.

At the next Brands meeting for the F2 Kentish "100", Stirling and I fought one of our fastest and closest races ever. Stirling in the Rob Walker Cooper and myself in the works car just broke the lap record all day long. I won the first part and Stirling the second, but he won overall on aggregate. Mike Hawthorn presented Stirling with the trophy after draining most of the champagne himself.

The World Championship that year lay between these two. They were great rivals but also got on pretty well. In fact we all did. We saw so much of one another, and so often travelled around together that there was a real bond between the drivers. It was a privilege to be part of that community.

I had co-driven with Stirling that year for the Aston Martin sports car team. In particular, in June, I had been teamed with Stirling in a works Aston Martin DBR1 for the Nürburgring 1,000 Kilometre classic. My only duty was to give Stirling Moss a break, maintain position and keep the car in one piece to hand safely back to him. He drove 36 of the 44-lap distance, which is why we won. I also co-drove with him at Le Mans, and fortunately it was Stirling who was driving when the engine blew up on the first evening, not me!

My first Italian Grand Prix at Monza was forgettable. Starting from the penultimate row of the grid, I clouted Olivier Gendebien's Ferrari, which had stalled on the second row. So I was out of the race before it had really begun.

The deciding race of the World Championship would be the Moroccan Grand Prix at Casablanca. Stirling Moss did everything he could, qualifying his Vanwall on pole, leading throughout, and setting fastest lap. But all Mike Hawthorn needed to do to win the title by one point was to finish second, and he did that comfortably when his new team-mate, Phil Hill, waved him past.

I was driving in the Formula 2 category, trying to race the other 1500s while keeping out of the way of the Formula 1 fast men who were lapping us regularly. I clinched the Formula 2 Championship there by winning the class with Bruce McLaren second. The worst thing that weekend was the sight of Stuart Lewis-Evans's crashed Vanwall, lying on its side on the verge with a cloud of dust drifting away. As I came by Stuart had just gone off (due to the car's engine seizing and locking the rear wheels) and I could see him just starting to scramble out. The next time round, however, his car was just a huge fireball. Stuart suffered terrible burns from which he died a few days later, back in Britain. Soon after, Tony Vandervell withdrew his Vanwall team from racing regularly, but Stirling Moss's win at Casablanca had clinched the Formula 1 Constructors' Championship for them. Now Vanwall would be out of the equation for 1959, and Leonard Lee of Coventry Climax confirmed that full 2½-litre versions of the FPF engine would be supplied to us at Cooper Cars for 1959....

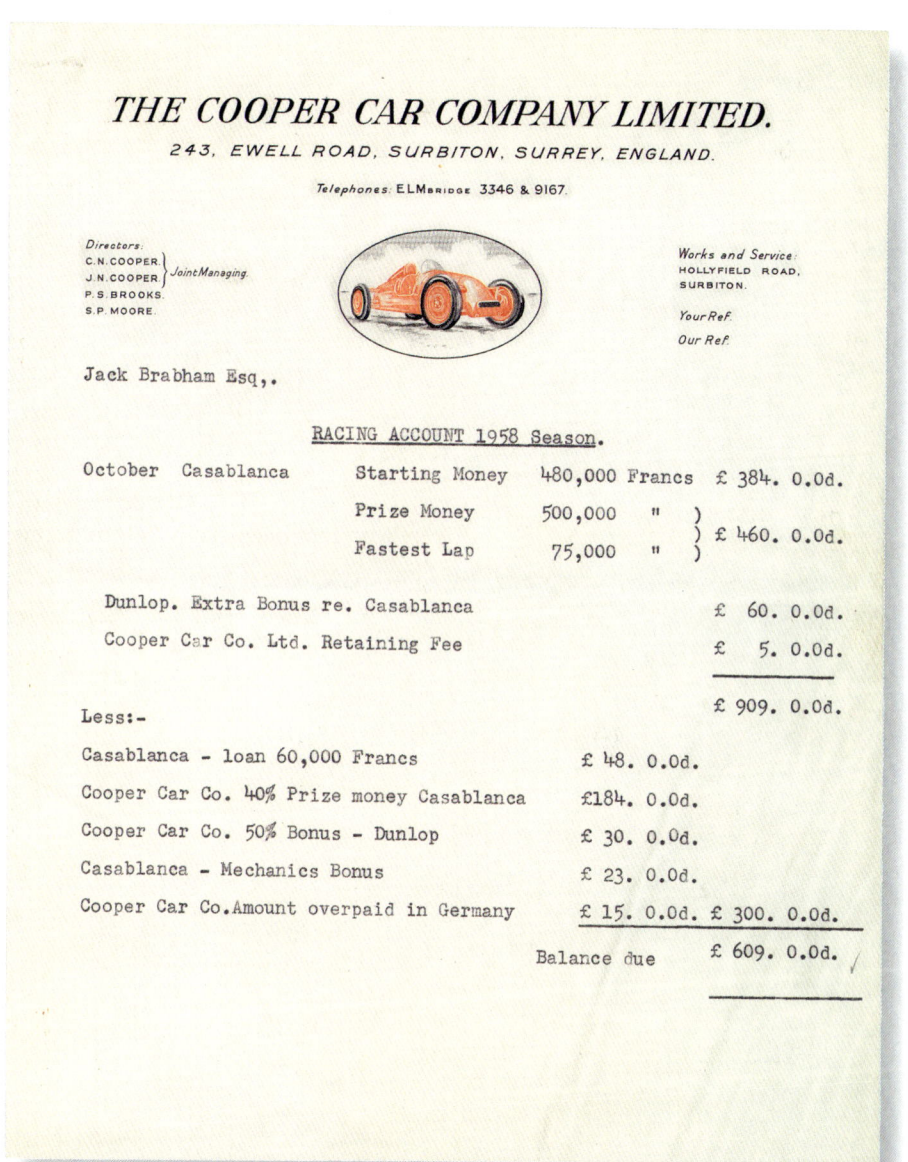

ABOVE

Can you sense Charlie Cooper's hand shaking? The head of the Cooper Car Company really was a great character. He loved his racing and enjoyed a win perhaps more than any of us. He loved to see the money coming in but he equally detested having to fork some out. Here's the racing account issued to me for the 1958 racing season. Not exactly earth-shaking but by the standards of the time it was pretty good.

CHAPTER 5

TUSSLE FOR THE WORLD TITLE

In 1959 the Formula 1 World Championship developed into a spectacularly hard-fought three-way war

A memento of a really rugged day's work. My stone-battered full 2½-litre works Cooper-Climax hammering down the finishing straight, away from the Reims circuit's last corner at Thillois, during the baking hot 1959 French Grand Prix. I've smashed out the perspex windscreen simply to get some cooling airflow on to my face and around the cockpit. My feet are being burned on the pedals, heated by hot air from the nose-mounted radiator, and the heat of its piping. I'm set to finish third behind the uncatchable V6 Ferraris of Tony Brooks and Phil Hill.

We were racing down under during the European closed-season of 1958–1959 when shocking news came through. Mike Hawthorn had been killed in a road accident. After winning the World Championship at Casablanca, he'd announced his immediate retirement. We all thought he was doing the right thing. He'd seen so many good friends die behind the wheel, not least his two Ferrari team-mates Luigi Musso and Peter Collins. Having been through so much, and having already lost his father in a road accident, it seemed cruelly ironic that he should die by hitting a tree in his Jaguar saloon, while larking about on the open road. But life and motor racing always goes on.

I couldn't wait to return to Britain, where Leonard Lee had agreed to provide full-sized new 2½-litre Climax FPF engines for our first serious attempt to win the Formula 1 World Championships. I was putting down real roots in Britain and was opening a garage business in Chessington, near Cooper's works. Bruce brought over a Kiwi friend of his named Phil Kerr whom I employed to run my garage.

At the same time Roy Salvadori had accepted a good offer from David Brown of Aston Martin to drive for their new team. Charlie and John Cooper agreed to take on my young New Zealand protégé, Bruce McLaren, in his place. Bruce had performed brilliantly in the "Driver to Europe" scheme Formula 2 car through 1958. He was now to join myself and the experienced American Masten Gregory in a three-car works team.

The scheduled Argentine Grand Prix was cancelled, leaving useful breathing space before the first European World Championship round at Monte Carlo in May. Our prototype 2½-litre Climax engine was delivered in March, while Masten and Bruce's cars were fitted initially with 1958-style 2.2-litre units.

For any Formula 1 races which Aston Martin did not enter, Roy was free to drive Tommy Atkins's private Cooper using a 2½-litre Maserati engine. Soon after I'd

LEFT
The Cooper Car Company's works Formula 1 team of the 1959 vintage. Left to right, Bruce McLaren, bespectacled Masten Gregory (the most fearless man I've ever known), yours truly, a typically ebullient John Cooper with his inseparable pipe in one hand (disregard his glass in the other), and his father Charles.

returned to Britain we were testing at Goodwood. Neither of us was quick and Roy put it down to wind direction, saying "It's a slow day". Masten Gregory blinked behind his thick spectacles and drawled, "It's a slow day all right, 'cause Moss and Brooks aren't here". That amused me, and really impressed Bruce. Masten's was a "no-excuses" attitude he would never forget.

Moss was to drive a Walker Cooper that year, fitted with another of the new Climax engines. Since Charlie and John had none of our precious uprated gearboxes to sell, Rob adopted a new Italian-made design by Valerio Colotti, formerly of Maserati.

Our latest works Coopers had double-wishbone rear suspension, in which a new upper wishbone instead of the transverse leafspring located the wheel uprights laterally at the top. Moss's Walker car retained the 1958-style system, with just a single lower wishbone each side, and the high-mounted leafspring controlling lateral movement up top. It was less precise, but worked rather better on tight and acrobatic circuits like Brands Hatch.

Compared to the conventional front-engined cars, our latest Cooper was tiny, punching a small hole in the air, so it would always be pretty quick on the straights. The car was light, so it braked and accelerated rapidly. I found it

RIGHT
My first Formula 1 win—receiving the *Daily Express* BRDC International Trophy from the Hon. Max Aitken, Lord Beaverbrook's son, at Silverstone during the 1959 May meeting. Until this time all Cooper's Formula 1 wins had been scored by Rob Walker-entered cars driven by either Moss or Maurice Trintignant. We had begun to feel like second-class citizens, racing our own works cars, and this win at Silverstone with the new full-sized 2½-litre Climax FPF engine installed, was a major breakthrough both for Cooper's, and for myself.

much easier to drive without throwing it sideways, where earlier Coopers seemed to lap faster the more you hung the tail out. The new 2½-litre Cooper was the first you could make understeer in corners.

And, as we would find, the greatest feature of Wally Hassan's full-sized new Formula 1 engine was its reliability, and if we had an Achilles heel it was our gearbox which the new 2½-litre engine's increased torque rendered marginal indeed. We would find that after each race the gearbox internals were good only as scrap.

We gave our new 2½-litre cars their debut at Goodwood on Easter Monday. Funny now to think this was only four years after I'd made my British debut there in that terrible old Cooper-Alta. It seemed a world away.

Moss beat me with the Walker car, but mine had F2-sized wheels and brakes, and 50mm Weber carburettors instead of the special new 58s we really needed. The Aintree "200" followed, where Masten used our second new 2½-litre engine, and my car was uprated with 58mm Webers, wider front wheels and tyres, and bigger brakes. Young Bruce would later write: "In practice Masten was warned not to do too many laps in case something fell off before the race...and broke the lap record! 'If that car's bad', he drawled, '...leave it bad!'" So he started from pole position, and led for a long way until his clutch broke. My new engine let me down with a head seal failure while Moss's latest invention, a Walker Cooper with 2½-litre BRM engine, led after Masten's retirement only for the poorly made Colotti gearbox to fail.

The May Silverstone meeting was the last of these "dress rehearsal" Formula 1 races before the Monaco Grand Prix. Moss drove a front-engined works BRM and started from pole. But I got a super start off the front row, Stirling had the BRM's brakes fail and spun off behind me, and I was able to run away to

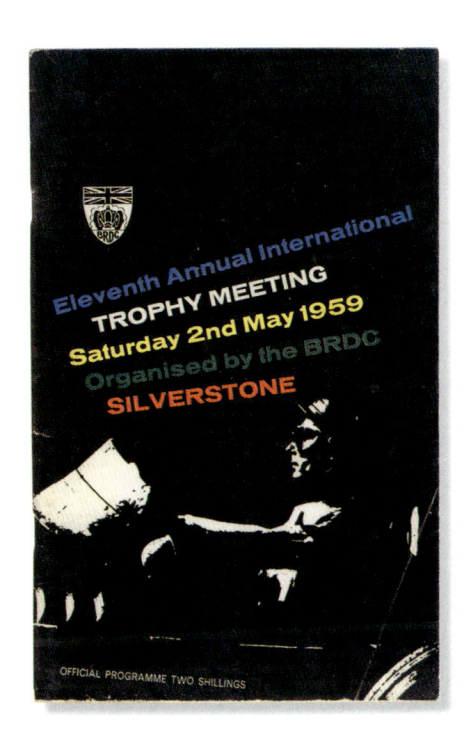

ABOVE
The 1959 BRDC International Trophy meeting programme.

LEFT
Here I am going for gold by hammering my works Cooper round the Monte Carlo street circuit during the 1959 Monaco Grand Prix. Glory be, we won!

score my first-ever Formula 1 race win and the first-ever for the Cooper works team.

That breakthrough victory was a real confidence booster, just in time for Monaco the following weekend. Again we ran our three works cars, 2½s for myself and Masten, and a 2.2 for Bruce. But at Silverstone Masten had crashed a Lister-Jaguar sports car, and he was battered and sore.

In practice I had a brush with the straw bales and found the foot pedals uncomfortably hot. Our mechanics Bill James and "Noddy" Grohmann fitted radiator heat deflectors overnight. In the race, Jean Behra's BRM retired from the lead and Moss took over in his Walker Cooper-Climax—the BRM-engined car having been abandoned. I was second behind Stirling but my car's gearchange was sticky, costing perhaps two seconds a lap in the tight hairpins. Worse, my foot pedals were scorching again. Stirling's race ended when his Colotti gearbox broke. As I inherited the lead I was wondering just how long I could keep going. My pedals were so hot I could hardly bear to touch them.

Late in the race, John began signaling that Tony Brooks of Ferrari was catching up. I just couldn't press the pedals any harder, the soles of my shoes were sizzling, the heat all but unbearable. But there was too much at stake, too much within reach, to give in. I just managed to hang on, and suddenly here was the chequered flag. Glory be, we'd won the Monaco Grand Prix!

And I found myself limping up to accept the trophy and laurels from Prince Rainier and Princess Grace. Old Charlie Cooper was beside himself, quivering with glee. That night we had an uproarious celebration at the race dinner in the Hotel de Paris, including a strawberry fight.

That fantastic start to the new season was followed by the Dutch Grand Prix, amongst the seaside dunes at Zandvoort. We should have won again. To conserve our borderline gearboxes we strapped small gravity-feed oil tanks above them, to top-up the oil level mid-race by pulling a cockpit lever.

Masten made a miraculous start from the third row to lead for the first 10 laps until his gearbox played-up, first Jo Bonnier in the BRM, and then I shot past him. Jo and I had quite a battle until I lost second gear. This was a disaster. It was vital for the tight Hunzerug turn behind the pits. Moss passed us both to take the lead, then lost it with yet another Colotti gearbox failure, and while Jo

TUSSLE FOR THE WORLD TITLE | 83

LEFT
Swirling round Monte Carlo's Station Hairpin in the Cooper with Ron Flockhart's front-engined 4-cylinder BRM following me through. Ron was a great friend. He'd been one of the first established British drivers I got to know when I first arrived in Britain in 1955 and he'd always been faultlessly supportive and helpful. He introduced me to private flying, and encouraged me to train for my pilot's licence, triggering a flying career which culminated in some 5,500 happy hours in command. Ron was killed over the Dandenong Hills in Australia in 1962 when testing his single-engined Mustang for a second attempt on the single-handed Sydney-London record.

FAR RIGHT
Spoils of war, Monte Carlo 1959 just before we left for home. My Australian journalist friend "Dev" Dvoretsky took this shot of John, myself and our ex-Aston Martin chief mechanic Bill James.

BELOW
Monaco 1959. Motor racing isn't an individual sport. The driver is alone in the cockpit but it's a team effort which puts him there. Once the team's success or failure is in his hands you'd be a hard man not to feel some responsibility.

went on to score BRM's first-ever Championship GP win after 11 years trying, I could only nurse my car home second, with Masten third.

There was a break before the French Grand Prix at Reims. Raceday there passed into history as probably the hottest ever. The road surface melted and cars sprayed chunks of asphalt in their wake. Our low-built Coopers put us right in the firing line, and the temperature in the cockpits was unbelievable.

Moss drove a front-engined BRM instead of his troublesome Cooper-Climax-Colottis. All three of our works Coopers now had full 2½-litre engines, but we couldn't touch Tony Brooks's V6 Ferrari for all-out speed. Yet, as early as lap seven, Masten was smacked in the forehead by a flying lump of tar, and was just able to reach the pits before collapsing. He'd just set a new lap record.

Bruce took a fearful battering in a duel with Olivier Gendebien's Ferrari. His goggles were smashed and he described his mask of sweat and blood as looking "like pink champagne".

My feet quickly blistered and towards the finish several drivers were just about semi-conscious. I reached out and broke my windscreen to get some air. Every time I got near another car I was showered with tar, grit, and stones. My Cooper's nose looked as if someone had fired a shotgun at it. Near the finish I was coasting into corners because it was too painful to brake. I finally finished third and the boys had to lift me from the cockpit.

Bruce placed fifth. He managed to climb from his car unaided. His Mum and Dad were there at the first overseas race they'd seen and as he removed his helmet he just burst into uncontrollable tears. They were staggered to see a Grand Prix develop into such a bloodbath and were really shocked to think they must all be like that!

The British Grand Prix was at Aintree. We now had gearbox oil pumps to help preserve the internals. Climax provided their only big-valve, straight inlet-tract Mark II-headed FPF engine, and I qualified on pole, made a good start, and led away. Masten covered my tail against Moss's pale-green BRM until his Cooper developed intermittent clutch slip on alternate laps which made the pit-crew rewind and shake their stopwatches every other lap.

The big drama, though, was tyre wear. We were all on Dunlops, but Aintree was very hard on tyres. With more power and torque than ever before, we needed bigger tyres but none were available, though I did put a thick-tread sports car tyre on my car's left-front. Even so, around half distance I could see that its tread was disappearing, so I changed my driving. The car was understeering, I had to induce oversteer by tossing it tail-out into the corners, to reduce the load on that marginal left-front. A tyre change would have been disastrous. We only had five-stud bolt-on wheels, instead of quick-change centre-lock knock-offs.

They waved a wheel at me, because Moss needed to stop in his BRM, and they had found his Dunlops badly worn. Fortunately, I'd already worked this out, but Moss's stop had removed the pressure, and I was able to ease to the finish with a completely bald front tyre. Bruce and Moss had a fantastic closing-laps battle for second place, both breaking the lap record, and Stirling just led across the line by a nose. Masten placed seventh.

For some reason that year's German Grand Prix was run on Berlin's AVUS track, with its amazingly tall, brick-paved banked North Turn. That banking was fantastically bumpy and not steep enough for the speeds we were doing. In those days we were not used to such high G-forces, at around 160mph (260km/h) our cars were squashed down onto the bump stops, and we were crushed down into our seats inside them. Every lap round the banking just left you glad to get to the other end. Even my crash hat squashed down over my eyes there! Fortunately our Coopers were always strong but from the moment practice began that weekend we all knew that anything could happen.

I was an eyewitness to two nasty accidents. In the supporting sports car race, with the brick banking slick with drizzle, the great French driver Jean Behra lost his Porsche and spun up into a wartime concrete block-house on the rim. He was thrown out against a flagpole, and killed instantly.

Next day in the Grand Prix I saw one of the biggest shunts ever as Hans Herrmann in the Moss BRM lost his brakes at the end of the straight heading into the flat hairpin at the opposite end of the course from the banking. He shot straight on through the straw bales and I nearly went off just watching his car—open-mouthed. The bales had launched it high into the air and it went somersaulting end over end in the most fantastic crash, throwing Herrmann out. Yet he immediately sat up, and watched the car bounce along on its own! Absolutely amazing!

Masten gave it a real go, running amongst the powerful Ferraris wheel-to-wheel at 180mph (290km/h), while I sat back. Masten's engine then sawed itself in half when a

BELOW
The 1959 British Grand Prix Trophy.

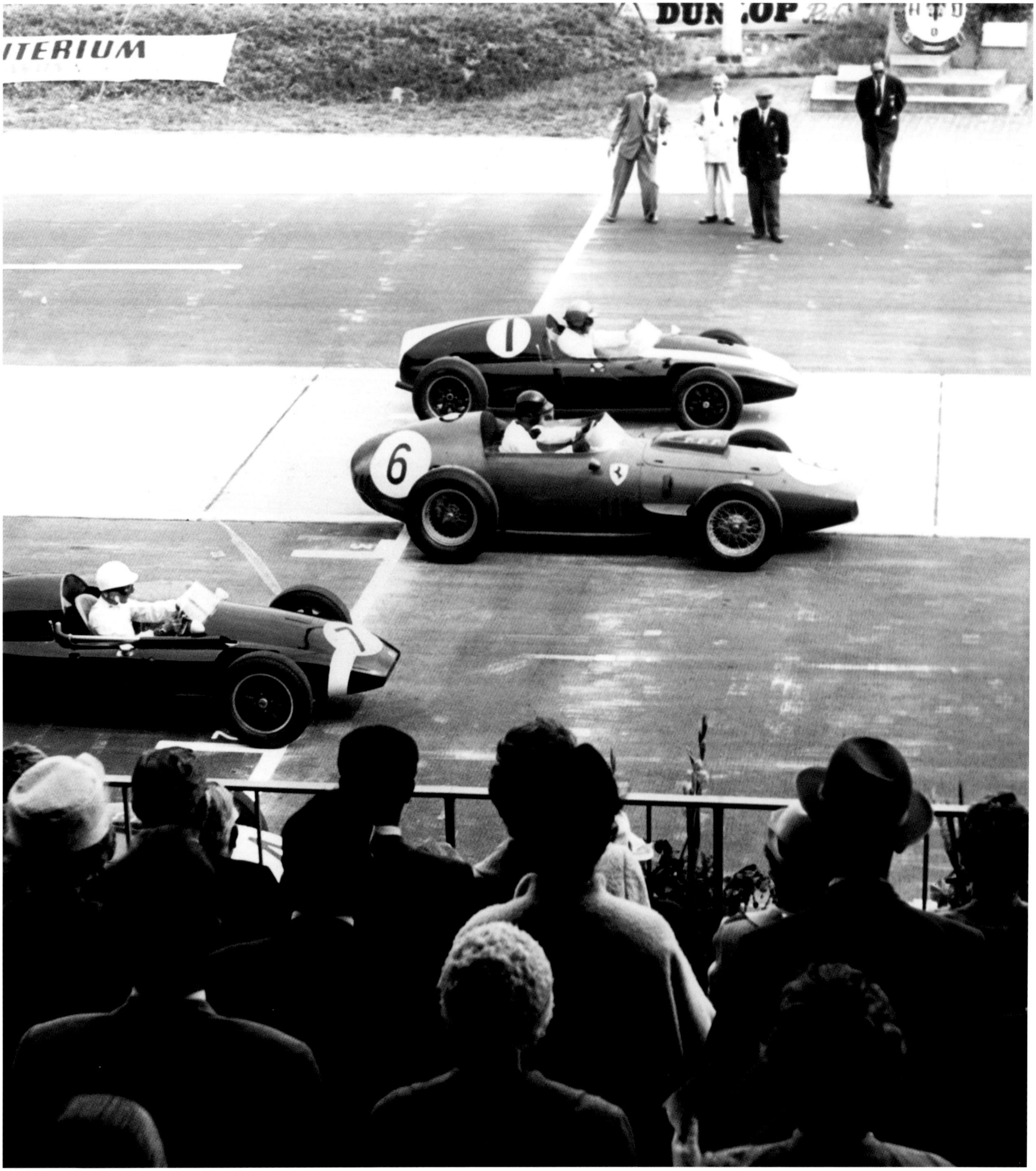
ITERIUM
DUNLOP

connecting-rod bolt snapped, and then my own car clattered and died—its step-up gears stripped. Moss's revised Cooper had broken another Colotti gearbox and Tony Brooks won again for Ferrari. So now he, Moss, and I were all in contention for the World Championship.

The Portuguese Grand Prix followed at Lisbon's Monsanto Park circuit, another dicey venue, really, lined by trees, bales, and drainage gulleys. I was persuaded to attend a bullfight on our first evening, and when we got there I was left to pay the taxi fare. I pulled out my wallet, paid the driver, and never saw my wallet again. My pocket was probably picked at the bullfight, which didn't appeal to me anyway, and I lost my driving licence and other papers, as well as money! I wasn't best pleased, then next day some of us went down to the beach at Estoril, I took out a canoe and when I returned to the beach through the surf it got caught by a big wave, and its keel tore my big-toe nail clean off. My feet had a tough time that season.

I had my toe bound up, and practice ended with Stirling on pole in the Walker Cooper (with further-modified Colotti gearbox) from Masten and myself. Early in the race I had a nasty experience when a small boy, perhaps only seven or eight, ran across the track in front of me, and I had only just missed him. An omen perhaps about what was to come.

I had led initially, but Stirling came by entering the hairpin. A few laps later I repassed, but about a lap after that he passed me again. We were having a great scrap when, on lap 24, we were lapping backmarkers, one of them for the second time. His name was Mario Cabral, a local Portuguese sports car driver who had been put in one of the private Italian Centro Sud team Cooper-Maseratis to give the crowd some home interest.

Going down into the hairpin I was right up Stirling's exhaust, ready to out-brake him into the corner, but Cabral was on the right-hand side of the road. As I was only inches off the back of Stirling's car, he probably saw only the blue Walker Cooper in his rearview mirror. As we passed, he swung back to latch on behind Stirling, so his car just knocked mine straight off into the straw bale barrier on the left, and suddenly I was airborne.

As I went up over the bales, to a great height, I remember seeing about a 30-foot (10-metre) drop into a gulley with trees at the bottom. Two things saved me. One, I hit a telephone pole perhaps two-thirds of the way up. And two, I didn't have a seat belt.

The car ricocheted off the pole, which it felled, and I dropped out onto the road just before the car landed upside down and then slid about 50 yards (45 metres) inverted which made a real mess of it. If I had been strapped in, I would have been killed for sure. And thankfully I'd hit that telephone pole just off-centre because if the car had hit it dead-centre I'd have been thrown against the pole, rather like poor Behra at AVUS.

As it was, I went tumbling down the middle of the road and it wasn't until I'd stopped rolling and sat up that I realised where I was. I looked round to see Masten's Cooper heading straight for me!

I scrambled desperately to one side and he shaved past so close I felt the breeze. Helping hands quickly sat me on a bale where I realised I was only winded and dazed. Amazingly, nothing seemed broken. My immediate reaction was to see if I could restart the car, but it was a total wreck. I wanted to assure our people I was OK, but then an ambulance arrived and the medics began insisting I climb aboard. It then set off on what was one of the most frightening rides of my life, siren wailing, heading to the city hospital with the driver really going for gold. It was unbelievable. The tyres were squealing, I was being tossed around from side to side, it was even more frightening than seeing my team-mate's car aiming straight between my eyes!

At the hospital they found I had suffered nothing worse than a beating. John then arrived with Betty, and

ABOVE
The sight of Hans Herrmann's pale green BRM smashing itself into a heap of scrap during the 1959 German GP has been etched indelibly into my memory. I'm just out of picture here, on the track proper, just behind the straw bale barrier to the left, gawping as his car smashed through the straw, tripped, somersaulted, and threw him out in a heap. He got away with it—amazing!

LEFT
Whenever I see a photograph with Formula 1 Ferraris in it I recall just how much I really relished beating those bastards! But I didn't manage it this day. Here's the start of the 1959 German GP on the incredibly dangerous AVUS track in Berlin with me, Dan Gurney, and Stirling Moss. Tony Brooks's Ferrari tucked down at the foot of the picture, would win.

ABOVE
The 1959 Portuguese Grand Prix programme.

RIGHT
A council of war at Lisbon's Monsanto Park circuit before the 1959 Portuguese Grand Prix. That's Roy Salvadori to the left (who'd left us to drive the new Formula 1 Aston Martin that year and who would finish sixth in it) while to the right is John Cooper with our mechanic "Noddy" Grohmann behind. This is not going to be a great day for me…For the first time in my career I'd be leaving the circuit in an ambulance. At the time this picture was taken Colin Chapman was still preaching how wrong we were to ignore traditional front-engined configuration and to be messing about with the Climax engine in the back.

the doctors reluctantly consented to them taking me back to our hotel. We flew home next day. My escape had been really miraculous, especially in that darned Portuguese ambulance.

Meanwhile Stirling had won with the Walker Cooper with Masten second. When I saw him back at the hotel I asked, "What were you doing—coming straight for me?" and he explained, "When I came over the rise and saw the pole you'd hit lying there with its wires down across the circuit I thought it might be a power pylon, so I took my feet off the pedals, and hands off the steering wheel in case they were live!" I should have known better than to expect sympathy.

I was still able to bounce back six days later in the Formula 2 Kentish "100" race at Brands Hatch, when our Formula 2 Climax-engined Coopers faced Stirling's almost all-conquering Borgward-engined Walker team version. We beat him, which was really satisfying because we out-engineered him. I set up our car for the tricky little circuit with single-wishbone rear suspension, a high second gear, and a low third against Stirling's car which had the more powerful fuel-injected Borgward engine. It also had a five-speed gearbox and the latest double-wishbone rear suspension. I was able to hare around, tail-out in stable slides while Stirling said later, "It's not so much getting the tail out, as getting it back again." I took first from Graham Hill's front-engined Lotus with Stirling somewhat cheesed-off, third. I had raced at Brands earlier that month with a double-rear wishbone car and had concluded the older set-up would be better. It worked beautifully, and John rode around on the back of my car on our victory lap, clutching the trophy.

But having scored no points in Germany and Portugal, where Moss had begun winning again, it was important to recover quickly. For the Italian Grand Prix at Monza I was fighting fit, but Masten had baled out of another crashing sports car during the Goodwood TT and had hurt himself. So I was to drive Bruce's normal car while he took over Masten's.

Walker arrived with Moss's Cooper wearing centre-lock knock-off rear hubs in case they should need a tyre change during the race. I think they'd miscalculated, because it was the left-front tyre which would take a caning, not the rears, and their front wheels (like all of ours) were still bolt-on.

The Drivers' Championship lay between Moss, Brooks, and myself. We qualified in that order. For the race I again fitted a sports car Dunlop tyre with full 8mm tread on the left front but right at the start Tony's Ferrari clutch burned out. His team-mates Phil Hill and Dan Gurney led in their Ferraris, with Moss just behind them, while I sat back, conserving my tyres. When the big front-engined Ferraris made their inevitable tyre-change stops Stirling was away to win non-stop. Phil Hill finished second and I was third with my tyres worn out. But the great news for John and Charlie was that Cooper had just clinched the Formula 1 Constructors' World Championship title. They were literally on top of the world.

One final Drivers' Championship round remained. Stirling, Tony Brooks, and I had each now won two GPs that year, and the title would be decided between us in the inaugural United States Grand Prix, to be held at Sebring in Florida on 12 December, two months after Monza.

In the interim, the Oulton Park Gold Cup was won by Moss from me. I ran my own 2.2-litre Cooper in another non-Championship F1 race at Snetterton, finishing second again, this time behind Ron Flockhart's front-engined BRM.

To beat me to the Drivers' Championship title, Stirling had to win at Sebring and make fastest lap which then scored an extra point. If he won but I set fastest lap I would be Champion. Tony's task was harder, he had to win and set fastest lap with both Moss and myself placing lower than second. If I finished second behind Tony we'd tie on points, but the title would be his since he would have won three GPs to my two. We pondered the

LEFT
The shape of the telegraph pole which saved my life is crushed into the nose of my shattered Cooper after the big Portuguese GP shunt in 1959. I was really happy not to have been wearing seat belts. If I'd been strapped into the car I'd have been killed for sure. As it was, my team-mate Masten Gregory nearly ran over me after I'd landed in a heap in the middle of the track. Some you lose, some you win.

ABOVE
Greeted in the Monza pits after the 1959 Italian Grand Prix—Stirling has just won in the Walker Cooper, and I've come home third behind Phil Hill's Ferrari; Cooper have clinched the F1 Constructors' World Championship. On the right there's my team-mate Bruce McLaren, Ken Tyrrell is beyond him. We hadn't won the race, but we had our first World title.

possibilities. Obviously that fastest lap could be the key. Masten was very fast indeed on his day, John decided to concentrate on running just two cars, and so told Bruce he would be stood down for the race. But by late November it was clear that Masten had still not recovered from his Goodwood shunt, so Bruce got the drive in this crucial decider.

To be honest, I wasn't bothered about the outcome, because I just did not believe my luck could hold and bring me the title. But it was frustrating to have to wait until Sebring. I had various business irons in the fire on which I had expected to concentrate after Monza. My new garage in Chessington was about ready for opening, the lease on our rented house in Dorking was up, and I wanted to find a new home to buy. Then rumours began that the Sebring race would be cancelled. Even after we shipped the two works cars in November, it seemed uncertain whether the race would take place or not. BRM and Aston Martin both opted out, and we waited to see what Ferrari would do, were they sending their cars or not? Then there was another rumour that Tony Brooks was going to retire in any case, because his wife Pina was expecting a baby. I think the only person who was desperately keen to race at Sebring was Stirling Moss. That was understandable. For four consecutive seasons he'd had been runner-up in the Drivers' Championship, three times to Fangio and then to Mike Hawthorn. He'd been bridesmaid so often and this was his chance.

Finally it was confirmed that the Sebring race was on, and I was then offered an entry in the Bahamas Speed Week at Nassau, the week before Sebring. I'd never raced on that side of the Atlantic and fancied some low-key practice to get back in the racing groove. I shipped out the Cooper Monaco sports car powered by a 2-litre Climax engine, recently purchased from Noddy Coombs, and which I intended to sell straight after the race. My own cars were looked after by a quiet, chain-smoking Aussie mechanic named Tim Wall, an ex-Rob Walker man. He went out to prepare the Monaco. John and I would fly down later following an Esso function which we both had to attend in London on 3 December.

Immediately after that reception we dashed to Heathrow, to catch a BOAC Britannia to Nassau, where we landed two-and-a-half hours late. By the time we reached the aerodrome circuit official practice had ended. The organisers, however, gave us a special half-hour extension in which I took out the Monaco, only to find that John Coombs's blokes, who had prepared it in Britain, had fitted the final-drive reduction gears the wrong way round. Noddy Coombs had assured me the 25- and 28-tooth gears had been fitted, which they were but upside down. This geared the car for a slow, tight circuit instead of Nassau's fast open course. I was running out of revs, everywhere.

We stripped the gearbox that night and swopped the gears round. Next day, against meagre opposition, I came through the five-lap preliminary race to challenge the leader, British privateer Mike Taylor. But halfway round lap four, as I moved out to pass him, a stone was thrown up which hit me straight in the left lens of my traditional RAF-issue "Mark IX" goggles. They were meant to be safety glass, but the lens shattered, sending splinters straight into my eyeball. I was whisked off to hospital after finishing, where a doctor spent over an hour painstakingly picking shrapnel from my eye. I saw a specialist that night who told me I'd been very lucky, but there was one tiny piece he couldn't get out, and in fact it's there to this day.

I'd always been blessed with exceptional sight, but that night it seemed as if my World Championship hopes, perhaps my entire career, were in jeopardy. I rested on the Saturday before Sunday's big Nassau Trophy feature event, and although my eye still ached, my vision had cleared, and I finished fourth.

The doctor persuaded me to stay for a couple more days. When we eventually flew to Miami on the Tuesday night my eye was still bloodshot and sore. John and I finally arrived in Sebring around midnight Wednesday, with first practice beginning next day.

Sebring's race circuit was just a barren, dead-flat aerodrome. It was littered with corroding military aeroplanes and the 5.2-mile (8.4-kilometre) road circuit was marked out by cones and sandbanks.

Noddy Grohmann was already there with our two works Coopers, while the Walker team turned up with a "Moss special" for Stirling; their own Cooper fitted with coil-spring rear suspension, in place of the well-understood transverse leafspring type. Rob Walker said Stirling, who had designed it, would have to say that it was an improvement.

On the first practice day I concentrated on setting-up my car. I believed that as long as I qualified on the front row I'd be all right. And of course, I never believed in wearing out my car before any race. Experience proved that tyre wear would not be a worry, but while trying to set-up the suspension, I ran wide out of one corner and dented one side of the bodywork against half-buried marker tyres. On the second day, for the first time in my driving career, I failed to see oil dropped on the circuit. Never before had I missed seeing that unmistakable

BELOW
Typical '59 Cooper-Climax behaviour, waving its inside front wheel through a quick corner. We just couldn't persuade that model to keep all four wheels on the ground. The first Formula 1 Cooper to do that would be our new *Lowline* quickly built at the start of the following year. This shot shows me at Oulton Park, second to Moss in the 1959 Gold Cup. The Cheshire parkland circuit was one of my favourites.

THE JACK BRABHAM STORY

RIGHT

By 1959 Formula 1 standards this was a crowded starting grid. Here we are, all lined up, and ready to go in the 1959 United States Grand Prix at Sebring, Florida. This was the deciding round of that year's Drivers' World Championship. I'm about to slither down into the driving seat of my Cooper (8) while watching Stirling stepping into his Rob Walker team car to my left. That's John walking across the front of my car in his straw hat, while "Noddy" Grohmann stands by my car's tail. Harry Schell's Cooper (19) has been wangled onto the front row of the grid thanks to a practice time achieved by short-cutting the hairpin! Maurice Trintignant's second Walker Cooper (6) is being lined-up, and then there's the flotilla of those darned front-engined Ferraris. We fixed them, didn't we?

sheen, and I slithered off to dent my car's nose against a rubber cone. Then my engine ran hot, its head seals were failing. So we worked late that night to remove the head and fit new seals. But it was too risky to rely on that car for the race, so I swopped cars with Bruce.

He then put a couple of laps on what had been my car to see if he wanted to make any adjustments to it. Within half a lap its crown-wheel and pinion broke! I took out what had been his car and found it didn't handle at all well. We checked it that night and found the chassis was twisted. I played around with the suspension to compensate, but next time we ran it the brakes juddered violently. We then checked the gearbox and found its mainshaft was cracked so our spare gearbox had to be fitted. For us, Sebring just seemed to be going from bad to worse.

We all worked on the cars (John, Tim Wall, Noddy, big Mike Barney, Bruce, and myself) until 1am race morning. Dr Frank Falkner, an English paediatrician working in the US who was an old friend of John's, then shooed Bruce and I off to bed. The boys finished the cars overnight, Bruce's first, then mine by mid-morning.

Before we lined up there was a colourful, carnival-style pre-race march-past of a "mixed" band complete with "majorettes". This seemed really over the top and comical to we visitors from sober Britain.

On the starting grid, Harry Schell's 2.2-litre private Cooper was suddenly wheeled into what had been Tony Brooks's place on the front row. Tony had badgered the inexperienced organisers into suddenly accepting a very quick practice lap he'd posted. In fact Tony had set that time by taking a crafty short-cut between the cones before the hairpin, a move which the observers had not reported. Poor old Tony found himself relegated to row two, which incensed Ferrari team manager Tavoni. The din and arm waving was quite something. But Harry stayed on the front row, and Tony's Ferrari was kept back on row two.

At last, we started our engines, and the race was started. I made another great start, but after barely 100 yards (91 metres) here was Stirling's Scots-blue Cooper, passing me like a rocket! Pre-race, John, Bruce, and I had decided to follow whatever pace Moss might choose. If he drew clean away early on I would simply let him go. It would make no sense to risk my car by chasing Moss flat-out early on with full tanks. But the way Stirling screamed

BELOW
Flagfall for the 1959 Drivers' World Championship decider, Sebring, Florida. Stirling (right) and I set off side-by-side with our main rival Tony Brooks's Ferrari (2) putting its V6 power down right behind. The first few laps would more or less decide the race.

by actually left me feeling comfortably relaxed. I could not believe he would get far.

Stirling was always "A Racer". He just loved a real old dice and he never really adopted his old mentor Fangio's dictum, "To finish first, you must first finish". What hope did his Colotti gearbox have here?

Bruce shot past me onto Moss's tail. Just as I was beginning to feel smug about Stirling's risky pace I nearly had a heart attack. My engine fluffed onto three cylinders, stammered for about 100 yards (90 metres), then miraculously chimed-in again on full song! I repassed Bruce in the hairpin and as we all completed that first lap my other Championship rival, Tony Brooks, pulled straight into the Ferrari pits. He had been shunted by "Taffy" von Trips, his own team-mate and he came in to have his car's suspension inspected. Stirling was pulling out two seconds a lap. I resolved that if he got too far ahead I'd either have to risk it and give serious chase, or let Bruce by to see what he could do. But on lap 6, as I went through Webster's Turn, there was the blue Cooper, off the circuit. I assumed he'd spun off and as I repassed the pits John Cooper just signalled me "P1". Next time through Webster's, the blue Cooper was still there, abandoned. Moss was out, let down again by that Colotti gearbox. Brooks was delayed, but I had great respect for his abilities, and his V6 Ferrari was always fast.

He was running ninth. John gave me no sign that the Ferrari was a threat. I was leading Bruce by about 10 seconds, so I eased my pace, and he closed up. Cliff Allison's Ferrari was running third. Maurice Trintignant closed up on him in Rob Walker's remaining Cooper, so Cliff then began to close up on our two Coopers.

John signaled us the news. I speeded up but around lap 20 Cliff's clutch began to slip and his bolt was shot. "Taffy" von Trips and Trintignant were promoted to third and fourth, with Tony Brooks now fifth. Trintignant was lapping really quickly in his effort to deprive us of points and thereby give Stirling his last slim chance of the title. He took third place and began to close, but the gap was big enough for me to maintain a consistent pace.

John Cooper kept signaling Trintignant's progress and I was constantly calculating time lost against laps remaining. Maurice set fastest lap but I felt pretty comfortable we could maintain our lead, regardless. After all the pre-race frights and dramas it really was turning out nice again.

Just as insurance, with a half-dozen laps left to run, I pressed a little harder in my now fuel-light car, and Bruce kept station on my tail. Everything seemed just great. My tyres had plenty of rubber left, the car had never been hard-pressed, and the sun was shining. That lovely, dependable Climax engine was barking away perfectly behind my shoulders.

Any racing driver is always tensely attuned to possible mechanical failure when it really matters. At that moment, however, I felt as confident as I ever could. Now a handy (and lucrative) Grand Prix win and the Drivers' World Championship both seemed to be in the bag.

I nodded to John as I flashed past the pits for the final time, into the last lap. It was a fantastic, euphoric experience. I was just thinking of that chequered flag, barely a mile to run when my engine stammered and fluffed. It fell onto two cylinders, cut, spluttered, and died. The car had run out of fuel.

When the engine died I was cornering at about 70mph (110km/h). I automatically flicked the gear lever into neutral and then coasted along to the last corner.

Bruce, of course, had almost fallen over me as I slowed. He now surged alongside, looking across open-mouthed, plainly wondering what the hell I was up to.

With much arm-waving and shouting, I told him to get on with it. Go for the flag. Bruce just couldn't grasp what had happened and said later he had vague ideas of stopping to help!

Just before Trintignant could catch us, Bruce twigged what was needed, and shot off. Trintignant then passed me as I coasted along, the Cooper rattling and swishing along the concrete runway, losing speed all the way.

There was a slight incline up past the pits. When the car was some 100 yards (90 metres) short of the flag it sighed to a stop. After thinking of Monaco '57 I scrambled out, wrenched off my helmet and goggles, then began to push.

Tony slammed past then I just got my head down, put my back into the job, and pushed. I kept on pushing.

My heart was pounding. It was hot and humid. I was aware of marshals around me, urging me on. And I could hear the crowd shouting, cheering, and clapping. I'm told they went wild.

Motorcycle cops arrived. It was really bizarre. Here I was trying to push my Formula 1 car to the finish of the World Championship-deciding Grand Prix, with a motorcycle escort.

Dean Delamont ensured I received no help. If anybody else had laid a hand on my car I would have been disqualified. And then I'd reached the line and someone was waving the chequered flag. John and the boys were jumping up and down.

I have few clear memories beyond flopping down beside the car, gasping for breath, and gulping down a cup of Coca-Cola offered by John. I was surrounded by a forest of legs. The crowd was cheering, laughing, and congratulating me. I was finally helped into organiser Alec Ullman's caravan where I was at last able to crash out for 15 minutes or so, just to catch my breath.

Bruce, aged 22, had just become the youngest-ever winner of a Championship-qualifying Grand Prix, by just six-tenths of a second from Maurice Trintignant, with

BELOW
"Stand back, don't help him!" Outside assistance could have scuppered my hopes and got me disqualified after my Cooper ran out of fuel on the final lap at Sebring. I'm hot and bothered here. The finish area concrete was slightly uphill and there's not much fuel left in my personal tank either. I'm just pushing for all I was worth. The outcome of the World Championship was, at this point, in the lap of the gods.

BELOW
It hasn't yet sunk in, has it? Just about completely done in, I have just pushed my car past the chequered flag at Sebring to finish fourth behind my team-mate Bruce McLaren, Maurice Trintignant, and Tony Brooks. It's another Cooper-Climax 1-2-3 finish, beating Ferrari, and I'm Formula 1 World Champion for 1959.

Tony Brooks third. My efforts had secured fourth place. And then it dawned on me. I really had won it. I'd won the title. I was World Champion! Bruce came in, smiling but dazed. He just kept saying, "I can't believe my luck." Then it was out to face the press. The sun was setting, TV lights, and flashbulbs were flaring. There seemed to be dozens of microphones shoved under my nose and everybody was shouting questions. It seemed a complete zoo. I was asked to take an overseas telephone call from one of the London Sunday newspapers and the reporter asked if I'd like him to tell my wife I'd won. My answer was simply, "yes please".

I finally got back to my room in the Harder Hall Hotel, and soaked in a hot bath, in peace, analysing my day. Bruce's car had finished with nearly 4 gallons left. He might have saved, at most, a couple of gallons by slip-streaming me most of the way. I'd been told there was no sign of a leak. But then there was that strange misfire and fluffing I'd experienced briefly just after the start? Perhaps fuel from the brimming tanks had gushed from the overflow pipe behind my head and spilled into the carburettor intakes, making them run over-rich? That would create the effect, which had so quickly cured itself. But what I think actually happened is that John, my old

LEFT
A memento of Sebring '59, dedicated to me by American-resident British paediatrician Dr Frank Falkner who was a friend of John's and who handled many of our team affairs whenever we raced in the USA. Bruce McLaren (left) will become the youngest ever winner of a World-ranking Grand Prix, and I will become the first Australian ever to be World Champion Driver.

LEFT
London celebration with John and Charlie Cooper at the World Championship awards presentation…three happy blokes.

friend, our team chief, had simply got in a muddle while the cars were being fuelled. He had miscounted and one churn too few had been loaded in my car. John always told a different story, explaining how we would run our fuel consumption tests in practice, and then base our calculated fuel load for the race upon them. "Then," he would say, "to be on the safe side I'd always add a couple of gallons just for luck. At Sebring I vividly remember Jack saying, 'I don't want to lug all that lot around' and he had the extra couple of gallons drained off again".

I really don't remember that, but a couple of gallons would certainly have done it. I think John simply miscounted and if I then had a couple of gallons drained off the effect would have been the same.

No matter, the Cooper Car Company had finished that season as 1959 World Champion Formula 1 Constructor and I had finished it as World Champion Driver. You wouldn't believe it.

1959 2½-Litre Cooper-Climax T51

Having found their feet in regular Formula 1 competition through the 1958 season, using 1.96 and 2.2-litre versions of the Coventry Climax FPF 4-cylinder racing engine, the Cooper Car Company works team was provided with full 2½-litre versions of this proprietary racing engine for 1959. Leonard Lee, head of the Coventry company, authorised manufacture of these full-sized contemporary Formula 1 units for supply to Cooper, the Rob Walker team (for Stirling Moss), and Lotus. In 1959 Brabham scored his maiden Formula 1 race win at Silverstone on 2 May in the T51, and his first World Championship-qualifying Grand Prix victory at Monaco on 10 May.

TECHNICAL SPECIFICATION

Manufactured by the Cooper Car Company Ltd.

Engine: Coventry Climax Type FPF in-line 4-cylinder; 2 valves per cylinder; 2 overhead camshafts; bore & stroke dimensions 94.0mm x 89.9mm, displacement volume 2,495cc; Power output circa 239bhp @6,750rpm.

Transmission: Cooper Citroen-ERSA 5-speed and reverse.

Chassis: Tubular spaceframe. Suspension; independent front suspension by wishbones and co-axial coil-spring/dampers; rear by wishbones and transverse leafspring with outboard telescopic dampers.

Brakes: Discs all round.

Wheels: CCast magnesium-alloy to Cooper spoked design.

Tyres: Dunlop Racing.

1959 2½-LITRE COOPER-CLIMAX T51 | 99

RIGHT
The fishlike Cooper-Climax Type 51 was the smallest and most compact Formula 1 car of its period, thanks to its rear-engined configuration with the big 2½-litre Climax 4-cylinder engine behind the cockpit. The bodywork is all aluminium, with separate nose, engine cowl, side panels, and undertray.

BELOW
The Formula 1 Constructors' World Championship-winning Cooper-Climax of 1959 displays its compact and sleek, yet still rather deep-chested profile. Note its bolt-on spoked Cooper cast-magnesium wheels and the way in which the aluminium body side panels enclose separate strap-on aluminium fuel tanks along both sides of the cockpit.

RIGHT
The Cooper-Climax T51 punched what was regarded at the time as the smallest possible hole through the air. The nose-mounted radiator was linked to the engine via lengthy feed and return water pipes which passed along both sides of the cockpit. The dry-sump engine oil tank hung immediately behind the radiator, ahead of the driver's foot pedals . All three heat sources bled hot air back into the cockpit around the intrepid driver. No full-length Grand Prix victory in one of these tightly-tailored little cars came easily to the driver.

RIGHT
Earlier model Cooper Formula 1 and 2 cars had used a single lower wishbone as here to locate the bottom of the rear suspension hub-carrier, while the transverse leafspring provided the upright's lateral location up top. During 1959 extra upper wishbones were adopted to provide better geometry control, while the leafspring was give a measure of free lateral movement which greatly improved the T51's cornering behaviour. There still remained, however, considerable room for improvement.

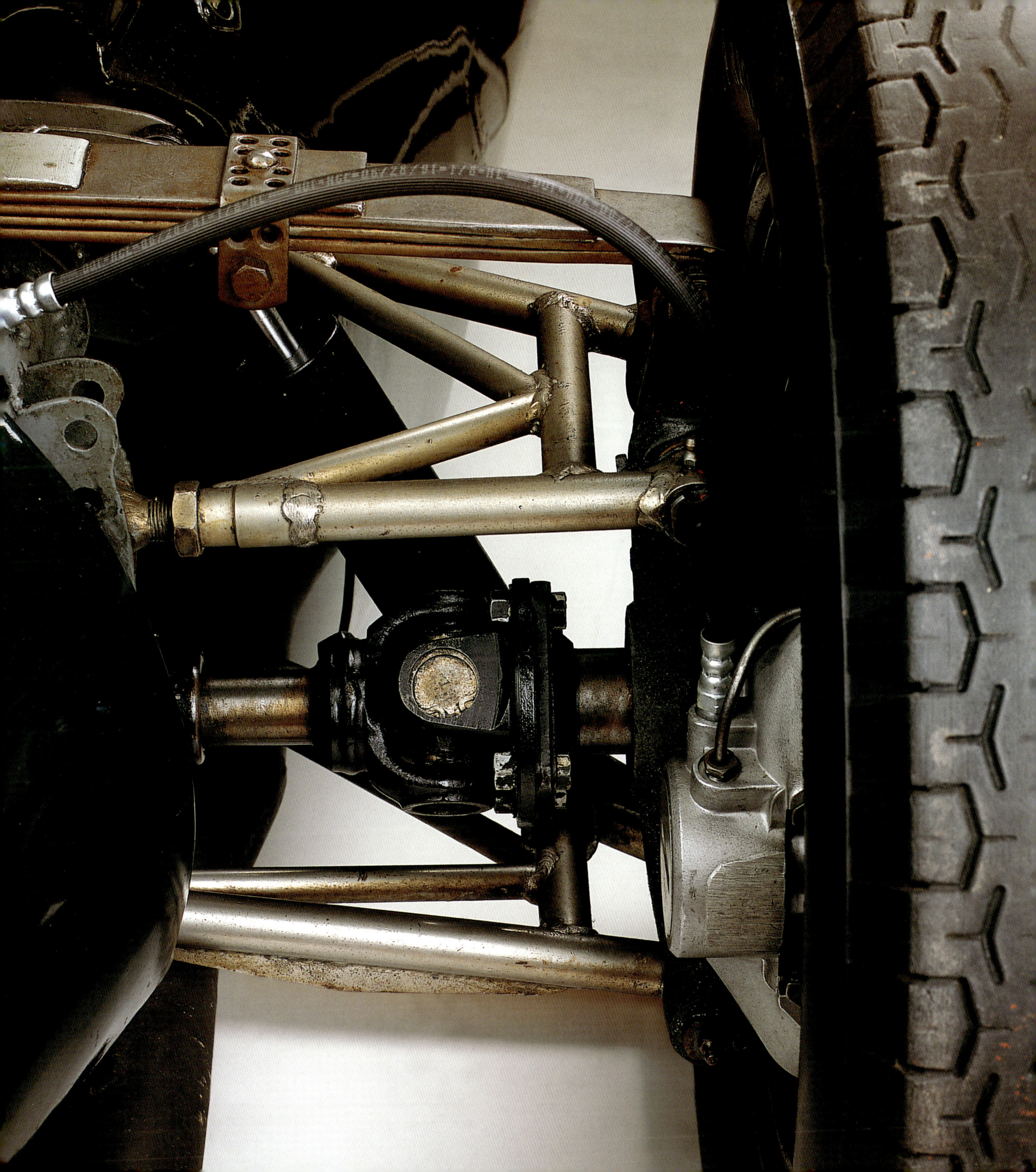

CHAPTER 6
TASMAN INTERLUDE

Racing back home in Australia and New Zealand provided an annual escape from the British winters

Racing back home in Australia and New Zealand, between November and March, became an enjoyable and often pretty successful part of my annual programme. Here we are with the works 2.2-litre Cooper with Esso's enthusiastic background support, at Albert Park before the 100-mile Melbourne Grand Prix in November 1958. With me (centre to right) are Esso's man, Reg Thompson and, with his inevitable cigarette, Tim Wall.

The northern hemisphere's winter months were obviously high summer "down under" in New Zealand and Australia. International races had been run there since the early 1950s, centred initially around the New Zealand Grand Prix. Other races would be promoted to take advantage of the presence of visiting "name" drivers. The extra events in New Zealand, then Australia, would become first "the Tasman series" and from 1964 "The Tasman Championship" which really took off.

The promoters catered for contemporary Formula 1-style cars. The rules, however, would be relaxed enough to admit local talent, mostly in second-hand Formula 1 and 2 cars, plus a few home-grown specials.

After my 1955 season in Europe I'd taken my Cooper "Bobtail"-Bristol back home. I'd won the Australian Grand Prix with it before its gearbox left me to spectate at the New Zealand GP.

At the end of 1956, I took home with me my works "Bobtail"-Climax sports car for the Olympic Games Australian GP meeting in Melbourne's Albert Park. Meanwhile, the prototype Formula 2 Cooper that I'd driven at Oulton and Brands Hatch, was shipped direct to Auckland for the New Zealand GP, along with my greatly unloved Maserati 250F. Charlie Cooper let me take the cars home, on the strict understanding that I would not be bringing them back. I'd find buyers and return only with cash in hand! At Albert Park I won in the "Bobtail", then took it to the new circuit being opened at Phillip Island. At the new circuit I won two races in the day.

After Christmas I hopped over to Auckland where I drove the new little F2 Cooper, instead of the big

LEFT
Spot the future. That's me on the left in the tiny little early Formula 2 Cooper-Climax, sneaking up on Peter Whitehead's apparently gigantic Ferrari *SuperSqualo* under braking in the 1957 New Zealand Grand Prix at Ardmore. On the right is local man Syd Jensen in the ex-Salvadori F2 prototype Cooper, while thundering along behind is Reg Parnell in a sister *SuperSqualo* to Whitehead's. This was "free Formula" racing with knobs on. Our little 1½-litre Coopers racing against the 3½-litre 4-cylinder sports-car engined Ferraris. It was in the supporting sports car race at this meeting that I witnessed Ken Wharton's fatal accident.

BELOW
Typical of the New Zealand circuits we raced on as International visitors. This is the aerodrome course at Ardmore, outside Auckland in the North Island. This was home to the New Zealand Grand Prix until 1963 when it moved to the new artificial road circuit around Auckland's horse race course at Pukekohe. The Ardmore course was marked out on the wide, crumbling concrete runways by oil drums and straw bales. The control tower is visible in the background beside the pits. That's where Ken Wharton's Ferrari *Monza* had slid wide into the straw bales in front of me, and flipped.

Maserati, in which I was terrified of breaking something expensive. The baby Cooper was much less likely to bite me in the wallet.

I was preparing my cars in local RedeX man Geoff Wiles's back garden when Pop McLaren, the garage owner from Remuera, arrived with his teenage son, Bruce. They'd come to see the Coopers and Bruce was wildly enthusiastic and eager. Bruce was studying engineering, and really knew his stuff. I also met his friend Phil Kerr who was racing a Ford Zephyr, and talking of coming to Britain. For any colonial keen on motor racing Europe was Mecca.

That 1957 New Zealand GP meeting at Ardmore included a supporting sports car race. I was running the "Bobtail"-Climax, against British star Ken Wharton's exotic Ferrari *Monza*. Ken had shone in everything from driving tests and mud-plugging trials to International rallies, sports car races, and Formula 1. He was quite a hero figure to me.

He had a Maserati 250F for the GP, but first he took off to lead the sports car race with me hanging on behind. I was pressing him hard, with little real chance ever of passing him, when he got into a big slide in the last left-hander, and lost control of the big Ferrari. It slewed inside the marker bales, reared up and rolled right beside me. I saw Ken in his trademark yellow shirt come flying out, then I was past but plainly he was going to be in great difficulty. It really shocked me. It had been such an enjoyable race until that moment, then in a split second this.

I think I finished the race but Ken had been killed. In the GP the little F2 Cooper was nothing but trouble. Old Reg Parnell won in a Ferrari *SuperSqualo* but Ardmore was sadly overshadowed that year.

The Lady Wigram Trophy race followed at Christchurch. The aerodrome course there was always dangerously marked by water-filled oil drums. Peter Whitehead won in the sister *SuperSqualo* to Parnell's, but this time I managed second place, and won the sports car event too. Racing around the houses in Dunedin, I then chased Reg hard until I overshot a corner, and lost time down an escape road.

Pop McLaren bought the "Bobtail" from me, while I took the F2 car back to Australia for the 1957 Grand Prix on an airstrip at Caversham, Western Australia. It was barely three months since the 1956 edition had been run at Melbourne in November. Stan Jones's Maserati 250F won, from Lex Davison's Ferrari, and my tiny Cooper third. I had found a buyer for it, in local racer Alec Mildren. Charlie Cooper would be proud of me.

Meanwhile, Rob Walker had invited me to join him in Sicily, for the start of the new European season. As we have seen, events would develop from there.

Through 1957 young Bruce McLaren wrote to me in Britain, telling me of progress with my old "Bobtail" and about the new "Driver to Europe" scholarship scheme for which he was competing. I offered to take out a pair of single-seat Coopers for the 1958 International races, one for him to drive. Charlie and John backed the idea, but of course on the usual basis that on no account should I bring either car back.

I built up a 2.2-litre Climax engine for myself, and put a 1½-litre, which we had stretched to nearer 1.7, in the other car for Bruce. My fifth New Zealand GP was run the day before the 1958 Argentine GP in Buenos Aires, which Stirling Moss would win in Rob Walker's car, and I also won.

Young Bruce was second behind me in the preliminary, but while warming-up his car pre-GP its gearbox broke. I had a spare which we tried to scramble into his car. In those great days it was typical that the Kiwi organisers should find all kinds of spilled oil on the circuit causing the start to be delayed, and Bruce was just tightening the last gearbox bolts when we finally set off. He joined in about half a lap behind, but hastily-tightened bolts vibrated loose and his gearbox lost all its oil. At the victory dinner that night he was declared winner of the "Driver to Europe" scholarship, which he thoroughly deserved and he would go on to great things.

He won a locals-only race at the dangerous little Levin circuit the following weekend, where I won the feature, but down at Christchurch both of us had gearbox trouble. After a brief trip to Australia I returned to New Zealand for the International at Teretonga on the extreme tip of the South Island. That circuit was surfaced with particularly abrasive shingle. To find some traction we fitted Michelin X tyres at the rear, retaining our normal Dunlops only at the front. The Dunlop rep was philosophical, "If you win at least we can still say Dunlops crossed the line first!" he said.

That would have been nice, but I'd mislaid my usual driving shoes and drove instead in ordinary ones which had a pronounced welt protruding around the sole. I was chasing Ross Jensen in an old Maserati 250F when I got the welt trapped between throttle and brake pedal. Then I had one hell of a moment, shooting off across the grass on the fastest corner and nearly overturning. I would never race again in ordinary shoes. I sold that car to a local racer, Merv Neil, and for the third time headed north to start the European season.

In November 1958 Melbourne's big Albert Park meeting saw Stirling Moss and I facing one another in Rob Walker and private ex-works Coopers respectively. The Melbourne Grand Prix was run in two 25-mile (40-kilometre) Heats and a 100-mile (161-kilometre) Final. Stirling won his Heat and I won mine at a slightly higher speed, so I started on pole for the Final. But I just couldn't hold him, he won and I finished second. Against Walker Racing our Cooper works team would just have to try harder during 1959 and we did.

First there was another New Zealand GP at Ardmore, another Cooper-Climax 1-2-3; Moss, Brabham, McLaren. Stirling had been leading his preliminary race when his

ABOVE
Typical "International series" racing in New Zealand, 1959 Lady Wigram Trophy. I'm threading my 2.2-litre Cooper (4) around Frank Cantwell's 3.4-litre Tojeiro-Jaguar sports car (6), Johnny Mansell's Maserati 250F, and Bob Gibbons' ear-splitting aero-engined Lycoming Special. Chasing me hard is Ron Flockhart (1) in the works BRM. We had a tremendous battle, which Ron won, with me finishing 2nd. He'd led the first seven laps, I took over until lap 24, then Ron until lap 38, and finally from lap 47 to the finish. Even after losing you remember a race like that as fun.

ABOVE
One of my most successful Tasman racing Coopers was the 1959 2½-litre car I shipped down for the January–March 1960 events. At Ardmore we won the New Zealand Grand Prix with Bruce McLaren second. This was the perfect launch pad for him to announce his engagement to Patricia Broad of Timaru. We were both clocked at 145mph (235km/h) through the speed trap on the back straight. At Christchurch I then won the Lady Wigram Trophy at my fourth attempt and it was my first win in the South Island too.

car broke a drive-shaft. I had a spare with me which I naturally gave to Rob for Stirling's use since I didn't need it. Their car was back together just in time for the GP, and so Stirling won on my driveshaft. I couldn't complain. The press made a fuss about my "sporting gesture" which was really no big deal, just the spirit of the age. It would have been a dull race without Moss, and if I'd won it, the win would have been empty.

It was on that trip at Teretonga that, after I'd won a preliminary Heat, Bruce simply slaughtered us all to win outright. He ran single rear wishbone suspension, mine had double rear wishbones, and the older system's inherent oversteer was better suited to Teretonga. Bruce would later write how we raced there wheel-to-wheel. "For the first and only time in my career [Jack] nodded me through" he wrote, and added how, after his win, I was "...strangely quiet...and has never waved me past since, when we have been in equal cars. It was the first time I had beaten him fair and square and I was pleased with myself". Honestly, he had good reason to be.

When I next flew to Sydney for a summer season's "Tasman" tour I was reigning World Champion. While our Sebring cars had been shipped home the other two works Formula 1 cars had been shipped out to Auckland for the 1960 New Zealand GP. Running mine on methanol fuel, I qualified on pole and beat Bruce in his home Grand Prix by just six-tenths of a second. Stirling's transmission collapsed, his goggles had been smashed, and his face cut by flying stones. He shouldn't have come so close.

I scored another win in the Wigram Trophy at Christchurch before Bruce and I flew off separately to Argentina. I also had another Cooper in Australia which I then drove to win at Orange before selling it to fellow Aussie driver Len Lukey. In October I made a flying visit, with a second World title to my name, and won at

LEFT
Everybody and his brother having a real go on the opening lap of the 1960 NZ GP. That's home-town boy Bruce leading in his Cooper (47) from Moss in the red-nosed pale-green Yeoman Credit Cooper (7), my car (4) wagging its tail, while to the left on the tight line is the great English globe-trotting privateer David Piper in his ex-works front-engined Lotus 16. More Coopers, Maseratis, and Ferraris follow on.

BELOW
The NZ GP starting grid here looks lost on that great broad runway, but the spectacle of this kind of tight-packed 4-by-4 starting grid must have been greater than that of a modern wide-spaced Formula 1 2-by-2. While we've gained a lot in safety over the years, we've certainly lost something in pure excitement. Perhaps that's easy to say when you've survived it?

Bathurst in my old 1959 works car. Life was hectic and my ability to sleep on airliners proved a major bonus.

Our 1961 programme yet again commenced with the New Zealand GP. John flew out this time to run the works *Lowline* cars for myself and Bruce, while Ron Flockhart drove our spare. When Bruce's engine starved at the end of the final straight I narrowly beat him again and Ron was fourth. I was on a winning streak as next day in the Bay of Plenty I hooked a 206lb Mako shark. That was another ambition fulfilled.

At Christchurch the Wigram Trophy race was ruined by torrential rain but I managed to surf home first again just ahead of Stirling in a damaged Walker Lotus. In Sydney a new motor racing circuit had just opened at the Warwick Farm horse-race course (a kind of Australian Aintree) and the Warwick Farm "100" was run there in fantastic heat (110°F) which literally cooked my chances while Stirling won in the Walker Lotus.

MINOR FORMULA FUN

Virtually throughout my racing career I enjoyed the minor-Formula races which filled-in the racing calendar's vacant weekends between Grands Prix.

From 1956–1961, these 1½-litre Formula 2 events not only developed the driver, they also advanced the car. If it hadn't been for 1½-litre Formula 2 racing through the late-1950s it's quite probable that for the British teams like Cooper and Lotus there wouldn't have been any 2½-litre Formula 1 development either.

The first Cooper-Climax single-seater was built in 1956 to race in a brief series of "dress-rehearsal" 1½-litre Formula 2 races. These were organised in Britain in anticipation of the FIA's new International class of single-seater racing which was being introduced for the years 1957–1960. Initially in the earliest races I drove stripped-out works Cooper "Bobtail" sports cars, while Roy Salvadori drove John's prototype slender-bodied open-wheeler. I drove a second open-wheeler from the Gold Cup forward, and then we got down to serious competition in "proper" Formula 2 from Easter Monday Goodwood, 1957. It proved to be a very successful class for us. We won a lot of races, while the British *Autocar* Championship and French "Grands Prix de France" Formula 2 series both came our way. In 1959 our Cooper-Climax domination was seriously challenged by fuel-injected new Cooper-Borgwards driven most notably by Stirling Moss in Rob Walker's famous Scots-blue colours, and in 1960 they fielded loaned works Porsches against us.

I had such fun racing in Formula 2 that by 1960 I would run my own Cooper in the class. The car was prepared for me by Tim Wall. The category finally lapsed at the end of 1960, when its 1½-litre capacity ceiling was adopted by the FIA as the new Formula 1 class. Many of the old European Formula 2 events which we had contested for the past four seasons thus became non-Championship Formula 1 races, but we could look back on some great competition, and considerable Cooper success.

My first decent performance in Formula 2 had been fastest lap at Brands Hatch in the last "rehearsal" race of 1956. But I began the 1957 season well with 2nd at Easter Monday Goodwood.

I then won my next three races in a row, at Brands, Crystal Palace, and Montlhéry outside Paris, set fastest lap at Reims, won again at Brands, was second, and set fastest lap at September Goodwood. Then I discovered the Oulton Park Gold Cup really was gold, by winning it at the Cheshire circuit.

As we spent more time racing seriously in Formula 1 in 1958 my Formula 2 programme was a little less hectic. I still won the Lavant Cup Formula 2 race at Easter Goodwood, and then the Kent Trophy at Brands Hatch.

Competition was even stiffer against the Walker and BRP team Cooper-Borgwards in 1959, but we still ended the season with another Lavant Cup win and victory over Stirling in the Kentish "100" at Brands Hatch, a success I really enjoyed because it was just a matter of days after my huge accident in the Portuguese Grand Prix. Finally in 1960 I won at Brussels and Pau. The 1½-litre Formula 2 had indeed been good for me, and for Cooper. Formula 2 had indeed been good for me.

That tour ended in Tasmania, at the fantastically dangerous, but wonderful, Longford country road circuit where my *Lowline* was lapping at an average 108mph (175km/h) and I saw 168mph (270km/h) on the "Flying Mile" straight. But a driveshaft joint failed, and Roy Salvadori won in our "old nail" spare car. I thought that was poor reward for my having shown him the way round in practice.

Although I was an ex-Cooper works team driver by the time we returned to Auckland for the 1962 New Zealand GP, I arrived there in my lightweight 1961-season works car, fitted with a 2½-litre Climax FPF engine in place of its new Formula 1 1½-litre unit. Bruce drove Tommy Atkins' *Lowline* with 2.7-litre Indy-sized FPF engine, but it poured with rain and newly-married Bruce found himself on the wrong side of the course markers in the spray. My gearbox broke a selector, while Stirling won in the latest Walker Lotus.

It rained again at Levin, but I won there, and when the sun shone at Christchurch, Stirling beat me into second place. Bruce in the Atkins *Lowline* then beat both of us at Teretonga. Back in Sydney I led the Warwick Farm "100" until my gearbox split, leaving Stirling to win again in Rob's 2.7-litre *Lowline* Cooper (he had a choice of Walker Lotus or Walker Cooper, lucky beggar). Roy had a terrible shunt in a Bowmaker team Cooper, and was very lucky to suffer only concussion. My mechanic Tim Wall then cannibalised his gearbox to put my car on the grid for the following race at Lakeside, Brisbane, enabling me to win again.

Next stop was Longford, Tasmania. John Surtees had flown home to get married, and had returned with his new wife Pat, in time to beat me in his 2.7-litre Bowmaker *Lowline*. We hit 171mph (275km/h) along the straight. That was the race in which Lex Davison had an almighty shunt just before the trackside Railway Hotel. He clambered out of the steaming wreck, stumped straight into the bar and ordered a Scotch!

That tour of '62 then ended at Melbourne's Sandown Park circuit, where John Surtees and I again became involved in a rare old dust-up. I just managed to win by eight-tenths of a second.

In fact that would prove to be my final serious home appearance behind the wheel of a Cooper-Climax. Those cars had carried me to more success than I could ever have dreamed possible over 11 long years of racing on five Continents.

The next time I would race down under it would not be in a Cooper but behind the wheel of a Ron Tauranac-designed "Brabham" car.

FAR LEFT
Roy and myself in our Coopers, in March '61, enjoying a weekend's racing at the remote Hume Weir circuit near Albury on the NSW/Victoria border.

BELOW
At Melbourne's Sandown Park in '62 with Lance Reventlow's rear-engined Scarab InterContinental Formula car. It used a lightweight Buick V8.

I like this shot: myself as leader of the pack on the opening lap of the 1960 Gold Cup race at Oulton Park. There's a real galaxy of talent here. I'm being chased by Jim Clark and Innes Ireland in their rear-engined works Lotus 18s, Bruce McLaren in our second *Lowline* Cooper, Jo Bonnier's BRM, Stirling Moss's Walker Lotus, John Surtees's works Lotus, Graham Hill's BRM, and my old mate Roy Salvadori in Tommy Atkins's private Cooper. All of us but Roy would win Grands Prix, and there are four World Champions here, but I'd lose this race to Moss!

CHAPTER 7

DOUBLE WORLD CHAMPION

Winning the 1959 title might have been construed as good fortune, in 1960 there was still something to prove

After Sebring our team split up. Bruce flew home to New Zealand where he was properly greeted as the youngest Grand Prix winner in history, while Tim Wall caught a plane to Australia, and the British members of our party and I caught another back to London. There we enjoyed a heady round of receptions and functions before I went home to Australia for Christmas and quite a welcome. Only five years had elapsed since I had first set out for Europe, a lot of water and so many racing miles, had flowed under the bridge since then.

Charlie Cooper was perhaps most proud of his company's World title. Our team secretary at Hollyfield Road, Andrew Ferguson who organised travel and bookings, amongst other duties, went with him to a British Racing Drivers' Club reception at the Washington Hotel. Charlie was a tough old Londoner, born and bred, and he was standing sipping cocktails when Earl Howe and Raymond Mays of BRM, who was pretty posh himself, came up to shake hands. "Congratulations Charles, absolutely delighted for you," they said in their public school tones. Small talk began—not Charlie's strong suit. He stood there for a while, silent, uncomfortable, and then to keep his end up he suddenly said, "'Ere, 'ave you 'eard the one about this Irishman wiv 'is dog—really good joke this is."

That was typical, but what also was typical was his conviction that since the recipe that we'd been developing for years had worked well enough to bring us the World titles, there could be no reason to improve upon it now. His war-cry was, "Why change it when we're winnin'?" But John, Bruce, and I all knew that we had to. We dared not stand still.

The same was not true of Cooper's designer, Owen "The Beard" Maddock, a part-time jazz musician who, if anything, was even more steadfastly conservative than Charlie himself. We'd had many animated discussions about new developments on the cars and Owen would argue black was white to stand his ground. Most of all he staunchly protected his curved-tube Cooper chassis concept, in which the main chassis tubes closely followed the lines of the bodywork, to save extra attachment framework. I knew that straight tubes could provide a stiffer, lighter structure, but no way would Owen accept that and our argument went on for ages with Charlie consistently backing "The Beard".

After the International races in New Zealand the new year's World Championship series began that February in Buenos Aires, Argentina. Inter-Continental flights were always gruelling in those days. I met up with John, Charlie, Noddy, and tall Mike Barney in BA, but it was Bruce who had the worst trip. He'd spent two days flying from Auckland to New York only to find his Argentine connection had been cancelled. He just missed a PanAm Boeing and found himself instead on a decrepit twin-engined DC3 Dakota, which creaked down to BA in a further 36 deafening hours. Upon arrival he was limp as a dishrag and slept for 20 hours before the Argentine Grand Prix practice began!

Meanwhile, we were more concerned by the fact we had no cars. These had been shipped out on the SS *Scottish Star* but one of her engines' giant pistons had collapsed at sea. John was on a wind-up telephone at the Autodrome, seeking news from the organising Club. He spoke no Spanish, and they had no English. Often excitable, John suddenly exploded in frustration, tore the entire telephone set off the wall and hurled it to the floor, scattering bells, springs, and Bakelite everywhere. But still no cars.

BELOW
Owen "The Beard" Maddock was Cooper's chief designer during the entire period I was with them from 1955–1961. I found him even more conservative than Charlie Cooper himself, which really is saying something, but his greatest work was the "C5S" Cooper gearbox which we used in the 1960 Lowline Coopers and on which our second World Championship really depended. It did the job brilliantly. One time a job applicant was described to Charlie Cooper as having a beard, and Charlie replied "Oh Gawd, we don't want 'im then, I 'ave enough trouble wiv the one I've got!".

ABOVE
Young Bruce being wheeled back into the pits after winning the 1960 season-opening Argentine Grand Prix in Buenos Aires, his second consecutive Grand Prix victory after Sebring at the end of the previous season. Look at the delight written all over the faces of John Cooper (left) and Charlie Cooper (right). If I couldn't win a race I enjoyed few things more than seeing Bruce do it.

Late on the Saturday afternoon the boys were standing on the dockside, peering hopefully into the River Plate haze. At 5.15pm the ship drew alongside, and by 7pm we were unloading the cars from a hired truck at the Autodrome, 20 miles (32 kilometres) away. Bruce and I rushed round for a few brief laps of practice. Another final session was provided on the Sunday morning and with tyres scrubbed, brakes bedded in, and Thermos flasks of iced orange juice fitted in the cockpits we lined up for the race, with ambient temperature hovering around 110°F.

The sensation at the practice had been Innes Ireland in Colin Chapman's latest Formula 1 Lotus, the Type 18 which like our Coopers, had its Climax engine mounted in the rear. It was ultra light, very compact, and incredibly ugly, but its very rigid chassis was composed of entirely straight small-gauge tubes. Typical of the era, while I had been cooling my heels without a car, Stirling and Rob Walker had let me drive his car for a few laps, just to see which way the circuit went.

On the opening lap I led into the first corner despite having muffed my start for the first time in ages. I went hurtling down the inside of everybody into that first turn when, you wouldn't read about it, a photographer just stepped out to take a shot. He was right there, on my line, about three or four feet out from the kerb, eye to viewfinder. I braked furiously but of course nobody would give me room to dodge around him. He just stood there, totally engrossed in his photograph, and I must have brushed his trousers. Out of that corner I was more like 10th than first.

Next time round, out on the backstretch, there was another photographer flat on his stomach, on the outside kerb, right at the point we drifted out to. These Argentines were something else!

Innes was leading in the new rear-engined Lotus and I was running fifth, when I heard a clatter behind me and the reduction gears on the gearbox broke due to faulty heat treatment. I retired to the pits, where I spent much of the race watching a series of furious fights erupt in the grandstand opposite. Ultimately it seemed 50 or 60 people were involved and bodies and seats were flying around—amazing.

Stirling took the lead after Innes spun only to break a wishbone, a very unusual failure on a Cooper, which gave Jo Bonnier's BRM first place, from Innes and then Bruce third in our second works Cooper. But the BRM broke, Innes's steering tightened up, and then we were frantically waving "FIRST" signals at Bruce and he won his second consecutive World Championship-qualifying Grand Prix, by 26 seconds.

This was terrific. I was so pleased for him, and for our team, but the writing was plainly on the wall for our old cars. The front-engined BRMs had out-cornered us and they had a new rear-engined car on the way, while the latest rear-engined Lotus looked a real threat, with a definite edge under acceleration and immense potential.

We then flew north for a *Formule Libre* race on city boulevards in Cordoba, which was also unbelievably hot. When we got to Cordoba airport for the flight back to BA, our plane's port-outer engine ran rough when the engines were started. Engineers were called out. They proceeded to take off the cowlings and began fiddling about. Eventually we had to disembark and return to the terminal. We hung about, watching through the windows, and eventually saw the mechanics just look at one another, shrug, and refit the cowls. We took off with that engine sounding as rough as ever. I was a flyer myself by that time, and was a very unhappy passenger all the way.

The Cordoba race was run in even higher temperatures than in BA, and I had to retire from the lead with my car's fuel system vapour locked. Bruce hit a straw bale and split his car's oil cooler, and Trintignant won in the Rob Walker Cooper from Dan Gurney, second for his new team, BRM.

On the long flight back to London I sat with John and had a real heart-to-heart about the season ahead. We were both desperately keen to defend our Championship titles. I told him "We've really got to do something or we'll be left for dead this year", and we began planning a new car right there on the airliner. We landed at Heathrow on March 17, and what would become known as the *Lowline* Cooper, for our 1960 title defence, would be on its wheels and making its racing debut at Silverstone on May 14. The old makeshift gearbox was already being replaced, Owen Maddock designing an all-new five-speed purpose-built transaxle with fully dry-sumped and pumped lubrication system. It would be made for us by Jack Knight's little specialist works in Battersea. It was an expensive exercise which we would never have got past Charlie, but for John managing to lose the expenditure amongst the accounts until it was too late for his Dad to say "No".

Where the new car was concerned, Bruce's college technical drawing experience was enlisted to lay out suspension and accessory blueprints. I spent hours studying sketches and thinking, and John chased progress. We wanted to change to a coil-spring rear suspension but when Charlie heard this he was adamant we must maintain the old transverse leafspring option, just in case the coils didn't work. He also insisted that only one new car should be built and a second would only follow for Bruce if, and when, the first was proven. It was blindingly obvious that if the prototype might only just make Silverstone then it would be suicide not to lay down a second car until so late in the season, so the boys began to build one secretly.

Perhaps most significantly we finally broke down Owen Maddock's resistance to straight chassis tubes, the engine mounted one-inch lower and the driving position was more reclined and slightly further back than in the 1957–59 cars. Dunlop had produced lower-silhouette tyres demanding wider wheel rims.

I believe the *Lowline* was the first really good Grand Prix car that Cooper produced. We would even find it had quite a good body shape for straightline speed, where it could out-perform Ferrari, Lotus, BRM, everybody.

Meanwhile our European season commenced with a series of Formula 2 races, at Syracuse, Brussels, and Pau.

ABOVE
A programme from the 1960 Brussels Grand Prix.

BELOW
OK I admit it, the old speedway crouch was still there. Here I'm in the Formula 2 Cooper-Climax on my way to winning the 1960 Brussels GP.

I won the latter pair, and felt on pretty good form. I was certainly looking forward to completion of our new car, and spent every spare minute in the Formula 1 team's new workshop in Langley Road, Surbiton, just up the hill from what was now purely the design and production works in Hollyfield Road.

The prototype *Lowline* was completed as a runner around 9am on Friday, May 6. It was taken straight to Silverstone and by 2pm I was out in it, lapping faster and faster. Within 10 laps it was two seconds inside the Formula 1 lap record, and we ended up six seconds faster than ever before. Bruce later wrote: "The grin on John's face was only excelled by that on Charles's, who promptly claimed the coil-spring rear suspension as his own idea!" That sounds about right.

But Charlie was nobody's fool. He wrote on the test report "3/4 of circuit resurfaced and new D9 speed tyres (2 sec each?)." He was crediting four seconds of our improvement to the combination of resurfaced circuit and new Dunlop tyres, but he was still delighted with the two-second gain left. And so was I.

Practice for the BRDC International Trophy began on May 12. It rained and remained wet next day, Friday 13th, when Harry Schell crashed fatally at Abbey Curve. His

RIGHT
Sometimes when you lose a race it's written all over your face, and almost every time you win you can't help smiling. Spot the losers here on the Brussels GP podium in April 1960. That's Stirling to the left, and Maurice Trintignant to the right. Another good day at the office.

Yeoman Credit team Cooper was hardly damaged but it had rolled over and landed on its wheels again while poor Harry had been thrown out and broke his neck. He was Franco-American, a larger than life character who'd always been a real tryer, and I'd counted him as a friend ever since I'd arrived in Britain. He had been a very popular guy.

Then, in the race that Saturday (because we didn't run major races in Britain on Sundays then) Innes Ireland was just uncatchable in the rear-engined works Lotus and won handsomely. I finished second and Bruce in his just-completed second *Lowline* way behind after a stop to free a sticking throttle. My new car's handling wasn't quite right yet and Innes beat me fair and square. Behind us in the Formula 2 category the latest New Zealand "Driver to Europe", a husky but rather introverted young chap named Denny Hulme, won in a Cooper.

The Monaco Grand Prix followed. Charlie in particular was hurt by news that Rob Walker was buying one of the new Lotus 18s for Moss, in place of their Coopers. Charlie didn't rate Colin Chapman and his fragile products, and was never afraid to say as much. Now he felt Rob had deserted to join the opposition.

Bruce and I both knew we'd have our work cut out to beat off not only Innes and the works Lotuses, but also Stirling in one of these darned biscuit-box things. We had to improve our new cars' handling before the opening Grand Prix of the European season, in Monaco. In preparation for the tight street circuit we tested at Brands Hatch, and concluded the ride height had been about an inch too high, roll seemed excessive, and we dialed-in oversteer and retuned the Weber carburettors for added low-speed torque.

In Monte Carlo practice was fraught, especially for Bruce who nearly failed to qualify after spinning and smashing a wheel at the Gasworks Hairpin, then having the official timekeepers miss some laps. His gearbox bung then dropped out and he coated the course with oil, and had to make a final desperate qualifying attempt on his own slick. It was only later that night, when the organisers re-checked their timing tapes, that they included him on the grid, in 11th place. Moss put Rob Walker's brand-new Lotus on pole position, and I lined-up second fastest in my new *Lowline*.

It rained on raceday after about 30 laps. I was chasing Moss's Walker Lotus in second place, but since he was unfamiliar with his new car in the wet I was able to overtake him. Then I stupidly spun at the bottom of the hill after Ste Devote corner, and Stirling nipped by while marshals were heaving and shunting my car back and forth. In any case, I'd clouted a trackside kerb and wall, dislodged my rear anti-roll bar which got trapped under the car, and its chassis was twisted. Bruce had been delayed but fought back into third place before spinning off beside me. Now I directed him back into the race, and, realising there would be few finishers, disentangled that anti-roll bar and rejoined the race myself. Bruce finished second, despite spinning again when his goggles

ABOVE
The business end of our new *Lowline* Cooper-Climax F1 car out on early test at Silverstone. It showed promise and gave us high hopes for the coming season in Europe. The chassis frame features straight tubes, there's the new "C5S" gearbox (left) and new coil-spring rear suspension about which Charlie was so dubious.

steamed-up, and, although I took the finish flag, I was judged too far behind to be classified. Stirling had won this debut race for his new Walker Lotus and Charlie's face told the story.

The Dutch Grand Prix was only a week away, and my car had to be taken back to Langley Road, rebuilt, and rushed to Zandvoort in time to practice on the Thursday. Noddy took it upon himself to do the work single-handed, and it was ready in time. However, the trailer carrying the car became unhitched from behind our transporter on the way back though France and the boys didn't miss it for a few miles, until Mike Barney glanced out the cab window, and realised from the shadow they had no trailer and *Lowline* attached any more! They retraced their route, and finally found some puzzled holiday-makers inspecting the car, on its trailer, at the end of the long swathe it had

RIGHT
Locking-over the handsome *Lowline* Cooper into *La Source* hairpin, the slowest point on the Spa-Francorchamps circuit, during the 1960 Belgian Grand Prix. The car's fine shape made it exceptionally quick in a straight line and for the first time we had a Cooper whose nose didn't lift alarmingly at high speed. We're going to win this one.

carved through a roadside cornfield. Fortunately for us, it had stayed the right way up.

At Zandvoort I was quite happy to qualify in the middle of the front row splitting the Lotuses of Moss on pole and Innes Ireland outside me. I led away with Moss close behind until I cut an apex out on the swerving backstretch, and one of the kerb stones must have been loose, because my wheel hooked it up, straight into Stirling's path. It burst his front tyre, and could have taken either the wheel off, or his head! He seemed to think I'd done it on purpose. Regardless, he had to stop to change wheels and I was left untroubled to win the Dutch Grand Prix, my first of the new season and the first for our new *Lowline* Cooper.

The Belgian Grand Prix followed at Spa. The second practice day was hot and the circuit of course was fantastically fast, demanding, and dangerous. Then Stirling's Walker Lotus lost a wheel and crashed violently just after the Burnenville curve. When I came out of the corner to see waving yellow flags and marshals running across the road, he was lying on the verge. We all skated to a stop and did what we could to help. He was obviously badly hurt, having trouble breathing, and his legs were a mess. We were frightened to move him and it was ages before an ambulance arrived. He'd broken both legs, his pelvis, and even his back. Moss would be racing again within eight weeks.

The specialists at St Thomas's Hospital in London did a fantastic job of patching him up, and Stirling's will to recover was incredibly powerful. He always had immense stamina and his whippet-like fitness obviously helped.

But while the Moss shunt was being sorted out, nobody seemed to notice that another Lotus 18 had gone off on

BELOW
Photographers could stand amazingly close to the trackside by modern standards, and this Geoffrey Goddard shot was taken with a normal lens, just straight down into the *Lowline's* cockpit as I nearly clipped his toecaps at *La Source*. Here's further proof of "the Brabham crouch".

RIGHT
My team-mate Bruce McLaren going well through the high-speed curves of Spa during the 1960 Belgian Grand Prix when I led him to the finish in a *Lowline* Cooper first and second place finish. This was a deeply satisfying result for our Cooper works team, but the circumstances of that tragic race, with two drivers dead and two badly injured, just left an empty feeling. Look at the wheel angles Bruce's Lowline was adopting. It might have been the best Cooper yet, but it still wasn't particularly sophisticated.

the return leg of the circuit. This was Michael Taylor's private car, and he'd had his steering column break as he entered another very fast corner (apart from one hairpin they were all fast at Spa) and his car had just torpedoed off into the woods. He too was badly hurt, but it was amazing he survived at all.

Even worse followed in the race. While we did just fine (I won with Bruce second for a crushing *Lowline* Cooper 1-2) a promising new young English driver named Chris Bristow crashed his Yeoman Credit Cooper at Burnenville while deep in a frantic battle with Willy Mairesse's Ferrari. He was killed on impact and six laps later Lotus works driver Alan Stacey went off at Malmedy and was killed as his Type 18 somersaulted down into a trackside field and burned out. This time the car wasn't to blame, it appeared he'd been hit in the face by a bird which probably knocked him out before the car went off. This was just awful. Alan had been another nice guy, and he actually had an artificial leg and used to claim he was the only Formula 1 driver whose socks were held up by drawing pins.

Although we had now won two GPs in a row and won well, that Belgian GP weekend was best forgotten. The next World Championship round was the French at Reims. Tony Brooks's Ferrari lap record there from the previous year was 2mins 19.4secs and now our *Lowline* Cooper proved so well suited to the bullet fast straights that I ended up on pole position with a best lap in 2:16.8. This was regarded very much as a Ferrari circuit, well suited to their V6 front-engined cars, but I always relished taking Ferrari's trousers down, and the race became a ferocious duel between my green Cooper and Phil Hill's Italian-red charger. We had a fantastic scrap for 29 long laps, during which Phil, at one stage, opened-up his Ferrari's snout against my rear wheel. We finally left the lap record at 2:17.5–135.8mph (219km/h), and the *Lowline* was screaming along the downhill Soissons Straight at some 180–190mph (290–310km/h).

LEFT
I just loved defeating Ferraris, I really loved it, ever since that day back in 1955 when I'd visited the Maranello factory with my introduction from the Shell people in Australia and they'd said, "Who?". Here, I'm turning my *Lowline* Cooper into Thillois Corner at Reims during the 1960 French Grand Prix, with "Taffy" von Trips's V6 Ferrari on the inside. Late in the race his team-mate Phil Hill would almost torpedo me amidships at this very point.

Phil and I slipstreamed one another furiously, tucking our cars right up as close as we could behind the other, whoever was ahead, and then pulling out to slingshot ahead, whereupon the other would tuck in behind. On one lap I'd just leapfrogged past Phil on the straight and was braking hard on the left side of the roadway into the right-hand Thillois Corner which led onto the finishing straight. I was set up to lock across right-handed to clip the inside apex when, fortunately for me, I glanced in my rear-view mirror.

I could hardly believe my eyes. Phil's Ferrari was avalanching up inside me with all four wheels locked, streaming blue smoke without a hope of stopping. If I'd locked-over normally into the corner he'd have tee-boned me for sure, but having seen him coming I just kept straight and "whoompphhh" he hurtled past, straight as an arrow, at least 50–60mph (80–97km/h) faster than I, and careered straight up the escape road heading towards Reims city centre!

So then it was three in a row for that season—the *Lowline* Cooper and I had just won the French Grand Prix. Bruce finished third and the previously so unfortunate Yeoman Credit team Coopers took second and fourth places, driven by Olivier Gendebien and Henry Taylor, making it a 1-2-3-4 success for Surbiton. Charlie was pretty cheerful by this stage of the season.

We went to Silverstone as winners of the previous year's British Grand Prix, and there I felt on the crest of a wave. I'd always been confident in the way we prepared our cars, and the thought we put into setting them up, and now I was also very confident of my ability to race against anyone driving almost anything. I led away from three works Lotus 18s, driven by motorcycle World Champion

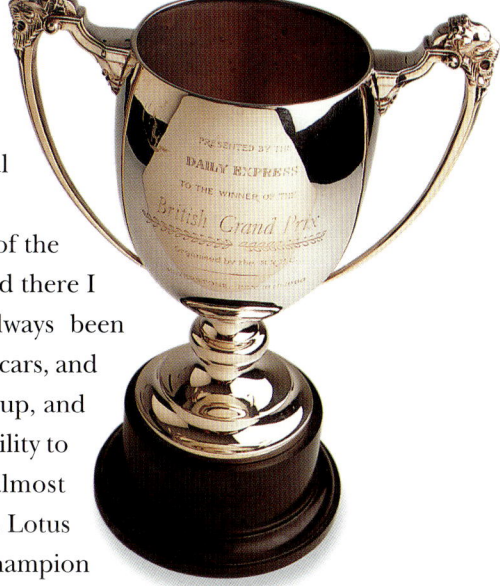

BELOW
The 1960 British Grand Prix trophy.

RIGHT

Flat-out at Silverstone during the 1960 British Grand Prix. I'm chasing desperately hard after Graham Hill's late-starting BRM, which had come through the field and shot straight past me, to my intense disgust. I'm lapping David Piper's privately-entered front-engined year old Lotus here. I was able to apply real pressure to Graham which ultimately caught him out when his BRM's brakes played-up, and suddenly I'd won my second consecutive British Grand Prix. I was really pleased to see him spin. That made my day!

BELOW

The programme from the 1960 British Grand Prix.

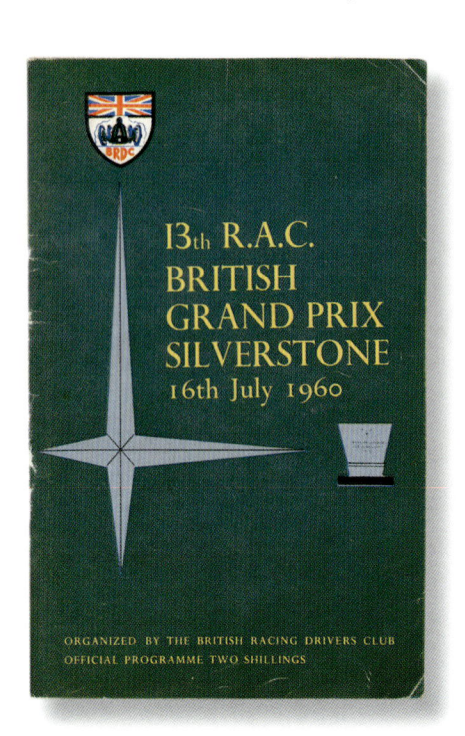

John Surtees in his first four-wheeled racing season, young Jim Clark, and the May Silverstone winner, Innes Ireland. But the real threat was to come from Graham Hill's new rear-engined BRM which they'd been developing progressively through the early races without much sign of success. Now Graham had stalled at the start and got away dead last. Graham was perhaps the most coldly determined driver I ever faced, and now he simply hacked his way back past the entire field, and on lap 55 of the 77 he barged his way past me to take the lead. His car was going like a rocket and plainly had a lot of power. I think it suddenly dawned on him that he was actually leading the British Grand Prix for BRM, the much-criticised and controversial "British Racing Motor."

John was madly urging me on, pointing to the laps remaining slot on the signal board—time was running out. So I pushed hard and began pegging Graham back. I reckoned I'd be within striking distance by the last lap when, with six to go, Graham dived past one backmarker too many as we hurtled into Copse Corner. His car's brakes had been going away for some tim, and now they caught him out. I saw the BRM's hunchbacked tail bobble and yaw and then he was broadside ahead of me. Smoke streamed off the tyres and he spun across the verge and crashed backwards into the earth bank. I'd been just 1.6 seconds behind him, looming large in his mirrors, and I must admit that when he handed me my fourth consecutive GP win of the season like that, it was a relief. On the other hand did I feel like a bit of a bully? No, not at all.

That year's Portuguese Grand Prix was run on the rugged street circuit at Oporto, with its mixture of fine surface, cobble-stones, and tramlines!

Stirling was back in a fresh Walker Lotus, but the sensation of practice was Surtees who out-qualified us all to put his works Lotus on pole position, in only his third Grand Prix. This time I had my Portuguese incident on the second lap. The long straight ended in a left-hand corner heading uphill along the tram lines, followed by another left-hander in which the tram lines went straight on, off the roadway being used as the circuit.

Dan Gurney was leading in his BRM and I was booming along third just behind Moss and felt that I could take him. I moved inside, intending to outbrake him into the next corner, but my tyres got onto the tramlines and slid on the polished metals. It became apparent to me I wasn't going to make the turn.

I weaved from the inside to the outside between Dan and Stirling, and shot straight on, slithered virtually to a halt, turned around 180-degrees, and rejoined eighth, right on Bruce's tail in the other *Lowline*. I moved past him and retirements up ahead elevated us to third and fourth behind John Surtees's now leading Lotus, and Phil Hill's Ferrari. I managed to nip past Phil and on lap 36 John overshot a corner as his foot pedals were slippery with leaking fuel, and he split his Lotus's radiator. I was back in the lead, with Bruce second in my wheel tracks, and so we scored the fifth consecutive *Lowline* Cooper victory of that year. Now I was virtually assured of back-to-back World titles as only Bruce could challenge my points total, and even then only by winning both the remaining Italian and United States Grand Prix.

But then political troubles intervened as the Italian organisers insisted upon using the combined road and banked speedbowl circuit at Monza and the British teams boycotted the race.

After our experience at AVUS the previous year, banked tracks were considered entirely unsuitable for modern lightweight Grand Prix cars. Ferrari were left with a walk-over 1-2-3 victory at Monza, and I was World Champion Driver for the second successive season, and the Cooper Car Company had successfully defended its Constructors' Championship title.

Moss's Walker Lotus beat me in the Oulton Park Gold Cup, before I returned home to Australia in October, racing my old 1959 works car at Bathurst where I was able to win again. One week later we reported for duty at Watkins Glen in upstate New York for a non-Championship 100-lap "International Grand Prix". I led initially until I was baulked by a backmarker, which gave Jo Bonnier the lead in his Yeoman Credit team Cooper before I caught up and managed to repass him. Moss, however, pressed ever closer in the Walker Lotus and I couldn't hold him off. He won with my *Lowline* second again, as at Oulton Park.

BELOW

On the way to my fifth successive World Championship-qualifying Grand Prix win of the 1960 season, at Oporto in Portugal. One of my more exciting races after the city's tramlines took me most of the way to the tram terminus, I finally inherited the lead when John Surtees's foot slipped off an oil-covered brake pedal, ending a terrific drive in his works Lotus. It could have happened to any of us.

ABOVE
The 1960 Danish Grand Prix Formula 2 trophy.

November then saw the second Formula 1 United States Grand Prix run at Riverside in California. This was to be 2½-litre Formula 1's swansong race, because new 1½-litre rules were taking effect on January 1, 1961.

After I had run out of petrol at Sebring the previous year, John made absolutely sure it wouldn't happen again and filled my car's tanks were filled to the brim.

Raceday was very hot and sunny, and as the car stood on the starting grid so the tanks warmed up and the fuel load expanded which sent AvGas dripping out of the overflow pipe. I made a good start and was pulling away but overflowing fuel was "scent-spraying" in the airstream out of the breather, back across the engine. As I changed up onto the main straight the exhaust probably spat back and ignited the leaking fuel.

I was hurtling down the straight with flames all around me in the cockpit. I sat up and hunched forward against the wheel while I tried to stop. But by the time I had actually stopped the only fire still burning was in the engine bay, where the wiring-loom insulation was alight. I trundled round to the pits where we shifted the breather and tidied the wires with insulating tape, and I rejoined the race.

But the electrics were damaged, the engine wouldn't run properly and I had an unhappy and fitful drive to salvage fourth place. Stirling won, Innes Ireland was second, and Bruce third.

While I think that John had miscounted his fuel churns at Sebring and left me one short, here I think his zealousness over-corrected. If he had not been so conscious of loading every last ounce of fuel we might have won that race easily.

I managed to finish that year, and the 2½-litre Formula, with my second World Championship title, and Bruce McLaren was runner-up behind me. He'd had a great year, as had the Cooper Car Co, but undoubtedly there were clouds gathering on the horizon.

The new year would see 1½-litre Formula 1 racing introduced. While Ferrari and Porsche had ideal new engines already well developed and race proven, nothing could be further from the truth where the British teams were concerned.

Entering 1961 we were all looking down the gun barrel, and the finger on the trigger was Enzo Ferrari's.

LEFT
Fellow Australian Tim Wall was personal mechanic on the cars I ran on a private basis through 1960–1961, and he stayed with us until the end of 1965 when he went off with Dan Gurney for the 1966–1967 Anglo-American Racers Eagle operation. Tim had been Stirling Moss's mechanic in Rob Walker's private team in 1958 and was immensely capable. The only problem was his chain-smoking, which as a lifelong non-smoker I always detested. I told him repeatedly it would kill him one day, and, very sadly, this proved to be true. Johnny Schonberg died the same way. Amongst my boys only Gary smoked and I told him I'd be attending his funeral one day instead of him attending mine. He paid close attention and kept smoking. I disapprove.

SPORTY CARS IN AMERICA

BELOW
A handshake from my successor as World Champion Phil Hill after I won the 1961 *Los Angeles Times* Grand Prix for sports cars at Riverside Raceway in California. Part of my prize was this enormous Pontiac Grand Prix which had been used as the pace car at the start. I didn't fancy shipping it all the way home, and when I was made a decent offer for it, within the hour it was sold and both the purchaser and yours truly went home smiling. Prize money for first place was $6,925, plus another $200 for pole position. This American way of racing really was quite attractive.

A weekend without a race was a weekend without an earning opportunity, and so throughout my career I was not alone in racing something, somewhere, at almost every opportunity. This had been particularly true during the formative years of my career, and when I was leading the Cooper Formula 1 team we still competed regularly in Formula 2 and, when the opportunity presented itself, in sports cars too.

The original centre-seat *Bobtail* Cooper sports cars had really reached the end of their frontline life by 1957, and it was the single-seater Formula 2 cars developed from them which filled almost every non-Grand Prix weekend of our sporting life through 1957–1958. In the absence of a current Cooper sports car that latter season I enjoyed my works drives with Aston Martin, but then for 1959 Cooper's at last announced a replacement for the successful little *Bobtail* cars, and John named it the *Monaco* to commemorate our maiden Grand Prix win in Monte Carlo that May.

The Cooper *Monaco* recipe was much the same as the little *Bobtail* with a Coventry Climax FPF engine mounted in the rear and driving through the normal Cooper gearbox. But this time the cockpit opening extended full-width, with regulation side-by-side seats for driver and notional passenger. Initially 2-litre FPF engines would be fitted, but with the FPF now available in full Formula 1 2½-litre size we would soon be fitting these units as soon as any became available. Subsequently the engine would grow to a maximum possible 2.7-litres, and it would be fitted into Cooper *Monaco* sports-racing chassis.

The British motor racing calendar was particularly busy at that time, and early-season was always enjoyable with a

SPORTY CARS IN AMERICA

series of non-Championship Formula 1 race meetings which started at Goodwood on Easter Monday, and then ran through the Aintree "200" and May Silverstone meetings, to resume in September with the Oulton Park Gold Cup International and then a race at Snetterton in Norfolk. The supporting programme at each of these meetings usually included a sports car race in addition to one for production saloons and later there'd be extra events for Grand Touring cars and schoolroom Formula Junior too. At these non-Championship race meetings the Formula 1 drivers would often turn out in the sports, saloon, and GT races as well, which was often really enjoyable sport in which we could really let our hair down, and earn money too.

I had a Cooper Monaco built for my own use which was entered for me by John "Noddy" Coombs, a former

BELOW
Me in the 2.7-litre Cooper Monaco sports car which Hap Sharp lent to me for the 1961 Riverside classic. I narrowly beat Bruce McLaren in a sister 2.7-litre Monaco.

SPORTY CARS IN AMERICA

ABOVE
Trying hard at Riverside, 1960, in Briggs Cunningham's one-off Le Mans Jaguar, the prototype "E2A" which was a kind of all-independently suspended halfway house between the 24-Hour race-winning D-Types of the 1950s and the forthcoming new E-Type production sports cars of the 1960s. "E2A" was hefty and outclassed, but nonetheless an interesting car.

owner-driver who had become a prominent Jaguar dealer and racing team patron, based in Guildford, Surrey. While my car used the 2-litre Climax engine, Noddy had a sister car into which he had a 2½-litre Maserati engine fitted for my old friend and sparring partner Roy Salvadori. We had some fantastic battles with each other and the front-engined works Lotus 15 sports cars which were driven by Graham Hill and Cliff Allison.

Stirling Moss later had a sister *Monaco* built-up with a full 2½-litre Climax engine fitted and we had a great battle, which he won, dammit, in these cars at Karlskoga, Sweden, in the summer of '59. That trip also took in a meeting at Roskilde in Denmark, a tiny little track around a former gravel pit, where we both shared wins. Karlskoga was a real eye-opener to me, not least when I was walking down the main street after dinner one evening and found a Swedish couple having it away, regardless of passing pedestrians, over the bonnet of a parked VW Beetle. That was my first visit to Scandinavia and I found their way of life quite intriguing. She was a big girl, too.

I drove my Coombs-entered *Monaco* with a 2½-litre engine fitted in the Goodwood TT but went out early with suspension trouble. And then we ran it in the Bahamas Speed Week at Nassau when I nearly lost my eye, just before the World Championship-deciding United States Grand Prix.

Sebring was my first taste of racing in America, and obviously it worked out well for us. Late in 1960, Scottish entrant David Murray sent his Ecurie Ecosse team's *Monaco* over to America to race at Watkins Glen, and in the West Coast Professional series races at Riverside and Laguna Seca. Each paid well. Roy drove the Ecosse car at the Glen, where he finished third, and then at Riverside

SPORTY CARS IN AMERICA

he spun and stalled at the start before fighting back right through the field to finish sixth. David Murray then invited me to drive the car at Laguna Seca, a tight little circuit on the Monterey peninsula, but its tyres were slit by stones before brake trouble put me out of the running. Stirling ran there in a new rear-engined Lotus, the Type 19, which Colin Chapman christened the *Lotus Monte Carlo* after their 1960 Grand Prix win there, and to take the Mickey out of our Cooper *Monaco* which had been named for similar reasons the previous year.

Then during the autumn of 1961, my works Cooper team-mate Bruce McLaren was preparing to take out a *Lowline* Cooper single-seater (owned by "Tommy" Atkins) to New Zealand and Australia for that winter's racing and Climax agreed to rebuild what had been my 2.7-litre Indianapolis "500" race engine for him. Bruce then figured that this big engine, fitted into the latest 1961 *Monaco* chassis, would make a terrific proposition for the US West Coast Professional sports car races on his way "down under".

Meanwhile, I had done a deal with the enthusiastic American owner of a private *Monaco*, Hap Sharp, who would become famous as Jim Hall's partner in their innovative Chaparral sports car company, to fit what had been my practice Indy "500" 2.7-litre engine into his car which I would then race against Bruce at Riverside Raceway, in the roasting Californian desert. The race was sponsored by the *Los Angeles Times* newspaper. It was the biggest American road race of the year, attracting huge crowds which far exceeded any yet seen at a Formula 1 United States GP.

I fitted sticky-compound Dunlop D12 rain tyres for qualifying, and earned pole position which paid $200. Stirling was driving a Lotus 19 and both he and Bruce considered using D12s for the race, but figured it would be too hot for them to last race distance. In fact, the thermometer hit 103°F on raceday but Hap Sharp's *Monaco* was really light. I took the gamble on fitting D12s for the race, and when Bruce's car blew water onto its rear tyres in the closing stages I was able to nip by after conserving my tyres, and won.

In fact I won $7,000, plus bonuses, plus a Pontiac Grand Prix sedan which I'd sold within the hour, without ever driving the car.

That was a great trip, and it was one of my final outings while I was still a factory Cooper driver. I had increasingly campaigned my own Cooper cars in between works team commitments but now, at the end of the 1961 season, I had decided that my future lay elsewhere and the time had come to leave the team which had for so long seemed like home, and in which I had made some wonderful lifelong friends.

BELOW
At speed at Riverside in my 2-litre Cooper Monaco, not in the major *Times* Grand Prix but at the other end of the year in April 1960, on my way back to Europe from the Tasman tour races back home in New Zealand and Australia. Here I finished 6th, and then sold the car to a former fighter pilot from Sacramento named Sam Weiss. Tragically, he crashed fatally in the car at Laguna Seca.

CHAPTER 8
INDY AND ALL THAT

Launching Cooper's rear-engined revolution in America's Indianapolis 500-Miles—the world's richest yet most conservative motor race

It was the 1959 Indianapolis 500-Miles race winner Rodger Ward who encouraged us to build a Formula 1-based Cooper-Climax to attack the world's richest single motor race in 1961. Here, pre-race, John Cooper and I say "cheese" for the camera with Rodger. Rodger was a great help to us, warned the Indy establishment that their front-engined cars were looking down the gun barrel, and like a number of other Indy regulars he was completely unstinting in the advice he gave about that peculiar place, and its strange brand of left-turn-only motor racing.

Income was always an important factor and at Sebring 1959 I'd had my first insight into the American way of racing. The nation's most prestigious motor race was not a Grand Prix at all. It was the Indianapolis 500-Miles speedway classic, and by the late 1950s the prize money paid for first place was a staggering $338,100, easily sufficient to make anybody think.

At Sebring, the reigning Indy winner, Rodger Ward, ran a tiny little dirt-track midget car powered by an Offenhauser engine. Rodger believed that this little car's good power-to-weight ratio could prove competitive against all these visiting Europeans with their fancy Formula 1 machinery.

I liked Rodger the moment I met him. He was a racer to the core, and told us how we were wasting our time. His midget car's cornering power would more than compensate for our F1 cars' extra horsepower.

The next day he, Bruce, and I arrived together at the first corner of the track, and just as we jumped from brake to throttle pedal and streaked away from him, he was astonished! To his enormous credit, he took it well. It really opened his eyes to how Formula 1 cars could corner. And then he said that such a car could absolutely set the Indianapolis circuit alight.

Rodger worked on us throughout our stay in Sebring. We became intrigued by how well one of our cars might go at Indy—which was a rectangular speedway, 2½ miles (4 kilometres) to the lap—with just four shallow-banked left-hand turns. It had an antique brick-paved surface rather than tarmac, from which came its nickname, "The Brickyard".

John Cooper's US-based friend Frank Falkner set about organising an Indy visit for us, which we made next time we raced in the US, in October 1960. I flew to Indianapolis direct from winning at Bathurst in Australia. Rodger met me and took me straight to the Speedway, where John and Noddy were waiting with my Formula 1 *Lowline*. Rodger drove me round, showing me the accepted racing line through the four near-identical banked turns. In fact what he was showing me was the line all the regular Indy racers aspired to in their heavy front-engined, 4.2-litre Offenhauser-engined Roadsters.

Under Indy regulations, everybody had to pass a standard driver's test for newcomers, or "Rookies" as they

LEFT
My first experience of the four banked Indy Speedway turns came late in 1960 in my Formula 1 *Lowline*. I was surprised to be confronted by the Speedway's "Rookie" driver's test rules and got into terrible trouble with the stewards when I inadvertently broke their speed limits. *Road & Track* magazine later published a photograph of me apparently picking my nose while driving round, the tongue-in-cheek caption suggesting that even a World Champion should show greater respect. After all, to generations of middle Americans, Indy was "The Big One".

BELOW
Our tailor-made Indianapolis Cooper-Climax outside the Cooper racing shop in Langley Road, just up the hill in Surbiton above the production car factory in Hollyfield Road. This shot plainly demonstrates the car's Formula 1 *Lowline* heritage with its straight frame tubes having long replaced the old traditional curvy nonsense, and the all-wishbone and coil-spring suspension front and rear. My cockpit is equipped with United States Automobile Club regulation safety belts, which at the time I would never have dreamed of wearing in Formula 1, and the engine is the first big new 2.7-litre Climax FPF.

called us. I settled into my Lowline and took it out onto the huge Speedway to warm it up.

I swear that's all I was doing, yet my second lap averaged 128mph (206km/h) and suddenly the officials were leaping up and down waving flags of all colours, and I was ordered in. The elderly Chief Steward was a pre-war driver named Harlan Fengler who gave me one hell of a rocket for going too fast, too soon. The normal Rookie test began with a "115mph [185km/h] acclimatisation phase", yet in the Cooper tooling around at 125mph (201km/h) seemed unbelievably slow.

But I politely covered eight laps around 115mph; then Fengler let me skip the 120mph (193km/h) phase, so I ran 10 at around 125mph. This was a very strange experience, and the USAC officials and Indy regulars all thought our green Cooper was not only weird, but dangerous because at superstitious Indy, anything painted green had been taboo for years!

They called it a "Funny Car". Few seemed willing to listen to Rodger who even then was telling them to watch out, "just wait 'til this Aussie guy stands on it."

Fengler allowed me to skip the 130mph (209km/h) phase, before it began to rain so we stopped (nobody ran at Indy if it rained) and went for lunch at the Holiday Motel. When we returned to the pits, word had got round and several Indy regulars had arrived to watch this strange green "bug" drone round their Speedway. I covered 16 more laps, and Clay Smith, the official timer, said I'd run spot-on 142.857mph (229.906km/h) for three consecutive laps. Pole position for that year's "500" had fallen at only 146mph (235km/h), so they were all pretty excited about that.

I couldn't understand all the fuss, I'd seen only 6,400rpm before the shut-off point at the end of each straightaway, and the following day, with a lower back-axle ratio, we ran faster still, hitting 6,800rpm on the back straightaway. I was able to run 11 laps with a best in 143.6mph (231.1km/h), and after a bit of suspension adjustment we managed 144.834mph (233.088km/h) which would have qualified our merely 2½-litre car eighth amongst 33 4.2-litres on that year's "500" starting grid. Of the drivers watching, only Rodger Ward and Tony Bettenhausen had ever lapped faster—and it was "their" track. Plainly then, this Formula 1 technology had something to offer.

The really significant factor was that the Lowline had equaled the fastest ever time set through the quarter-mile long first turn, 6.5 seconds. Revealingly, our time from the exit of Turn Four down the straight to the finish line was a two full seconds slower than any self-respecting Indy Roadster. Our little Formula 1 car was plainly cornering competitively by front-engined Indy Roadster standards, but they would eat it alive down the straights.

Some of the Indy establishment plainly felt threatened. They knew how our rear-engined revolution had rendered traditional front-engined cars obsolete in Formula 1. Now they found themselves looking down the same gun barrel. But generally they were wonderfully friendly. Rodger drove our car briefly and was amazed by its smooth ride and stability. He added, "Damn shame it hasn't got more steam!"

John and I discussed prospects for entering the following year's "500". Our Climax engine burned AvGas petrol at 12 miles (20 kilometres) per gallon while the big American Offenhausers burned alcohol brew at 2–3mpg. That was to our advantage, but Dunlop's road racing tyres were plainly inadequate for Indy due to their relatively soft compound and flexible casing, which caused tremendous heat build-up. Through the Speedway's four left-hand turns we'd worn through the right-front Dunlop in only 12–20 laps. For the 200-lap "500" this would mean 10 tyre-change stops, a hopeless disadvantage. Frank Falkner then introduced us to Jim Kimberly, the Kleenex millionaire and a great racing enthusiast. On the spot he offered to sponsor a tailor-made Indy Cooper to run the following year. We flew to Chicago to finalise the deal, and when John left Jim's office he had the biggest grin on his face I'd ever seen.

Calendar pressure posed the biggest problem, because Indy practice and qualifying clashed with the Monaco GP. Jim Kimberly just insisted, "No problem", and offered private air travel to connect with the trans-Atlantic flights. Everything just seemed relentlessly positive which suited us just fine. It was an exciting proposition and the money looked great. Back in Britain, John badgered Coventry Climax to build us the biggest 4-cylinder FPF engine they could achieve. They reluctantly agreed and the final result emerged at 2.7-litres, producing around 251bhp on a 50/50 Avgas/methanol fuel mix. In the engine's mid-range it developed around 25-horsepower more than our standard 2½-litre Formula 1 versions.

Early in 1961, when we sent our serious entry for a "Kimberly Cooper Special" to USAC, there were many Americans, and genned-up ones at that, who did not expect us to qualify, even with a car specially designed for the job. Producing the car was a real rush job.

I dashed over to Indy two days later (changing out of my racing overalls in the plane which I'd caught immediately after the International Trophy race at Silverstone). But the effort was negated by rain that Sunday morning and, as we'd discovered before, nobody runs at Indy in the rain.

Fortunately the track at Indy had dried by the afternoon when the drivers' tests began. The car went very well and we had to do very little to it, apart from changing the suspension's anti-roll bars. The engine seemed strong, and a second engine was being prepared in time for the race.

LEFT
John and myself (hidden in the cockpit) with the new Indy Cooper during its press launch in 1961. Heavily worn regular Dunlop Racing tyres are fitted but the big USAC regulation "nerf" bar around the tail is entirely distinctive, as is the chassis and body offset to the left for the left-turn-only Speedway, with shorter suspension wishbones and drive-shaft on the left side compared with those on the right.

132 | THE JACK BRABHAM STORY

ABOVE
This is why the Indianapolis Motor Speedway was nicknamed "The Brickyard". By 1961 most of the Speedway had been tarmac surfaced but for tradition's sake much of the pit straight retained its pre-war surface of red brick setts. Here the car is fitted with the special asymmetric tyres, developed by Dunlop, slick-treaded on the inner half and standard on the outer.

We then had two days rained out and couldn't run again until the Wednesday morning, the day before first practice at Monaco. We managed two hours practice that morning, clocked at 146.4mph (235.6km/h). If we could average more than 144mph (232km/h) for the required four-consecutive official qualifying laps we would be assured of a place on the "500" starting grid.

We then rushed off to Monaco, for first practice there, and dashed back across the Atlantic for Indy qualifying that Saturday. It was then vital I should qualify right at the start of the first Indy session so I could hop the first plane available to return to Monaco in time for the Grand Prix that Sunday.

But Indy qualifying is a tense and critical business. Once committed to the four-lap run there would be no opportunity for a second attempt, so if you failed to run quickly enough you could be out of the race until the following year. One safety valve was that if, after three laps, you realised you weren't going quickly enough you could pull in and take another run later. But in my case I had no such luxury, because I could not afford the time to go to the back of the queue and run again.

I played it carefully, and my four laps averaged 145.144mph (233.587km/h), which put me on the fifth row of the grid. It was then back to Monaco, race there, race in the Dutch Grand Prix at Zandvoort the following weekend, and then back to Indy for "The Big One", this time with Betty and our new baby son, Gary. He seemed to sleep on planes just as well as I do.

We fitted the second engine for the race because although the first one was still running beautifully, it had done quite a high mileage, and the fresh engine gave seven more horsepower. So we set off with around 258bhp, against the quicker "Offy" engine's 430 or so.

We had to alter the fuelling positions because the fuel would not go in quickly enough. We also had to alter the screens, because during the trials I found that the rush of air nearly blew the top of my head off; it was so bad it gave me neck-ache. But the modifications worked.

On the night before the race, John, Jim Kimberly, Vic Barlow—Dunlop tyre engineer—and our pit crew all got together to discuss strategy. Dunlop had produced special asymmetric-tread tyres for this unique left-turn only challenge, but they had retained normal road-racing construction and compounding. Vic Barlow was adamant we'd need three pit stops, while we hoped that the 33-car

ABOVE
Honking on through Indy's Turn One, the 2.7-litre Kimberly-Cooper-Climax was as quick as any of its opposition through these turns but just lost out to the 4.2-litre Offenhauser-powered traditional American roadsters along the straights.

LEFT
I've always enjoyed a joke but I've seldom been reduced to such helpless laughter as I was by the "Clown Prince of Indy", Eddie Sachs, in our Cooper's garage in the Speedway's "Gasoline Alley" paddock. When word got round that Eddie was talking to the visitors, a crowd began to gather. The bigger the audience grew, the more he warmed up. I wish somebody had a tape-recorder there. His performance was absolutely priceless.

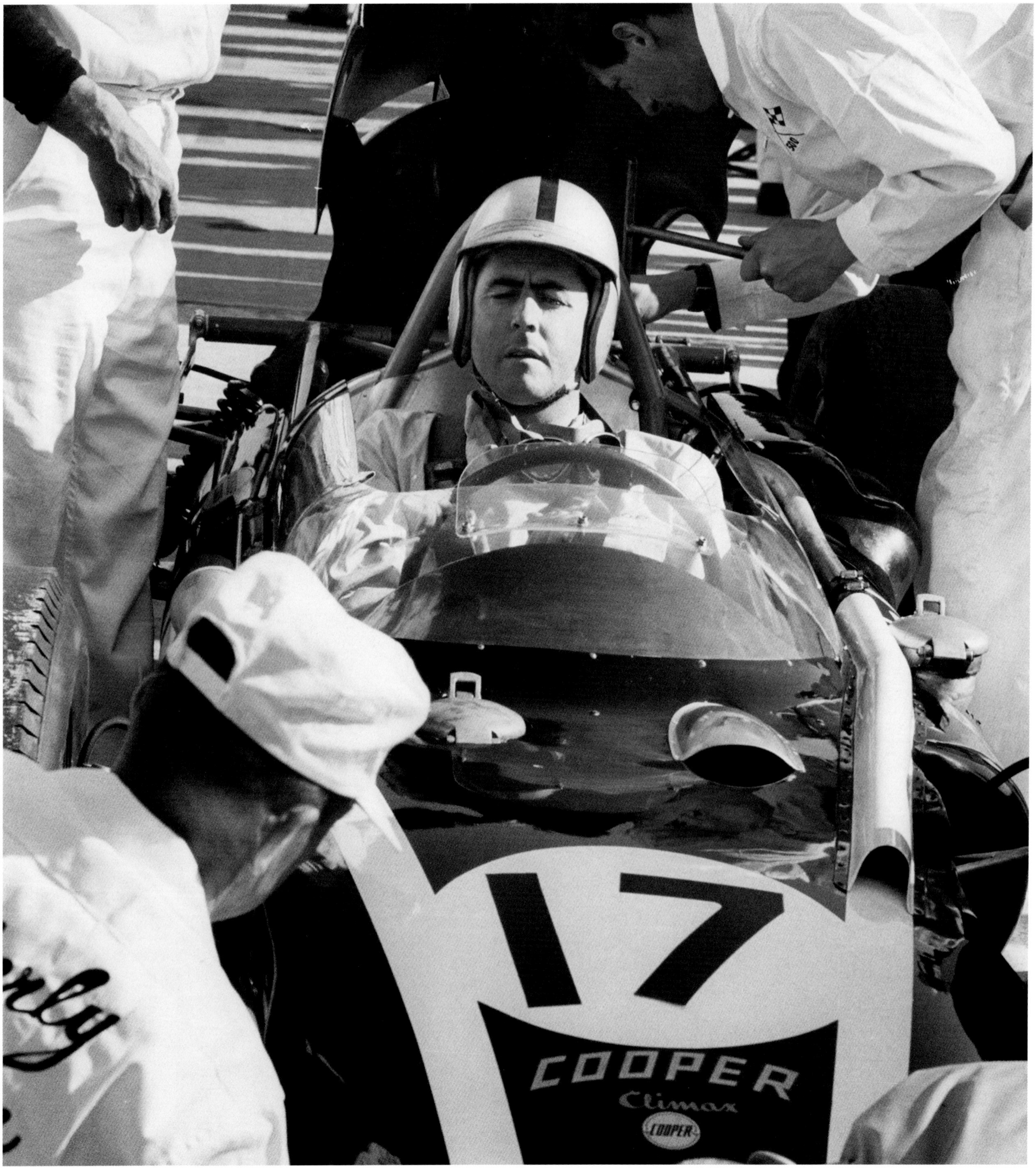
17
COOPER
Climax
COOPER

field would lay down sufficient rubber on the course to enable us to stretch our tyre life to only two. If that had worked out we would have had an enormous advantage.

I felt unusually tense as we prepared to start. The pre-race razzmatazz was extraordinary and the jam-packed 300,000 crowd was something entirely new to me. The pace car led us round for two laps at around 50mph (80km/h), made sure everyone was lined up exactly in our 11 rows, three-abreast. It felt rather odd as the race began to be grumbling round towards the rolling start with my eye-line virtually at hub level to all these great, growling front-engined cars around me. The alcohol fumes coming out of their exhausts smelled like boot polish, snagged in the back of my throat, and made my eyes water. But as speed built up this improved, and then the pace car pulled smartly off to release the field on the starter's green flag, and I found myself running flat-out in America's greatest race.

It quickly adopted a pattern in three groups: the faster boys pulling away out front, a second group behind with me in the middle, and the tail-enders in a third bunch behind us. It was impossible to make up any places for at least 30 laps, because though the Indy cars were going slowly round the corners they were just too quick for me down the straights. I simply could not get by.

Frustrating though this was, I was pretty impressed by the USAC regulars' driving as they diced hub-to-hub at enormous speed. Everyone seemed very courteous indeed. We visitors had heard numerous lurid stories about Indy's dangers, and had seen a lot of spectacular crashes there on film and TV.

But I soon found it was not half as terrifying as I had feared it might have been. In the first 30 laps or so, when the cars were all bunched quite tightly, I never saw a single incident that looked at all dramatic. But after the first pit stop and four or five laps of my second stint, while I was trying to pass a car into the finishing straight, all that suddenly changed.

The engine of the car ahead blew up and sent it spinning down the straight in a cloud of tyre smoke, bouncing from wall to wall and showering broken bits across the track in my path. Luckily, the Cooper braked well, I aimed for a narrowing gap between the spinning car and the outside wall, and just got through. Next time round, to my total amazement, I had to pick my way through the debris from several cars strewn around as five more Indy Roadsters had become involved after the Cooper had nipped through.

Those Indy cars were so committed to a pre-set line, and so unmanouevrable in an emergency, that should anything go wrong ahead of them then the drivers merely became passengers. It really surprised me at the time.

During my opening stint my tyres had worn out four or five laps earlier than anticipated. After my first stop at 42 laps I rejoined, determined to conserve these over-soft Dunlops, eager for only one more stop. This was another mistake, because in the interests of tyre conservation I slowed too much. Although I came in the second time after lap 110, we were not going to manage without a third stop. Had we planned three stops I would have pushed much harder throughout, which should have put us further up the leader board.

But then our pit stops were shockingly slow, mainly because the hub-nut on the offside rear wheel had been damaged in the first stop. The American crewman had put it on cross-threaded and then hit it with his hammer—hard! It jammed in place and then had to be hammered off, and the damaged thread filed true. Thereafter it had to be hammered all the way off and hammered back on again in every wheel-change. This meant 64-second stops, compared with 20–30 seconds for most of our rivals, and at Indy speeds that meant losing considerable distance.

If I'd only run harder from the start, and had three scheduled stops without wasting time, I think we would

OPPOSITE
Time to be serious. Hard work during practice and qualifying on pitlane, Indianapolis Motor Speedway.

BELOW
Time to get a grip. The American pit crew hired by Jim Kimberly for our 1961 assault upon the 500-Miles cost us dear when a rear hub nut was replaced cross-threaded, and then hit hard with a hammer. It was largely because of this, in combination with Dunlop's poor tyre wear, that we could finish no better than ninth.

RIGHT
Blasting past the pit wall at around 170mph (270km/h) in the Kimberly-Cooper wheel-to-wheel with Ebb Rose driving a Porter-Offy. It's notable how we took our regular Formula 1 pit signalling kit with us. There was no "MOSS" competing in the Indy "500"—that's one major race that Golden Boy never attempted. If he'd ever tackled it in a decent car I'm confident he would have stood American motor sport on its ear.

RIGHT
Rapid refuelling in the Indy pits didn't help when that damaged rear hub nut had to be hammered all the way off, and all the way back on again. See my string-backed driving mittens? I always liked to retain proper feel on the steering wheel, and to do so I cut the fingers off regular gloves to make simple mittens, with the normal leather palm protection only. Early on I seldom raced with gloves at all and my hands were hard enough never to blister, but I wore these mittens in racing for the majority of my career, though for sure they're banned today.

have finished sixth or seventh, which would have been really something, but as it was we finished ninth.

But even so, that special Cooper went like a bomb. We never put a spanner on it mechanically throughout the whole 500 miles. All that "Noddy" had to do when I came in for refuelling and wheel changes was to give me a glass of water, fresh goggles, and another stick of chewing gum. The engine was absolutely perfect, running just as well at the end as at the start.

Biggest problem for me was the rubber dust, which made me as black as the ace of spades, and rarely would I be so glad to have a post-race shower. We needed competitive power but most critically there's no substitute for decent tyres, and the makeshift Dunlops might have cost us the race. We should have run standard Indy Firestones, no question, but that was contractually impossible at the time.

Anyway, it really triggered the rear-engined revolution in Indycar design, we picked-up around $9,000 in prize money—on top of a lump sum from Jim Kimberly which financed the car—and it had been a terrific experience. I would return.

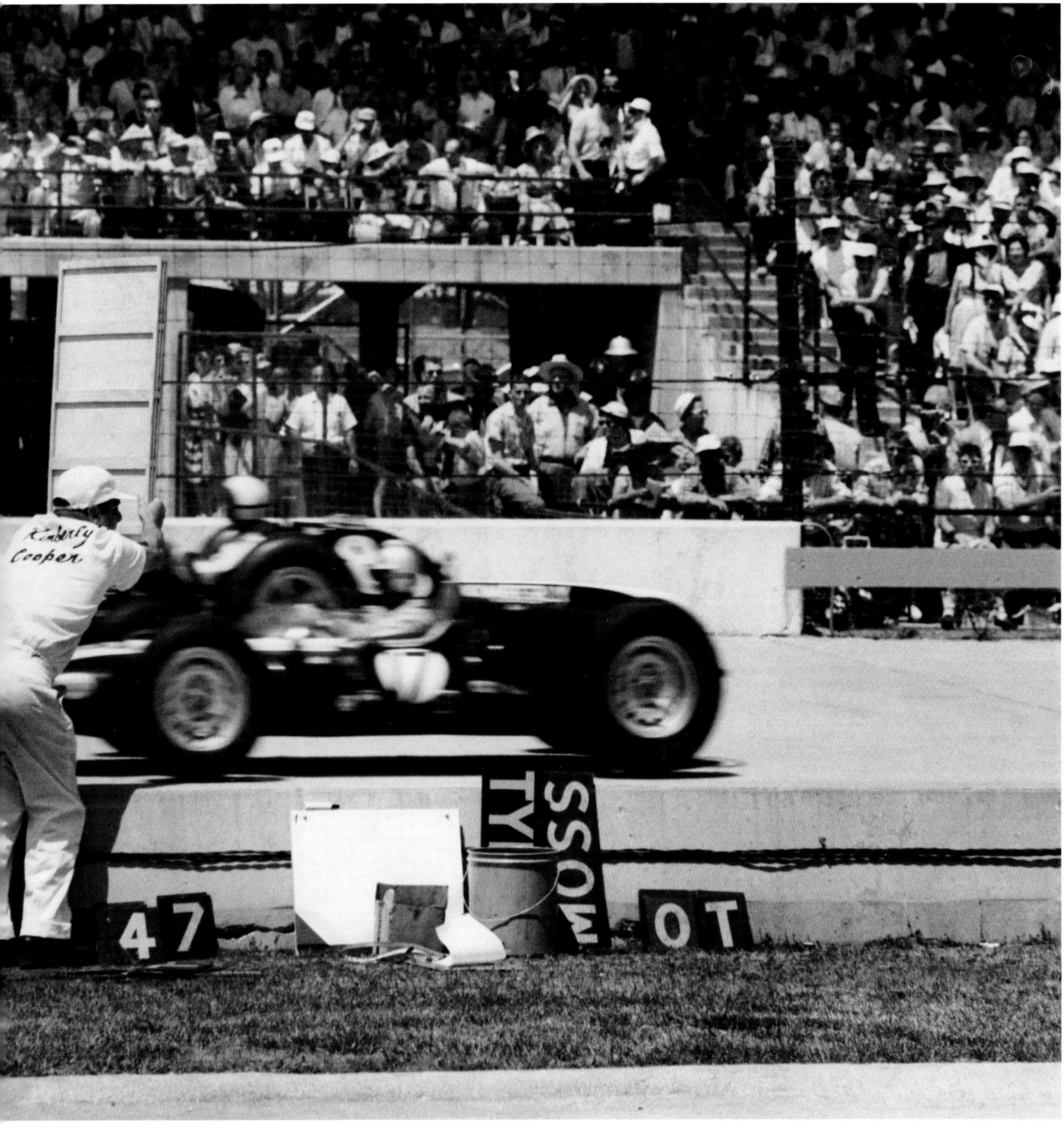
Kimberly
Cooper
47
OT

Motor dealer to the gentry and celebrities—at my Chessington garage business with British movie comic Norman Wisdom and one of our wares—the handsome Sunbeam Alpine.

CHAPTER 9

Cooper On The Cliff

Victims of their own innovation, Cooper's star waned as others forged ahead and thoughts turned to independence

By the start of 1961 I was rapidly coming to the conclusion I should set-up my own racing car company, whose activities would extend to Formula 1. I had been frustrated by the battles to push through the new Lowline Cooper early in 1960 against Charlie Cooper's constant bleats of, "Why change it when we're winnin'", and, "It's going to cost 'ow much?!!!"

In many ways Charlie was a terrific old boy, often gruff on the exterior while as soft as butter on the inside, especially with his animals and his grandchildren. But when it came to staying on the tightrope at the top of Formula 1, he was often an obstacle.

John, in contrast, was a great ally. His enthusiasm was always infectious but he was also a worrier and often inclined to fuss.

Owen Maddock, as Cooper's chief designer, was if anything even more conservative than Charlie. He'd really dig-in his heels to prevent changes. I couldn't believe it when he took up gliding as a hobby. I was pretty sure old Owen would find some situation in which he'd convince himself he was right regardless of what the flight instruments or even any basic sense of self-preservation might be telling him. Sure enough, he had an enormous shunt in a glider, which he fortunately survived, but it sidelined him for quite a while.

Meanwhile, back in Australia, my old associate Ron Tauranac had continued, together with his brother Austin, to develop and build his own Ralt racing specials throughout the 1950s. When I had first met him, Ron was working for Colonial Sugar Refining, and he was later seconded to an outfit named Quality Castings. He had just recently married his wife, Norma, when he began building his latest Ralt in the spare room of their new house. That car worked pretty well. Somebody persuaded him to sell it, and he then used the money to lay down a production line of five similar cars.

When I thought our rear-engined Coopers' handling would be improved by lowering the Climax engine, I had

LEFT
The way forward, we thought, with Bruce McLaren taking over the prototype Coventry Climax V8-engined Formula 1 Cooper on test at Silverstone in July 1961. This eight-cylinder 4-cam engine had been developed for the new 1½-litre Formula 1 which had replaced the old 2½-litre class that season. Now I was poised to give the car and engine its racing debut in the German Grand Prix at Nürburgring.

RIGHT
Rare sighting—the Ron Tauranac smile. This great Australian engineer had been a trusted collaborator and advisor to me ever since the early 1950s. When I brought him over to England in 1960 he was the only man I would have gone into partnership with, building our own racing cars for customer sale…and for me to drive in our MRD "Brabham" works team.

OPPOSITE
I met New Zealander Phil Kerr through his great boyhood pal Bruce McLaren. Phil became manager of my Chessington and later Woking garages, before going off to join Bruce in the embryo McLaren racing team. Here we are in Cooper days in the hillside paddock at Brands Hatch, soon after Phil's arrival in England.

penned-over an *Autocar* magazine drawing of the car's rear end, and mailed it to Ron requesting comments. Ron not only designed a pair of step-down gears and a bell-housing which would do the job for us, but went ahead and had it made in Australia. When I returned there at the end of 1957 I collected the bell-housing, took it back to Britain with me, and Cooper adopted it for use in our 1958 cars. When we were scheming the new Lowline Cooper early in 1960 the first person I contacted was Ron, and again he had a design input into that car's new coil-sprung rear end.

Ron's design and manufacturing capabilities were always central to my growing ideas of independence. As 1959 World Champion, my new garage business in Chessington had got off to a good start and during that winter into 1960, I was able to offer Ron a job in Britain.

He had just laid down his five production Ralts but now he accepted my proposal to come over, initially for six months. Quality Castings kept his Australian job open for him, but in effect he would never return. Betty and I put him up initially, together with Norma and their small daughter Jann who quickly followed, before they rented a flat over a shop in Surbiton. At my Chessington garage we sold Rootes Group and Standard-Triumph cars, and also a *Jack Brabham* tuning kit for the Sunbeam Rapier, I thenn got Ron to convert the latest Triumph Herald saloon to use a single-cam Coventry Climax engine. We uprated its brakes and suspension to match, and the *Jack Brabham* Herald-Climax emerged as a very useable hot-rod, with a 0–60mph (0–97kph) time of around 11 seconds—as good as an Austin-Healey 3000 sports car. In all we would sell around 100 of them.

Ron was absolutely the only bloke I'd have gone into partnership with. He was conscientious to a fault, and peerlessly straight. We were going to build racing cars which Ron would design with a degree of input from me. But I was in a tricky situation, because Cooper's bread and butter was manufacturing production racing cars for customer sale. I was still contracted to them as number one works driver for 1960–61. I could not be seen to be setting up in competition. But John and I were very close, and I talked it through with him, and he not only understood what I intended to do, but appreciated why. He was sad about it, but sympathetic. We were still enjoying tremendous success together and I think he was prepared to enjoy it while it lasted. With my engineering and manufacturing experience John must have known I would either eventually want a share in the Cooper Car Co., or begin doing my own thing. We agreed to keep this to ourselves, and definitely not tell Charlie—who wouldn't have been so accommodating. What's more, it was important that Ron should maintain a low profile, particularly when seeking parts from suppliers we shared with Cooper. Gossip about any orders he might place which could be construed as being parts for a new production racing car could have lit a fuse.

Looking forward to 1961, we decided to build a design prototype single-seater racing car for the contemporary schoolroom-class of Formula Junior. Engines in that class had to be production based, with no more than four cylinders and no overhead camshafts. By 1960 the British racing car industry was taking a stranglehold on the world market. Formula Junior that year was bitterly hard fought, essentially between Cooper and Lotus. Now Ron was drawing a car to present serious competition to them both. It was his first water-cooled racing car design and his first with the kind of modern lay-down seating position we'd used in the *Lowline* Cooper and which Colin Chapman would take to extremes in his Lotuses. Ron had very advanced ideas on suspension geometry to get the best from available tyres. Now he would introduce the first fully-adjustable anti-roll bar suspension on a production racing car, enabling its handling to be optimised on any circuit.

To build the car, we moved into a room at the back of a garage on the Esher bypass, much closer to home for us both. Ron tried to teach himself to weld the prototype chassis before we gave the job to a specialist kit manufacturer, Derek Buckler, and swore him to secrecy.

Our new car grew slowly while I continued my Cooper career and Phil Kerr ran Chessington for me. It was mid-summer 1961 before the car was ready, and Ron sold it to a visiting Australian racer from Tasmania, named Gavin Youl. We called it the *MRD* after the initials of our new company, which we'd entitled Motor Racing Developments Ltd. Gavin kicked off with a couple of respectable second places in a club meeting at the little Mallory Park circuit, before running our new car in Goodwood's big Tourist Trophy meeting in August. So far nobody had publicly connected his new Formula Junior car with me.

He was running it for the first time with the latest 1,100cc Ford engine developed by John Reid's Holbay company, and he ended Saturday practice on pole position! Then the car caught fire—Ron rushed it back to Surbiton, rebuilt it, and then whisked it back to Goodwood for the race.

The car wasn't quite right but Gavin still finished fourth in his Heat and then second in the Final, beaten only by well-regarded Lotus driver Alan Rees. Gavin was considered a novice in comparison—so our new MRD car took the credit.

Some people were beginning to make the connections, and in the monthly column which Alan Brinton ghosted for me at the time in *Motor Racing* magazine I explained:

"The *MRD* is a little project on which Ron Tauranac, an old friend of mine from Australia, has been working. Ron and I have enjoyed playing motor cars for several years and I felt that his talent was being wasted in Australia. So I was delighted when he decided to come to Britain to work for us. His particular flair is in the suspension department. The *MRD* is pretty

ABOVE
Gavin Youl in our prototype MRD FJ car leaving the Goodwood chicane during the FJ race supporting the 1961 RAC Tourist Trophy.

BELOW
A programme from the 1961 French Grand Prix.

conventional by today's standards, but I think that some of the detail work is not too bad. We will be making a few models in kit form for a firm in Australia, and I suppose that if there is a demand we might consider making some for the British market at a later stage. Anyway, the car has had an encouraging start, and I must say that it is very pleasant to have toys of your own to play with."

John and I had already broken the news to Charlie Cooper that I would be leaving at the end of that season. Predictably the old boy was very upset, regarding my decision as a betrayal. Forewarned, John wished me well, but perhaps not too well because in motor racing only successful cars attract customers, and he was naturally worried that in future years MRD might take a share of Cooper's already diminishing market. He was having enough trouble fending off such rival marques as Lotus and Lola... and he was right to be worried.

Meanwhile, the 1961 season was pretty much a disaster for us. F1 had been diminished from 2½-litre rules to just 1½-litre, and a new minimum weight regulation made these less powerful cars heavier than their predecessors. They were far less challenging to drive.

The British teams had all protested about these rule changes, and there had been a move to perpetuate the old cars in the new InterContinental Formula which led a very brief life that summer of '61—only in Britain—although its maximum 3-litre engine limit was also adopted in New Zealand and Australia, where it would survive into '63.

While our British teams had been fussing, Ferrari and Porsche had just got on with developing powerful new engines and rear-engined cars through 1½-litre Formula 2's final season, in 1960. We had done pretty well against them there with our 1½-litre 4-cylinder Climax engines, but it was plain that these were at the end of their development—while Porsche and especially Ferrari (with their V6-cylinder design) still had untapped potential.

The development of suitable British multi-cylinder (actually V8) Formula 1 engines began late, and so we entered into the 1961 World Championship season knowing full-well we would be handicapped and that the promised new V8s from Climax and BRM would not emerge for months.

The only way to compensate for lack of horsepower was to build a new Cooper which was even lower and also slimmer than the Championship-winning *Lowline*. We used a new 6-speed gearbox to make better use of the small Climax engine's rev range, but we had at best 151-horsepower against probably 180 for Porsche's air-cooled flat-4 and 185 for the latest wide-angle Ferrari V6.

We raced these new 1½-litre cars for the first time in the non-Championship Aintree "200" at Liverpool. It rained, Dunlop's new D12-compound wet-weather tyres worked well, and I led Bruce home in a Cooper 1-2—a terrific start, in the absence of both Porsche and Ferrari.

From Aintree we flew straight out to Syracuse, Sicily, where three days later Porsche and especially Ferrari brought us crashing down to earth. An unknown Formula Junior novice named Giancarlo Baghetti appeared there in the prototype new V6 Ferrari. He was making his Formula 1 debut, and just blew us all away! I'd sent my own private *Lowline* out there and I was first "Brit" home, fourth behind Baghetti and the two works Porsches driven by Dan Gurney and Jo Bonnier. Roy finished fifth in a Yeoman Credit team Cooper, and we'd both been lapped. Our worst fears were being realised.

The rest of my Formula 1 season wasn't memorable; ignition trouble at Monaco, outclassed sixth at Zandvoort, fourth in a minor race at Brands Hatch, engine blow-up in Belgium where "the Sharknose" V6 Ferraris finished 1-2-3-4, while in the French race at Reims I retired to save the engine when my oil pressure zeroed—only to discover it was the gauge which had broken.

It then rained for the British Grand Prix back at Aintree—we used the D12 wet tyres again—and I finished fourth, behind a 1-2-3 Ferrari parade. With the Climax 4-cylinder engine we just could not compete. But by that time Wally Hassan's prototype Climax V8 was ready for testing. We ran it at Silverstone in the back of a specially adapted chassis, then took it to the Nürburgring for the German Grand Prix.

We had various teething troubles, but the new V8 gave us another 8mph (19kph) down the long straight. Then Vic Barlow of Dunlop broke the bad news. At practice wear rates our rear tyres would not last race distance. Weather next day was forecast as "changeable"—rain was expected. Dunlop had D12 wet-weather tyres available, but only six of them—not even two full car sets! I couldn't believe it.

They gave one full set straight to Stirling, so I went to the startline with the other two grippy wet-weather tyres on the front of my V8 Cooper and standard tyres on the rear. The track was dry when we started and it was a wonderful feeling as I let the clutch in and the Cooper shot away like a shell. I led round the first 180-degree right-hander, then around the left-hander behind the pits,

ABOVE

Apart from running too hot and threatening continually to boil, the brand-new Cooper-Climax V8 seemed pretty promising during sunny practice at the Nürburgring. Here I'm aiming it into the concrete banked *Karussel*, you had to ensure you kept your car tucked in on the tight line, if you popped a right-side wheel over the lip of the banking you'd spin away your chances in an instant, straight through the outside hedge.

ABOVE
A programme from the 1961 German Grand Prix at Nürburing.

RIGHT
Non-Championship Formula 1 racing didn't involve any World title points, but offered a pretty good start and prize money, and often some darned good sport. Here in the Austrian Grand Prix on the NATO aerodrome at Zeltweg I'm running third in my own *Lowline* Cooper behind young Jim Clark's leading works Lotus 21 and John Surtees's Bowmaker-Yeoman team Cooper—with Innes Ireland right up my car's exhaust in the second works Lotus.

over the little bridge and then downhill through the swerves into the forest. It was there, just as I was turning into a left-hander, that I hit a wet patch under the trees. The front end's D12 tyres bit and turned, but the rear end didn't and in correcting the slide I ran wide and crashed straight through the hedge running along the side of the track.

I popped out the other side still travelling very fast and found myself straddling a ditch! I was desperate to keep my wheels tracking each side of it, because for sure if one side had dropped down into it the car would have tripped and overturned. But as I was whizzing along like this my left-side wheels were actually in the back of the hedgerow. Roy who was following couldn't stop laughing afterwards because he said when he arrived on the scene he just couldn't figure out what had happened to the hedge—there seemed to be a wave running along it, shaking the foliage so violently! It was in fact me—careering along out of sight on the wrong side of it.

Although damage to our new car wasn't too bad, I just couldn't get it back through the hedge onto the road. So that was the end of my 1961 German GP.

In the Italian race at Monza the V8 engine blew out all its coolant: but I'd led briefly before witnessing the aftermath of the second lap collision between Jim Clark's Lotus and "Taffy" von Trips's "Sharknose" Ferrari in which poor Taffy—a nice guy—was thrown out. He and 14 spectators were killed.

Taffy had been favourite to clinch the World Championship there. His team-mate and only rival for what had been my title was the American Phil Hill—and Phil won the Grand Prix and the Championship, but what should have been his great moment had been marred. Phil is one of the most thoughtful and earnest top drivers I've ever known, and he deserved better—as did Taffy. That was another sad weekend.

For the Oulton Park Gold Cup I ran what had been my works Slimline 4-cylinder car as a private entry and finished second behind Stirling in the four-wheel drive Ferguson, making the most of its remarkable traction on the damp track. We then took the V8 car to Watkins Glen—latest home for the United States Grand Prix—where I was able to qualify on pole by a clear second. I had a real go in the race and pulled out seven seconds over Stirling's Walker Lotus in three laps before the water temperature shot off the dial. John had one of his big panics after I dived into the pits. He yanked off the water filler cap and of course released a fountain of steam and scalding water. I was out of the car and John dropped the cap which clattered down into the cockpit under my seat. I'm afraid I grabbed him by the legs and jammed him up and down in the cockpit on his head bawling, "Cooper! Where's the cap???!!!!" But in fact the water pump spindle had sheared. That was the end of not only my United States GP, but also of my Formula 1 career in Coopers.

One moment of that race stayed with me. When the car first boiled it gushed water onto the back tyres as I was going down into a right-hander. The car slid towards the edge of the track, and continued sliding—until two of the wheels slipped off onto the dirt. Just at that point there was a corrugated metal crash barrier which I just grazed at about 70mph (113kph) before lurching back onto the track. It was so nearly the end of more than just my works Cooper career.

But by this time the little car which was the foundation of our new Brabham marque was already out and racing in Formula Junior. And with Ron Tauranac hard at work, our new independent company, Motor Racing Developments Ltd, was about to find its feet.

COOPER PRIVATEER, 1961

Through the first season of 1½-litre F1 racing I entered my own Cooper in suitable non-Championship F1 races and the short-lived 2½-litre Inter-Continental Formula

When (what had been) the old 1½-litre Formula 2 engine restriction had been broadly adopted as the new Formula 1 for 1961, many of the old European F2 events consequently became non-Championship F1 races. Even there our Coopers began to be upstaged—not only by the V6-engined "Sharknose" Ferraris whenever one appeared, but also by the latest from Lotus. I ran my old *Lowline* Cooper as a personal private entry in non-Championship Formula 1 and maximum-3-litre InterContinental Formula (ICF) races through that year.

Tim Wall prepared the car for me in the back of the Repco company warehouse in Victoria Road, Surbiton. The Australian outfit Repco derived its name from "Replacement Parts Company" which manufactured not only components to fit imported production cars but also some of the world's best balancing equipment, for which they had a considerable market in Britain. I had been on good terms with Repco for years. The plan for that season was to run the Lowline with alternative 1-litre F1 and 2-litre ICF engines installed as appropriate. First I drove Tommy Atkins's pale-green sister car—which Bruce would later take over—with the big engine fitted to win the ICF season-opener at Snetterton, but in my own car the little F1 unit's water pump then failed at Pau in France on Easter Monday. Six days later I won the F1 Brussels GP on the Heysel circuit. The larger engine then went back in for the final British ICF races, in which I notched one final win in the Lowline at Brands Hatch. We returned to non-Championship F1 in June at Brands, without luck, then in August at Karlskoga in Sweden, and Roskilde in Denmark. Gearbox troubles put me out of both events, and then at Modena in Italy I finished fifth after further trouble, while at Zeltweg aerodrome in Austria, Innes Ireland's works Lotus beat me into second place. Pretty much the whole the 1961 season had felt like that—us languishing in second place. I never did think much of finishing second.

Part 3
BRABHAM RACING ORGANISATION

Our first full season of "Brabham" Formula 1 racing came in 1963 with my old prototype Brabham-Climax BT3 from 1962 superseded by lighter, more tidy new BT7 spaceframe-chassised cars which we ran for Dan Gurney and myself under the "Brabham Racing Organisation" banner. Liveried in Australian dark green and gold I like to think we always turned out a well-prepared car, but in general our experience with the Coventry Climax V8 engines was a bitter disappointment. Here I am cornering one of the later team cars at Zandvoort's Tarzan Loop during the 1963 Dutch Grand Prix.

CHAPTER 10
A WINNING PARTNERSHIP

With Ron Tauranac at the helm, Motor Racing Developments Ltd takes off as the "Brabham" marque is born

Testing was the key to all we did with our Motor Racing Developments'—built Brabham cars. Here's Ron (left) and myself with our first prototype F1 Brabham-Climax BT3 during its second test outing, at Brands Hatch in late-July 1963. Harry Spiers of Climax is fiddling with the 1½-litre V8 engine. We're actually running the car from the layby behind a barrier on the outside of the track at the crest of Paddock Hill Bend. It was closer to our transporter and so was much more handy than working from the regular pits.

I remained under contract to the Cooper Car Co. until 31 December 1961, and continued to test the Climax V8-engined car to help sort out some of its teething troubles. I was going to be a Climax V8 customer, so was keen to see it running well.

Meanwhile, Gavin Youl had shipped the prototype MRD Junior car home to Australia, where it was welcomed as the very first Australian racing car ever to have competed in Europe! In March '62 he won the Australian National Formula Junior Championship at Catalina Park, bringing MRD both our first victory, and our first title.

Ron was relieved, but I'd always had confidence in his abilities. Our own new Brabham Formula 1 car project took second place to Ron's developed FJ design for customer sale. We set up production in a small factory we'd taken beside the Wey Navigation canal at New Haw, near Byfleet, in Surrey. Now we adopted "Brabham-Tauranac" or "BT" type numbering for MRD cars. In recognition of Repco's support—and mindful of that French pronunciation of MRD—we marketed our new cars as Repco Brabhams. Gavin Youl's prototype became the Brabham BT1, the 1962 production Juniors became BT2s, and our prototype Formula 1 car would be the BT3.

Initially I planned to buy the best available Formula 1 car for the early-season races. I actually hoped to run a Lotus down-under in January/February, but had to use the old Slimline Cooper instead. I'd ordered a new Lotus 24 with Climax V8 engine but it was delayed so I bought a

BELOW
Before we finished our own F1 car, I drove "off-the-peg" Lotuses in the early part of the '62 season. We started with a 4-cylinder Type 21, then replaced it with another assembled from parts, and took delivery of this Climax V8 spaceframe Type 24. As delivered it was dreadful, but we progressively beefed it up and won the Copenhagen GP. Here in the British GP at Aintree I finished 6th.

RIGHT
Every Formula 1 Lotus I ever tried to drive was incredibly cramped. I was no slim whippet but I was slimline compared with Lotus founder Colin "Chunky" Chapman seen here trying to squeeze himself into his new monocoque-chassised Lotus Type 25. Those riveted sheet-metal pontoons along each side provided his chassis' torsional and beam strength, whereas Ron preferred easily-repairable welded multi-tubular spaceframes for our "Brabham" chassis. I'd have gone monocoque for our Formula 1 cars earlier than we did, but Ron wanted to keep our works cars as close as possible to what we sold to customers, which was fair enough. Colin was obviously a fine engineer, but unfortunately he cut things too close to the bone sometimes, and several Lotus cars broke with tragic consequences. If we'd been able to mix in a barrel the best of Ron Tauranac with the best of Colin Chapman we'd have seen something really formidable!

4-cylinder 1961-model Lotus 21 instead. First test at Goodwood, I found one needed a shoehorn to fit into it—Colin Chapman seemed to build cars for midgets. But its ride was softer than any Cooper, its steering lighter and its handling good.

Only a few days later Tim Wall was fitting the car's battery in the Repco warehouse when his spanner shorted-out against one of the aluminium fuel tanks. Thankfully, the tank was almost full at the time, because if it had only contained vapour it would have exploded. But the short-circuit melted a hole through the aluminium below the level of the petrol inside, which began to spray out—on fire!

We rushed around grabbing extinguishers and had the fire contained but only until each extinguisher ran out, whereupon the spraying fuel repeatedly re-ignited. It was a race to see which would run out first—the leaking fuel or our supply of extinguishers—and we lost. With all extinguishers used it became a furious fire, and the fire brigade arrived too late to prevent it not only destroying my uninsured new car, but also blackening most of Repco's stock. Four days later I was at the season-opening Formula 1 race at Snetterton, waving the starting flag. Jim Clark won handsomely in his works Lotus-Climax 24 V8.

Ron and I had engaged an Aussie to drive our works Brabham Junior—Frank Gardner, technically proficient, very quick, and one of motor racing's born characters. While Ron, myself, Tim Wall, and Roy Billington were all pretty taciturn. Frank could have any audience in hysterics. Although much of his language was completely unprintable I'd defy anyone not to laugh, he could be hilarious.

Colin Chapman loaned me parts to assemble another Lotus 21, which Tim, Roy, and Stan Ellsworth flung together for the following weekend's Pau Grand Prix. My race ended with run bearings after only four laps.

The Aintree "200" was just six days away, and as I flew Tim and the spare engine back home in my Cessna 310

ABOVE
Ready to begin our second series of tests with the prototype Formula 1 Brabham BT3, in the Paddock Hill layby at Brands Hatch—the control tower and pits visible in the background. Just to be different, Ron and I had chosen turquoise-blue and gold for our new car's paint-scheme. Everybody seemed to think it was exceptionally pretty. From this angle that's certainly true. Even the cast-alloy wheels were Ron's design.

ABOVE
Prototype Formula 1 cars and the German Grand Prix at Nürburgring weren't a very enjoyable mix. After poking the prototype Cooper-Climax V8 through the hedgerow in the *Hatzenbach* in 1961, here in our prototype Formula 1 "Brabham" during the wet 1962 race I was fighting a losing battle against massively over-strength throttle return springs. I gave up before I might do the car—or myself—an injury.

twin, Roy transported the car there by road. We had to cobble together an engine, missed Aintree practice that Friday, and Colin Chapman and Jim Clark let me try their Type 24 briefly. Again I found it as tight as a sardine can. Jimmy had said he didn't mind me trying his car as long as I didn't exceed 7,000rpm. I said, "Oh, I didn't know you couldn't use 11,000." He nearly had a fit. Next day, my own 4-cylinder Lotus stripped its gears.

A brighter moment at Aintree was the supporting Formula Junior race, in which Frank Gardner seemed set to win—only to spin off just before the pits. We walked over just as he was retrieving the car, and somebody called, "Give 'im a rocket, Jack!" None was necessary—nobody was more disappointed than Frank. In any case, next day we heard that our first paying customer—Frenchman Jo Schlesser—had scored our maiden European race win, at Montlhéry in France.

The boys then completed our new Lotus 24 V8 just in time for May Silverstone practice, working feverishly in the Lotus factory at Cheshunt. While they snatched sorely-needed sleep I towed it there on a trailer. It had been set-up by guesswork, the rev counter failed, and only experience enabled me to nurse it home sixth. But it was nice to see a chequered flag again.

After the fire we were always playing catch up. We only just got to Zandvoort in time for the Championship-opening Dutch Grand Prix. I qualified on row two but only to be shunted out of the race after just three laps by Ferrari's young Mexican driver, Ricardo Rodriguez. I had realised my Lotus was much faster than his V6 Ferrari through a downhill right-hander. So next time round I pulled out wide to pass and he promptly spun across my path. I had no chance.

Further Ferrari difficulty followed at Monaco. The first corner was the tight 180-degree Gasworks Hairpin, and Willy Mairesse—the Belgian Ferrari works driver—broadsided into the corner like a madman, causing a chain reaction behind him. I had almost stopped, when Richie Ginther's BRM hurtled past with its throttle jammed, clattering into cars left and right. I emerged fourth, but braking into the Station Hairpin here was Mairesse again, spinning his Ferrari in my path. He just blocked me off against the trackside wall. I couldn't move until he moved, but he just sat grimacing at me, and I

LEFT
Ron's new Brabham BT3 design was roomy and extremely comfortable for me. After having been roasted by generations of Cooper and most recently Lotus cars all the pipe runs between engine, radiator and nose-mounted oil tank were isolated from yours truly and open to the cooling airstream. The Climax V8 engine's distinctive high-set twin megaphone exhaust tail-pipes really set off the ensemble from this angle. In this car I would become the first Formula 1 driver ever to score World Championship points in a car bearing his own name (three points for 4th place in the 1962 United States Grand Prix at Watkins Glen). With it slightly modified and repainted dark-green-and-gold for 1963 I would become the first Formula 1 race winner driving "a car of his own"—at Solitude, outside Stuttgart in West Germany.

could only shake my fist back and bawl at him to shift himself.

Eventually, I managed to work my way up to third but I was hindered by another car leaving the pits, which let Phil Hill's Ferrari get by. He was flying, but couldn't quite catch Bruce's latest Cooper V8 and Graham Hill's works BRM V8 ahead of us. Graham should have won but his new engine ran out of oil with the finish almost in sight. Bruce just held off Phil to win, and I was already out—because soon after passing me, Phil had half-spun in the Casino Square, and I'd bent my Lotus's suspension and split its radiator against a kerb avoiding him.

I placed second in the Mallory Park 1,000 Guineas race, behind John Surtees's new Lola-Climax V8, before we returned to Spa for the Belgian Grand Prix. There the Lotus's handling was simply evil—demanding the full road width at 150mph (240km/h)! I came sixth and scraped a solitary Championship point—my first since leaving Cooper. The boys straightened-out the Lotus's bent chassis in time for a non-Championship race at Reims, which became a thoroughly enjoyable dice between myself, Graham Hill's BRM, and Bruce's Monaco-winning Cooper-Climax. Reims was the home of high-speed slipstreaming and we played the game to its limits. We knew each other well and it was terrific fun: wheel-to-wheel, nose-to-tail, absolutely flat-out for long periods. I set off knowing I'd have to switch to reserve fuel on the penultimate lap. But in the heat of battle I forgot! Lying back in the Lotus I couldn't pick out my pit signals on every lap, and after finishing fourth I told the boys next time they should throw a fuel funnel at me.

That year's French Grand Prix was run at Rouen. The road there dived downhill past the pits through a very fast and demanding section. In the race I went hurtling down there with Dan Gurney right behind in his works Porsche, but my Lotus seemed to be bumping badly at the back. I turned into the next right-hander—still travelling very quickly downhill—and nearly lost it in the biggest possible way. Dan shot by, gesticulating wildly, and with the bumping intolerable, I stopped to find a rear damper mount had broken clean off. That year's prime Championship contenders, Graham Hill and Jim Clark, both struck trouble, and Dan survived to score Porsche's maiden (and only) major Grand Prix win.

BELOW

Ron in typical pose, completely absorbed in the task at hand, trial-installing a slave engine in a customer's new Brabham sports-racing car at our factory in New Haw. Many customers bought chassis from us to carry engines of their own choice, and the quickest way to tailor their new frames to suit such engines was to offer one up and see how it fitted. Ron could be a hard taskmaster to our staff but he led by example and the customers generally thought the world of him. So did I.

Back home we put a major effort into completing our own prototype Brabham Formula 1 car. We were hoping to finish it in time for the British Grand Prix, again at Aintree, but I'd had the Lotus delivered there as insurance, and drove it home fifth, with my right foot blistered on a hot pipe. My driving shoe was so charred I binned it.

Our new BT3 was completed the following Wednesday, and we ran it briefly at Goodwood before engine trouble. The Lotus's V8 engine was fitted and further testing at Brands Hatch confirmed that here at last was a modern Formula 1 car into which I actually fitted. Its cockpit wasn't too hot and most critically it handled beautifully. Ron really knew his stuff.

We took it straight to the Nürburgring for the German Grand Prix, but the V8's bearings ran on my first full lap, and my spare engine was still unwell in Coventry. Wally Hassan, Peter Windsor-Smith, and Eric Burton of Climax built-up a hybrid engine from the top end of mine, and the undamaged bottom-end of a Team Lotus engine, which had dropped a valve earlier. It ran as rough as old boots, but enabled me to qualify, and my own spare engine was flown into Cologne that night. After another all-night session fitting it, I started from the back of the grid, and found I could run with anybody—and especially enjoyed passing a couple of Ferraris, my favourite target!

But our assorted dramas had left me with a lashed-up throttle linkage, with extra springs to ensure it would close safely. In fact it demanded so much pressure to hold it open I thought my right foot would drop off. Throttle-balance in corners was a real challenge. I couldn't continue with the throttle so stiff, and retired.

A non-Championship race followed at Roskilde, in Denmark, where I used the Lotus 24 in a real old carve-up with Masten Gregory in a similar UDT-Laystall entry. The Lotus handled perfectly and I won both Heats and the Final, scoring my first Formula 1 victory as an independent. For me this was a breakthrough because some people were beginning to think that since leaving Cooper's I'd achieved next to nothing. Was I a busted flush? I didn't think so.

Back home, we put the Roskilde-winning V8 in the new BT3 for the Oulton Park Gold Cup. I qualified on row two, only to find that the brake pads had worn out after 40 laps and race distance was 73! We couldn't do a thing about it because the 9-inch (23cm) diameter disc brakes we'd chosen—with our small 13-inch (33cm) front wheels instead of the more conventional 15-inch (38cm) size, were simply too small. I nursed it through the race and was fortunate to inherit third place.

We then fitted 10½-inch (27cm) front discs to the BT3 and altered the spring rates to stiffen it up; it had been a little too softly-suspended. We tidied-up the body and these changes all seemed beneficial.

Meanwhile, I had bought a sports-racing Lotus 23 for the lucrative North American "Fall" races. It was a tiny little thing, powered by a 1½-litre Holbay-Ford 4-cylinder engine, and for its debut I made my first trip to Canada, to the Canadian GP, at Mosport Park. The '23 was great fun to drive, and on a wet track I was able to battle with the big Lotus 19s and Cooper Monacos for second place. When the track dried power told, and I finished fourth and won my class which paid for the trip.

The United States Grand Prix at Watkins Glen then provided another landmark. Our BT3 went really well for the first time, I shared fourth-fastest practice time with Dan Gurney's Porsche and we had a real ding-dong throughout with Bruce in the Cooper. Right from the start I found myself occasionally hurtling into corners in neutral. The gearchange rod was rubbing against one of the fuel tanks and selectors turned out to be loose on the selector rod, inside the Colotti gearbox. But I'd finished fourth, so our new marque had scored its first Formula 1 Constructors' Championship points.

I ran the Lotus 23 sports at Riverside, without much luck. Dan Gurney went like the wind there in a Lotus 19, and we discussed his joining my team for 1963 Formula 1. He was absolutely one of the world's top drivers. Porsche had told him they were pulling out of Formula 1. He was a free agent, a good bloke, and considering his burgeoning talent, he wasn't expensive. He said he'd think about it, and come back to me.

At Laguna Seca I had a super dice with the American Porsche driver Bob Holbert who beat me in our Heat, but in the Final another good scrap between us ended when my engine sprang an oil leak. I sold the Lotus 23 there to Gordon Richardson.

A new non-Championship Mexican Grand Prix was introduced that year. Local hero Ricardo Rodriguez—only 20 years old—was the crowd's favourite, driving a Rob Walker-entered Lotus 24. Tragically, he seemed over-excited, and during practice he crashed and was killed.

I qualified on row three but the start was crazy. The 1-minute board was showing when Jim Clark began signaling frantically because his engine wouldn't start. The officials let his mechanics struggle to restart him

ABOVE
At his best, Dan Gurney was one of the world's most formidable racing drivers. He could be unbelievably quick, and we were genuinely thrilled when he agreed to join us for F1 1963–1965. When his mind was focused on driving he was capable of shattering performance. But perhaps too often his mind would be distracted by some perceived technical shortcoming or problem, he'd lose his focus and his real class would not shine through.

BELOW
Testing, testing, always testing….Here's a typical scene at a deserted midweek Goodwood in 1963. This is our first prototype Brabham sports car, the BT5 ordered by private team patron Ian Walker for his Aussie drivers: Paul Hawkins (left) and Frank Gardner (arms folded talking to me, with my crash helmet and goggles). On the right is the quiet, thoughtful, rugged figure of our works Formula Junior driver, the Kiwi, Denny Hulme.

while our engines continued running and getting hotter and hotter. The Lotus lads finally had to push-start Jimmy's car, with everybody else's engines boiling furiously, and fists waving. Old Reg Parnell, running John Surtees's Lolas had been furiously urging the starter to drop his flag, when three cars—including John's—burst into flames! Reg instantly began trying to stop the starter from dropping his flag. He did so regardless, and we staggered off the grid in mixed clouds of tyre smoke and steam. I led briefly, before engine temperature soared, so I eased back to finish second.

Back at Byfleet, Ron and the boys were completing our first "Tasman" car which I would run in the winter races down under, commencing with that year's Australian Grand Prix on November 19. This new BT4 car was very similar to the BT3, but with smaller fuel tanks, 15-inch (38cm) wheels all round and a big 2.7-litre 4-cylinder Climax engine driving via a Colotti gearbox. We shipped it out on the *Canberra* and I would fly out for the race before the concluding Grand Prix of the Championship year, in South Africa.

The titles would be decided there at East London between Jimmy Clark and Graham Hill. My BT3 handled well enough to compensate for the gearbox jumping out of third and fifth, and I finished fourth—to add more points for "Brabham-Climax". Jimmy's Lotus broke, enabling Graham Hill and BRM to take the World titles. Judging the season overall they deserved it.

I'd just checked into our East London hotel when I got a cable from Ron, telling me that our new Kiwi driver, Denny Hulme, had won at the Boxing Day Brands Hatch race meeting in our 1963 prototype Formula Junior car. We couldn't have wished for a better sales boost, and for Formula 1 through 1963–65, Dan Gurney had also agreed terms with us just before I left for South Africa.

Ron's new 1963 Formula 1 car was a development of our prototype BT3, which I kept as team spare. The new BT7 was to be lighter, and would use the latest Climax V8

engine with Lucas fuel-injection in place of the old Weber carburettors. Dan was exceptionally tall, which meant his car had to be 2-inches (5cm) longer. My BT3 was lowered and lightened. We trimmed about 55lb (25kg) off it, and first time out in this format at Easter Monday Goodwood—fitted with a short-stroke Climax engine on Weber carburettors—it felt terrific. However, an ignition wire came adrift, and I finished sixth. The Formula Junior result there cheered us up—Frank Gardner first in his Ian Walker-entered Brabham, from Denny Hulme, second in our works car.

I missed the Aintree "200" after qualifying on the front row because a Climax V8 piston shattered, and we ran out of time to repair it. I had been eager to give Dan his Brabham debut in his new car at May Silverstone, but now we only had one engine and he was too big to drive my car. I wrote at the time in my *Motor Racing* magazine column about his "big frame and farmer's feet". They were huge!

So I ran alone at Silverstone where practice, unfortunately, provided a pointer to what lay ahead. My rebuilt Climax engine broke a cam follower. I rushed up to Coventry where the second engine had been hurried through. The boys fitted it overnight, but it had been so hastily flung together it was down on power. In the race I was just thinking fifth place was acceptable, when the engine began cutting out due to a fuel surge as the level in the tanks dropped. So I spluttered home seventh, completely unimpressed.

We were desperate for an engine to complete Dan's car in time for Monaco, but it didn't arrive until the preceding Sunday. Thursday practice at Monaco then began badly. We had tremendous trouble merely starting my engine in our garage, and as I drove it down to the pits it would barely run on all eight cylinders. We wasted time checking the ignition when in fact the head had dropped off an exhaust valve and had been blown clean out of the exhaust!

We only had the two engines so I told Wally Hassan there what had happened, we whipped out my damaged unit and loaded it into the Cessna which I flew direct to Coventry where Climax had been warned to stand by. They pinched a cylinder head from our third engine which was then being reassembled. I flew the rebuilt V8 back to Nice that Saturday, but the moment I landed I was told that Dan's engine had just broken a valve-spring, dropped a valve, and blown up in a big way! I seldom swear. At that moment it seemed the only thing to do.

There we were, Monaco GP next day—two cars, and only one fit engine. Dan had qualified well, he deserved the engine, so it was fitted into his car that night. Next morning Colin Chapman heard of our predicament and

ABOVE
Shakedown laps—one of the many thousand I drove at Goodwood through my frontline career, in this case trying the new Brabham BT5 sports car before delivery to the Ian Walker Racing team. We prided ourselves on being able to sort out spring and damper rates, anti-roll bars and braking ratios, etc to a decently raceworthy point, from which customers could then carry on with their own development to suit their own preferences. Up until 1970 I did the basic testing—to arrive at an acceptable factory specification—on every Brabham customer model that Ron ever designed and MRD ever built.

offered me his spare Lotus 25—the latest monocoque-chassised car with which Jimmy Clark was already on the crest of a wave, winning almost everywhere.

That was a great gesture by Colin and I was delighted not to miss the race, but I can't say I liked his car. If I thought my tube-chassised Lotus 24 had been cramped, this Lotus '25 simply redefined the term. Its German ZF gearbox had a weird "upside-down" change pattern, and while I thought Dan's feet were big, Jimmy's must have been microscopic! The 25 seemed to have terrific traction, and it cornered well, but the gearbox got stuck twice in fifth and I had to stop to have it fixed, and finished way back.

We were pioneering the use of a new five-speed gearbox—based on a Volkswagen casing with gears and internals made by Mike Hewland's specialist company. It had performed well on my car at Silverstone but Monaco is exceptionally punishing on transmissions and Dan's stripped three teeth off its crownwheel. He was very encouraging, however, and was confident he'd had pace in hand.

In the Belgian race at Spa my run ended with fuel starvation, but Dan, meanwhile, ran comfortably second behind Jim Clark for many laps only to be caught and passed in torrential rain just before the end by Bruce McLaren's latest Cooper. Dan was driving virtually blind. He couldn't see a thing and frankly I was delighted to see him survive in one piece rather than go off the road trying to defend second place.

During the Dutch Grand Prix practice at Zandvoort he suffered yet another Climax engine failure, while I was running-in my brand-new sister car—our second works

RIGHT
Denny Hulme at speed in our works-entered Brabham Formula Junior car had a very successful 1963 season. At Easter Monday Goodwood he was narrowly beaten—by 0.8 of a second—by our previous year's works driver Frank Gardner driving Ian Walker's customer Brabham. At the Aintree "200" meeting he turned the tables and beat Frank by nearly 19 seconds, and here at May Silverstone he beat David Hobbs' Lola by 0.8 of a second. Formula Junior racing was close, hard, and hectic, and Denny won six times while Brabham customer cars driven by Frank, his Ian Walker team-mate Paul Hawkins, and Frenchman Jo Schlesser, won nine more major European races between them.

team BT7. But our expected spare engine hadn't arrived from Coventry Climax and I telephoned Phil Kerr at Chessington to collect it early on the Saturday. He raced up there, put the rebuilt engine in the boot of his Ford Zodiac, and delivered it to us in Zandvoort that evening. The moment we looked at it closely our faces fell. This was our first new Climax V8 with flat-plane crankshaft, which demanded a different exhaust system, and different oil inlet pipe—no way would it fit into Dan's chassis. Tim, Roy, and Noddy managed to strong-arm it all into place by race morning. I held a strong second behind Jimmy's Lotus 25 before a throttle spring broke, so I had to slow which let Graham Hill pass and get away in second place. I was then ripping past the pits at over 150mph (241km/h) into the 180-degree Tarzan Loop when the other throttle spring snapped. Fortunately I'd had the forethought, after the first failure, to double-check the ignition switch, and I'd already made a couple of practice grabs for it, just in case.

Now, as I hit the brake pedal the throttle remained wide open with the engine screaming flat-out, and I found myself hard on the brakes with my front wheels locked solid, pluming smoke, and the car hardly slowing at all. I dabbed the throttle hoping it would return. It did not, so I knocked the ignition off, and just barely managed to stay on the road before heading back to the pits on the ignition switch. Every time I flicked it on the engine screamed instantly at full throttle, so my progress back to the pits involved a serious of maniacal lunges, then silence with me hard on the brakes, then another deafening lunge! During all these antics I'd twice dropped off the edge of the track, which had cracked the chassis frame. In fact it was sitting too low. After that race we jacked-up the ride height a little.

Dan, meanwhile, had been charging round until the boys noticed a fuel line sagging dangerously low beneath his car. Afraid it might chafe through they signalled him in. The sagging pipe was quickly taped up, but the stop dropped him from fourth to eighth, but he tigered back to finish second! At last his true talent had found some Brabham reward.

The French Grand Prix at Reims the following weekend left just two days for repair and preparation before we set off and arrived late. Dan managed barely 20 minutes practice, and myself only 14, but he qualified on the front row with me on row two. In the race another ignition lead vibrated off my car, while Dan actually yanked the gear-lever out of his, yet still finished fifth.

We were beginning to show consistent qualifying pace, and both got on to the front row for the British Grand Prix at Silverstone. As icing on the cake Denny Hulme qualified our Junior on pole for his race there, and on that Saturday morning I arrived just in time to see Denny destroy the Junior. I then led the Grand Prix for the opening three laps before Jimmy blasted past on Hangar Straight. It was plain that Team Lotus's Climax engines had an edge. Secondly, his Lotus 25 was an exceptionally slim pencil, punching a smaller hole in the air than

ABOVE
A programme from the 1963 Dutch Grand Prix, held at Zandvoort.

ABOVE
Sleek 1963 Brabham-Climax BT7—Dan's car in the pits at Monaco, an early disappointment in what proved to be a very disappointing debut season for us as a two-car Formula 1 works team. Ron was one of the first designers at that period to test his Formula 1 car full-size in a serious wind-tunnel—the Motor Industry Research Association facility at Lindley in the English Midlands. The original BT3's nose line had generated too much aerodynamic lift. As revised for 1963, our cars were pretty good in this respect, and efficient and slippery in a straight line.

our Brabhams. And thirdly, Jim Clark was driving the car, and he was quick.

We settled down, with Jim drawing away in the lead and myself and Dan running confidently second and third. Everything seemed fine until just after Copse Corner when my engine fluffed onto seven cylinders. I had never worn earplugs when racing. I always had an ear for my engines (which ended up literally deafening me) and now I was able to switch off in time to save this one further piece of costly damage. A cam follower had seized and was holding a valve open. Just as I was walking in, thinking that at least Dan's second place seemed secure, his flat-plane crank Climax V8 exploded. That engine had propelled him to second in Holland and fifth in France, but now it was history—destroyed in the most costly blow-up I'd ever known.

Having once been Climax's favoured customer, it was galling now to realise how much we were receiving second best. Where the 4-cylinder Climax FPF engines had been virtually unbreakable, the Climax V8 was, in my experience, never much good. It was rough-running,

never really nice to drive, and worse, its reliability, in our cars at least, was often abysmal. They were meant to be safe to over 10,000rpm. At that Silverstone race my rev-counter telltale was left at 9,800rpm and Dan's at only 9,700—yet both engines had broken.

Because of these failures our two-car entry for the non-Championship Solitude Grand Prix in Germany the following Sunday was cut to just the old BT3, for me. I used my Reims engine, and in practice qualified second to Jimmy's inevitable Lotus, which then did us all a favour by breaking a drive-shaft at flagfall.

I then had a terrific battle with Trev Taylor in the second Lotus, before it also failed, which left me in a comfortable lead, despite the circuit becoming incredibly oily. For once both my car and the Climax V8 held together, and you can imagine how it felt when I passed the chequered flag at last, and "Brabham-Climax" had scored our first Formula 1 race win. It wasn't a World Championship round, it wasn't a full-blown Grand Prix, but it proved we had a car capable of winning. That was a great moment, and I relished it.

After a week in the baths at Baden Baden I was a few pounds lighter for the following German Grand Prix. My Solitude-winning engine had gone into Dan's car, while I would use my repaired Silverstone unit. Both of them popped and banged in practice but we thought we'd cured the problems as we went to the starting grid on raceday. My engine then refused to fire and I lost a lap while we changed the Lucas OPUS electronic ignition transistor box. We came to detest that system, which was commonly lampooned as Lucas "'Opeless" ignition, but at the time it was the only game in town.

Later in the race everything ran well, but the lost lap was never recoverable. Meanwhile, poor Dan had a miserable time, his engine spluttering after the opening half-lap and despite a string of stops exploring both ignition and injection nothing could be found, and he finally gave it up.

A Championship calendar gap followed before the Italian Grand Prix, but there was to be no rest for me, I filled in with a hectic schedule of "earning opportunities" on successive weekends. While the mechanics transported the cars around by road, I commuted in my Cessna 310 and between us we managed to rack up a really enormous mileage.

At Karlskoga, Sweden, in pouring rain, I drove Dan's BT7 to lead the works Lotuses into the penultimate lap of Heat One. Then the engine cut dead—low on fuel. Jimmy's and Trevor's Lotus 25s swept by, and I managed to salvage third place. They only had to follow me in Heat Two to ensure themselves victory on aggregate time. I won Heat Two but was officially placed third for the combined race overall.

Dan was back in the States, so I gave Denny Hulme a Formula 1 outing in my old BT3 at Karlskoga, and, typically competent, he brought it home fourth. My own BT7, meanwhile, had been trailered straight from the Nürburgring to Sicily for the Mediterranean Grand Prix at Enna. That circuit was fantastically fast, 3 miles (4.8 kilometres) to the lap and shaped like an egg encircling Lake Pergusa. It was virtually flat out all the way. Horsepower was critical, and when my engine went woolly I faded back through the field, made a fruitless pit stop, and finished last. The filter in the fuel-injection system's high-pressure pump, known as the Lucas "bomb", had become blocked. Lucas advised its customers not to change these filters until fuel flow became plainly compromised because the pumps were usually less reliable once dismantled and reassembled.

BELOW

Good friends together—even after I'd left Cooper I remained on extremely good terms with the team, and particularly with my former protégé and teammate Bruce McLaren. Here at Zandvoort I'm holding the inside line with Bruce outside me in his latest 1963-spec works Cooper. Both cars use multi-tubular spaceframe chassis, and both are powered by Coventry Climax V8 engines. As both Bruce and I would discover, Climax engines supplied to Team Lotus for Jim Clark's use were rather more Climactic than ours! Where I had been the favoured driver with Cooper from 1959-61, the wheel had moved on. We just had to try harder. By the end of this 1963 season Bruce would be following my lead into founding his own team and building his own cars.

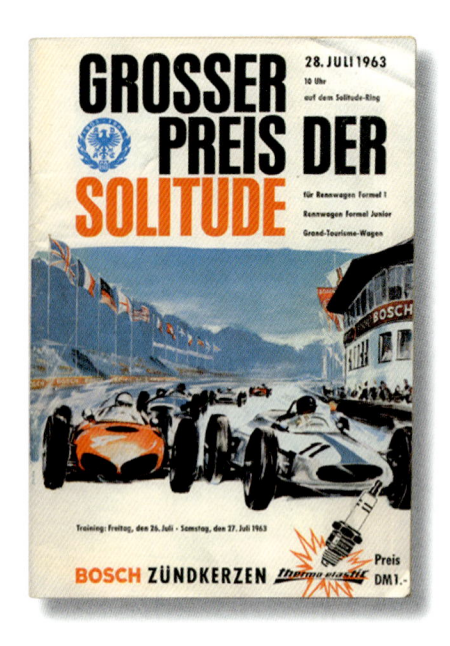

ABOVE
A programme for the non-Championship Solitude Grand Prix in 1963.

This had plainly been our problem at the Nürburgring, and if we'd only realised we would have got Lucas to change the filters and perhaps have had more luck at Enna. It was all part of a painful learning curve.

During that race Trev Taylor had led Team Lotus with their Formula Junior star Peter Arundell driving the other car in Jim Clark's place. Pete had gone very well, while Trevor had survived a fantastic shunt when he'd been stunned by a stone thrown up by Bandini's BRM. He'd been hit while exiting the curve before the pits, and his car shot up a bank at about 140mph (225km/h), before flying back across the track inverted with him falling out before it crashed down and then somersaulted, rolled, and cartwheeled the length of the pits. It ended up shattered and burning while Trev had tumbled along the track to end up in a sitting position—head lolling, and briefly unconscious—by the finish line. Incredibly, he didn't break a single bone and next day I flew him and Peter back to Britain in the Cessna. We were all glad to leave Sicily for other reasons: each of us suffering from tummy bugs. That gipsy existence was not all roses.

Back at Byfleet, Ron was putting the finishing touches to two new sports cars—the Brabham BT8s—which would use the 2.7-litre Climax FPF 4-cylinder engine for the big-money American "Fall series" races. After a couple of days home I took Betty, Geoffrey, Phil Kerr, and his wife Valerie with me to Ollon-Villars for the five-mile against-the-clock "Swiss Mountain Grand Prix". I used my Enna car with a new Lucas "bomb" installed, and won my class there. We then swopped the BT7 for my old BT3 brought out to us at Ollon and moved on to Zeltweg aerodrome for the non-Championship Austrian Grand Prix. That race was run in an oven. Jim Clark charged past me only to go out with a broken oil pipe. I then had quite a battle with Innes Ireland's private Lotus 24 until it faltered and I was left to score our second win, by five clear laps.

I'd originally intended to enter just one car at Monza, for Dan but the organisers then offered more realistic starting money so we sent two. They insisted on using their full Autodrome circuit, including the banked high-speed track. We all knew what punishment that could inflict on modern cars and protested bitterly, but because of that I took the more heavily-built BT3 for myself, and we raised the spring-rates and fitted more robust bump-stops on Dan's regular BT7 which we also fitted with an additional fuel tank beneath his knees so he could complete the long race non-stop.

Thankfully, after several cars had broken in first practice, the banked track was closed and the race run instead on the level Monza road course. Dan then starred in a fabulous flat-out battle for the race lead with Jim Clark and Graham Hill, and after Graham's BRM dropped back Dan had a real go at the Lotus only for his engine to cut—blocked fuel filter trouble yet again, but it was a different filter this time! I suffered similarly just when I seemed set for a third place finish, and I finally had to settle for fifth.

We only identified this problem after our return from Italy at the Oulton Park Gold Cup. After practice there we were allowed to run a private test on the back straight. The Lucas boffins isolated a pressure drop between the inlet and output ends of the fuel metering unit. The filter inside it had not been routinely changed because they had assumed there was no chance of any muck getting through from the main filter—wrong! This piffling problem in a part costing pennies had wrecked too many races for us, but that's motor racing.

Dan's transistor ignition failed on the Oulton Park startline, costing him a lap, and he then spotted oil spraying onto the exhaust pipes. We found a cracked cylinder head had let water into the sump, pressurising the lubrication system. I ran a flat-crank Climax engine for the first time in a home race, but it had been assembled with a new set of camshafts, one lobe on which had been improperly hardened, so it wore down as the race progressed and lost power. I was pretty unimpressed.

We flew our cars to Watkins Glen for the United States Grand Prix and endured another troubled practice period: Dan requiring an engine change while my V8's fuel injection ran far too lean, not liking American gasoline. On one lap Richie Ginther's BRM and I were circulating in close company when we shot over the blind hump beyond the pits, flat-out. There, blocking the road before us, were the two works Ferraris, side-by-side, at about 15mph (24km/h)!

John Surtees's had broken its suspension, and his teammate Lorenzo Bandini had slowed down to enquire after him. Both Richie and I had huge moments in avoidance, careering way off the road, fortunately without hitting anything hard. We were not particularly impressed.

In the race Dan ran with the leading bunch, and after an initial delay I was able to catch up—until my engine began to misfire. I fell back into a dice with Jo Bonnier, whose Rob Walker Cooper had the edge along the straights while I knew I could corner faster. I finally made a determined effort to overtake him at the end of the main straight, but left my braking too late, and visited the countryside. Again I was able to rejoin, and lucky eventually to finish fourth.

The Mexican Grand Prix then closed 1963's Championship calendar. There I had more transistor box trouble before my car ran pretty well in the race, enabling me to come through from a poor grid position to run third, headed only by Dan in second place and Jim Clark—that man again—in the lead. Suddenly I caught up with Dan who seemed to be craning up out of his cockpit like an ostrich. I was wondering what the hell he was up to, and later discovered he thought his car's fuel pressure had fallen too low, so he tried to turn on the tap for the top auxiliary tank. But the top tank wasn't actually fitted in his car that weekend, and the tap had been taped-up. However, Dan managed to rip off the tape and turn the tap, which promptly gushed fuel over his legs and when he tried to turn the tap off again, it jammed open! He had to stop at the pits and his second place became a distant sixth, while my distant third place became an eventual second.

It had been a difficult season. We had scored our first (albeit minor) Formula 1 wins for Brabham-Climax, but we had undoubtedly under-achieved at Championship level, and had not provided Dan Gurney with the equipment his talents deserved. That first full season of racing the Formula 1 Brabham cars left us with the hurtful knowledge that we could, and should, have done better.

LEFT
Opening shot in the battle to become the first-ever racing driver to win a Formula 1 race in a car bearing his own name. I lead in BT3 through the first corner of the 1963 Solitude Grand Prix on the challenging (and dangerous) public road motorcycle circuit outside Stuttgart in Germany. I'm being chased here by Jo Bonnier in Rob Walker's private Cooper, Trevor Taylor's works Lotus 25, and Chris Amon's red-nosed Parnell team Lola—all with Climax V8 engines—then Innes Ireland's pale-green monocoque BRP-BRM. Jim Clark's Lotus had sheared a drive-shaft joint on the startline and I made hay while the sun shone!

1962 1½-Litre Brabham-Climax BT3

The first Brabham Formula 1 car, designed by Ron Tauranac and completed in time for its debut in the 1962 German Grand Prix driven by Jack Brabham. He subsequently used it to finish 3rd in the Oulton Park Gold Cup, 4th in the United States GP—in which Jack became the first driver ever to score World Championship-qualifying points in a car bearing his own name—2nd in the Mexican GP, and 4th in the South African Grand Prix.

In 1963 Jack drove the BT3 again to win the Solitude and Austrian Grands Prix, and finish in the 5th Italian GP, 6th at Goodwood Easter Monday, and 7th at Silverstone International Trophy. Denny Hulme drove it upon his Brabham Formula 1 team debut to finish 4th at Karlskoga *Kanonloppet*, Sweden.

TECHNICAL SPECIFICATION

Manufactured by Motor Racing Developments Ltd.
Engine: Coventry Climax Type FWMV 90-degree V8-cylinders; 2 valves per cylinder; 2 overhead camshafts per cylinder bank; bore and stroke dimensions, 63mm x 60mm, displacement volume, 1,494cc; Power output circa 157bhp @ 8,500rpm (in 1962 tune) or circa 190bhp @ 9,500rpm (in 1963-season tune).
Transmission: Colotti 5-speed and reverse.
Chassis: Multi-tubular spaceframe. Suspension: independent front suspension by wishbones and co-axial coil-spring/dampers; rear by wishbones, links, radius rods and co-axial coil-spring/dampers.
Brakes: Discs all round.
Wheels: Cast magnesium to Brabham design.
Tyres: Dunlop Racing.

1962 1½-LITRE BRABHAM-CLIMAX BT3 | 165

ABOVE
Ron Tauranac's suspension design abilities were second to none. His Brabham BT3 all-independent suspension enabled Jack to make the most of Dunlop tyre grip, 1963–1964.

BELOW
When Jack Brabham and Ron Tauranac set up Motor Racing Developments to build their own racing cars in 1961 they adopted this gorgeous turquoise-blue and gold livery which the BT3 was the last to wear before, in 1963, their works cars went to Australian dark green and gold.

LEFT
The Brabham BT3 was quite a capacious car. It had a Coventry Climax V8 engine installed behind the driver with its twin megaphone exhausts (as seen here) emerging above the bodywork around the preferred Colotti or Hewland gearbox.

166 | THE JACK BRABHAM STORY

RIGHT
The simple cockpit of the 1962 Brabham-Climax BT3 in which Jack scored his first Formula 1 "Brabham" victories.

LEFT
Upon its introduction at the German Grand Prix in 1962 the Brabham BT3 was one of the most handsome of all contemporary Formula 1 cars.

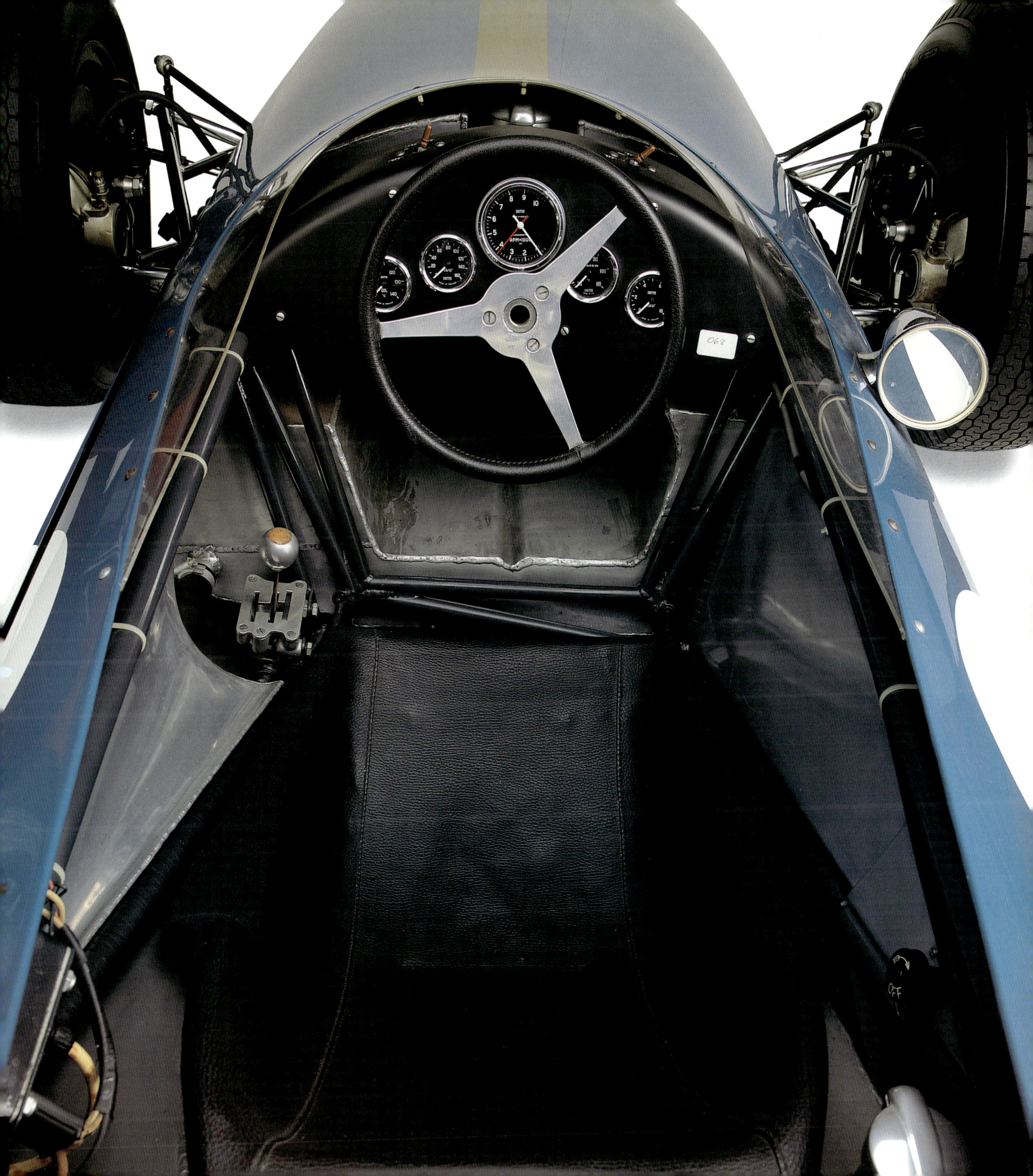
RPM×1000
068

CHAPTER 11

CHAMPIONSHIP CHALLENGERS

The Brabham marque's first World Championship Grand Prix victories, and an amazingly narrow escape in the Indianapolis 500-Miles

Dan on form—driving brilliantly in the 1964 French Grand Prix at Rouen-les-Essarts, Dan Gurney brakes down into the *Nouveau Monde* hairpin at the bottom end of the circuit. He's on his way to scoring our first-ever World Championship-qualifying Grand Prix win for the Brabham Racing Organisation. I'd finish third behind him. This was a great day for our little team, and it did much to compensate for continuing disappointments in so many other races.

We had much to prove as we began the 1964 season. Ron's production designs for 1-litre Formula 2 and 3 single-seaters, and now the sports-racing cars, were generating a full order book, while the new Formula 1 season began on a depressingly rainswept March day at Snetterton.

I made a bad start and drove virtually blind through the spray and murk. Dunlop had introduced squat new "doughnut" 13-inch (33cm) diameter R6 tyres for Formula 1, and my 1963 BT7 car was fitted with these new wide R6s at the rear, but old narrow 4.5-inch (11.4cm) tyres at the front. The moment I hit deep water the rear tyres would aquaplane, while the narrow fronts cut through. I spun three times, finally hitting a bank backwards.

We ran a new 1964 chassis frame, at Easter Monday Goodwood, using old '63 body panels and tanks but with suspension accepting 13-inch (33cm) wheels and the latest tyres. We also used the latest Hewland HD "Heavy Duty" five-speed gearbox.

I ran with Graham Hill and Jimmy Clark, and on one lap Jimmy almost spun leaving the chicane, so I nipped by. Then I began to pick back Graham when a rear wheel split at Madgwick. My Climax V8 engine there was a beauty, going better than any I'd used before.

We were building two completely new team cars that were even lighter, with slimmer bodywork and tanks. Meanwhile John Zink, an American USAC entrant, had commissioned MRD to build a 4-cylinder Offenhauser-engined car which I would drive for him in my second Indy "500".

I'd driven Alan Brown's gigantic Ford Galaxie saloon at Snetterton and we'd actually won outright, despite the rain! In fact the two-tonner handled amazingly well on Dunlop R6s and my winning average speed was actually faster than Innes Ireland's BRP-BRM had managed in winning the Formula 1 race.

"Brownie", the owner, was thrilled, and I drove for him again at Goodwood during Saturday practice for Easter Monday. Out of the chicane on one lap I thought something felt odd. I braked a little early into the next corner, Madgwick. Sure enough, I had a puncture, the tyre collapsed and the car careered straight off into the bank,

BELOW
Testing again, Goodwood again, and it's also raining again. I'm showing off the new 2½-litre Climax FPF-engined "Tasman Formula" Brabham to the cameras. We found a ready market for these big-engined "four-bangers" amongst our old sparring partners in Australia and New Zealand. Great drivers who bought and raced them would include Lex Davison, Bib Stillwell, David McKay, and Frank Matich. I would have liked to have seen more of them follow me into European and worldwide international racing. The 1950s Aussie racer Stan Jones's son Alan did just that, and became Australia's first F1 World Champion since me.

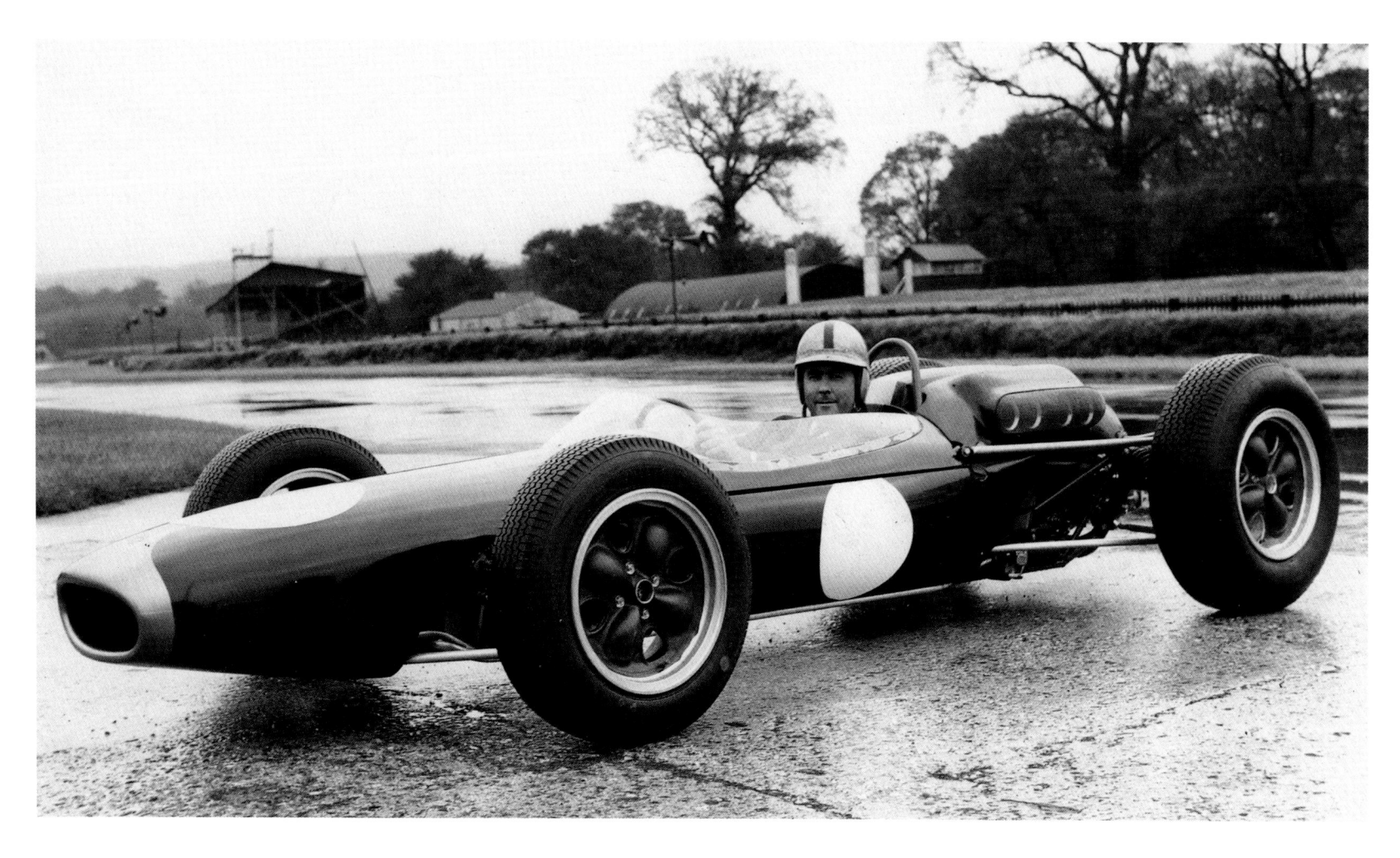

reared up, and rolled right over. I looked out the side window and found myself eye-to-eye with a group of white-faced spectators!

I was walking back to the pits when I saw Brownie scampering towards me. I said something like, "I'm all right," but without looking at me he ran straight past bawling, "How bad's my car?"!

To be honest, it wasn't too good.

A lot was happening through those first few months of 1964. I had been invited to visit Honda in Tokyo after the Australian races. They were keen for help in racing their little production sports cars in Europe. I must have driven around 100 laps at Suzuka in the two sports Hondas offered. With little twin-overhead camshaft engines delivering around 60 horsepower they sang along very happily at 8,000rpm, sounding like sewing machines, and had a 5-speed gearbox which was rare in road cars around that time.

A Honda engineer rode with me. His name was Yoshio Nakamura, and although we slithered around on the damp track, he just sat there silent. When he got out his only comment to the Honda people was, "...his driving was very skilful!" He had certainly taken it all in and I was extremely impressed by their experimental section. They also let me loose on some of their racing motor bikes, 50, 125, and 250cc jobs, on a motorcycle test circuit beside their experimental department. It was immediately obvious that if Honda ever got their cars going as well as their bikes then we would all be in trouble. They seemed to rev to around 18,000rpm. At first I couldn't get the hang of it, because whenever it dropped below 11,000rpm there seemed to be no power at all. The Honda 250 must have been hitting 130–140mph, which was quite exciting.

When I asked if I could try the bikes, Mr Nakamura was most accommodating, issuing instructions which ended with the ominous comment, "...and have amburance

RIGHT
On my way to my first Formula 1 race win of 1964, narrowly leading Jim Clark's brand-new Lotus 33 during the non-Championship Aintree "200" race at Liverpool. We had a rare old dice before he was accidentally put off line by a back-marker in the frighteningly quick ess-bend at Melling Crossing and crashed into the straw-bale barrier there. I was really relieved to spot him walking back across the infield, obviously safe and sound.

stand by". This was the beginning of good relations with Honda which would endure.

Back in Britain the Formula 1 Aintree "200" began with more Climax engine trouble. Then for the race Graham Hill blasted away in his new monocoque-chassised BRM, with me clinging to his tail. The BRM looked very untidy, Graham obviously struggling to make it stop. After a few laps I slipped by. Then my pit signals warned me that Jim Clark was closing up in his brand-new monocoque Lotus 33.

He was soon right behind, and we were going like the clappers. He couldn't get past for quite a time. I felt as if my car was steadier through the very fast left-right flick at Melling which was, in fact, a swine of a corner, one of the most difficult in Britain. It was certainly no place to make a mistake.

Jimmy finally passed me. He was trying really hard, looking untypically ragged. After a while I tailed him very closely round Bechers, slipstreamed him onto the Railway Straight and breezed ahead just before Melling. It then seemed as though I could pull away, and then he wasn't in my mirrors any more.

I had lapped a backmarker entering Melling, who let me by but didn't see Jimmy and pulled back across his line. Jim had to dodge, and crashed very heavily into the straw bales.

I kept pressing, but couldn't see him in my mirror. That really bothered me—was he alongside? I couldn't work it out, until next time through Melling I saw his crumpled Lotus and was very relieved to see him walking towards the pits.

This left me unchallenged. Dan, meanwhile, had broken a universal coupling, but he was happy about his car, and happy that we had won, and won well.

May Silverstone then produced an epic battle! My Brabham-Climax and Graham Hill's BRM were really closely matched, and we had a rare old dust-up. I realised that come the last lap my only chance would be to slipstream him through the second-last corner, the left-handed Abbey Curve, and then give it everything before the final right-hander at Woodcote, just sawing through on the outside if he quite properly protected the inside line—which I presumed he would.

For several laps towards the end I'd lined-up to try passing him on the inside, and sure enough he covered that line. But running round the outside in that

ABOVE
Aintree "200" casualty, 1964. The crushed and twisted monocoque chassis of Jimmy Clark's brand-new Lotus 33 lying where it came to rest beside the track at Melling Crossing. Damage like this to an aluminium stressed-skin monocoque chassis was very difficult and time-consuming to repair. When my Brabham's tubular spaceframe chassis was just as severely damaged at Solitude that year we simply sawed-off the mangled back end and welded-on new tubes to suit. Within a week it was fit as a fiddle again.

LEFT
Ah yes…the way it was! An intrepid photographer gets a viewfinder full of Dan in our works "Monaco-nosed" Brabham during the GP there in 1964. After my debut victory here five years earlier, Monte Carlo had never been particularly lucky for us. Nothing would change.

INDY FIREBALL 1964

Masten's words really burned into my mind. I never thought anything could terrify him. And here he was describing the Thompson car as terrifying?

So it was back to Indy for the "500" itself. One thing had already made a really big impression on me. My old Cooper team-mate Masten Gregory was there, trying to qualify one of Californian hot-rodder Mickey Thompson's radical new ultra low-slung small-wheeled cars. "Oh really," I'd said, "What's it like?" Masten pulled a face and said, "It's absolutely an accident going somewhere to happen. Under full tanks it's totally terrifying…".

By missing qualifying that first weekend—which decided the front rows of the Indy grid—I was lining up further back which meant that Cobra sports car driver Dave Macdonald was ahead of me in one of these ultra-low Thompson cars. All the way round the rolling lap before the start—mindful of Masten's warning—I just kept my eyes riveted on that red car, knowing it was brimful of fuel. It was visibly very unsteady. I did not take my eyes off it.

We came out of Turn Four, green flags and we were racing. My eyes were still glued on that odd-looking car a couple of rows ahead. Dave Macdonald nearly lost it in Turn Two, but caught it. In Turn Three he was again all over the place. Then, coming out of Turn Four, it happened. Dave's ultra-low Thompson car flicked broadside, and he lost it.

Instantly, I hit my brakes. Dave Macdonald's car speared down to the inside. The ultra-low Thompson car impacted against the concrete wall and exploded like a napalm bomb. The car then ricocheted back up at an angle leaving a blindingly bright wall of orange flame across the course. Eddie Sachs simply could not stop. He smashed straight into Macdonald's car, and his own car's fuel load exploded too. He didn't stand a chance.

Despite braking so hard, I just seemed to be accelerating through a funnel between roaring flame and the outside wall. I managed to slow just enough to dodge left through the fire at right angles before the burning wrecks. I was through it literally in a flash, and apart from running over some debris emerged unscathed. The race was stopped.

To this day I'm confident that Masten Gregory's pre-race words saved my life. Tragically Dave Macdonald died of his burns a few hours later, while Eddie Sachs—poor Eddie, the "Clown Prince" of Indy who had helped make my debut at the famous circuit there in 1961 so enjoyable—had been killed instantly.

The blast of heat as I drove through those flames had been like opening the door of an oven—I never wanted another experience like that.

We prepared to resume racing in the positions held when the race was stopped. The car then went pretty well, and I began picking up places. But it wasn't long before I noticed the undertray was filling with fuel from a leaking tank. It was probably punctured by debris.

After 83 laps I made my first refuelling stop and the instant the tap opened fuel just gushed from the split in the tank. Not wanting any more fire I retired—and would not return to Indy for several years.

125–130mph (201–209kph) curve was always a dicey business. I tried a ploy; I eased back on the penultimate lap and Graham seemed to swallow it, I sensed he thought I'd shot my bolt.

On the last lap, however, I shot through Club Corner absolutely flat-strap and closed on him into the following left-hander at Abbey. I could see he was prepared for me to try the inside move into Woodcote. As he held a tight line to the right I just barely braked at all and launched myself into a kamikaze-style slide round the wider, outside line which came off, but only just!

As we flashed across the timing line my car's nose was just ahead, and I promptly went straight off, bounding along the left-hand verge, hanging on for dear life. I survived—and was thrilled. It was our first Formula 1 Brabham win on home ground.

More Lucas trouble ruined Monaco for me, but I didn't have time to brood on it. Early next morning I was flying back to Gatwick to catch a plane for my second attempt at Indianapolis.

There I found our new Brabham-Offenhauser BT12, the *John Zink-Urschel Trackburner*—in deep trouble. To meet my Formula 1 commitments, it was vital I should

LEFT
This Bob Tronolone shot taken at Indy '64 captures my John Zink-owned Brabham-Offenhauser running nose-high at speed, dwarfed by the pursuing Watson-Offy roadsters of Lloyd Ruby and Parnelli Jones. John had absolutely insisted we should use soft F1-type spring and damper rates in our car—he was convinced that would be the key to Indy success. He was wrong, but we bowed to his greater Indy experience. We didn't catch up until just after the 1970 "500" when I finally appreciated how stiff your car had to be to make it work at "The Brickyard". Until then—and A.J. Foyt's help in testing—we simply lacked the mileage to know any better.

FAR LEFT
The obscene fireball engulfing the colliding cars of Dave MacDonald and Eddie Sachs on the opening lap of the 1964 Indianapolis 500-Miles. Both drivers were killed, and I've somehow come through it all without hitting anything too hard—standing desperately on my Brabham-Offenhauser's brakes. If it hadn't been for Masten Gregory's pre-race tip off I'm convinced this catastrophe would have had my name on it. Almost 40 years later, the memory remains so vivid that just the sight of such photos still makes me go cold.

qualify on this first of the two Indy weekends. If I failed I'd have to return for a second bite, giving access only to the rear rows of the starting grid, on the second weekend.

Firstly, we found fuel surge interrupting pick-up from the tanks. The car was oversteering wildly, and we finally fitted a front anti-roll bar like a crowbar, three-quarters of an inch in diameter! Certainly it improved things, though the big Offy engine at the back still gave oversteer. Lack of track time didn't help—neither John Zink's absolute insistence we fit Formula 1-rate springs and dampers. They weren't man enough at Indy. I was also rather disappointed by the engine's power. It didn't go like a mad dog, as I'd expected, though I was still timed at 186mph (299kph).

Just before qualifying, the engine picked-up dirt in its injection system. By the time we had fixed it, time was short, and I was desperate to run. Another would-be qualifier volunteered his place in the queue but even this didn't quite cut it. The driver ahead of me wasn't quite far enough round his "coming in" lap when the whistle blew at 6pm, and I had just missed out by about 10-15 seconds.

That was one of the big lows of my racing career, because I knew I'd have to return during practice for the Dutch race at Zandvoort. I explained this to the officials, but they just shrugged, "That's how it goes".

So I flew back from Indy that Tuesday night, qualified during the Friday session at Zandvoort, then left Amsterdam at five in the afternoon to return to Indy, via New York. I snatched a night's sleep and reported to the Speedway next morning. Yellow caution-light delays were followed by another disaster when a wheel hub nut flew off one of the cars as it came by the pits and struck Denny Moore, our engine man, in the chest. He was lucky the nut only struck him a glancing blow, but even then it broke some ribs. If he'd been standing square-on it would have gone straight through him.

In consequence we found ourselves queueing to qualify without the car warmed up. Since it was 11am, and I was due to catch my return plane at noon, I had to set a competitive time first time; there was no room for mistakes. The Offy engine was pulling 5,800rpm as I exited Turn Four (1,000rpm below its limit)—and I just went for it.

RIGHT

This is Dan stranded out near Stavelot Corner on the Spa-Francorchamps circuit after his works Brabham has run out of fuel after he had totally dominated the 1964 Belgian Grand Prix from the fall of the starter's flag. He was absolutely supreme in our car that day and this was a bitter let-down. Jim Clark came round on the cooling off lap and coasted to a halt, also out of fuel, at the same place. Jim had no idea he'd inherited first place and had actually won the race until someone drew his attention to the public address commentary they could all hear over the spectator enclosure loudspeakers. Dan was owed a Grand Prix victory, and it came in the French GP at Rouen.

We had decided that four laps at 151mph (243kph) would be the minimum to be confident of qualifying, so I had a board numbered "151", which could be displayed if I was beating that target. Things went OK on the first lap, but I on the second I went a little low in one turn and lost 300 revs. The speeds of my four laps were: 152.801mph (245.910km/h), 152.078 (244.746), 152.878 (246.034), and 152.259 (245.038), an average of 152.504mph (245.432km/h). There was still something in hand, but I'd had to make sure I didn't drop it.

I dashed off, with a police escort, at 11.30 and made the plane with a few minutes to spare. I landed at Schiphol, Amsterdam, at 7.40am on Dutch Grand Prix morning, sleeping so deeply across three seats that the stewardess hadn't even woken me for breakfast. I needn't have bothered—early in the race my car's distributor drive sheared. I'd already seen Dan's car stopped at the pits, and found he'd broken his steering wheel! He looked a big strong bloke, and he was!

After Indy, back at familiar Spa, the Belgian Grand Prix provided further disappointment. Dan had been in fantastic form during practice. We'd soon discovered in '63 that the key to Dan running well was to get his head straight pre-race. If he believed his car was right he was mighty! If the least thing niggled him, or put him off, he just wouldn't go as well. I remember in testing one time, he reported the car's handling was "nearly there", and then requested another $\frac{1}{8}$-inch adjustment on the rear anti-roll bar. Now by that time I'd probably had more experience of setting up racing cars successfully than anyone else in Formula 1. I'd challenge any driver of that era to spot the difference made by an $\frac{1}{8}$-inch change on an anti-roll bar. Half an inch maybe, one inch definitely, but not one-eighth!

Anyway, we fiddled about behind him, did nothing, told him we'd made the change, and off he went to set another fantastic time, returning with that dazzling grin, chuffed to bits.

At Spa '64, his head was absolutely straight. He loved his car and was demonstrably miles quicker than everybody else. He was absolutely blitzing that race—until with just three laps left he stopped at the pits shouting for more fuel, his engine was beginning to starve. No Formula 1 car of that era was equipped for rapid refuelling. The boys had a churn of fuel behind the pits, not on the pit counter. Jim Clark slammed by to take Dan's lead, and as they dived for the fuel Bruce McLaren's Cooper took second place. Dan knew if he hung around much longer he'd lose all chance so he rejoined, shouting that he'd be back at the end of the lap. Sadly, his engine died on the Masta Straight, and he coasted to a halt at Stavelot—robbed of the Grand Prix triumph that his magnificent drive totally deserved.

The French Grand Prix returned to Rouen that year, where we first confirmed we could run our tanks down to as little as half-a-gallon before the engines began to starve. Dan again went well behind Jim Clark's Lotus for the first 30 laps, with me third.

When Jimmy's Climax engine holed a piston, Dan was left with a minute's lead from me, but I was in a tremendous scrap for second place with Graham Hill's BRM and Peter Arundell's second works Lotus. Graham found a way by, Pete dropped back and I broke the lap record to reel-in Graham's BRM again. But we finished in that order, and Dan had won!

This was fantastic. For the first time a "Brabham" had won a World Championship-qualifying Grand Prix, and our team cars had actually finished first and third, setting the new lap record. I would have loved to have followed Dan through into second place but my engine was never on top form with a hesitancy between 7,000–8,000rpm.

ABOVE
That's me, blurring past our pits in second place in the 1964 French Grand Prix at Rouen-les-Essarts—with Roy Billington holding out my pit signal—7 seconds up on Graham Hill's BRM and Pete Arundell's works Lotus. Graham caught and passed me, and I came home third, but Dan had scored our first-ever "Brabham" victory in a World Championship-qualifying Grand Prix.

BELOW
Literally going for gold in the 1964 Oulton Park Gold Cup for F2 cars. My Brabham BT10 beat Jim Clark's Lotus 32. Both cars used virtually identical single-cam 1-litre Cosworth-Ford SCA engines. Half of that year's F2 races, 16 in all, were won by our chassis, driven by myself, my team-mate Denny Hulme, or privateers Jochen Rindt, Alan Rees, and Jo Schlesser.

At Brands Hatch for the British Grand Prix, onlookers concluded I was trying to wear out my fresh engine, I did so many laps scrubbing in new tyres.

Racing tyres in those days were almost immortal. The set I'd just replaced had done both the Belgian and French GPs! It was ridiculous, really, because here I was virtually wearing out my car merely to achieve optimum wear on a new set of tyres.

Early in the race Dan was screaming into Stirling's Bend, with Surtees's Ferrari and myself right behind him, when his ignition amplifier burned out. His car faltered and he threw up his hand in warning. John was too close and actually clipped Dan's gearbox, while I only just avoided tagging the Ferrari's. Dan limped round to the pits and despite rejoining was out of contention. I was running third behind Clark and Hill when my car began to slide in right-hand corners.

Dodging around Surtees earlier I'd straddled a kerb which had graunched underneath. A fuel tank had split and leaking petrol that had collected in the undertray had been sprayed out onto the rear tyre in right-hand corners, but not in left-handers. Late in the race fuel level had fallen below the split, no leak, no handling problem. I finished fourth.

It was back to Stuttgart and the Solitude race the following weekend. A fast road circuit, lined by ditches, trees, and road-signs, and it rained. The organisers waited 20 minutes for a violent shower to pass. By the time they started the race, surface water was cascading from the surrounding slopes, and rivers were running across the track.

Sure enough, after about one-third of the opening lap Bandini's Ferrari began to spin in the middle of the pack. He was right in my path, rotating like a lawn sprinkler, with columns of water showering up from his tyres. It seemed he was going to spin straight down the middle of the road so I cut to the left, but the Ferrari abruptly spun my way and we clattered wheels—so violently that one of his balance-weight clips transferred itself onto one of my rims. The impact threw me straight off the road and, while he bounced back and struck other cars, I found myself diving down into a ditch, then up and out, straight for a telegraph pole into which I smashed in a soggy shower of tuffets, rainwater, and bits of Brabham car. The impact chopped my car's rear wheels and gearbox clean off, and twisted the chassis frame.

I jumped out as bits of other cars came raining down around me. In the middle of the road was the biggest tangle of Formula 1 cars I'd ever seen. It was a miracle nobody got hurt. A little further on Graham Hill and Innes Ireland had an independent accident of their own. Back at the startline the pit crews and crowd saw Surtees and Clark scream by leading nobody.

Back at Byfleet, I was thankful Ron and I had retained multi-tubular construction, because a monocoque structure would have been irreparable. As it was we cut the mangled frame in half and welded-on a completely new back end in time for the German race at the Nürburgring where my final-drive packed-up and Dan's engine blew a head seal.

The first Championship-qualifying Austrian Grand Prix at Zeltweg brought more disappointment, and at

ABOVE
Trying out the old hard stare technique which so seldom worked on any of the hard-boiled drivers involved in top-level Formula 1 racing. This is the 1964 Austrian Grand Prix—the first (and only) F1 World Championship-qualifying event to be held on the frost-heaved, rippled, and bumpy aerodrome circuit at Zeltweg. I'm on the outside in my Brabham-Climax, and that's little Richie Ginther (4) running hub-to-hub in the monocoque works BRM V8. Richie would run one of our Brabham sports cars in US West Coast professional races equipped with the first enlarged version of the 1^1/$_2$-litre BRM engine, reaching towards 2-litres.

ABOVE
During his three Brabham seasons (1963–1965) Dan Gurney generally drove as well as our equipment would allow him to. While Ron and I were developing during 1965 the new Repco V8-engined cars which we'd be using in the New Year's forthcoming 3-litre Formula 1, Dan was also laying plans—like Bruce McLaren—to build and run his own F1 project, the Anglo-American Racers Eagle.

Monza my engine holed a piston and I watched while Dan fought a tremendous scrap for the lead with Surtees's Ferrari. It was one of his best drives, until his alternator belt broke, causing his battery to flatten. The lead across the finish line had changed 22 times between them. After 63 fantastic laps he hurtled into the pits where cold water was poured over the fuel pump, but he finally popped and banged home tenth—poor reward—and too typical of our Climax V8-engined period.

Formula 2 provided some consolation. In three races on successive weekends I managed to win at Albi, Oulton Park, Montlhéry in France, and won the French Formula 2 Championship title, again. Of the six rounds Brabham cars had won four, Lotus and Cooper one each. At Watkins Glen both our engines failed, while the Mexican Grand Prix closed that season and would decide what had become the most dramatic battle for the World titles since my first win in 1959.

Jim Clark of Lotus, Graham Hill of BRM, and John Surtees of Ferrari were the contenders. We simply aimed to put them all in context by winning the race. In fact Dan and Jimmy showed a clean pair of heels, and entering the final lap Jim looked set to win both the race and his second successive World title, but his engine had run out of oil and failed halfway round. For once luck was on our side, and Dan sailed by for his and our second Grand Prix win—compensation, in some measure, for being robbed of what should have been his Belgian GP victory.

Graham had been sitting comfortably in third place—good enough to secure a second World title for himself and BRM—when he was put out by Bandini's Ferrari. Bandini seemed set to have an accident, trying repeatedly to dive inside Graham's BRM in the hairpin which was never really possible. He finally made one lunge too many, ramming the BRM's rear wheel and spinning Graham backwards into the trackside barrier. The impact closed-up the BRM's exhausts, and with his engine barely running Graham limped into the pits to have the pipes broken off and the stumps opened-out. The result was that John Surtees and Ferrari nicked the World titles.

A few weeks later, back home in Britain, I drove myself to hospital in some discomfort, where that night a surgeon whipped out my appendix. Dan Gurney flew over in December and tested his new BT11 car in preparation for the new year's South African Grand Prix on January 1. He'd relied on his old BT7 for most of the season and hadn't wanted to risk racing the new one until it was properly sorted out.

I intended to run a team of three cars at some races—with Denny Hulme stepping up from his "day job" as my regular Formula 2 team-mate. Climax were producing a 4-valve per cylinder (32-valve) version of the normally 2-valve per cylinder (16-valve) V8, and also had a complicated flat-16 cylinder under development, for which Ron had designed a special new chassis, our BT19.

We started the season unreliably in South Africa, and for the first time in many years I missed the New Zealand races. MRD's order book was absolutely bulging and our Byfleet works was bursting at the seams. I did do the Australian races, and on the way tested one of our

Formula 1 cars on Goodyear tyres at Riverside Raceway, in California. It had been a struggle to make ends meet financially ever since I had gone independent. Now we had signed-up with Goodyear exclusively. They had little road racing experience and were eager to learn. At last I felt our team was properly funded.

At Goodwood over Easter I'd been fitting modified suspension to my car, and was reaming-out a hole in one of the front uprights when the sharp reamer slipped and opened my left thumb to the bone, requiring four stitches. Luckily it wasn't my gearchange hand, but the steering wheel vibrating against it made that an exceptionally painful race. I was told my driving looked rather ragged. I'm not surprised.

At May Silverstone I managed to displace John Surtees's Ferrari for second behind Graham's BRM, and then eased him out at Stowe Corner to take the lead. He repassed me before the next turn, at Club, but by lap eight I was ahead again and was able to drive away.

My Climax engine was singing just beautifully and the car's handling was as good around Silverstone as I'd ever known. The only blemish was occasional difficulty engaging top gear. I noticed occasional smoke in my mirrors, it worsened, and my heart sank. A pinion bearing had collapsed and the gearbox casing split, leaking oil onto the exhausts. I retired with the back of my car in flames and Denny Hulme—having a Formula 1 chance that weekend—was also out, with a failed V8 rear oil seal. That race was the first Formula 1 event ever to be won by BRM's promising new signing—a young Scot named Jackie Stewart.

Our first new 32-valve Climax V8 was delivered barely in time for the Monaco GP. In wet practice the V8 didn't impress low down in the rev range, I took pole position briefly, before Graham bumped me back in his BRM.

Everything looked good until a half-hour before the start when the Goodyear rep declared, "We're afraid you're only going to do 80 of the 100 laps on the tyres you've got on the car". He wanted me to remove my scrubbed tyres and fit a fresh set. I wasn't keen, and in fact started with three fresh tyres and one scrubbed one on the right-front. This lost me 15-16 seconds to the BRMs of Hill and Stewart before the new rubber wore-in and I could at last push hard.

I got on to the tail of the two Ferraris in time to see Graham manhandling his BRM out of the escape road at the harbourside chicane. That had cost him the lead. Soon after, I found Jackie Stewart facing the wrong way, having spun his BRM at the Casino. I had already passed Surtees so only Bandini lay ahead of me, and I finally succeeded in elbowing past him under braking for the Gasworks Hairpin.

Then my rev-counter stopped working. No problem, I was well in the groove by then and raced on, changing-up at the familiar landmarks. But part of the rev-counter drive had come apart and jammed between the rev-counter gearbox and camshaft, which popped the counter gearbox off the back of the engine.

This allowed oil to pump out, and in the *Tabac* Corner my engine locked-up, and I declutched only just in time to

ABOVE
The 1964 Easter Monday Goodwood race for F1 cars. I'd just got myself into a position to intrude upon a scrap for the lead between Graham Hill and Jim Clark when my new wide-section "doughnut" nearside rear tyre burst, here at Madgwick Corner.

BELOW
A rare sports car outing for me in the prototype Brabham-BRM BT8 sports car at the 1964 Goodwood Easter Monday meeting.

RIGHT
The round-the-houses Monte Carlo street circuit was always one of the hardest on the entire Formula 1 calendar. Driving at competitive pace around the streets and quayside involved completely relentless attention and effort—and the smallest mistake could bend the suspension or break a wheel against the kerbs. Everywhere there was something hard to hit but it was a great challenge in glamorous surroundings which most of us enjoyed. Naturally, drivers enjoy it more when they win. Here I am in our works Brabham-Climax BT11, in practice for the 1965 Monaco Grand Prix, diving into the *Tabac* left-hander on the harbourside and poised to qualify briefly on pole position before Graham Hill's BRM bumps me back into second place on the front row of the grid. The race? Forget it…

LEFT
In the pits at Clermont Ferrand during the 1965 French Grand Prix meeting. I look happier than I really felt in my unaccustomed role as team manager. When the penny-pinching organisers refused us a three-car entry, I stood down to give Denny Hulme his World Championship-level chance in our second car, and he grasped it with both hands.

save myself from crashing into the wall there—a bitter disappointment.

At Spa, in the rain, Dan had a few inexplicable moments during his early laps and was unsure of his car's handling. Unlike this race the previous year, his head wasn't right that day. Towards the end I nearly caught Bruce's Cooper but there was so much spray I couldn't see a thing if I closed within 300 yards (274 metres). I settled for fourth behind him.

One horrible sight during that race was Richard Attwood's Parnell team Lotus wrapped around a telephone pole and on fire. The pole seemed to be right in the cockpit. It looked unsurvivable, but in fact Richard had miraculously escaped with bumps and minor burns. I requested three entries for the French Grand Prix at Clermont-Ferrand, but they refused. Two only they said. I had promised Denny more Formula 1 drives. Since he'd won the F2 race at Clermont the previous year I stood down, to give him a run. His car was carefully set-up with painstakingly chosen gear ratios and he set quickest time in first practice! This was my first experience of being team manager while other blokes drove our cars. During practice, the moment they started lapping quickly I felt an irresistible urge to call them in! In the race, Dan had a plug lead fall off, then another plug oil up, while Denny—after early delays—finished fourth.

The British Grand Prix was a shambles for us. Dan's 32-valve engine blew-up on the warming-up lap, so I handed him my 16-valve car for the race. The engine wasn't much good, tall Dan didn't fit the cockpit, yet still finished sixth. Denny's car, with an oily, down-on-power engine, broke its alternator drive belt and flattened its battery.

And so it went on, a sequence of disappointments. In between times that season I'd had a few drives in Alan Brown's latest American saloon car—a Ford Mustang—and I managed a pleasing win with it at Brands Hatch on August Bank Holiday Monday. The trophy and garland were presented by Miss World, which also perked me up. I would win again in that car at Oulton Park, only to be told later we'd been disqualified because some non-homologated parts had been found in its engine. If the car had been properly scrutinized before the race we could have changed the offending parts. That really annoyed me.

ABOVE
Dan in our works BT11 during the 1965 French Grand Prix at Clermont-Ferrand. I'm afraid it was a typically troubled race for him that season and he was out after only 16 laps, but we managed to put a more reliable car under him through the second part of that season and he finished 3rd in three consecutive races—the Dutch, German, and Italian GPs and then added two 2nd places in a row in the United States and Mexican GPs. His drives in Italy and Mexico in particular were brilliant.

At Monza, I was team manager again. The only way we could negotiate a three-car entry was to provide a car for Milanese ex-Ferrari driver Giancarlo Baghetti. The organisers offered good start money, and he went quite well before missing a gear and blasting his engine apart. Denny drove my normal car but its front suspension mounts cracked and he wisely came in to investigate. Dan made a tremendous start from the fourth row of the grid, and became instantly embroiled with the leading bunch.

From my newfound vantage point, Monza's slipstream racing was fantastic to watch. I never believed Dan would be able to hold the front-runners. He compensated for his lack of power down the long straights by storming every corner, knife-edging his car through with minimum possible slide to conserve his impetus. He finished third behind the twin BRMs of Jackie Stewart and Graham Hill —the little Scot having outfumbled Graham in the final corner to score his maiden Grand Prix victory. Dan raved afterwards about the car's handling. "How was the engine?" I asked. He replied, "All the power of a VW". Watkins Glen was better. Dan and I finished second and third. We'd arrived with our two cars and four engines. The 32-valver again disappointed, down on power and leaking oil, so we replaced it with a 16-valver on the night before the race. We both had trouble disposing of Bandini's flat-12 Ferrari, and then the race lay between Graham Hill—shooting for his third consecutive United States GP win for BRM—and our two Brabhams. Rain showers played their part. In the first Graham slithered off and I led, for about half a lap, but entering the hairpin by the pits I just couldn't stop and slithered onto the muddy verge. I didn't spin but had trouble finding sufficient traction to rejoin. After the second shower it began to dry and Graham just powered away from us, but Goodyear were very happy with our 2-3 finish on American soil, on their tyres.

Our cars had always gone well at Mexico City. The twisty course put as much accent on handling as power, and handling was our forte. But Richie Ginther's V12 Honda was the star—developing fantastic power and quite uncatchable. It was his greatest moment and his first GP victory. We were very happy for him and for Honda.

But personally that final race of the 1½-litre Formula was a great disappointment. Just as I braked for the banking on the opening lap the cockpit filled with smoke. A cam-cover gasket had blown, spraying oil onto the hot exhausts. I was able to watch Dan have another terrific drive. He had told me he would not be driving for us in 1966, he planned to follow my lead and build his own cars, so this was his farewell outing in a Brabham—or so we thought at the time.

First he sorted out Jackie Stewart, which we had come to realise took a bit of doing, and then Mike Spence's Lotus, and he then took second place behind Richie's Honda. The last 15 laps of that Mexican GP were amongst the most exciting I'd seen. The lap record stood at 1 minute 58 seconds. Dan put in eight successive laps at 1:56 or under. He left the record at 1:55.84, but Richie drove a beautifully judged race. He prevented Dan from closing to within striking distance until the final lap, by which time it was just too late—and these two great American drivers came home in that order. With close ties between ourselves and Honda on Formula 2 engines, and Dan and Richie being such old friends and former Ferrari team-mates, Mexico '65 provided a memorable finale to five seasons of 1½-litre Formula 1 racing.

LEFT
Driving in a full-length Grand Prix is bloody hard work! I stood down from the French race to give our minor-Formula works driver Denny Hulme his chance in frontline F1. He did very well, as I was confident he would. He finished 4th.

BELOW
After winning the first F1 race in which he ever competed (Syracuse, 1961) and then the first World Championship GP in which he ever competed, Giancarlo Baghetti always seemed jinxed. Here at Monza in the '65 Italian GP we were persuaded by the organisers to let him drive our third car, while I stood down to give Denny another drive. Baghetti qualified 19th and our Climax engine exploded behind him after 12 laps.

CHAPTER 12
TASMAN INTERLUDE II

From 1962–1969 the Brabham marque shone in racing down-under, particularly when driven by the man himself

A typical mid-'60s Tasman racing scene. This is the 1965 New Zealand GP at Pukekohe in which I wasn't involved, but our cars were. The entire front row are using 4-cylinder 2½-litre Climax FPF engines, and the two red cars are both customer Brabhams (left) Lex Davison in his own *Ecurie Australie* car, and (right) Graham Hill in David McKay's *Scuderia Veloce* entry. Between them, and shading them both off the line is Jim Clark's works Lotus. Graham will win, with Frank Gardner 2nd in Alec Mildren's entry, and Jim Palmer 3rd in his own car—a Brabham 1-2-3.

In November 1962, we took our first *Formule Libre* Brabham BT4—fitted with a 2.7-litre Climax FPF 4-cylinder engine out to that year's Australian Grand Prix at Caversham aerodrome, near Perth in Western Australia. The trip began with the discovery that our new car wouldn't fit into the hold of any of the planes flying into Perth. We had to shoe-horn it into a Boeing 707 by removing all the suspensions and putting the chassis on a couple of wooden skids like a sledge, which was inserted into the 707's hold with the suspensions and wheels packed in around it. Roy Billington had already flown out from Mexico City to assemble the car once it arrived.

My 2.7 Climax engine broke in practice. Fortunately, Bruce McLaren loaned me the 2½-litre unit from his sports Cooper Monaco, and we worked through the night to fit it. We finished the job at 7am race morning, and I went to the grid without a wink of sleep. I was intent upon putting up a decent show in my first race in a Brabham car on home soil.

Bruce and I had a tremendous battle until nine laps before the end we came up behind Arnold Glass, the Sydney motor dealer, in his Buick V8-engined BRM. Bruce got by just before a corner, and I followed through thinking Arnold had seen us both. In fact he hadn't seen me at all, and pinched me off against a half-tyre corner marker, which smashed my car's nose and split my radiator. I was pretty unhappy about that, but Bruce had certainly loaned me a decent engine!

After the South African Grand Prix the overseas brigade arrived in Auckland only at the last moment before the 1963 New Zealand GP. The old Ardmore aerodrome circuit was being replaced by a brand-new one purpose-built around the perimeter of the city's Pukekohe horse-racing track. My engine had been flown out brand-new which gave us another all-nighter fitting it in time. I became one of the first retirements, with a blown cylinder head seal. Those 2.7-litre Climax engines were pretty marginal, there just wasn't enough metal left in the block once it had been bored out from 2½-litres to 2.7.

I had two cars available on that tour, one for New Zealand, one for Australia. The latter was on a ship which was diverted to collect passengers from the crippled *Canberra* liner at Malta, so suddenly it would not be arriving in Melbourne, which is 600 miles (960 kilometres) from Sydney, until 8 February, the opening practice day at Warwick Farm...in Sydney.

Meanwhile, in New Zealand we raced and won at Levin the weekend after Pukekohe. Down at Christchurch, the Wigram Trophy saw drama involving our D12 tyres: could they survive the 150 abrasive miles? I was leading comfortably when my engine broke piston rings which burned off oil. I had to top up, losing 80 seconds, and finished a distant second behind Bruce's Cooper.

Bruce scored his third consecutive win at Teretonga, where I'd led the first 20 laps before he slipped by and I couldn't repass. I then had a puncture. The tyre was slowly deflating for the last 10-15 laps and it gave out with two laps to go, but I managed to hobble round the last half-lap to finish. Bruce did me a favour by lapping me just before the line, which meant I qualified for fourth place money instead of fifth.

Once we got to Melbourne, our Australian-leg car's ship didn't arrive until the Friday before the Sunday race at Warwick Farm. We got it unloaded at 4pm that afternoon, rummaging down past Donald Campbell's *Bluebird* land speed record car stowed above it, plus a mass of material from the stranded *Canberra*. There wasn't a plane leaving for Sydney capable of carrying the car until 10pm that evening. Our original schedule had allowed Tim Wall a clear 10 days to prepare the car. Now we had less than 10 hours. We got it to the Farm circuit on the Saturday morning, and lost the first of the two half-hour practice periods due to an electrical short. I spent the second session scrubbing in tyres and tuning the engine. I would start from the back of the grid, but the car felt good and so long as I didn't lose too much time chipping my way through from my lowly starting position I felt pretty optimistic for the race.

I'd never previously enjoyed good luck at "The Farm". That year was different. I was able to slice clean through the field to run second behind John Surtees's Bowmaker team Lola. He spun while leading, and on lap 31 of the 45 I was able to slipstream him down the main straight, outbrake him at the end, and take a decisive lead. The crowd went potty for their "local boy", which was really heart-warming. I was dog-tired at the end, and particularly pleased that David McKay had finished fourth in my New Zealand car which he'd just bought and Bib Stillwell was fifth in our prototype *Formule Libre* Brabham. I then flew back to pressing business at Byfleet.

For the start of the down-under season late in 1963 we shipped a brand-new Repco Brabham with big Climax engine to Frank Matich in Australia. First time out he had a tremendous battle with Bib Stillwell's 1963 car at Warwick Farm. It could have seen a Brabham 1-2, but instead they collided. Frank telephoned me in Britain to tell me all about it. I then sat by the phone awaiting Bib's call…it followed. This time he was the one who'd been pushed off. All racing drivers are the same!

The new Tasman Formula Brabhams were based upon Ron's Formula 1 designs, with 15-inch wheels all round and small 16-gallon tanks against 30-gallon required for Formula 1.

A new "Tasman Formula" had been agreed for 1964, limited to 2½-litres, so the big old unreliable 2.7s were ruled out. Repco in Melbourne were meant to be building me a new 2½-litre Climax engine in time for the New Zealand GP on 11 January, but it failed to arrive so I had to use the sports car Climax engine we'd installed for initial testing in Britain. My car handled well and I was able to hold off Bruce's latest Tasman Cooper for the opening race laps, but soon he was by and away.

Around half-distance Matich's engine blew-up, covering the braking area at the end of the straight with hot, slippery oil. I arrived, poised to lap backmarker Tony Shelly, who chose a nice dry part of the track, leaving me the oil slick.

He drew ahead, and I slotted behind to follow him through the next two corners. I assumed he'd let me by under braking again, but he stuck to his line and we hooked wheels which sent me into a flat spin at an altitude of about 6–7 feet! It knocked a wheel clean off my car, which Roy Billington had to rebuild quickly for Christchurch the following weekend. It would be three years before I'd drive again in a New Zealand Grand Prix.

Denny Hulme had finished second in my 1963 car, he was fastest in practice at Wigram, and won the first preliminary heat there, while I beat Bruce in mine. In the

Final, Denny and I took off, and seemed to be clear of all opposition as far as my pit signals were concerned. I wondered what the hell could have happened to Bruce, when with 12 laps to run he suddenly appeared on the boards—only 5 seconds behind, and closing!

Then I came upon a slow backmarker, sticking right on the racing line, and within two corners Bruce was with me. I tried to run around the outside of the backmarker before the next hairpin, but he hadn't seen me, moved wide and ran me off the road. This resulted in me veering onto the gravelly verge, and spinning. Denny chased after Bruce, but his engine ran its bearings and Bruce won from a red-faced me—with Denny coasting home third.

I flew home to London for the Racing Car Show, to hear that my old Cooper mechanic—Noddy Grohmann—was dead. He'd worked a typical, totally committed 16-hour day on our new year's Formula 1 cars before complaining of a headache, and setting off home to Godalming. In fact he was suffering a cerebral haemorrhage. A police patrol found him slumped in his Mini, parked off the road, and concluded he was drunk. He was put in a cell in Godalming police station, and died there. He was only 32. We couldn't believe it. He'd been a great character, and when Dan Gurney had signed on with us he'd said, "It sure is an honour to have my car prepared by him." In fact we were blessed throughout my career by some pretty darned good mechanics. Noddy had been one of the very best.

On the Australian leg of that tour I managed to win at Sandown Park in Melbourne, Warwick Farm at Sydney, and Lakeside, Brisbane, in succession. I was keen to make it a clean sweep at Longford, Tasmania, but stripped my crownwheel and pinion after three laps, when I was leading by four seconds. Fortunately Graham Hill was there in David McKay's latest Repco Brabham, and he managed to win for us. I used the Repco-built short-stroke Climax engine only in the Australian GP at Sandown Park and the standard 2½-litre Climax elsewhere. It was good enough.

In 1965 I couldn't afford the time to do the New Zealand races, so had to settle for the Australian rounds only. I had two Repco-prepared Climax engines, using the first with 230bhp at Warwick Farm and the short-stroke 235-horsepower sister engine at the other two races. At "The Farm" everybody's stopwatches put me on pole position apart from those which mattered—the official timekeepers'. I had to start from row two, which cost me about 10 seconds in the opening laps. I managed to pull back some 7 seconds on Graham Hill and Jim Clark ahead, but with about 15 laps to run I realised my new Goodyear tyres weren't going to last if I kept pressing so hard. For the last 10 laps they were completely bald, but on the second-to-last corner of the final lap Graham lost it so I inherited second behind Jimmy's Lotus.

Goodyear responded with new-compound tyres for Sandown Park, and on them I was able to win a great duel with Jimmy. My only problem that day was tremendous cockpit heat. During the race I lost nearly 6lbs in weight.

Longford in Tasmania was always a course on which it was positively dangerous to mix 1½-litre class cars with our big 2½-litre front runners. I was locked in a really ferocious dice with Bruce and Phil Hill in their Coopers, Graham Hill's Brabham, and Jimmy when I moved to lap a backmarker into one of the few tighter corners. I was

LEFT

Longford, Tasmania, the Tasman racing circuit we drivers always recall with pursed lips—a fantastically fast public-road course which was a little too narrow for comfort with cars of widely differing speed potential. I'm on the centre of the front row here as the 1965 Australian Grand Prix field sets off. On the left is Bruce McLaren's "Cooper" built by his own new team, and on the right is Graham in David McKay's sister Brabham to my works car. Bruce and I will have a terrific dice until I'm swept up an escape road by a backmarker. After a quick stop to check for damage I finished second. Lex Davison had crashed fatally at Sandown Park, and here his protégé Rocky Tresise died too, his crashing Cooper also killing a photographer. A motorcyclist had also died in a supporting race. There was a down side…but we always accepted it.

BELOW
Having fun at my home Sydney road circuit—Warwick Farm—in the 1967 Australian Grand Prix. The car is our Brabham BT23A, powered by one of the first centre-exhaust Repco V8 engines, in this case in 2½-litre Tasman Formula trim, while full 3-litre Formula 1 versions would power our World Championship cars through the coming season. It would bring us our second consecutive Formula 1 Constructors' Championship, and my team-mate Denny Hulme his Drivers' title—at my expense! Ron's cars could be beautifully balanced to drift like this under power…but here I'd finish fourth, behind Jackie Stewart's BRM V8, Jim Clark's Lotus-Climax V8, and Frank Gardner's 4-cylinder Brabham-Climax.

outside him into a right-hander but he left his braking too late and slithered straight on, which hustled me off down the escape road. I wasn't best pleased, and rejoined, repassed Graham and Phil, and then Jimmy but I couldn't do a thing about Bruce who won with me a rather hot and bothered second.

I wasn't going to compete in the 1966 Tasman Championship, but at the last moment received a series of frantic phone calls from Australia asking me to run in the last two rounds of the series, (as related later). In 1967 I returned to Australia. At Pukekohe my Repco V8-engined car left the road on spilled oil in the preliminary heat and bent its suspension. We got that repaired just in time for the GP—driving 20 miles (30 kilometres) from Pukekohe to a garage where we repaired the car and got back just in time for the feature event's warm-up lap, but as we moved off it was obvious a drive-shaft was out of alignment. Although I took the start to show good faith the shaft inevitably failed within five laps. I had put the V8 into Denny's car, who had already had to retire his old borrowed Brabham-Climax when a stub axle broke after 50 laps, having run third at one point.

Jimmy Clark's 2-litre Lotus-Climax V8 won the next three Kiwi races consecutively while Denny ran our Repco V8-engined Brabham. I didn't drive again until the Australian round at Lakeside, Brisbane, where I finished second to Jimmy's Lotus 33. Neither Denny's car nor mine could compete on traction, while the works Tasman 2-litre BRMs burst their gearboxes. Jackie Stewart persuaded his BRM to hang together in the Australian Grand Prix at Warwick Farm, where the best I could manage was fourth, with my rear tyres completely bald.

Melbourne was Repco's home town so we were determined to shine at Sandown Park. I won the preliminary race there and broke the lap record but we changed the engine before the main event, suspecting a broken timing chain. After leading for the opening eight laps my engine cut dead. We'd unwittingly crimped an ignition flywheel pick-up wire during the engine change, and it had broken. Jimmy had clinched the Tasman Championship, but there was still the trip across the Bass Straight to Longford. There I won the first heat from Denny, and in the Final Jackie Stewart made a very gentle start to preserve his BRM's gearbox. I was away and clear, leading from start to finish, and setting a new lap record.

I didn't run in the 1968 Tasman Championship until rounds six and seven at Warwick Farm and Sandown. I'd flown myself out from Britain delivering my old Queenair to its new owner, Bib Stillwell. Roy Billington was already in Melbourne, assembling our latest Tasman car, equipped with a magnesium-block Repco motor and small Formula 2-type Hewland FT200 gearbox.

I sorted the car in testing at Oran Park, some 15 miles (25 kilometres) from "The Farm", on the preceding Wednesday, but the engine wouldn't run properly. On the Thursday we tested at "The Farm" and changed the fuel injection system in search of a cure. I then made myself popular by larding the circuit with oil from a serious leak in the front crank seal.

On a very hot race morning I was late arriving at the circuit. We had removed the troublesome magnesium-block engine overnight and replaced it with a standard unit flown up from Melbourne. At first light I tried it out at Oran Park, but another oil leak began. We also had a tyre drama going on. Our Goodyears had been delayed in Customs, I tried Firestones, and found the locally supplied Dunlops wouldn't survive race distance on the abrasive surface.

I was in the second group pursuing the leaders when, on lap six, I slithered off on oil at the northern crossing and was launched off an earth bank. After a four-point landing the car felt OK, so I carried on. By half-distance I was fifth but then had to pit for a gallon and a half of Ampol oil, but it was leaking away and I finished seventh. I'd set a new lap record. Stirling Moss presented me the fastest lap trophy, suggesting I'd taken over as Champion oil dropper where Maserati had long since left off.

Repco provided the first 830 crossflow-headed low-level exhaust system engine for Sandown Park. Combined with fresh Goodyear tyres it enabled me to qualify on pole, in temperatures of 107°F in the shade and 142°F on the track surface. On raceday it hit 95°F at 8.30am and 110°F in the pits before midday. My car's radiator was punctured early on, and the engine boiled itself to death. We didn't go to Longford.

I didn't run in the 1969 Kiwi races, and although we sent out a new Formula 3-based BT31-Repco V8 car intended in time for the Warwick Farm "100" in February, its freighter was delayed. We didn't clear the car through Customs until the following Wednesday and then it had to be assembled in time for the Sandown race. Finally, we rushed it to the little Calder circuit outside Melbourne on the Friday. It was a tiny little thing, which made all our preceding Tasman cars seem huge. The engine bay had been tailored to accommodate the Repco V8 two-cam 830 engine with lightweight block and crossflow cylinder heads, outside exhausts.

Right at the end of Sandown practice a crack developed in the leading edge of its tall strutted wing, and while Jochen Rindt qualified his latest Lotus 49T on pole just marginally quicker than Chris Amon's V6 Ferrari, I qualified fifth fastest. I couldn't keep Jochen and Chris in sight during the race, and cruised home third. Then I hopped on an airliner, bound for Johannesburg and the South African Grand Prix. I would not drive in another Tasman Championship race, but in 1969 ran the BT31-Repco in the Bathurst "100" on the fabulous Mount Panorama circuit and won easily. That success finally signed off the Repco Brabham story—and my single-seater racing career on home soil—on a high note.

ABOVE
Over the top of Mount Panorama at Bathurst, 1969—this is our little Formula 3 chassised Brabham BT31 with 2½-litre 4-cam Repco V8 engine—the last of the works Repco Brabhams and my last hurrah in frontline single-seater racing on my home soil. Against relatively feeble opposition it was a comfortable win—but it has saddened me for decades now to see how single-seater racing in Australia declined through the 1970s-80s-90s from the extraordinary heights that we—and Australian racing fans—used to enjoy.

CHAPTER 13
CHAMPIONS OF THE WORLD

With a Melbourne-built V8, Brabham take both the Formula 1 Drivers' and Formula 1 Constructors' World Championship titles

Rounding Thillois corner at Reims during my winning drive in the 1966 French Grand Prix. I'm poised to become the first driver in history to win a premier-level Grand Prix in a car bearing his own name and run by his own team. My car is the Repco Brabham BT19 with Australian-made two-cam 3-litre V8 engine based on an American Oldsmobile F85 light-alloy block. In Ron's lightweight, good handling tubular spaceframe chassis it proved good enough that summer to win four consecutive Grands Prix. We were on our way to our third World title.

Our prototype Repco V8 engine arrived at Byfleet just days before we were due to leave for the Rand Grand Prix in South Africa. Ron had modified the chassis he'd designed for the flat-16 Climax engine to suit. The engine developed around 290 horsepower, but before I could do much with it I left for Johannesburg. I drove a new Brabham built for local entrant Aldo Scribante, powered by a 2.7-litre Climax FPF engine. I took pole position, then fought a real battle with local star John Love in his ex-Bruce McLaren Tasman Cooper. I won and set fastest lap, about 2 seconds quicker than the best ever achieved in a 1½-litre Formula 1 car. We were around 18mph (30km/h) faster down the straight and the car was then turned over to Scribante's driver, Dave Charlton, for local Championship racing.

Our new Repco V8-engined Formula 1 car was almost complete, and on the Wednesday after the Rand race we tested at Goodwood, managing around 25 laps before it rained! My best time was a 1:18.7—extremely encouraging. We shipped the car next morning for the non-Championship South African Grand Prix at East London on 2 January.

That new engine was sweet as a nut up to 8,000rpm and pulled really well from only 3,500. I saw 160mph (257km/h) down Goodwood's Lavant Straight and in East London practice I felt almost indomitable. Ours was the only new-Formula 3-litre there and it ran trouble free. I thought the Hewland gearbox might be marginal, so started very gently. Down the straight I saw 150mph (241km/h) against 143-ish (230km/h) in our old 1½-litre cars and I drew away from Mike Spence's 2-litre Lotus-Climax V8, which was pressed by Denny in our second-string car, using a 2.7-litre Repco-built Climax 4-cylinder. Denny's gearbox then broke, so badly that only the battery box prevented its back half dropping onto the road! He dumped oil everywhere, but three laps later, with only nine to go, my new engine cut absolutely dead.

The drive belt for the injection metering unit had dropped off, due to part of the little universal joint driving the unit's rotor having broken off inside and jamming the works, making the unit itself seize and throw its drive-belt. Despite this double disappointment, we'd made a terrific Repco Brabham 3-litre debut. Though extra power was enjoyable it also made the car more difficult to drive. Consumption was around 7mpg (10kmpg) against 9–10mpg (15–16kmpg) for the 1½-litre Climax V8s, but we were already hearing talk of as little as 4mpg (6kmpg) for our more exotic F1 rivals...which was fascinating.

I had planned to miss the Tasman races that year, but suddenly I was receiving frantic phone calls from my old Australian friend and de facto manager there, Reg Thompson, inviting me to Sandown Park, Melbourne, on

BELOW
This was the new Repco Brabham BT19 V8's encouraging debut in the non-Championship 1966 South African Grand Prix at East London, when I led most of the way until another minor mechanical problem caused the engine to cut out, because the fuel injection metering unit was no longer metering its fuel. This car's unique chassis frame included some oval-section tube instead of our normal round-tube material, and its swept-down nose and upswept rear lip to the engine cowl are evidence of Ron's attention to aerodynamic detail. Both the Repco V8 engine and those distinctive exhaust megaphones were Australian-made—the latter by my 1950s on-track rival, Len Lukey.

27 February and Longford, Tasmania, the following weekend. Repco were keen for me to run their new 2½-litre Tasman Formula V8. The new car was not due back from South Africa until 7 February, so we hastily booked air-freight transport. Taking the car out engineless helped as it was very much lighter and therefore cheaper to ship.

So I returned to Melbourne, but at Sandown Park in first practice the 2½-litre V8 didn't sing. Overnight we found its injection system was not properly calibrated, and next day I finished third from the back of the grid in the preliminary race, and vitally set fastest lap which earned pole position for the feature race. I was flying for the first 5-6 laps when a driving-key sheared in the oil pressure pump and I had to retire. Our start had been delayed by a shunt in the supporting race. The hold up meant my oil got cold and on the first lap the oil pressure was off the clock!

We had learned a valuable lesson and Repco just had time to repair the pump and fit fresh bearings before we caught the ferry to Tasmania. The long straight at Longford really gave the top-end horsepower of the works BRM V8s a big advantage. It was very hot and my V8 ran hotter than hoped, so I drove on the temperature gauge, easing off whenever the needle soared!

Where the 2½-litre Repco gave me around 237bhp, the 2.1-litre BRM V8s gave 250-plus. I had a very quiet run into third place behind Jackie Stewart and Graham Hill.

On my way out to Australia, I called at Honda's in Japan where new Formula 2 engines were being prepared for our new season, starting on 2 April—my birthday—at Oulton Park. The first Honda engine had reached us in mid-March, and I managed a brief test in a general practice session at Brands Hatch short circuit—amongst Minis and Ford Anglias—and lapped 0.8 second inside the lap record. The Honda F2 engine in its latest form was shorter-stroke than the 1965 version, which made it shallower, so we could mount it upright, instead of canted in the chassis. This improved the car's balance and

RIGHT
Filling the camera here at Silverstone during the 1966 BRDC *Daily Express* International Trophy race which I won on the BT19's British race debut. The best part of that day for me was that John Surtees's new 3-litre V12 Ferrari had been loudly tipped as the pre-race favourite—we out-qualified it to put our new Repco Brabham on pole, and led the entire distance, won by 7.4 seconds and set a new lap record at 117.34mph (188.84km/h). It's marvellous what you can look up in the record books…Forgive me a little gloat—I just loved beating Ferraris.

although the engine wasn't a lot more powerful at the top end of its rev range, it gave about 10 extra horsepower lower down and was much more drivable, something that I had impressed upon Mr Nakamura would be the key to success. Many engine designers seemed to think races were run on dynamometer test beds, where peak horsepower decides the winner. But we didn't race dynos, we raced cars, and drivability would often make an engine of lower outright power, but with more in the mid-range, unbeatable on all but the very fastest circuits.

At Goodwood a long test produced eight successive laps inside 1:23. I was beginning to like the new car a lot. I qualified on the front row beside Jim Clark's latest Lotus at Oulton Park, but raceday dawned—to snow. The race was cancelled. With some fine tuning to the rear suspension we tested again at Goodwood, and I lapped in 1:21.8, while Denny turned a "22" in his sister car. On Easter Monday we both enjoyed trouble-free drives in the feature Formula 2 race, to finish 1-2. That year's Formula 2 turned into complete Brabham-Honda dominance.

We had been building a new sports-racing car—the Brabham BT17—and Repco shipped a brand-new 4.3-litre V8 to us for the car's entry in the Oulton Park Tourist Trophy. The preceding week was almost sleepless. I crawled into bed at 4.30am one morning and 5.30am the next, then up and back to the works at 8.00am. I wasn't popular! Roy Billington got home at 7.30am after one all nighter, flopped into bed, couldn't sleep so went out and mowed the lawn instead.

I managed third fastest practice lap at Oulton and led the first Heat briefly until Denny blasted past in Sid Taylor's 6-litre Lola-Chevrolet. This left me in second place but then my engine cut completely. I then realised the electrical master-switch had popped out—so I snapped it back in and the engine struck up again, before a terminal oil leak developed.

We had an entry in the Formula 1 Syracuse Grand Prix in Sicily. I wasn't licenced to fly my Cessna at night but managed to talk Hugh Dibley—the Lola driver who was also a BOAC airline pilot—into flying us down to Rome. We were very late flying into Catania, and then at Syracuse my engine survived a dismal lap and a half due to an internal water leak, and Denny's lasted only a few minutes more.

May Silverstone held promise. I had seen the new Ferrari V12 at Syracuse and wasn't confident I could beat

THE REPCO V8 ENGINE

Through the first season of $1\frac{1}{2}$-litre F1 racing I entered my own Cooper in suitable non-Championship F1 races and in the short-lived $2\frac{1}{2}$-litre Inter-Continental.

When Leonard Lee announced that his Coventry Climax company would not build racing engines for the new 3-litre F1 of 1966, we had to look elsewhere for motive power. Ron and I contacted Repco in Australia. I believed the new Formula's opening races would see the big teams in development trouble with over-sophisticated new engines.

Repco of Melbourne had taken over the old Climax 4-cylinder FPF engine stock and its servicing for Tasman racing. By 1964–1965 they were keen to defend their market with a replacement engine. I pointed them towards a V8, perhaps based on a production cylinder block. A cast-iron "stock block" would have been too heavy, so I hunted down a suitable aluminium one.

In Japan in 1964, I inspected an alloy V8 Prince block—but with wet cylinder liners it looked too fragile. I then examined an alloy GM Buick block in a GM distributorship near Los Angeles Airport. Someone there suggested a near-sister unit, developed for a stillborn Oldsmobile project. It had one extra stud retaining each cylinder head. That offered greater potential. One cost pennies, and I took it back to Melbourne, and outlined a programme to Repco's boss Charles McGrath. The Oldsmobile block could provide a $2\frac{1}{2}$-litre V8 for Tasman racing, and a 3-litre F1 V8 for us. It'd be a modest unit, with chain-driven single overhead camshafts and two valves per cylinder, but it should provide decent torque and driveability—we might just get lucky.

Repco's consulting engineer was Phil Irving—an Australian of enormous experience, particularly with Phil Vincent on his world-famous motorcycles. Phil began drawing in Australia, then came to Britain for 1965, taking a flat near Croydon where we spent hours in the evenings looking over his shoulder as he drew the first engine. Ron advised on location of ancillaries etc, so this new V8 would fit our cars ideally.

The first Repco V8 racing engines used original Oldsmobile blocks modified in Melbourne. We stiffened the bottom end with a steel plate with apertures allowing the con-rods to pass through, and to which the big-end bearing caps were bolted. It produced a rigid, reliable, yet lightweight unit which was powerful enough!

Initially we used Daimler con-rods. Repco then produced tailor-made block castings for 1967, and we should have continued with that year's 2-cam 16-valve V8s through 1968 as well. Unfortunately everybody else was using four camshafts and four valves per cylinder, and we thought we had to follow to keep competitive. In retrospect I'm confident that if we had just relied on the ultimate 2-cam 16-valve unit we could have run hard for a hat-trick of World Championship titles in 1968 as well. As it turned out, the 4-cam Repco V8 would be a disaster in 3-litre Formula 1 trim—but a very strong unit as a 4.2-litre V8 for Indianapolis track racing or a 5.1-litre for sports cars, in which form it revved more slowly, sparing its fragile cam-drive gears the high-speed vibrations which in F1 destroyed them. But for two seasons, 1966–1967, Repco and Brabham had been on top of the world.

BELOW
With the B19 in the Silverstone pits, May 1966, the Lucas blokes inspecting our baby, the Repco V8 engine. See the plastic "Tudor" washer bottle hung alongside the Hewland gearbox? It was the lightest (and cheapest) way to provide the catch-tank demanded by the regulations to prevent oil overflow dropping on the track. Back in the 1950s we'd had no such niceties and the tracks were often larded.

John Surtees in it, but felt we'd at least be competitive. In fact I got a flying start, led into the first corner and never looked back, lowering the Formula 1 lap record to 1:29.8 and winning comfortably, while Denny was fourth in our 2½-litre 4-cylinder Climax-engined car. My Silverstone Repco V8 was producing 278 horsepower and when we arrived (late) in Monaco after a seaman's strike, a new 300bhp unit had arrived from Melbourne. Unfortunately a wire had been crimped too tightly on to an electrical system terminal, and had been cut in half so the engine refused to run on more than six cylinders.

We refitted the Silverstone engine—on a non-transistorised ignition system—but overnight I caught some local bug and felt horrible next morning. Ken Tyrrell toured the local chemists' shops for medicine, which I guzzled down. I still felt awful as the race began, but it was all over after 17 laps—the reverse-gear idler bearing failed in the gearbox, and I came to a grinding halt jammed in second.

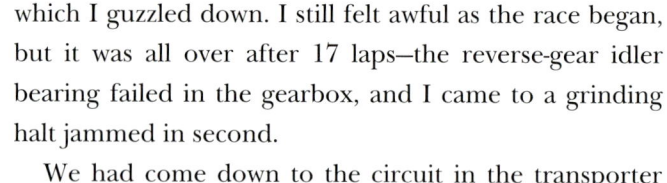

We had come down to the circuit in the transporter from our hotel at Cap d'Ail. I couldn't wait to get back into bed, but couldn't find a taxi anywhere with the race still in progress, and eventually caught a bus—the first time I'd ever returned from a Grand Prix by public transport. I flew the Cessna home next day, but spent two more days in bed.

Our F2 Brabham-Hondas were churning out almost 150bhp and, at Crystal Palace on Whit-Monday, Denny and I enjoyed another 1-2. We had four of those engines, and my Palace unit had not been touched since winning at Zolder, while Denny's had done both the Zolder and Barcelona races. People began complaining we were spoiling Formula 2. They hadn't complained the previous year when we'd plugged away fruitlessly with the original Honda engine.

I drove a Ford Mustang in the saloon car race. I couldn't do anything about Roy Pierpoint who won in the smaller Ford Falcon, but had a hell of a dice with a young Belgian boy named Jacky Ickx, driving a Lotus-Cortina. He was right up my exhaust pipes coming out of South Tower corner, and on one lap got by, though I had sufficient power in reserve to squirt ahead again across the finish line.

We then took my BT19-Repco and Denny's stopgap Brabham-Climax 4-cylinder to Spa for the Belgian Grand Prix. We seemed to have fixed a V8 problem with rising crankcase pressure due to misplaced breathers, and further Goodwood testing had also given us confidence to race the latest Hewland DG300 gearbox. Dan Gurney used one of these in his new Eagle Formula 1 cars, and was touched that Mike Hewland should have identified it by his initials. Mike told a different story. He had it on his drawing board when somebody walked into his office, looked over his shoulder and said, "What's this, a different gearbox?". So "DG" it became.

I never thought we had sufficient horsepower to compete at Spa, but in first practice only John Surtees's V12 Ferrari was faster. Everybody was disappointed by the top speed of the new-era 3-litre cars, concluding that the frontal area of the latest fat tyres was holding us back. In the 1960 Cooper at Spa, on 60 fewer horsepower, I'd seen 178mph (285km/h). My 1966 car would only do 172. Lap times were a different story, for these modern cars were very much faster through the curves, and also accelerated and braked more quickly.

It always seemed to rain at Spa, and for the 1966 GP we didn't bother to get a met forecast, just keeping our fingers crossed. About an hour before the race we went round the circuit on a parade lap. The surface looked fine, clean, and dry.

But by the time we rolled on to the grid, the skies were clouding over, and unfortunately not every driver realised it was already raining out on the far side of the course. Apparently the PA system was telling spectators it was raining at Malmedy, but we couldn't hear it, and no-one thought of clueing us in. They even declared it a dry race!

That 1966 Belgian GP opening lap was a memorable experience I never wanted to repeat. I think if I had been on the front row instead of the second I might well have been first to reach the top of the hill at Les Combes, since my car accelerated so well on full tanks. Anyway, I actually crested the rise third behind John Surtees and Jochen Rindt, the Austrian driver in his big works Cooper-Maserati V12. I was intent upon maintaining contact at the start of the long Masta Straight, but first we had to dive downhill and through the very fast right-handers at Burnenville and Malmedy.

Burnenville—with its downhill approach where you dived in blind between a stone barn on the left and a pub on the right—was probably Spa's most difficult corner. I was just set-up into it when I realised the road was shining. There had just been a shower. It was difficult enough to survive Burnenville in the dry, but in the wet—unexpected—it was lethal!

We were all doing about 135mph (215km/h) when we found our cars sliding. I was in a desperate situation, being drawn as if by a gigantic magnet straight for the barn on the left. For the second time in my career I really did think, "This is it," and felt my nerve ends freeze for the impact...but I was still finger-tipping the steering and modulating the throttle, fighting to save myself.

I don't quite know how, but the car began sliding slightly more sideways before nudging a rear wheel against the flat trackside coping, not really a kerb, just a different-surfaced edging. It was just sufficient to kick the car straight enough to save it—I missed some straw bales by about an inch, and the tyres then gripped and snapped the car back across the road. I used maximum steering lock and after at least a quarter of a mile as a virtual passenger the car settled, running straight and stable—on a now increasingly wet track.

I drew in a deep, deep breath—marveling I was still alive to do so. I was still chasing Jochen Rindt—who'd survived a similar fright—down into the tricky kink between the houses in Masta hamlet. Frankly I couldn't see any way he was going to make it, he was going so fast. So I had already begun rolling on to the brakes when his big bottle-green Cooper yawed, slewed, and began to rotate like a top.

I've never seen a car spin so violently, nor so many times. I had a grandstand seat. Amazingly, he kept tracking through the corners on line while actually spinning end-for-end. His head was snapping like a ballet dancer's to keep track of where he was. But, embarrassingly, I was catching him up, because his spins were slowing him down more quickly than my brakes were doing for me! As he finished his last spin, I so nearly tagged him, but at the last instant the Cooper-Maserati slewed right, and I just nipped by on the left.

Back at Burnenville next time round there were yellow flags, cars, and debris all over the place. At the entry to the

ABOVE
Team-mates—myself with Denny Hulme. The big, quiet Kiwi became a formidable and most reliable driver, and would take the Drivers' World Championship title away from me in our second car in 1967. Some likened his looks to the kid's comic character "Desperate Dan". Denny wasn't like that, he knew exactly what he was doing—I never saw him desperate.

RIGHT
Team-mates again—here Denny and I are in our Formula 2 Brabham-Honda BT18 works cars at Reims during the memorable French Grand Prix weekend. No, we're not just shaking hands, my engine has died during practice and he's towing me home to the pits. That was the last thing that went wrong that fantastic weekend. I would win in both the 1-litre Formula 2 and 3-litre Formula 1 cars, and Denny would finish 3rd behind Mike Parkes's 2nd-placed Ferrari (I love that phrase) in the Grand Prix.

FAR RIGHT
I ended up with three Drivers' World Championship titles and feel I missed out on a fourth in 1967, and perhaps a fifth in 1970—but here's the real thing, five-times World Champion Juan Fangio. I'd raced against him during his swansong appearance in the 1958 French Grand Prix at Reims. Now he was one of the first to wish me well on my first Championship-qualifying round win in our own car.

Masta kink one BRM was upside down on the left, a second was parked nearby, and Jackie Stewart's was lying smashed on the right. Somehow John, Jochen, and I had all survived the sudden shower while almost everybody behind had gone off in all directions. After all this I merely concentrated on staying on the road, and finished second behind Surtees's big Ferrari, scoring our new Repco V8s first World Championship points.

Back home the boys got a new BT20-Repco V8 car ready for Denny in the French Grand Prix at Reims. These new cars were based on the old 1½-litre BT11s, but with 15-inch (40-cm) wheels and 38 gallons (170 litres) fuel tankage, but I would stick to my hybrid BT19.

At Reims we were also running our Brabham-Hondas in the supporting Formula 2 race. During practice, my original Honda engine lacked power down the straight, so when it broke I was happy to replace it. The other engine wasn't much better, but the Japanese mechanics stripped it in a heroic 14-hour all-nighter, and had it fighting fit for the race that Saturday.

I anticipated stiff competition from some of the quicker Cosworth-engined cars, particularly from Rindt and Alan Rees in the Roy Winkelmann team Brabhams. Cosworth had definitely closed the power gap on us, but I managed to break the tow and get away. Towards the finish my only real worry was that I might run out of fuel, but everything turned out nice again, and I gained another dominant win.

I was on row two for the Grand Prix next day, peering up the 36 exhausts of the Bandini and Mike Parkes Ferraris, and the Cooper-Maserati which John was driving, having sensationally just walked out of Ferrari. I reckoned they had around 60-horsepower more than my Repco V8's best, so I was determined to stay in their slipstream if humanly possible. In fact John was soon in trouble, and I managed to squeeze past Mike Parkes round the back to slipstream Bandini.

My car was handling well enough to gain a little each lap on the right- and left-hand curves before Muizon corner at the start of the Soissons Straight, which put me close enough to maintain the tow right down into Thillois. But when we lapped a couple of backmarkers Bandini broke clear. I managed to pull away pretty comfortably from Parkes, but could not catch the Italian leader up ahead.

I knew Bandini would keep on charging, but trying to catch him would do nothing more than compromise my car. So I drove at my own pace, awaiting developments, and sure enough—suddenly there was Bandini, stopped beside the road at Thillois.

So then I was in the lead. The first driver ever in a car bearing his own name to lead a Championship Grand Prix. Parkes began to close, but I wasn't worried. I calculated the seconds he was gaining against the number of laps remaining, and the answer left me feeling almost serene, because I knew my Brabham-Repco had a little pace left in reserve.

And then I saw the chequered flag, and I'd not only won my first major-league Grand Prix since 1960, but also become the first driver ever to do so in a car bearing his own name. Denny coaxed his new car home third after stopping out on the circuit, and our little team could not have wished for better. That was such a special weekend—it made all the toil, effort, and disappointments seem worthwhile. One of the first people to congratulate me was John Cooper, another was Dan Gurney, and then Colin Chapman...we were engulfed, but that's the way it still was then in Formula 1.

We had always felt that our recipe of a simple, light, good-handling car with decently-drivable torque rather than sheer outright horsepower would do well on the more twisty, acrobatic circuits. That year's British Grand Prix was being run at Brands Hatch, ideal for us, and we prepared for that race fresh from our Reims win, and feeling very confident.

The Brands circuit was never in a condition for fast times, with oil dropped everywhere during practice. My fastest practice time (which I never approached in the race) was set on day one, but I always recall that 1966 British GP for the oil—it was like a skidpan out there. Ferrari stayed away, which disappointed me. I'm sure that

ABOVE
Enjoying the spoils of a job well done—our mechanics with the team's converted coach transporter pose on the Reims circuit before the drive home. Onboard are hundreds of bottles of Champagne—which HM Customs would overlook.

FOLLOWING PAGE
The 1966 British Grand Prix at Brands Hatch—the Driver-constructors lead the way on the opening lap through what was then known as Bottom Bend—my BT19, trailed by Dan Gurney's new Eagle, Denny…and the rest.

CASTROL
AVON TYRES AVON
AVON TYRES
FERODO
DAILY EXPRESS
Motor
CASTROL
CASTROL
CASTROL
MINTEX
CASTROL

had they been able to run there it would have removed any doubt about our ability to see them off! That weekend everything seemed to go just right. After our experiences through 1962–1965 this was barely credible. Virtually nothing had to be done to our cars, we didn't even have to change any gear ratios from those installed at the works. I qualified on pole, and Denny was alongside me in his new BT20-Repco—and Dan's lovely Eagle-Climax was on the outside.

When it drizzled with rain at the start, even that wasn't a worry. Our Goodyear tyres were good both wet and dry. Initially Dan pressed hard, then Jochen Rindt in his Cooper-Maserati. But even in the wet I was able to lead at my own pace, with performance in reserve. As the track dried, Denny and I actually found our advantage growing. I found it a rather lonely race, at least until the boys signalled me that Denny had moved into second place around half distance.

He'd had a tyre change just pre-race, and during the reconnaissance laps couldn't decide whether his tyres were going to be good in the wet or not. It was only as his confidence grew that he began to motor well. His new car still hadn't been fully sorted out, but we finished as a Brabham-Repco 1-2, just like our Brabham-Honda season in Formula 2. I really began to wonder if I was dreaming some of this. It was an extraordinary experience...even Ron was seen smiling.

But still the pressure was unrelenting. We had just eight days before the Dutch Grand Prix. Luckily, both Repco engines were OK, and at Zandvoort my BT19 went beautifully, both during practice and the race. Denny wasn't so fortunate, because his engine destroyed itself during the final practice session—when absolutely flat-out between main grandstand and pits! We diagnosed big-end bolt failure and the worry was whether one of my engine's might be about to go too. We couldn't do anything before the race. I therefore decided to drop our "safe" rev limit by 300-400rpm.

Throughout the race, the vision of Denny's blow-up was at the back of my mind, but I needn't have worried. We later adopted better-quality big-end bolts and nuts, but short-term we fitted our spare V8 in Denny's chassis overnight, and during race morning he did his best to run it in.

John Frankenheimer's MGM film unit was shooting footage for *Grand Prix* at the time, and less than two hours before the GP started, several of the competing cars went out for a filming session. Denny was poised to join them, when the reverse-gear idler shaft in his gearbox burst its way through the side of the casing.

We had no time to change the gearbox, so instead we put aluminium sheet on each side of the hole and a draw bolt through the middle to hold them together, then sealed everything off with some Japanese "goo". In the race this terrible lash-up worked perfectly, but his engine's ignition system packed up instead. We had run first and third, with Jim Clark's 2-litre Lotus trapped

ABOVE
Denny in his new BT20-Repco, topping Paddock Hill on his way to 2nd place in the 1966 British Grand Prix at Brands Hatch.

BELOW
Second consecutive Grand Prix win at the 1966 Dutch GP at Zandvoort. The BT19 was beautifully balanced and I loved its readiness to drift through fast curves.

ABOVE
Old Father Tyme—you should've seen the faces of everybody at Zandvoort when I limped to my car with this hook-on beard, using a jack handle as my walking stick. It was nice to show them all how life can begin at 40 by achieving our hat-trick win.

FAR RIGHT
Pre-German GP '66, in the pits at Nürburgring, comparing notes with Goodyear tyre technician Bert Baldwin.

between us, for many laps, but it was never as easy as Brands had been.

The circuit became even more oily and treacherous than Brands, and the extra power I had compared with Jimmy's special 2-litre Climax V8 just couldn't be used. So I decided it would be better to follow Jim than have him pursue me. I was content to let him lead while I waited for the surface to clean up. It didn't work out like that at all because more oil kept going down. At the time I thought that whoever was dropping so much oil would surely run out before the end, but more than one car must have been at it—no single oil tank could have held so much.

So I had to get stuck in. I pulled back Jimmy's lead, and found I could catch him, but I could see a haze blowing back from his Lotus, and retook the lead as he sailed into the pits for attention. After this I had no trouble and again it was a wonderful feeling to see the chequered flag flash by for the third Grand Prix in a row.

Incidentally, since I'd passed my 40th birthday that April, I had been reading a lot of newspaper stories about my being "the old man of motor racing" so before the start I walked to my car using a jack handle as a walking stick, and wearing a long, luxuriant clip-on beard. It raised a laugh. I certainly didn't feel old, and thought it would be good to make my point. Fortunately our race performance underlined it.

Three consecutive Grand Prix wins was fantastic. Harking back to 1960 in the *Lowline* Cooper, frankly this was better than I had hoped. At the start of the year I thought we might perhaps pick up one or two early races, because I couldn't see anyone—except perhaps Ferrari—sorting out their more complex new 3-litre cars until later in the season. But by Zandvoort it was beginning to look as though we might keep competitive, because that Repco V8 was proving just ideal. The higher-powered cars were expected to overwhelm us in the Italian Grand Prix at Monza, but the autodrome actually had more corners than Reims, so we did perhaps have a chance...even there in Ferrari's back yard.

I was looking forward to the Nürburgring—Brands Hatch on steroids—it should suit our cars pretty well, I thought. Until that time I had never enjoyed much luck at the German circuit, other than winning there as Stirling's understudy in the works Aston Martin sports car in 1958. How much racing cars had changed in the eight years since then!

Certainly practice there did not calm any apprehension we might have felt. Denny's engine had an internal blanking plug drop out, wedge itself between a couple of con-rods, which consequently wanted to go round and round together, so snapped. The resultant blow-up was even worse than Denny's Zandvoort disintegration, completely wrecking the Repco 620 block. But the nice thing about those production-based engines was that a new bare block cost about £11, while the basic Daimler con-rods were £7 each—it was almost poor-man's Grand Prix racing.

Irrespective, the replacement engine wasn't run-in. So Denny had to try for a decent grid position while running-in a fresh V8 on the last day of practice. We were naturally concerned about blanking plugs falling out in the other engines, so we secured them with grub screws. We needn't have bothered, because when we stripped all the engines the following week, only the one that failed had that particular type of plug.

My gearbox gave trouble in first practice, with the reverse gear hitting the layshaft. The second gear we had fitted for the Nürburgring was too big in diameter, and that failure cost me the rest of first day's practice. Next day I qualified on the front row and was quite happy sitting out the rest of the session in the pits until everyone else began flying and my time was bumped off the front row. So I rushed out again determined to improve, but didn't survive even the first lap. I broke fourth and fifth gear selectors—we later found they'd been formed from a bad batch of steel—and if I hadn't gone out to do that extra stint that failure would surely have put me out of the race on the opening lap next day!

Initially I thought the failure had been caused by faulty heat treatment, embrittling the metal. So we took all the gearbox dog rings into the little galley section in our transporter, and gave them some softening treatment over the gas ring. It was rather like cooking tea cakes, turning them over from time to time and seeing if they were done by the colour!

On raceday I managed to make a pretty good start from the second row. The circuit was wet, it was showery, and I was determined not to find myself driving blinded in someone else's spray. So I went for it, dived into the first corner third, chopped past Bandini's Ferrari for second, and closed on Surtees's tail in the leading Cooper-Maserati. Conditions were variable all round the 14-mile (20-km) circuit. Some sections were almost dry, others merely wet and several absolutely swimming. Out of the final right-hander before the long hump-backed straight I managed to get a good run on John's car and towed past him before the swerves leading out onto the broad pit straight. He tucked right in behind my gearbox past the pits and dived ahead under braking into the South Curve. This wasn't going to be easy.

I trailed him back behind the pits, down through the *Hatzenbach* and then—just beyond the Foxhole section—we came into a little right-hander. He got the Cooper crossed-up and I managed to dodge alongside and out-drag him to the next corner. My Goodyear tyres seemed to have an edge over his Firestones and just prior to the

FAR RIGHT
The golden helmet I wore in 1960, together with overalls and gloves from this period.

race we had made extra tread cuts in the tyres which I think did find me extra traction. For sure I had a more comfortable drive than John did in his Cooper but Denny's luck was out. His engine's badly adjusted timing-chain broke, due most probably to the hasty installation after all our practice dramas. And now that summer I'd won four Grands Prix in a row.

Three days later I was on an airliner to Australia, to race my BT19-Repco at the new Surfers' Paradise circuit near Brisbane. We had merely fitted a fresh engine in the car, and faced Jackie Stewart in David McKay's 2½-litre Brabham-Climax. I started the preliminary 10-lap race from pole position, led into the second lap—and my engine's distributor drive broke. That was disappointing, but I went down to Melbourne to see Repco, and spent a couple of valuable days with them.

I was back in Britain the following Thursday, then flew to the Karlskoga Formula 2 race next morning. Jim Clark went very well in his Lotus there—but Denny and I managed another Brabham-Honda 1-2. We felt by that time it was almost our right.

Monday morning back to Britain, Tuesday evening off to Finland for a new Formula 2 round at Keimola—run on Wednesday night. Situation normal—our Brabham-Hondas 1-2 again. Bank Holiday Monday Brands Hatch, the Guards Trophy for sports cars. Our little-used big-banger sports car had a completely rebuilt engine with "60-thou" over-bore, increasing capacity to 4.4-litres from 4.3. A top ring land cracked while I was running-in, we didn't have a spare engine, so the only thing we could do was fit a 3-litre Repco V8 for the race. I started it up in the pits, went to drive it to the starting line, and the ignition system failed. We had become so used to all the breaks going our way that season, that this was like a dowsing with ice-cold water. It reminded us of some motor racing realities we might have been in danger of forgetting.

For the Italian Grand Prix we took three cars—my regular BT19, Denny's BT20, and the just-completed second BT20. The latter still wasn't quite complete when we arrived.

In first practice we both had handling problems, since we'd fitted new springs without the time to set-up the chassis on them. On my very first lap I'd sailed straight on

LEFT
After you Alphonse—the pack jostling into the South Curve at the start of the 1966 German GP. That's the rear tyre of John Surtees's Cooper-Maserati just leading out of the picture (right) with me leading the pursuit. Jim Clark's Lotus (1) is trailed by Dan's Eagle, Jochen Rindt's Cooper-Maserati is (twin white stripes) behind me with Mike Parkes's Ferrari (10) to the right. Denny's striped helmet is just visible beyond Dan (left).

FAR RIGHT
Do as I do son, but not what I do. Geoffrey really wanted to race, and built himself a very substantial American career: 1981 CanAm Champion with a Lola, 10 Indy "500"s, including 5th place in 1981 and 4th in 1983, four-time IMSA GTP Champion 1988–89–90–91, but ultimately winning the Le Mans 24-Hours in a Peugeot in 1993. And in 1997 he and David together co-drove a BMW saloon to win what had become Australia's greatest race—the Bathurst 1,000.

RIGHT
The Brabham Racing Organisation's 1966 World Championship-winning team in our race shop at New Haw. We are (left to right) Bob Ilich from Perth, Western Australia, New Zealander Roy Billington, Hughie Absalom (Pom), three more Kiwis—John Muller, Cary Taylor, and Denny—then myself and Ron from Australia, John Judd (Pom), and Phil Kerr (Kiwi). Missing here is my fantastic BRO secretary, Christine McCaffrey, our absolute mainstay, without whom we wouldn't even have arrived at the races on time, never mind won any of them. She was absolutely brilliant for us, over many years. Given the chance, I'd race with them all again tomorrow.

CENTRE RIGHT
The 1966 World Championship presentation from Esso.

at the *Parabolica* Curve where, fortunately, there was an expansive run-off.

On the second day I did quite a few laps in the new BT20, which handled fine, but its engine wasn't as good as the BT19's. I qualified on row three, but I really wanted to be up with the boys when the slipstreaming began, and a tow from the front-row Ferraris would have been useful. I decided then to race the older chassis, and I had no problem as the race began in catching up with the leading, slipstreaming, bunch. By lap three I was second, right behind Surtees, and next lap I was leading. It seemed incredibly easy. I was only stroking the car, never above 7,600rpm, yet pulling away comfortably.

Then I spotted smoke in my mirrors. After just eight laps I whistled into the pits. The boys found an inspection plug had come adrift in the timing cover, losing a lot of oil—and I was out.

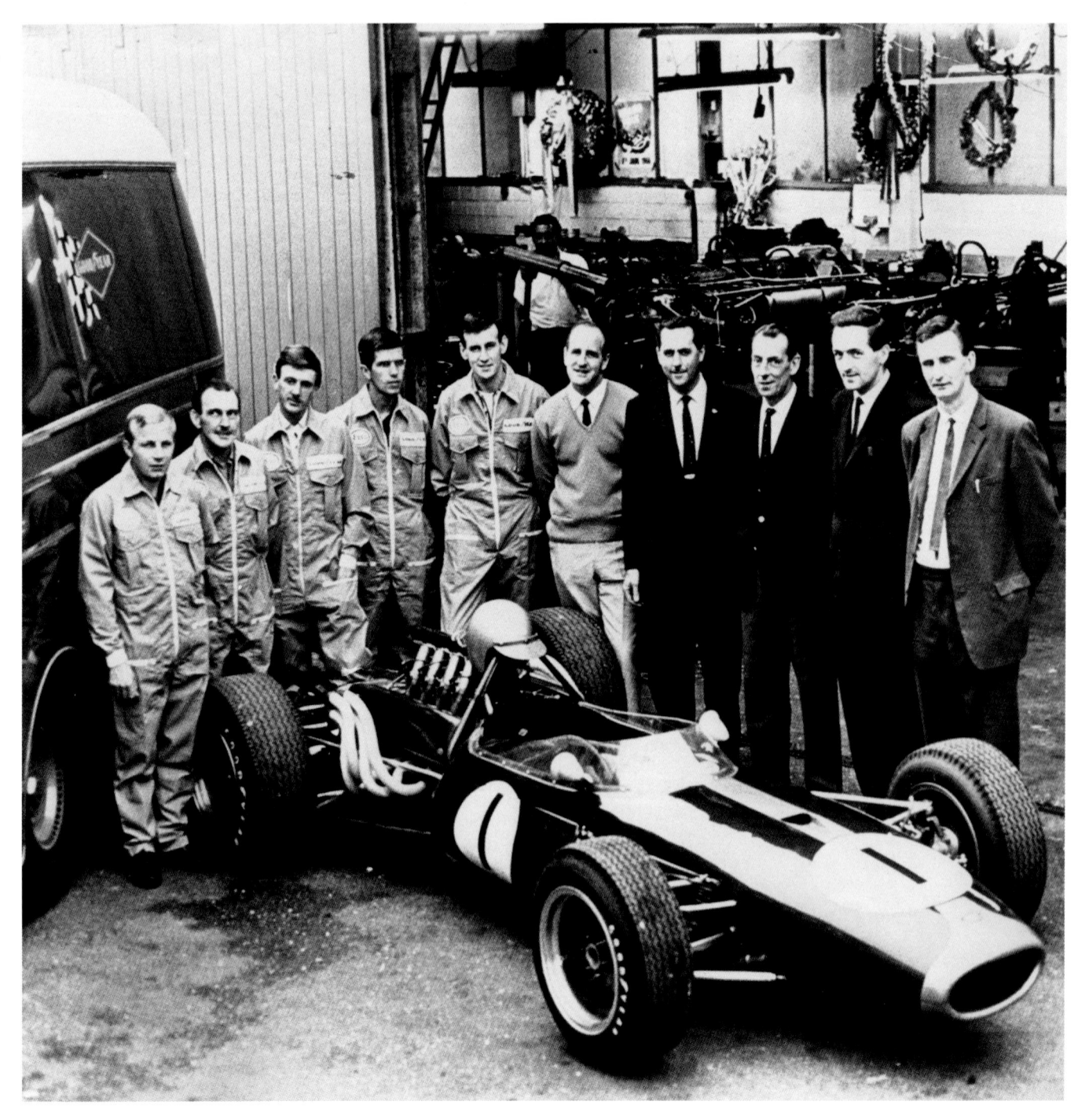

I then watched while the only drivers who could challenge my World Championship lead—John Surtees and Jackie Stewart—battled on. They both retired—and sitting there on the Monza pit counter I was suddenly World Champion again, for the third time, but how much I would have preferred to clinch it by winning that race.

Denny just failed to pip Mike Parkes's Ferrari for second place by three-tenths of a second. This was still a fantastic result though, I thought that was one of Denny's finest drives, because his BT20 was so out-gunned by Parkes's V12 Ferrari along those straights.

It's funny now looking back from a distance of nearly 40 years to recall my feelings that day. World Champion again, but this time in my own car—the car which Ron Tauranac had designed and built for me, and the car which we and our team had developed and run from stem to stern. Everything we had hoped for had slotted into perfect place. But we still had ambitions to continue racing, to win more races—and more Championship titles. The fire inside had not diminished, not one jot.

There was still races remaining to complete that fantastic Formula 1 season. The non-Championship Oulton Park Gold Cup was a complete Repco Brabham demonstration, as Denny and I not only finished 1-2 but shared fastest lap. We then made the annual trip to Watkins Glen for the United States Grand Prix, which I led early on from pole position, until a cam follower broke, while Denny's engine lost its oil pressure. Neither of us finished—quite a blow to our pride I must confess. And then in Mexico I led early on but just couldn't hold John Surtees's Cooper-Maserati once he'd found a way past me, and while he scored Cooper's first Grand Prix win in four years, I finished second, with Denny again third. What a year it had been.

CHAPTER 14
THE SEASON OF '67

Defending two World Champion titles—Repco Brabham again win one, while Jack loses the other to team-mate Denny

High flyer—Denny in our Repco Brabham BT24 on his way to victory in the 1967 German GP at the Nürburgring. This was a great 1-2 success for our Brabham Racing Organisation team and we scored similar 1-2s in France and Canada that season—in the correct order…yours truly first, Denny second. He still edged me out of the Championship that year, and Ron secured his back-to-back titles with MRD as Formula 1 Constructors' World Champion. These Formula 2-based BT24s were the best Formula 1 cars we ever built.

And so our team began the 1967 season as defending Formula 1 Constructors' World Champion. The new year's opening round was the South African Grand Prix at Kyalami—the high-altitude Johannesburg circuit replacing the old East London venue, down beside the Indian Ocean. My BT20 was flown down in virtual kit form and assembled there. Repco had fitted a new type of cam follower in my engine and in first practice a cam-follower guide came loose, fouled the camshaft, and damaged the head quite severely. We found a local machinist who turned-up some new cam-follower guides very efficiently, which we grub-screwed into place.

Denny and I both qualified on the front row, and with the track temperature up around 134°F we packed dry ice around the fuel tanks, rigged additional cooling ducts on both cars, and had lengths of 2½-inch (6-cm) diameter radiator hose directing cool air around the vital Lucas "bomb" fuel injection pumps.

Denny had really developed into a fine driver by that time and he completely dominated that Kyalami race. He led initially while I was wheel-to-wheel (literally) with John Surtees's big white Honda V12 for second. We touched at the end of the downhill straight and I fell back without losing third place. The second-place battle became really fierce between John, myself, and the Cooper-Maseratis of Pedro Rodriguez and Jochen Rindt. My engine began misfiring and I had to stop, rejoining with ice packed around my BT20's injection pump, and finished a distant sixth. Denny looked set to score his first Formula 1 win, until his brake pedal went straight to the bulkhead, he'd lost brake fluid. He was forced to make a long stop and finally finished fourth. Pedro Rodriguez inherited what would prove to be Cooper's last Grand Prix win.

The Tasman races followed, in which Repco introduced new "40-series" cylinder heads in which the ports were reversed, so that the inlets were on the outside of the engine. The exhausts all emerged from the top, in the centre of the engine's vee. These 40-series heads mounted on the established 600-series block, or Repco's own replacement block known as the 700-series—so by assembling different combinations of block and heads you could produce a "640" engine or a "740" engine.

Back in Britain we had a poor Race of Champions at Brands Hatch, more fuel injection trouble followed by an ignition wire coming adrift (again) while Denny's engine broke its timing chain. But we then dominated the Oulton Park Spring Cup charity meeting in a carbon copy of our Gold Cup performance the previous September. I won again, using 40-series centre-exhaust heads on a 600 block, with Denny second, and again we shared fastest lap.

At the Silverstone May meeting with an old 620 outside-exhaust engine I found I couldn't hold Mike Parkes' V12 Ferrari which just ran away with the race while I finished second. Both my engine and Denny's pumped oil out through the breathers, which was a mystery—it hadn't happened here the previous year and we using '66-spec engines again. Denny went off on oil at Stowe on the opening lap, denting the side of his BT20 and breaking an oil pipe.

BELOW
Repco V8 engine behind my shoulders in 1967, with young son Gary on my lap. He too would become a racer, building a considerable career and becoming the first British Formula 3000 Champion in 1989. That same year older brother Geoffrey won his second consecutive IMSA-GTP title in America and younger brother David the British Formula 3 Championship. That year I was a very proud father.

ABOVE

Arriving race ready in the pits at Monte Carlo before the 1967 Monaco Grand Prix. That's Denny leading the way in his outside-exhaust Type 620-engined Repco Brabham BT20, while I'm following in my sister BT20 fitted with Repco's latest centre-exhaust Type 740 engine. Denny will score his first World Championship-qualifying Grand Prix win…while my race will be extremely brief.

For Monaco I chose to race the old BT19 with the first type 740 3-litre engine installed, but the darned thing broke a con-rod on the opening lap. It threw me into a spin but curiously kept running on seven cylinders, and for once I really didn't appreciate quite what had happened so I limped back round to the pits, unaware I was larding most of the circuit with oil. I wasn't a very popular boy!

But meanwhile Denny danced around over the oil and cement-dust in his BT20 to score a superb victory, scoring nine Championship points, and winning his maiden Grand Prix at last to make up for his South African disappointment. That race was spoiled for everyone, however, by Lorenzo Bandini's fiery fatal accident when he just seemed to have worn himself out in his Ferrari pursuing Denny, and had misjudged the chicane and rolled.

Denny then went off to Indy where he finished brilliantly, fourth in the "500" driving an Eagle built by Dan Gurney's outfit, powered by a Ford 4-cam V8 engine. We took four cars to Zandvoort, our two BT20s, the old BT19, and Ron's prototype Formula 2-chassis sized BT24, but decided this new car wasn't quite ready to race just yet. I therefore drove the "Old Nail" BT19 instead, fitted with the centre-exhaust type 740 engine from the BT24. I finished second, but second to Jimmy Clark making his debut in the brand-new Cosworth-Ford V8-engined Lotus 49—which won first time out. The trouble for us was that the new design set entirely new performance standards, and it was plain that while I might have been worried about the bigger teams with their complex V12 and 16-cylinder engines the previous year. Here was a relatively simple but entirely state-of-the-art V8 which was going to make us really sweat.

Denny finished third there in his Monaco car, the last time we would run a BT20, and when he first drove it after his recent Indy experience he had to ask the boys to reassure him he'd driven it before, it felt so strange. This turned out to be because, unlike his Indy car, he found he could do anything he liked with the Repco Brabham, tossing it around with impunity.

He then took over my BT19 for the following Belgian Grand Prix, in which I gave the tiny little BT24 its race debut, while our newer BT20 was shipped out to South

Africa where it had been bought by Team Gunston for their national champion John Love to campaign.

At Spa both our engines drowned in their own oil with scavenge problems, which was disappointing. The bright side on a personal level was to see Dan Gurney score his first—and as it turned out, only—Grand Prix win there in his own Formula 1 Eagle. I knew how it felt to do that, and was really pleased for him. The fact that he'd won Le Mans for Ford the previous weekend capped that really memorable time for him. It couldn't have happened to a better man.

After Spa, the French Grand Prix at Le Mans (a weird affair run on a tight new circuit through the car parks of the 24-Hours course) was more fortunate for us. The new Lotus 49s driven by Graham Hill and Jimmy Clark were uncatchable, but they seemed to have very tender transmissions, and sure enough they dominated only until both went out with final-drive failure. Denny and I ran our two new BT24s together for the first time, and we were able to run away from the rest of the field—and it was quite like old times in Formula 2...Brabham and Hulme, 1-2. We'd modified the Repco engines' sumps and there was no repetition of the oil scavenging problem, the new cars' brakes were superb, and both just ran perfectly. It was another great weekend

Guy Ligier, a French privateer, bought Denny's old BT20 to replace his French-blue Cooper-Maserati in time for the British Grand Prix at Silverstone. Ligier became my favourite Formula 1 customer. He insisted I went out on the town with him one night in Paris, and we had a startling time—quite an eye-popper in fact for a colonial boy from Hurstville.

At Silverstone our works BT24s finished second and fourth, with Denny ahead of me and setting fastest lap. I came in for a bit of flak for having baulked Chris Amon's Ferrari for many laps but I honestly didn't know he was there—both my rear-view mirrors had fallen off! For much of the race I wondered what that strange high-pitched noise behind me might be!

In Germany, the Lotus 49s fell to bits under the battering from the Nürburgring surface and so Dan Gurney's Eagle seemed to have the race sewn-up until it broke while leading. This then gave Denny his second Grand Prix win of that season and myself another second place in his wheel tracks. When Denny stepped from his car after winning he caught the windscreen and broke it,

BELOW
C'mon Aussie—my former team mate (and long-time friend) Dan Gurney just shading me off the startline as the 1967 French Grand Prix begins on the short Bugatti circuit at Le Mans. I'm in my favourite Formula 1 Brabham—the wonderful little Formula 2-based BT24 with its centre-exhaust Repco Type 740 V8 engine. This is one race I'm going to win—and Denny will be second behind me in the sister BT24; another good day.

BELOW
Denny's BT24 is fuelled in the Nürburgring pits before the '67 German GP. He will score his second F1 win of that year, and I will finish second. We sat in these cars with aluminium fuel tanks strapped on each side, and that extra scuttle tank above our legs.

but even Ron didn't seem to mind, the team had done very well considering the pre-race drama we had suffered.

In practice I'd had quite a nasty moment when a rear suspension bolt broke at 150mph (240km/h), which left my car careering along on its belly for a very long distance. We changed all the bolts on both cars that evening and crack-tested everything—even the dampers. My new friend Guy Ligier was delighted with his new car, finishing sixth, scoring a Championship point.

For some reason the first Formula 1 Canadian Grand Prix had been slotted into the calendar between the German and Italian races. We therefore had to fly all our cars and kit across the Atlantic for it, then back again for Monza, before returning to America for the United States GP at Watkins Glen.

In preparation for that Canadian race one of our leading customers, former motorcycle racer Bob Anderson, was testing his Brabham-Climax 4-cylinder at Silverstone when he went off, hit a marshal's post, and was killed. Very much his own man, and a tough character, Bob had run a beautifully prepared car on a shoestring budget, and we were dismayed by this news.

The race at Mosport Park was run in torrential rain. Once again we profited from Lotus 49 failures. Our policy of careful preparation with small, simple, good-handling, lightweight cars paid off repeatedly that year. And so Denny and I scored our team's third 1-2 finish of that season, and this time I was ahead after Denny had stopped twice in the rain, first for a change of goggles, then for a visor, and he spun too.

The World Championship was developing into a straight fight between Denny and myself in our Repco Brabhams. But back in Europe for the Italian Grand Prix I found myself embroiled in a truly fantastic dice for what could easily have been my second consecutive GP win that year. Early in the piece we had spotted that Jim Clark had a rear tyre deflating on his Lotus 49. From right behind I could see it changing shape, and both Denny and I tried frantically to point out the problem whenever we could dart alongside. At last Jim got the message, and dived into the Lotus pits which left his new team-mate Graham, Denny, and I slipstreaming for the lead.

Denny's engine overheated and he dropped out, and then Graham's Ford engine exploded on the way into the 180-degree *Parabolica* turn leading round into the finish-straight. He spread oil all along the inside line, but the marshals promptly covered the spill with cement-dust to soak it up.

John Surtees's hurriedly built new V12 Honda showed good form there, and he had worked his way onto my tail, while my engine had over-revved slightly, losing its ultimate edge. Jimmy was driving an absolute blinder after his stop to change that punctured tyre, he'd regained an entire lap and passed us all to lead into the final lap. Less than two seconds covered Jimmy, John, and I as we screamed past the pits but then the Lotus abruptly hesitated and slowed, and was running out of fuel. In a flash John and I were past and dicing wheel-to-wheel for the win.

John's Honda led me out through the Ascari Curve down the back straight towards the *Parabolica* right-hander. He stayed wide on the left-side, daring me to take the inside line on that cement slick covering Graham's oil. I had no choice, of course, and I just stuffed it in there, knowing I'd be lucky to find some grip. It was a chance worth taking...but I found no grip at all. I slid straight on, John cut across behind my tail on his racing line through the right-hander and after a dicey bit of wheel twiddling around the outside verge I slammed back onto his tail. We blasted out of the *Parabolica* towards the finish line going absolutely hell for leather; he just had the edge, and beat me by a car's length—two-tenths of a second after 243 flat-out miles (390 kilometres) racing! It was a choker.

Denny had retired after leading when his car overheated, due we concluded to nothing less mundane than a water system pressure cap which was blowing-off too soon, but back at Oulton Park I won yet another Gold Cup. Frank Gardner drove our BT19 there, but retired from second place.

In the United States GP at Watkins Glen, we fitted 12-inch wide rear wheel rims in place of the previous 10-inch, while at the front we used narrower tyres we'd also run at Monza. The valve-gear failed on my engine in first practice, I ran our only available spare on the Saturday and then we fitted a fresh engine for the race, flown out to us that day. Denny's engine seemed to lose power early on, then cure itself and he wondered if he'd bent a valve at some point, which had later bent itself back straight again! I had a puncture, which lost me three laps, and Denny was signalled to ease off to preserve his tyres. Coming down the back straight on the last lap his engine began to starve and he coasted over the line, silent, to take third place. Had he stormed on at full pace, he would surely have run out earlier. We'd been quite unable to match the now reliable Lotus 49s, I finished fifth and the Drivers' Championship title then lay between Denny and myself into the last race at Mexico City.

I had to win to take what would have been my fourth World title, with Denny finishing lower than fourth, but he did the right thing and just glued himself to my tail, we finished second and third behind Clark's Lotus—although I had terrible worries about high oil temperatures—and Denny took his World Championship, with me as runner-up behind him. I was happy to see our cars, which Ron had designed so superbly, winning another Constructors' Championship. If I couldn't emulate my back-to-back Drivers' Championship success of 1959–1960, at least we had matched the Cooper Car Company's back-to-back Constructors' titles. One Formula 1 race remained that season, a non-Championship event at Madrid's new Jarama circuit, in Spain. I drove my old BT19 there—and I was blown off by Jimmy and Graham in the Lotus 49s, and finished third. I was best of the rest again—never a position I enjoyed. During the later part of that season—in between his Formula 1 commitments with us—Denny had driven the new Gulf-McLaren sports-cars in the lucrative new North American Can-Am series, as team-mate to Bruce McLaren. Of course they were both Kiwis, and old friends, and when Denny told me he had signed with Bruce for Formula 1 in 1968 it didn't really come as a surprise, and I wished him well.

For the new year—1968—our Brabham Racing Organisation would have a new second driver, and the man we chose was a driver already completely at home in Brabham cars. He was the King of F2, Jochen Rindt.

ABOVE
Cresting Deer's Leap at Oulton Park in Ron's wonderful BT24 design—and I'm heading towards my fourth Gold Cup win in Cheshire's non-Championship Formula 1 classic. I used to fly up to the picturesque Park and land in the neighbouring field. One year here, flying a Comanche with young Geoffrey as passenger, I arrived overhead quite late and didn't recognise the grass was wet until we touched down. The Oulton lake was rushing up, but I managed to tweak the Comanche slightly sideways to scrub off speed, and ended-up half-spinning it to rest with its wheels about 6 feet from the lakeside, and one wing projecting over the water. The memory's particularly vivid for Geoffrey.

FORMULA TWO WAS FUN 1964–1970

ABOVE
Our most successful year in Formula 2—and we had several good ones—was 1966 when our exclusive use of Honda's exceptional new 4-valve per cylinder roller-bearing 4-cylinder engine produced fantastic results. Here in my works Brabham-Honda BT18 I'm eyeing-up the next apex at Crystal Palace pursued by Alan Rees's Cosworth-engined Winkelmann team Brabham.

I had always enjoyed competing in motor racing's second division of single-seater racing, Formula 2. It was a 1½-litre class from 1957–1960, which then effectively became the new Formula 1 of 1961–1965. Established Formula 1 drivers in those days were "graded" by the FIA, which meant we were not allowed to compete in less than full International events, and definitely not in the new "schoolroom" class of Formula Junior. However, come 1964, the FIA replaced Formula Junior with two new rungs on the single-seater racing ladder—1-litre Formula 3 for racing cars with very modestly-tuned production-based engines, and 1-litre Formula 2 which still required production cylinder blocks, but permitted special cylinder heads and many other modifications providing more power. While in Formula 3 graded drivers were not allowed to compete, in Formula 2 we could race against private owners, new boys, and veterans alike. And a terrific class of racing it was too.

Through its first season in 1964, our cars, Lotus, Cooper, and Lola each enjoyed victory at some stage, powered every time by the Cosworth-Ford SCA engine. Most successful drivers were Jim Clark and myself, with four wins apiece. *Autocar* magazine backed a Championship based on the six British rounds, but that year's Formula 2 sensation was a self-confident 22-year old Austrian named Jochen Rindt. He drove a customer "Brabham" which BP Austria had helped him buy. Most of the time he looked completely out of control, an accident looking for somewhere to happen, but lap after lap he looked exactly the same, and we soon realised he probably wasn't going to fall off, and was really quick.

Over the British Whitsun holiday weekend he put his Brabham on pole at Mallory Park only to stall at the start and finish third, but at Crystal Palace that Monday he made no mistakes and beat Graham Hill's Noddy Coombs-entered Cooper. Such success by an unknown youngster in a customer car was fine justification for Formula 2.

Our works team Formula 2 season was also progressing well. I'd had my first bash—literally!—at it in Austria on 12 April at Vienna's Aspern aerodrome, one of the roughest tracks I ever raced on. In the very first corner Tony Maggs spun his Lola and knocked off one of my rear wheels. We managed to weld-up the wishbones in time to go again in

FORMULA TWO WAS FUN 1964–1970

Heat Two, which I won from Maggs and Dickie Attwood. This was the first victory for Ron's new Formula 2 Brabham BT10.

It was plain there was going to be some pretty hard and tight racing in Formula 2, because these underpowered cars were reasonably easy to drive. Everybody travelled at about the same speed down the straights, then just scrambled round the corners in a mob—so outright driving skill became the key.

At Reims that July, Denny Hulme and I ran our two Formula 2 BT10 works cars. There were 50 bottles of champagne for the fastest time set in the first half-hour of practice, and 100 bottles for anybody who managed to better that time. I set fastest time in the first half-hour to win the 50 bottles, but it proved so quick that try as I might I couldn't improve on it, and neither could anyone else—in effect I'd done myself out of 50 bottles of bubbly.

The fastest part of the Reims circuit was the long downhill straight—actually the main Reims-Soissons road—into Thillois Corner, down which our little 1-litre cars were hitting 142mph (229km/h). Slipstreaming effect could be felt at considerable range. To break another car out of your "tow" you had to pull at least 400 yards (435 metres) ahead of it.

Towards the end of the race Alan Rees, in Roy Winkelmann's private Brabham, and I had managed to break some 500 yards (545 metres) clear of the pursuing pack and he led into Thillois, the final right-hander entering the long, undulating finish straight. I was hoping to slipstream him out of that corner and slingshot ahead at the line, but he was playing the same game. We both crept unbelievably slowly round Thillois, and when he booted it for the line I couldn't quite get by and he won by half a length.

Earlier in that race we'd been involved in a slipstreaming bunch of at least eight cars. It had been really dangerous because it was so easy to be distracted by one and clip another. Peter Arundell had a terrible crash, which really ended what had seemed a potentially dazzling career. Denny in our second car finished fifth.

He then won at Clermont-Ferrand, beating Lotus's latest hope Jackie Stewart, while Frank Gardner's Brabham won a Heat at Enna, Sicily, and Jo Schlesser's won the Rome GP at Vallelunga. I won at Karlskoga in Sweden, Albi in France, the Oulton Park Gold Cup, and the final race of the year at Montlhéry. Ron was very good at sharing technical information and advice with our Formula 2 customers, and sometimes I wondered if that was wise—one or two them made me work really hard.

1965 season

For 1-litre Formula 2's second season, we had a secret weapon—a new Honda 16-valve engine. It seemed rather large and ungainly, the Japanese designers had some difficulty fitting its ancillaries neatly into the chassis, but Honda agreed to send over three technicians with the engines for the British and European season.

At Oulton Park the new unit refused to rev, and its in-house fuel injection leaned out in the race, which holed a piston. Denny pulled off a great win there with a Cosworth engine, but at Snetterton the Honda began to perform, though gearing was absolutely critical and I had to keep it above 9,000rpm to pull properly. Its throttle linkage then vibrated apart. After setting a new lap record I was out.

That original rod linkage was replaced by cables but engine vibration simply broke them too. This put me out at Pau, and sadly, those 1965-series Honda Formula 2 engines just didn't do the job. Through the 1965 season, both Brabham and Lotus Formula 2 cars won five races each, Lola three, and the small Alexis marque the other. Jimmy Clark drove the winning Lotus every time, while five different drivers won in Brabhams. Despite their greater frontal area and outboard-mounted spring and dampers interrupting airflow through the front suspension, our cars seemed aerodynamically better than the slimline Lotuses.

At Reims, Jimmy had used a Cosworth engine that claimed to deliver 130bhp, but beyond 140mph (225km/h) he was simply overwhelmed by both the Roy Winkelmann Brabhams of Rindt and Rees. Jimmy complained vehemently about the treatment they gave him—they really worked him over—but he'd been the first to laugh when Graham Hill had spun at Thillois after being hung out to dry on the outside line.

Journalist Bill Gavin wrote of that season: "For consistently splendid performances Jack Brabham was possibly the best. There's no getting away from the fact he is probably now a better driver than he was during his reign as World Champion. He really seems to enjoy F2 and tries his utmost on nearly every occasion." Nice of him to think so.

FORMULA TWO WAS FUN 1964–1970

In fact, while Jim Clark and Lotus won that year's *Autocar* Formula 2 Championship, Graham Hill was runner-up in one of our Brabhams owned and run by Noddy Coombs, Denny was third, and I placed ninth, after suffering all kinds of dramas with our new Japanese "secret weapon". The 1965 Honda engines were neither driveable nor reliable, but Mr Nakamura and his men listened to us, and would do a brilliant job in 1966.

1966 season

At the end of 1966, Formula 2 reporter Simon Taylor wrote: "Jack Brabham's driving skill and the power of the twin-cam roller-bearing Honda engine brought the Formula 1 World Champion a domination that was ever more marked than his run of victories in *Grandes Epreuves*. At the end of the 1965 season the Honda engine was just beginning to show its paces...in 1966 it was a winner from the word go, and failed to win only one race in which it was entered, by a fifth of a second. Brabham...won 10 out of that 13."

I'd retired twice, at Rouen and Le Mans, both times while leading, and, "...On both occasions Denny Hulme, the ideal team-mate, was ready...to take over the lead and win the race. Denny scored six second places behind Brabham...the spaceframe Brabham BT18 proved to be the perfect chassis to handle the Honda's power...and at Karlskoga Brabham switched to car No 'F2/1/67', the prototype BT21, which he continued to use for the rest of the season."

But one thing most reporters got wrong that year, was my reason for retirement at Rouen. It really impressed Nakamura and our mechanic Nobuhiko Kawamoto—who would rise through the ranks to become President of Honda. After retiring at the trackside, I fiddled about to remove the gear-lever retaining pin, and then carried the lever back to the pits. In front of waiting pressmen I handed it to Nakamura. The inference was that it had fallen off—our fault, not his. When the press had dispersed I put my arm round his shoulders and whispered the truth: "Your perishing engine broke its crank." I knew Honda was paranoid about mechanical failures being publicised, and I couldn't have done better on their behalf...they were more impressed with me than if I'd merely won another race for them.

Late that season Denny was driving Sid Taylor's big Lola-Chevrolet sports car in North American CanAm racing so we gave a promising young driver named Chris Irwin his F2 place. He finished third at Albi. Two of the three races our Brabham-Hondas didn't win went to Cosworth-engined Brabhams run by Winkelmann Racing and driven by Jochen Rindt and Alan Rees.

In the final race of the year at Brands Hatch, Jochen and I had a fantastic dice. I led the Final for the first 26 laps with Jochen right up my exhaust and often alongside,

RIGHT
Enjoying dominant performance—Formula 2 racing for me was racing for fun...and it was easy to enjoy the Brabham-Honda, as captured here by Nick Loudon's camera, it was the ideal racing package.

FORMULA TWO WAS FUN 1964–1970

until a backmarker momentarily baulked me, Jochen was by in a flash and try as I might I couldn't repass. A couple of times we actually plummeted round Paddock Hill Bend—a dicey corner at the best of times—perfectly side-by-side, with our wheels interlocked; unbelievable! But we had total confidence in each other—it was brilliantly enjoyable. I'd been baulked at the last gasp by backmarker Chris Lambert, who pointed to the left as we came upon him at Clearways, then moved left, shouldering me straight off onto the grass because I'd taken his signal to mean I should pass him on that side! Jochen was by, and there just wasn't time for me to catch him again. I was pretty unhappy about that. Poor young Lambert was killed later in a Formula 2 accident at Zandvoort. But for us and Honda 1966 had been a truly fantastic season...even better than for us and Repco in Formula 1.

1967 Formula 2

Formula 2 was revised from the start of 1967 season with new 1.6-litre regulations. The only viable engine became the latest 4-cylinder 16-valve Cosworth-Ford FVA.

It was absolutely Jochen's year in his Winkelmann Racing Brabham-Cosworth. He won nine of his 15 races, and took both the British and French titles. Our latest BT23 chassis was the dominant car, winning 11 of the 24 races, and Jochen's team-mate Alan Rees won the British *Autocar* Championship title. I did 15 races but suffered much engine trouble. I salvaged just two second places, at Langenlebarn in Austria and Hameenlinna in Finland, plus fourths at Zolder in Belgium and Madrid in Spain. Frank Gardner was our hope to win the non-graded driver European Championship, but he was edged out by Jacky Ickx, and also placed second in the *Autocar* Championship to Rees.

At Jarama for the Madrid round Frank had a very lucky escape when his onboard fire extinguisher got so hot inside his car that the bottle exploded in his cockpit. I was ribbing him about it in our pit garage immediately after the race when my car's bottle detonated as well! That really wiped the smile off my face.

My most vivid memory is of the Rouen slipstreaming battle between Clark, Hill, Rindt, and myself which we took turns to lead. We all noticed Jim's right-rear tyre going down, more of the rim becoming visible as the tyre changed shape. Jim was a genius driver but to me had no mechanical feel. As we swopped places we all took it in turns to point it out to Jimmy who was more untidy every lap. Rouen had very fast downhill curves just beyond the pits. Jimmy had just got the lead again and I decided no way could he stay on the road so I backed off and let them go. Sure enough, he lost it on the first left-hander and hit the barriers. They all shot by but, because I'd dropped back, his car bounced clean into my path so I knocked-off its nose and radiator, and cannoned to the inside, straddling a drain with me steering feverishly to prevent one side dropping in and turning my car over. Jim and I walked back to the pits together, a great relief to my parents who were in the stand opposite. The hysterical French commentary hadn't helped!

Jimmy would suffer another undiagnosed puncture at Monza that year, and at Hockenheim the following April he was killed by one. I'm convinced his ability to control whatever his car might do, regardless of his apparent inability to diagnose the cause, contributed to his death.

At the time I'd stopped racing in Formula 2, and I was actually airborne, flying myself back from Hamble near Southampton, when air traffic control broke the news to me. Jim Clark was dead. Absolutely unbelievable...that was a sad, sad day.

Out latest BT23C customer cars kept the "Brabham" banner flying high. Jochen's Winkelmann Racing car won six of the 17 1968 races, and Jonathan Williams another in a car entered by young Frank Williams.

During 1969 Jochen again dominated as a driver but this time in Lotus chassis. Leading Brabham driver was Piers Courage driving Frank Williams's BT23C and BT30 cars, and then in my final professional season in 1970, I returned to the fray more or less for old time's sake, driving my old friend Noddy Coombs's Brabham BT30 in three races only—at Pau (retired), Rouen (8th), and, finally, at Tulln-Langenlebarn in Austria. I finished 2nd in Austria to Clay Regazzoni's very quick Tecno in Heat One and then had a tremendous dice with Jacky Ickx's works BMW in Heat Two. I took the lead and drew away until François Cevert's Tecno came through with just three laps to run. Second place would have been fine, if I finished there I'd still win overall on aggregate but—on the very last lap, just as at Monaco and Brands Hatch in Formula 1 that year—my car faltered. An injector pipe failed, and Ickx's BMW screamed past. I finished 3rd in the Heat, so Ickx won overall and I was 2nd on aggregate. Which was how my Formula 2 career finally ended...darn it.

Jochen Rindt in full flight in our Repco Brabham BT26 during practice for the 1968 Canadian GP at Ste Jovite. He's hard on the brakes with his car nose down, tail up, pushing the normally dihedral centre-hinged rear wing into the anhedral position seen here, and about to qualify on pole position for the second time that season, the first time having been at Rouen for the French race, but every time our 4-cam V8 engine's unreliability will prevent real success. Jochen— killed at Monza in 1970— was a brilliant racing driver and a great bloke whose memory I really cherish.

CHAPTER 15

GOODBYE REPCO

A season of catastrophic unreliability ends Repco's memorable three-year Formula 1 career, but Jochen Rindt proves they can still shine

For 1968 Repco had two avenues of approach. One was for a short-stroke magnesium-block engine, and the other was for a daring new cylinder head design, using a radial valve disposition. The latter frightened Ron and myself since it would have a bunch of eight small-bore exhaust pipes emerging inside the vee, and four more exiting below the heads outside the vee on either side.

Back within the vee there would have been eight induction trumpets fighting for space with all those exhausts, plus another four trumpets outboard each side as well. This would have been an installation nightmare and we feared Repco's engineers were beginning to get carried away—losing sight of the simplicity which had served us so superbly for two seasons. The Repco engineers finally opted to combine the proven aluminium blocks with twin-overhead camshaft, four-valve per cylinder heads; without the complex radial layout, or the short stroke.

So the radial-layout type 50 heads were shelved, and Repco (who had a lot of originality inside them, fighting to get out) adopted a more conventional 60-series design, using twin overhead camshafts for each bank of four cylinders, and conventional four-valve per cylinder layout, with neatly tucked-away outside exhausts and the Lucas injection gear un-cluttered within the vee. They mounted these heads on the new 800-series block, which was fully 1½-inches (4-cm) shallower than the 600/700s. Despite having a hefty gear-train now to drive the four camshafts instead of the two-cam V8s' original, light and simple timing chain, the new 800-series engine was considerably lighter, and was suitable only for 2.5 and 3-litre capacities, not the big sports car 4.3/4.4-litres as before.

The first 800-series block to be raced was cast in magnesium and we used it in the 1968 Tasman series, but in Formula 1 it would eventually run out of water and become distorted. However, time spent on these developments cost the quad-cam Repco V8 programme dearly. Our 1968 season in Formula 1 subsequently staggered from problem to problem.

Ron had designed a new car The objective was to produce a lighter but stronger chassis using alloy-sheet stress paneling instead of tubular triangulation as before.

LEFT
The growing family—with Betty and the boys, Geoffrey, Gary, and David, at our home in Pyrford, Surrey, for some publicity shot or other. Even the most down to earth racing driver has to do these things from time to time.

ABOVE
Jochen diving into the *Tabac* left-hander on the Monte Carlo quayside during the 1968 Monaco GP. There he had qualified fifth and ran fourth in the opening stages before trying to overtake John Surtees's V12 Honda into Mirabeau. He locked-up his brakes on some oil and hit the barrier. I'd already retired with a rear radius rod detached. I'd been sitting on the starting grid when I noticed a bolt in the rear suspension without a nut. With the grid cleared, engines running, there was nothing I could do about it.

RIGHT
Guest driver—with his own AAR Eagle programme losing impetus, Dan Gurney rejoined us for the Dutch GP, driving the year-old spare BT24. He'd run as high as sixth for many laps but spun several times, partly due to his goggles coming loose, and ended up off-road, with sand clogging the throttle slides.

This allowed use of smaller-gauge, thinner-section tubes for the basic frame with riveted-on sheet paneling to stiffen it all up. It was a kind of move towards monocoque construction, while still retaining the simplicity and easy repair features of our spaceframe designs. In retrospect Ron thought it might have been cheaper to build a monocoque like everyone else.

Our new team driver in Denny's place was Jochen Rindt, the Austrian driver who had dominated Formula 2 racing in Brabham cars, and who was delighted to join us after three pretty fraught seasons with Cooper. I knew he was one hell of a driver, and we'd had some tremendous Formula 2 dices together. I was happy to race against him with one of his wheels almost in the cockpit with me, and vice versa it seemed. He was absolutely fearless, tremendously talented and just a really good bloke. Above all he was 100 per cent racer, through and through, and I was perfectly happy with that. I was confident that if we could provide him with the tools he'd do as good a job for us as Dan and Denny had before.

We ran the old BT24s in the Championship opener at Kyalami, where Jochen immediately finished strongly in third place. We then sold the old cars locally to Team Gunston for the Rhodesian driver Sam Tingle, and to the Lawson Organisation for Basil van Rooyen to race in their national F1 Championship series there.

Our new BT26 prototype made its debut in practice at Jarama in Spain where it blew-up when a valve insert dropped in, leaving Jochen in our sole remaining BT24 to retire when its Repco 740 engine lost oil pressure. He crashed the same car in the following race at Monaco, where I had to retire when a radius rod pick-up failed on the BT26.

This wasn't quite the season start we'd hoped for, but in Belgium we were able to run two quad-cam Brabham-Repco BT26s for the first time. Jochen's leaked its water and failed, while fuel feed problems ended my race. During practice I'd had another valve insert detach, and Repco decided the material was shrinking, causing the problem. So I flew home overnight, while John Judd and Norm Wilson (over from Melbourne) collected a new engine from Heathrow. We tore it down overnight with the help of Roy Billington and our machinist Ron Cousins came in to our Guildford race shop to fit the new parts. He'd been with HRG in the old days who did all the original Repco 620 work in Britain, and he'd joined our Brabham Racing Organisation when HRG gave up. I took the new heads home to heat in Betty's domestic oven. When she woke up next morning and found her house full of acrid fumes I was pretty glad to be going as deaf as I already was.

At Zandvoort, a wet Dutch Grand Prix saw Jochen showing his class in practice, qualifying on the front row of the grid, only 0.16 of a second slower than Chris Amon's Ferrari, while I got onto row two, but we nearly didn't make it at all.

Just after our transporter had left for Dover, a message arrived from Melbourne saying there was not enough static clearance between the pistons and the valves in the 860 engines, and that the two would meet when started-up. So I bought a suitable wood chisel from a hardware store in Guildford, and when we got to Zandvoort the boys lifted the cylinder heads and chiselled down the piston crowns to ensure just the necessary clearance. The error hadn't been big, but it could have destroyed both engines in a moment.

The alternator shafts on both cars were found to be dodgy, so we had to race without the rotors in place. My car's fuel feed system was still giving trouble, which meant I had to use the electrical pumps all the time instead of just for starting, which flattened my battery because it

LEFT
Heart of the problem—the troublesome 32-valve 4-cam Repco Type 860 engine in our 1968 BT26 car (foreground) contrasted against the still reliable World Championship-winning 2-cam Type 740 centre-exhaust engine in our spare BT24 beyond. The latest 3-litre Formula 1 engine's new gear-train driving the twin overhead camshafts per bank lived in a vibration period which destroyed the rearward cam followers. In contrast the enlarged 4.2-litre 4-cam Repco V8 for Indianapolis and its larger 5.1-litre sports-car racing sister operated in a lower rev range, in which the cam-drive gears survived.

BELOW
Our best race of the 1968 season was the German GP, run in appalling wet and misty conditions on the Nürburgring. Jochen had already done well by qualifying on pole at Rouen, now he was third fastest qualifier on the front row, and survived the race at last—glory be!—to finish third, and I was fifth. I always like racing in the wet. My greatest attribute had always been keen eyesight and I could read a track surface well. In the dry I could spot oil (well, most of the time!) and in the wet I was less wary than others.

wasn't being charged since the alternator was out of operation. In the wet, I spun and stalled, and couldn't restart, while Jochen just hated the conditions and gave up. Dan Gurney returned to our team for that race—his Formula 1 Eagle project being on its last legs—and he drove the spare two-cam BT24, left the road, got some sand in the throttles and after some hairy moments with them sticking open, also retired. Little Swiss privateer Silvio Moser—who had bought the ex-Ligier BT20—soldiered on through all this Brabham mayhem to finally finish fifth.

At Rouen, the French race was run in even heavier rain, but Jochen really set us on fire by qualifying on pole position, proving there was nothing wrong in principle with our quad-cam BT26. Unfortunately his fuel tanks split before he got into his stride, and my car's fuel feed problems persisted and finally put me out as well. We suspected that when the tanks in my car were full to the brim for the race, an air vent was becoming blocked and the engine pumps just didn't have sufficient suction to overcome the vacuum they were trying to create within the tank.

But we just weren't achieving anything. At Brands Hatch for the British Grand Prix my engine's right-hand exhaust camshaft threw its drive-gear after one lap (an assembly fault), and Jochen's car actually caught fire after a pump failure. In Germany we spotted a cracked titanium valve-spring retainer just 90 minutes before the start, there was a spare engine in the transporter and in a mad scramble we managed to swop over the two units' cylinder heads. The car was back together with 10 minutes to spare, and Jochen splashed round in the atrocious conditions which characterized that 1968 German Grand Prix, and he finished brilliantly third while I was fifth in our team's best race of the year. The cool, dank, dark, soaking wet conditions probably helped cool everything on our cars and the quad-cam Repco engines survived race distance for the first time.

We knew that Monza for the Italian Grand Prix would present an infinitely more gruelling challenge, and—sure enough—there my brand-new engine ran its centre main bearing, while Jochen's broke a gudgeon pin, which collapsed the piston, shattered a cylinder liner, and generally caused terrific damage as the engine exploded. In fact when my engine was stripped one gudgeon pin was found in three pieces; luckily I must have switched off literally a split-second before my engine would have destroyed itself.

Monza was unusual that very wet year in having been a dry race, and it was the first time that the Repco 860 engines had been run at anything like full-bore for any length of time. John Judd adopted replacement pins from a Petter diesel engine, which Ron Cousins again machined to fit, solving the problem. Cam follower wear had been found on the Alfa Romeo-made components which had been used since 740 days, and this now became the quad-cam engine's latest bug-bear.

But at Ste Jovite in Canada Jochen was again on terrific form, he ripped around to qualify on pole position yet again, only to have brake problems and overheating force him out of second place. I had a suspension failure. In practice Ron had asked me to try Jochen's car since it apparently "felt strange". A steering arm broke and I slid off and hit the bank.

That had been a bear of a year for us. We were eager to finish at Watkins Glen where the United States GP always paid well, but only if you finished.

Both of us used 1,000rpm less than the customary limit to conserve the engines, but mine broke a cam follower, and Jochen's threw a rod. The Mexican Grand Prix put the cap on that year, as Jochen's engine broke after only two laps, and I was nursing mine round in third place only to have excessive oil consumption leave my engine dry before the finish. As the oil pressure zeroed I switched off and retired, but was classified tenth and last.

That four-cam engine had always been unable to drain oil quickly enough from the heads. So much got trapped up there it caused extra leakage down the valve guides, and the BT26's oil tank just was not big enough to last the distance.

By that time I was queuing up to buy Cosworth-Ford DFV engines for the coming year. Gulf Oil—our new sponsor—were keen for their star driver Jacky Ickx to join us. Jochen had received an offer we couldn't match to sign for Lotus and Ford. So off he went, and in came Ickx. This wasn't quite the end of the trail for the Formula 1 Repco-Brabhams. The privately-owned BT20s and BT24s raced on through 1969–1970, and early in 1969 I would finish third in a Tasman round at Sandown Park, Melbourne, using a tiny Formula 3-based BT31 with an 830 V8 engine. Later that year I returned to drive the same car in the Bathurst "100" which I won easily to sign-off our Repco-Brabham story on a high note.

In reality, the 12,000-mile (19,300-kilometre) gulf between Repco in Melbourne and our race shop in Guildford had proved an insuperable obstacle to competitive race development.

Repco later rested on its hard-won double-World Champion laurels, and concentrated on the service of their Tasman and Indianapolis V8s, and production of a Holden-based Formula 5000 engine before becoming submerged in a chain of take-overs and mergers.

The modern ACL company fell heir to my old BT19, and occasionally today they invite me to demonstrate it for them. I am always happy to oblige.

LEFT
Studying the opposition in my rear-view mirror—ready to take to the Monza Autodrome circuit in practice for the 1968 Italian Grand Prix, ahead of a works Lotus 49. Colin Chapman ran three cars there—for Graham Hill (who would clinch his second World Champion title in the closing race at Mexico City), Jack Oliver who had taken the place made vacant by the death of Jim Clark that April, and American guest star Mario Andretti. The new front and rear wings—designed by BAC aerodynamicist Ray Jessop in conjunction with Ron—troubled me, but we had to keep pace with Chapman's daring. We discarded them here after a few practice laps.

1968 INDIANAPOLIS REPCO BRABHAM BT25

For 1968 Goodyear were keen that Brabham should return to the Indy fray, while F1 team driver Jochen Rindt was intrigued by the prize money offered. Indy racing ruled fuel tanks had to be sheathed in metal panelling, so Ron Tauranac designed a stressed-skin monocoque chassis structure in place of his normal multi-tubular spaceframe practise. Repco developed a special 4.2-litre version of the latest 4-cam 32-valve V8 engine. In the BT25, this power unit was slung in a tubular engine-bay frame. Jochen and Masten Gregory were listed to drive two BT25s but only Rindt qualified, 16th fastest at 164.144mph. And after just five race laps he retired with piston failure.

In 1969 two developed BT25s were driven at Indy by Jack and Peter Revson, who started from 33rd—at 160.851mph (258.865km/h)—yet finished fifth. Within weeks Peter drove in the USAC road races at Indianapolis Raceway Park and won one outright, finishing third in the other. In the "500" Jack's BT25 qualified 29th at 163.875mph (263.732km/h), but retired after 58 laps with ignition problems.

TECHNICAL SPECIFICATION

Manufactured by Motor Racing Developments Ltd.
Engine: Repco V8; 4 valves per cylinder; 2 overhead camshafts per bank; bore and stroke dimensions 96.2mm x 71.9mm, displacement volume 4,120cc; Power output circa 550bhp @ 8,500rpm on methanol fuel.
Transmission: Hewland 3-speed and reverse.
Chassis: Stressed-skin monocoque forward nacelle with tubular spaceframe engine bay.
Suspension: independent front and rear suspension by wishbones and co-axial coil-spring/dampers.
Brakes: Discs all round.
Wheels: Cast magnesium-alloy to Brabham design.
Tyres: Goodyear

1968 INDIANAPOLIS REPCO BRABHAM BT25 | 223

LEFT
The United States Auto Club's technical regulations enforced at Indy included requirement for the "nerf bar" protecting the car's tail and gearbox from damage which could create oil spillage onto the high-speed track.

ABOVE
Indy saw the invention of the racing rear-view mirror when the winner of the Speedway's inaugural 500-Mile classic in 1911, Ray Harroun, dispensed with a riding mechanic and drove his Marmon single-handed without the second man "on lookout". The BT25 sports its modern descendant.

BELOW
Ron Tauranac's first monocoque-chassised Brabham also displays his clear-sighted aerodynamic appreciation with its downswept nose form and modest, yet effective, "ducktail" spoiler on the engine cover. While the forward chassis nacelle is the stressed-skin monocoque, the BT25's engine bay was multi-tubular.

RIGHT
As sleek as could be, the BT25 was unusual for a Brabham in having its front suspension coil-springs and dampers tucked away inside the bodywork, out of the airstream through the front suspension members.

RIGHT
The BT25 was powered by a 4.2-litre version of Repco's 1968 3-litre "4-cam" Formula 1 V8 engine, with twin overhead camshafts per cylinder bank driven by spur-gears instead of the chains which the 2-cam World Championship V8s of 1966–1967 had employed.

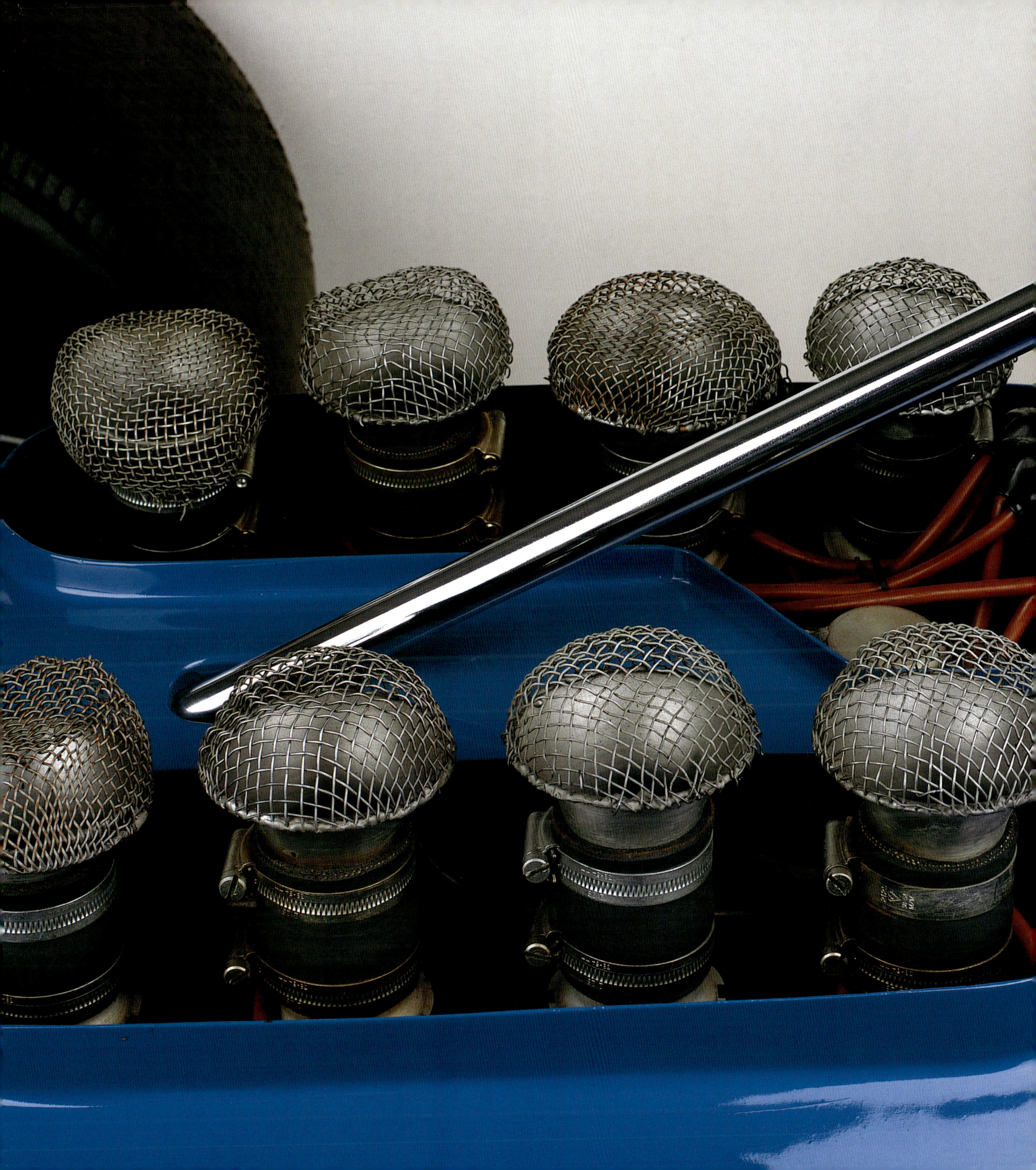

Hard-pressed after one of the nastiest frights of my entire career—when the rear wing collapsed on my brand-new Brabham-Cosworth BT26A—during the 1969 South African Grand Prix at Kyalami. Retaining his strutted wing is Chris Amon, in the latest V12 Ferrari.

CHAPTER 16

HELLO FORD

Cosworth-Ford V8 engines signal Brabham's return to form as Jack wins again at Silverstone, while two Grands Prix and the Gold Cup fall to Jacky Ickx

With Jochen Rindt leaving us after that solitary season of 1968, we had to find another driver. I'd been very impressed by the young Belgian, Jacky Ickx, who'd driven very well for Ferrari through that season. He had won the French Grand Prix and was in contention for the World Championship before crashing in practice in Canada, and breaking his leg.

Ickx was a fine driver, but on a personal level he and I never completely clicked in the way I had with Dan, Denny, and Jochen before him. Perhaps it was simply a generational thing. I was 43, rising 44, and he was 20 years younger. But he was also a native French speaker—and French-thinker—and we would have a small problem with conveying shades of meaning, particularly in technical terms where the cars were concerned. Ickx was also very self-possessed. He came across as being rather aloof. Perhaps it was shyness, I'm not sure, but generally I got on rather better with his father—the leading Belgian motoring journalist, Pascal Ickx. As a driver, Jacky plainly preferred to be team number one, and he would perform best when he was number one.

In fact he would get his chance that season, because just before the mid-season French GP I had a pretty massive shunt during Goodyear tyre testing at Silverstone, which broke my ankle and put me out of racing for a while. Running as our sole entry, Jacky Ickx immediately punched in some brilliant results—third in the French GP and second in the British preceding a great win in the German Grand Prix at the Nürburgring.

The Silverstone testing shunt—my worst since Lisbon '59—occurred in June, just after our return from Zandvoort, and it sidelined me until the Italian Grand Prix at Monza in September. I'd been in and out of the pits, testing various tyres. We were due to break for lunch when Leo Mehl of Goodyear asked if I'd quickly try a special ultra-light two-ply set. I'd got to the point where I could sometimes tell a new tyre wasn't going to work after the very first corner. Leo said, "Just one lap and come in" —I think they were pretty nervous of these very thin tyres. They'd marked the tyre positions on the wheelrim and when I returned one had rotated on the rim, bending the valve. They raised the pressures to provide a firmer seat on the rim, and said, "Just three more laps, Jack". Well, I didn't manage three laps.

I'd got as far as Club Corner where we used to blast through at around 115mph (185km/h), drifting out to within 6 inches (15 cm) of the earth bank at the exit. My Cosworth-engined BT26A carried me into the corner under perfect control, but three-quarters of the way through as I leaned on the left-front tyre, it popped off the rim and deflated!

With no front-end adhesion the car understeered straight into the bank, about 4 yards (4 metres) away. The impact smashed the left-front wheel into the side of the cockpit where it crushed the frame inwards, onto my legs. The car ended up 10-15 yards (11-16 metres) beyond its initial point of impact, at about 45-degrees with its shattered front end on top of the bank, its rear-wheels on the verge below. Miraculously, it didn't roll over, but the throttle was jammed wide open, and behind me the engine was absolutely shrieking. I was seeing stars and flashes of coloured lights. The pain in my twisted and trapped legs and feet was just unbelievable.

It was only a test day, and in those days we tested without marshals anywhere round the circuit. So I was absolutely on my own, with the engine hammering away. I twisted round in the cockpit and unfastened my belts, then tried to free my left foot which was jammed high-up in the corner. The undertray panel had popped down, which let my foot pass through, but then had snapped back, trapping my foot by the heel and back of my shoe against the chassis frame. I was desperate to kill that screaming engine but the switch was buried behind bent bodywork,

BELOW
Team-mates 1969—Jacky Ickx and I had relatively little in common, but after my Silverstone testing crash sidelined me for most of the season he put up some prodigious performances as our one-man Brabham team and won both the German and Canadian Grands Prix—and yet another non-Championship Oulton Park Gold Cup—for us.

RIGHT AND BELOW
My first Formula 1 race win since Canada 1967 was also my third BRDC International Trophy win, and the last of my career at both Silverstone, and on British soil. This time—to my intense satisfaction—the wings actually stayed on my BT26A.

and I couldn't get my fingers in to it. I could feel heat waves pulsing off the engine and visualised its exhausts glowing red. There was a terrible stench of fuel. Looking over the cockpit side I could see a spreading lake of petrol. I knew if it ignited I'd stand no chance. So I bent back the bodywork just enough to jab the kill-switch with a finger-tip, and the engine cut. The silence was utterly deafening. I made myself think clearly. Should I punch the onboard extinguisher right then, and so use up my one chance to douse a potential fire, or wait until one started and then punch it? If so much spilled fuel had flashed-off, no onboard system could have handled it. I'd fitted the system myself, I knew exactly where its nozzles pointed, and I had to quench those glowing exhausts before they could ignite the fuel. So I fired-off the system right then. And the exhaust glow was smothered.

My left ankle was completely numb. I couldn't move it. I couldn't twist it and simply couldn't free myself. To escape, I tried to wrench off bits of bodywork and broke away the steering wheel but really couldn't do anything. Just before I'd crashed I had been about to pass a saloon car. Now I heard him coming round on his next lap. He skidded to a stop and was the first to reach me. I explained we needed cutting gear and he shot off to the pits to bring the boys to my rescue. But by that time they were already on their way, wondering where the hell I'd got to. Senior mechanic present that day was a young chap named Ron Dennis who had joined us with Jochen ex-Cooper. He did a darned good job, organising extinguishers first to blanket the entire fuel lake surrounding the wreck, while others rushed back to the pits for tools and cutters. One spark and it could still have gone horribly wrong. Under Ron Dennis's direction, however, they very carefully cut the undertray trapping my foot, and after what seemed like forever I was free and on my way to hospital.

Once at the hospital the doctors discovered that about the last three-quarters of an inch of my left ankle bone had been broken clean off, and no way could they either splint it or relocate it. The whole foot was swollen, and the doctors decided it was better to delay any attempt to attach it, so I got a lift home. I got a second opinion from a consultant at St Thomas's who agreed there was nothing to be done until the swelling subsided. Five days later, they operated and fitted a 6-inch (15-cm) screw from the bottom, to hold it together while the bone knitted. I was left to hobble about for some weeks—and racing was out of the question—but it felt good just to be alive, and the screw's still there today.

Meanwhile our existing BT26 chassis had been converted around the engine bay to accept our new Cosworth-Ford DFV V8 engines in place of the unloved old quad-cam Repcos. First time out at Kyalami it was obvious Ron Tauranac had again got his sums right, because I qualified on pole—one-fifth of a second quicker than Jochen's new Lotus 49; which caused us both a smile.

I was chasing Jackie Stewart's blue Matra-Ford in the early stages when I had another big fright. There was a really fast right-hander on the back-stretch at Kyalami in which the quick way was to use the outside kerb to kick your car straight on the exit. Just as I clipped that kerb all hell broke loose! I couldn't have been in worse shape if I'd lost both rear wheels. It took me the entire road width and most of the following straight to catch-up with the car's cavortings. The tall strutted rear wing we were using had collapsed backwards, and had slashed the tyre adhesion instantaneously! I trundled into the pits where both front and rear wings were removed, but once I rejoined—freed of the wings' drag—my engine began over-revving wildly down the straight. In fact I was fastest through the trap there at 176mph (285km/h), but I retired rather than risk my expensive new engine blowing apart. Jacky Ickx, meanwhile, was pretty unimpressed when his rear wing also collapsed, his engine refused to restart in the pits and was found to be leaking oil, so he was out too.

The Race of Champions at Brands Hatch saw our rear wing mounts strengthened, but my run ended with a fuel leak and ignition failure and Jacky's with sticking throttle slides. Both our cars were further modified in time for the International Trophy at Silverstone—what had been the big May meeting, now run on gloomy, cold, and wet conditions on 30 March. Jackie Stewart popped his Matra onto pole but I lined-up alongside him, only one-tenth slower, with Chris Amon's Ferrari to my left, and beyond him—on the outside of the four-strong front row—Jacky in our second BT26A. Stewart had to start from the back of the grid, and I was away well. Jochen was delayed in his Lotus but battled back to finish just over two seconds behind, but the race was mine—my first F1 win since September 1967. Jacky Ickx was fourth. We were pretty happy about that.

ABOVE
For the first time since that horrible "fireball" year in 1964 I raced again in the Indy "500". Here I am passing the pits at around 190mph (305km/h) in our developed monocoque-chassised BT25 with 4.2-litre Repco quad-cam V8 engine. I'd qualified at over 163mph (260km/h) average—24th on the grid after the usual hurried qualification visits in between Grands Prix—but we'd fitted an American ignition system which we thought should be good, but without a chance to test it pre-race it proved hopeless, and failed during the 500-Miles.

The Spanish Grand Prix at Barcelona's Montjuich Park circuit opened the European second of the World Championship. Many of the cars carrying high strutted wings suffered catastrophic collapses there, none more so than both works Lotus 49s. First Graham Hill had an immense shunt in his and then Jochen had an even bigger one, somersaulting his car when its rear wing collapsed. He was knocked-out for a while, and suffered facial injuries and concussion. The tall wings would be banned after practice at the next race, in Monaco. Jacky had a wing collapse and finally broke a rear wishbone while my engine threw a rod when I was feeling pretty secure in third place.

Jacky and I qualified 7-8 at Monaco, but in the race he ran second for a long period before a rear suspension upright broke, while I only lasted 10 laps. I had been stuck behind John Surtees's BRM early on. He was always difficult to pass, and when I tried down the inside leaving the Portier, charging towards the tunnel, he'd just decided to wave me by, and moved aside. Unfortunately he'd waved me by on the left, not realising I was already committed to his right, so I rode over his gearbox, which plucked off one of my wheels and I was out.

At Zandvoort we had finished 5-6, Jacky leading me home—and then I went tyre testing at Silverstone. I was still limping when I returned to the fray at Monza in September, but I was stranded out on the circuit when a fuel pipe broke off the metering unit after only seven laps. Jacky made a second-lap stop to report fluctuating oil pressure and an oil leak, and trailed around the circuit before finally retiring.

This frankly wasn't good enough. We went to Mosport for the Canadian Grand Prix determined to do better. Jacky was on fantastic form there, qualified on pole, set fastest race lap, and punted Stewart's Matra off during a battle for the lead. He ran on to win while I had a fine dice with Jo Siffert and Graham Hill in their Lotus 49s, and passed both before they retired, then displaced Jochen for second at two-thirds distance. We ended that day with another Brabham 1-2, and again there was a lot of banter between Jochen and me, because I finished nearly six seconds ahead of him.

He hadn't been very happy at Lotus—we'd discussed him returning to our team. Seeing how well our cars were going, and knowing Ron had a brand-new monocoque design ready for 1970, he was up for it. I'd been under constant family pressure to retire, which my Silverstone shunt had merely increased. I'd have been happy to bow out with Jochen taking my place. So that had become our plan, and we'd shaken hands on it. Jochen Rindt would drive for Brabham in 1970.

But at Watkins Glen he broke the news that Lotus and Ford had made him a new offer he just couldn't refuse, including his own Lotus team for Formula 2 as well. He said he really wanted to accept it, and asked if I'd release him from our verbal deal. There was no way we could raise the funds to match that offer, so I said, "If you really want to stay with Lotus, I won't stand in your way...". Those are words I've bitterly regretted ever since. If I'd held him to our deal I'm sure he would have stood by it too, I'd have retired at the end of 1969, and he might still be alive today.

Jochen hadn't yet won a Formula 1 race. Veteran journalist Denis Jenkinson had bet his beard he never would. After Watkins Glen "Jenks" had to reach for his razor. Jochen won there, while Piers Courage proved his ability by finishing second in the private BT26 he was driving for the young Frank Williams. Surtees was third for BRM and I finished fourth. For over an hour Piers, myself, and Jacky had been racing within inches of one another, until Jacky's engine expired.

Ferrari had unveiled its new 3-litre flat-12 engined Formula 1 car just before the Italian race at Monza. It looked fabulous and between Monza and Mosport Park Jacky Ickx had told me he was leaving us, and would return to Ferrari for 1970.

Goodyear's latest tyres made all the difference in Mexico City, where Denny Hulme scored his first win of that year for McLaren with our Brabham BT26As second and third behind him, Jacky second ahead of me. I qualified on pole in practice but in the race my engine refused to pick-up cleanly. I had given Jacky our only special set of ultra-low gears, and my car was just too highly-geared to get away from hairpin quickly. But it was still a heartening note on which to end that year, and the magazines said things like, "Jack Brabham showed there is plenty of life in the old dog yet by earning pole position and finishing a strong third...".

I had told Betty and a few friends of my intention to retire at the end of that season, but Jochen's change of mind had altered the situation somewhat. I'd always felt I could still match my rivals in the right car on the right day. They talk about a fire still burning—well it certainly burned in me.

I felt confident our new monocoque would be competitive in 1970, and I had taken the plunge. I had rung Betty from Watkins Glen and talked her into the fact that I should drive for one more year. It was a long phone call and went over like a lead balloon!

Everything was settled, 1970 would be my 23rd and final season as a professional racing driver.

FAR LEFT
One of our year-old BT26 chassis was sold to Frank Williams for young Piers Courage to drive in Formula 1—using Cosworth-Ford V8 engines like ours—in 1969. He did really well with the car, finishing second here in the Monaco GP and ending the season second again in the United States GP. The following year at Monaco his Williams-run de Tomaso would get in my way entering the last corner, on the last lap. Piers crashed fatally in the Dutch GP—another young man from a wealthy background, with a beautiful wife and child, like Jochen Rindt, he had so much to live for. I preferred not to philosophise too much when I was racing.

LEFT
Jacky Ickx showing Jackie Stewart the way—our BT26A versus the Ken Tyrrell-entered Matra—on his way to wining the 1969 German Grand Prix. Jackie Stewart actually dominated that year's World Championship series to take the first of his three World titles…but on several occasions both Ickx and Jochen Rindt of Lotus really made him work for it.

1969 BRABHAM BT26A-FORD

Belgian driver Jacky Ickx won the 1969 German GP in this Brabham-Cosworth BT26A, and later also won that year's Canadian GP and the non-Championship Oulton Park Gold Cup.

These cars were Ron Tauranac's ultimate expression of multi-tubular spaceframe construction, with lightweight tubes stiffened by stressed-skin panelling. With the experimental Matra MS84 four-wheel drive vehicle these were the last tube-framed GP cars built.

The first BT26s in 1968 carried the Repco 4-cam 32-valve V8 engines but for 1969 two of the three existing chassis were adapted to accept Cosworth-Ford DFV V8 engines, forming the "A" variant. First time out in South Africa, Jack qualified on pole, and he then won the International Trophy race at Silver-stone.

Jack eventually sold the car to British collector, entrant, and Donington Collection museum founder Tom Wheatcroft, who has preserved it ever since.

TECHNICAL SPECIFICATION

Manufactured by Motor Racing Developments Ltd.
Engine: Cosworth-Ford DFV V8; 4 valves per cylinder; 2 overhead camshafts per bank; bore & stroke dimensions 85.6mm x 64.8mm, displacement volume 2,993cc; Power output circa 430bhp @ 9,000rpm on pump petrol.
Transmission: Hewland 5-speed and reverse.
Chassis: Multi-tubular spaceframe with stressed-skin stiffening.
Suspension: independent front and rear suspension by wishbones and co-axial coil-spring/dampers.
Brakes: Discs all round.
Wheels: Cast magnesium-alloy to Brabham design.
Tyres: Goodyear.

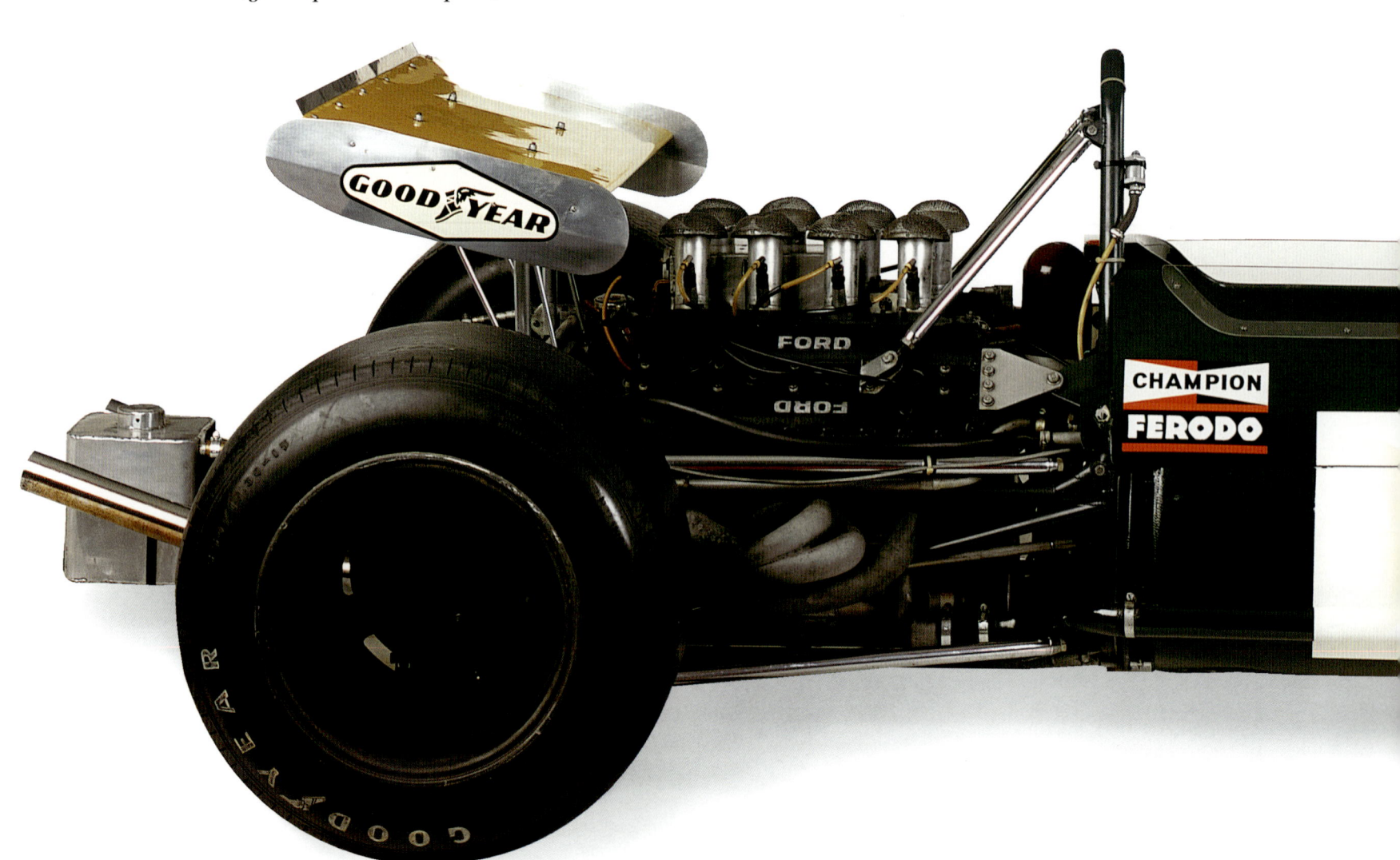

1969 BRABHAM BT26A-FORD | 233

ABOVE
An adjustable-incidence canard wing on the BT26A's nose used to match front and rear end aerodynamic downforce. This optimised the car's balance and handling. Ron and Jack were leaders in the appreciation of aerodynamic effect.

BELOW
The Ron Tauranac-designed Brabham BT26A was the ultimate expression of the multi-tubular spaceframe-chassised Formula 1 racing car. This actual vehicle, chassis serial BT26-4 is the car driven by Jackie Ickx to win the 1969 German GP and Oulton Park Gold Cup races.

LEFT
This view demonstrates the BT26A's bulged strap-on pannier fuel tanks, front and rear wings complying with the height and width restrictions applied by the FIA governing body from the 1969 Monaco GP forward (when tall strutted suspension-mounted wings were, thankfully, banned) and the car's Cosworth-Ford DFV V8 engine with Hewland gearbox projecting at the rear.

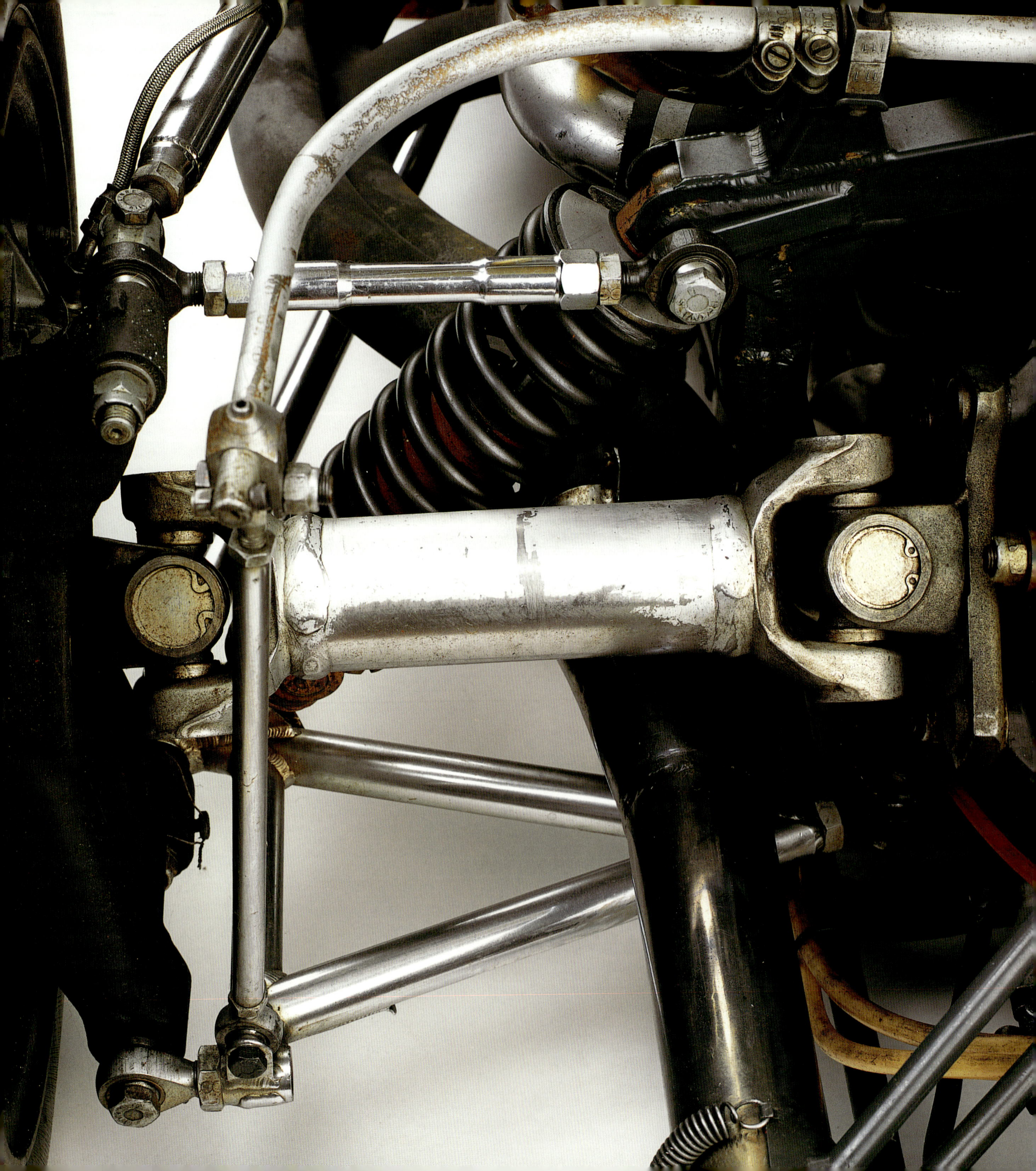

LEFT
Detail of BT26A-4's well-used and typically Ron Tauranac rear suspension, with curved anti-roll bar above adjustable single top lateral link, long trailing radius rods from the engine-bulkhead chassis section, hefty twin-universally jointed drive-shaft, and reversed lower wishbone (with its apex pivoting on the chassis) plus outboard-mounted coil-spring/damper unit.

LEFT
Fishlike aspect of the ex-Ickx Brabham BT26A with its aerodynamically effective thrust-forward lower nose lip, substantial wing area and somewhat "pregnant guppy" bulged midship tankage. It was in a sister car that Sir Jack survived his serious testing accident at Silverstone in 1969.

SPORTS-RACING SWANSONG

ABOVE
Prelude to another fright—easing the Agapiou brothers' ungainly Ford G7A CanAm car out of one of the Michigan Raceway's tight road-course corners onto the superfast banking....just before that left-rear wheel broke off. CanAm could be fun—as I discovered when Bruce McLaren loaned me his team's spare Chevrolet-engined M8B car during practice. To my chagrin I had to return to the Ford for the race, and it nearly bit me!

The weekend before the 1969 United States Grand Prix at Watkins Glen, I went to Michigan International Raceway for what was round eight of that year's CanAm sports car Championship. The series was a really big deal in the USA and Canada, utterly dominated by Bruce McLaren and Denny Hulme in their works McLaren-Chevrolet cars. Ford had decided they wanted to get a look in, so they asked me to drive a car based on their Le Mans-winning "GT Mark IV" chassis named the G7A which they'd apparently sold to a couple of mechanics—the Agapiou Brothers—for one dollar.

The Agapious had dropped into it—with Ford's apparent blessing—an all-iron pre-production prototype engine destined for really high-performance road cars of the Cobra persuasion. It was a 429 cubic inch V8 stretched to just over 8-litres and fitted with a tall fuel injection unit.

That engine had plenty of steam, but nowhere enough to make it raceworthy, because it must have weighed about half a ton. The car just wouldn't accelerate out of the slow corner going out onto Michigan Raceway's super-speedway banking. By the end of the banking section, where we had to dive back down onto the so-called infield "road circuit" it was going as quickly as anything present, but everybody was leaving me under that initial snap. The pit was full of suit-wearing Ford executives clicking stopwatches—evident they thought I was the problem.

In second practice one of the engine's road-type features—a pressed-steel rocker arm—was split by its pushrod. While it was changed I walked down to the McLaren pits, had a word with Bruce, and he let me try their spare orange McLaren M8B—with an alloy Chevrolet V8 engine. They put my number—"15"—on it and in three laps I was 3 seconds quicker than in the Ford G7A, and fourth quickest overall. Journalist Pete Lyons reported: "Back at his other number 15, surrounded by tall, well-dressed, silent figures, he gave nought but a business-like nod to the mechanics as he climbed in. Drop curtain as he drives off...".

The Ford execs who had been pressing me on why their G7A "supercar" had been so slow were suddenly very quiet. I'd also told one of them that if he'd had to run round the track with that amount of iron strapped to his back he'd have been pretty slow too. During the race, behind the pits into the corner leading onto the banking,

SPORTS-RACING SWANSONG

the Ford's brake pedal went straight to the floor. A quick pump brought it back, so I was able to slow for the corner. Going round the banking towards the next right-hander I was trying to reason why the pedal had gone to the floor, so braked early for the really fast corner leading off the banking. As I turned in, the Ford's left-rear wheel sheared off and I careered into the dirt. When the dust settled and I could see out, the wheel had done terrible damage to a car in the car park! The axle had broken and as it began to fail its movement had allowed the brake disc to knock-back the brake pads, allowing the pedal to flop to the floor! If I hadn't braked so early I would have had a really high-speed shunt and with that huge iron engine behind my shoulders that would have really hurt in the morning. Cary Agapiou said ever since he'd had the car it had used six-stud wheels, but just before the race Ford provided four-stud wheels.

After the United States and Mexican GPs, I returned to CanAm for the final round, at College Station, Texas, on another Speedway-plus-infield road course. This time Ford put me into British entrant Alan Mann's latest Group 7 car—using a 494 cubic inch alloy-block Ford V8 engine. I had a minor collision with a slower car during practice there but qualified pretty well, and then finished third in the race—behind Bruce who won his second CanAm Championship title in his works Gulf-McLaren, and Canadian McLaren privateer George Eaton. I'd have absolutely loved to have tackled CanAm in a Ron Tauranac-designed Brabham, but he would never play, I should've bought a car from Bruce!

For my last season's racing, in 1970, Matra made me an offer to join their World Championship endurance racing team. Their 3-litre V12-engined sports prototype cars were pretty competitive, and fun to drive. The best part of the deal was simply to fly in, find everything pre-arranged, sort out the car in practice with your co-driver, race, and then fly out again. Preparation and development were someone else's problem. It was liberating. I was teamed twice with Jean-Pierre Beltoise—in the Brands Hatch and Monza 1,000km races (finishing 12th and 5th to win our class) and three times with Francois Cevert—really quick, very promising—in the Daytona 24-Hours (10th), my fourth Le Mans 24-Hours classic (retired), and finally on 18 October 1970, in the Paris 1,000kms at Montlhéry—which we won! That was the final victory of my frontline career. I was happy with that.

BELOW
I felt like a privileged guest during my 1970 works drives for the Matra team in the World Championship of Makes races. It was a real novelty to be relieved of all other responsibilities—nice people, good cars—and the last win of my frontline career, in the season-ending Paris 1,000Kms.

At Kyalami in the 1970 South African GP. I've just taken the lead from Jackie Stewart's Ken Tyrrell-entered March, and we're off and away in our brand-new monocoque-chassised Brabham BT33, heading towards what proved to be my final F1 win. See the deformation on that right-rear tyre—I was still hanging the tail out. These cars generated a lot of "G" load and drivers had to be fit to endure a long race. They said I was an old man, but fitness was never a problem. I never visited any gym. For 23 years I kept fit just by driving, and working hard, eating simple food, and not smoking.

CHAPTER 17

FINAL VICTORY— FINAL SEASON

Ron Tauranac's first Formula 1 monocoque proves there's life in the old man yet—but South African success precedes repeated dismay before a fine French finale

During the late 1960s, motor racing became increasingly safety conscious. Ultimately, for 1970 regulation changes in Formula 1 demanded rubber bag safety fuel bags, within metal sheet skinning. Ron's 1968-1969 Indy Brabham BT25 had been our first stressed-skin monocoque car, rather than using multi-tubular spaceframe chassis construction. Now, through the closing months of 1969, the promise I saw in Ron's new monocoque Formula 1 design for 1970 was a major factor in persuading me to continue driving. Truth is, I probably couldn't face the fact that I'd miss out on driving it if I did retire.

We shook down this new Brabham BT33 monocoque car at Riverside in California, and we quickly corrected its few minor teething problems. I spent February in Australia, before the season-opening South African Grand Prix at Kyalami on 7 March. I was confident the car to watch that year would be the new flat-12 Ferrari. It was my aim to accumulate sufficient Championship points before it became truly raceworthy. Colin Chapman's much-rumoured "revolutionary" new Lotus 72 didn't trouble us greatly—we thought he would struggle developing it.

At Kyalami I felt confident of qualifying on pole, until our race engine's timing gears rattled when we fitted it for final practice. I had my original practice engine refitted rather than risk an entirely fresh one, untried.

My race nearly ended in the very first corner when Jochen banged his Lotus 49's wheels with mine, and I actually became airborne. I assumed I'd had it, but my new car survived with its left-front suspension not only intact, but unbent! I just felt my way round for two or three laps, unable to believe it. With confidence regained I went to work. I was running sixth but found it remarkably easy to peg back the leaders. Ultimately, I not only caught Jackie Stewart, leading in Ken Tyrrell's brand-new March, but felt I could pass him. While I was trying to do so, Jackie put a wheel off the road and hurled back a stone which cracked me on the cheekbone. Some uncharitable types suggested he'd learned a thing or two from me.

My face would carry the scar for years. But once I was ahead it was relatively easy to pace myself to the finish, and I became a Grand Prix winner again, first time out, in our brand-new car. It was just great.

I was determined to enjoy that last season as a full-time professional driver. Matra had offered me a World Championship sports car drive, which I'd accepted, and just turning up at Daytona, Brands Hatch, Monza, Le Mans, and Montlhéry to drive a car someone else had to develop and prepare was a rare luxury, which I really enjoyed. I also ran one last time at Indianapolis, and did three Formula 2 races in one of our customer Brabham BT30s entered by our old friend Noddy Coombs.

BELOW
Pursuing Jackie Stewart's March this time—at Jarama in the 1970 Spanish GP. I really thought another Grand Prix win was on the cards, when my new-model DFV engine's faulty crankshaft broke. That was the first disappointment of my retirement season. See my new US helicopter pilot's crash helmet? I'd been increasingly bothered by deepening deafness after years of racing without earplugs to monitor my cars mechanically. These helmets had ear defenders built into them which filtered sound without totally blanking it, an audible clue of incipient failure could still get noticed.

BELOW
My last Indy "500"—my Gilmore Broadcasting Brabham BT32 with 2.65-litre turbocharged, 930-hp Offenhauser 4-cylinder engine, qualified 26th at 166.397mph, dogged by an elusive ignition problem. By the time we thought we'd fixed it, the track had closed so I started the race with more power than the chassis could handle, but hit 224mph down the straights. The books say a piston burned with 25 laps left. In fact a gudgeon-pin broke and cut the engine in half! In tests we found at Speedway any oversteer was too much. We dialled-in total understeer. Any oversteer whatever and every turn would scare any driver. At the California "500" Lee Roy Yarbrough led with only nine laps to go when the engine blew again. We'd cracked Speedway Racing, but too late to exploit it.

For the Formula 1 Spanish GP at Jarama I used our first "10-series" Cosworth-Ford engine, the latest 1970-spec, but it seemed no better than our faithful old "9-series" 1969 units. After 200 miles (320 kilometres) in practice, it seemed reliable. So we left it in for the race since Jarama placed more emphasis on chassis than engine.

I made an indifferent start, which didn't bother me until an enormous shunt developed in front. Jackie Oliver's BRM broke a stub axle and slithered across the hairpin, to tee-bone Jacky Ickx's new Ferrari. Both cars ignited. While Oliver escaped unscathed, Ickx was dazed, then slipped as he jumped out amidst a huge blaze, and sat in burning fuel. His overalls were the latest fireproof Nomex type with protective under-layers, and although Jacky took a couple of months to recover his form, he and Ferrari quickly bounced back.

Extinguishing foam made the track there extremely slippery. Stewart's March led from Denny Hulme's McLaren second, just ahead of me. I was lining him up into the slippery hairpin when he nearly lost it under braking, I thought Denny was going to spin, and spun myself, while he caught his slide and pulled away. That silly mistake rather irritated me and I just tried too hard to recover. Coming off that same slippery patch soon after, I spun again. Jean-Pierre Beltoise got by and I then found his Matra immensely wide. I just couldn't repass, though my car was capable of lapping much faster. Jackie was drawing away, but Denny's car had broken, so if only I could have passed that wretched Matra I would have been second.

We were screaming round, with me trying to find any way around Beltoise, when I realised the Matra's slipstream actually smelled hot. Sure enough, its engine expired releasing me to charge after Jackie.

I began to reel him in, closed right up, and really began to pressure him. He was driving very defensively apart from along the main straight where his car was plainly faster. Obviously he wasn't going to give me an inch. I finally decided my only real hope would be to slipstream him as closely as I could down the pits straight, then outbrake him into the following long right-hander. We came streaking out of the last corner, with me putting everything into that bend in order get the best possible tow down past the pits. And with a terrific thump and clatter my new engine's crankshaft broke.

If only I could have scratched past Jackie, I'm confident I could have pulled away quite comfortably. Cosworth decided I'd been the victim of a bad batch of crankshafts. I've always regarded that 1970 Spanish Grand Prix as one that got away.

Monaco followed. After brake trouble I qualified only fourth, behind Denny's McLaren, and the Marches of Chris Amon and Stewart. Chris was right in my path at the start, slower away than Jackie who shot off pole into an immediate lead. I was effectively baulked and around Monte Carlo in a wide modern Formula 1 car there was precious little I could do about it.

I finally managed to outbrake Chris into the Gasworks Hairpin, and set about Stewart's lead (again!). Six laps later, his engine failed so I found myself building a comfortable lead. I knew this was probably my last season, and my last ever Monaco Grand Prix. I was pretty happy to ensure I kept the machinery comfortable, took no risks and finished. Perhaps that was always a weakness of mine.

Perhaps, to preserve a car or a small advantage, I would take it easier than I should. In retrospect, if I'd only pressed harder, built a bigger lead before nursemaid mode, I might have guaranteed another win.

Through half distance, I led Chris by around three seconds, but closing behind us was Jochen Rindt, in the elderly but well-sorted Lotus 49. Then it all backfired on me, because Jochen was on fire and catching me. I didn't worry, because from my pit signals I'd calculated his closing rate, and concluded he was running out of laps to threaten me seriously. Chris's March had broken, so Jochen was my only threat, and I felt supremely confident of holding him off.

However, into the last five laps I encountered the most shocking run of slow backmarkers of my entire career. On one lap I hurtled over the crest towards the Casino, to find Jo Siffert in Rob Walker's Lotus weaving side to side, trying to slosh his last remaining dregs of fuel into the collector system. I had to make a virtual crash-stop to avoid smashing straight into him, and then had to hover behind him. The flag marshals were waving flags, arms, shouting at him, pointing...but I still had to use the footpath to pass. I'd been lapping in 1:24—that lap thudded in at 1:29.3! And there in my mirrors I could now see a gleaming gold nose and red-and-white livery—Jochen was almost with me.

We blazed around then, Jochen scenting his chance, became eager to push me into the mistake I knew—with my experience—I should not make. I still had a handy little time cushion, small but big enough. Yet even starting my final lap I still felt I had plenty in hand. I'd told myself not to get excited and overdo it because as I flashed past the pits Colin Chapman was doing a war dance, making "come on" signs plainly for my benefit, long before Jochen was even in his sight.

I still felt in complete control until I reached the chicane for the final time, and just beyond it encountered three desperately slow cars bumbling down like walking wounded into the *Tabac* left-hander. I had virtually to stop again, and then I was onto the final curving stretch to the Gasworks Hairpin, after which it was a curving flat-out sprint to the chequered flag.

By this time my heart was thumping madly as I floored the throttle, and screamed round towards the hairpin, realising I now had a real problem on my hands, because Jochen was coming, I knew he was coming. In effect I was clearing the track for him. Any backmarker surprised to find me climbing all over them was warned that Jochen was coming through too. His exit speed from *Tabac* had been higher than mine. As we streaked into the braking area for the Gasworks turn he was almost in touch. And right in my path, in the middle of the road, I then found Piers Courage in Frank Williams's red de Tomaso, apparently coasting with a dead engine.

Well, that situation is always a lottery. As the overtaking driver, you never know which line the obstacle will choose. Should you take the inside line, or the outside, and in my case then—whichever I chose—I had to cover any attack that Jochen might make.

Trying to decide which line to take, I slightly overshot my braking point. I'd chosen the inside line—of course—but right there (as at Monza three years before) a trail of cement had been laid on spilled oil. My brakes locked-up, and I simply failed to take the corner.

With my front wheels locked, tyres streaming smoke, I slithered straight as an arrow—crunch—into the strawbale barrier. The impact was very slight, but my engine stalled, and I was stuck, unable to reverse out. Courage went by, Jochen went by—he could not believe his luck!—and I was desperate to avoid receiving outside assistance, for I could still salvage second place with its Championship points. An excited flag marshal made to push me back. As I saw him coming I'd just hit the starter button, thankfully the engine fired immediately, and I grabbed reverse. My engaging the clutch coincided exactly with the enthusiastic marshal lunging forward to push.

As my car shot backwards, the marshall's out-stretched hands encountered no resistance. So instead of pushing me back he launched himself into a swallow dive, straight onto my car's nose—full-length, flat on his face—right against my windscreen!

He was struggling to get up when I needed to engage first and rejoin. I jerked forward but could hardly rush off with him as a bonnet mascot. So I jabbed the brakes, which fired him into a heap on the roadway—in my path. He was completely flustered and at a loss what to do—just floundering there on the tarmac. And while he was trying to recover, I just had to sit and wait.

He'd inflicted more damage upon my car's nose than hitting the bales, but then I could charge off to take the flag, still—but only just—in second place, another six Championship points. This gave me 15 to Stewart's 13.

Jochen couldn't stop chortling about his lucky win. "Jack!", he guffawed, "What the hell happened to you?" He confessed he never thought I'd drop it—but I had. He'd covered his last two laps in 1:23.5 and 1:23.2—fabulous driving by any measure.

But within days came shocking news by any measure. Bruce McLaren—that great bloke whose career I'd done so much to foster—had been killed testing at Goodwood.

Just days before, we'd flown back from Indy together, and he'd told me he was going to retire from racing and concentrate on testing. "But that's the most dangerous thing we do..." I told him, with feeling. And now it had killed him.

At Spa for the Belgian Grand Prix, we were down on top speed—an insuperable handicap there. I could hold station with cars I was slipstreaming, but couldn't slingshot past them. Then I really worked at it, and slowly began to gain ground by tremendous effort, concentrating my hardest. I climbed from sixth to third, trailing Chris Amon's March and Pedro Rodriguez's leading BRM. I had settled for third when my car began to vibrate and thought a drive-shaft had gone eccentric. A mirror-check, however, showed they were true. So I selected neutral, eased the throttle, and the vibration faded with the engine. The clutch had shattered and was out of balance —and I was out.

My last Dutch Grand Prix was nearly one I did not live to see. After our performance deficit at Spa we tested pre-race in Holland. The best Goodyear tyre choice was then fitted to our second car, being driven that season by Rolf Stommelen. We had been expecting him to arrive, but he hadn't and with only half-an-hour left before the circuit closed, Ron asked me to try his car. It was fitted with new brake pads, new tyres, and the gear ratios had been changed from those I'd been using.

The first thing I found was that two second gears had been fitted, but no third. I scrubbed the tyres for a few laps before attempting a serious time. Entering a normally third-gear right-hander on Zandvoort's deceptively quick back leg I had to take it gently in fourth. If the proper gear had been available I would probably have been cornering fast enough to notice that my left rear tyre was deflating.

Then I was really on full song in fourth gear into the following left-hander, leaning heavily on the good right-rear tyre, so again I didn't notice anything wrong. But the instant I steered back to the right it became most evident there was something very wrong with my car's rear end.

It entered a vicious slide, and the deflated tyre left the wheel-rim, which then hit the road. The car broadsided into the sand, the wheel rim dug in and we flipped, rolling over and over into the wire catch-fencing in which it wrapped itself up, trapping me inside my cockpit, trussed up like the Christmas turkey. I might not (quite) have been stuffed, but I was terrified I might yet get roasted! Had any leaking fuel caught fire, there was no way could I have escaped.

This all seemed to happen quite slowly. Even the roll-overs had not been unduly violent. But the car came to rest inverted over a ditch, and I was hanging in my safety belts with just sufficient room to turn my head, a little. I killed all the switches, then began to ponder escape. Here I was in another test session—on a deserted circuit—out of sight of the pits, trapped in a crashed car. I really was getting too old for this! Everywhere I reached, my hands snagged in wire fencing. I'd have needed wire cutters to make my own way out.

I was increasingly anxious. I could smell petrol, and studied the extinguisher button. My finger was poised should fire break out. But I didn't fire it off, as I had at Silverstone. The fuel, however, was dribbling from the filler caps, and down onto the sand, fortunately for me, because there it was instantly absorbed.

At last I heard running feet and voices. Hands began to yank the wire away and untangle the car. I took that as my cue to twist my safety belt release—forgetting I was hanging by it—and dropped on my head, with my entire weight twisting my neck. The Dutch spectators then managed to raise one side sufficiently for me to wriggle out—but it had been another pretty scary experience, and although I was really unhurt I would have a stiff neck for a while.

Of course, it was business as usual the following weekend. In Dutch GP practice we had traction problems out of the corners which compromised our terminal speed down the long straight. I ended up on row five, and early in the race had my work cut out to keep up with my group. Piers Courage was running ahead of me in his Williams-entered De Tomaso, and as I came out of a quick right-hander on the back stretch I saw a huge cloud of dust flung up on the left, exploding into a gigantic fireball as I drew abreast. I heard it, and I felt the heat. It was like a furnace. And there beside my left-front wheel, bouncing along the trackside, was an empty crash helmet, silver-blue, Piers's. Next time round there was a terrific fire blazing, and I knew he could not have survived.

As the track grew oily, I made two stops to change punctured tyres, and was truly disheartened to see Jochen lap me—twice—in his latest wedge-shaped Lotus 72, in which he would win. My parents were at that race, and

FINAL VICTORY—FINAL SEASON | 243

LEFT AND BELOW
While the sun was shining everything seemed just fine leading the 1970 Monaco Grand Prix in the sparkling BT33. Monte Carlo was always hard work, with never a moment to relax, not a straight in sight, hard things to hit, the constant threat of mechanical failure, and nobody prepared to leave you in peace and let you win. But I really felt confident that another Grand Prix was ours—until the final lap. When I finally backed the car out of the barriers at the last corner—and shook off the track marshal who'd taken up station as my bonnet mascot—the BT33 looked a little less sparkling.

had been laughing with Piers and Sally Courage that morning. I'd survived my Silverstone testing shunt, and had been lucky again here, but Bruce—who they had known so well, and so long—had been killed, and now Piers Courage too. My father had always been my staunchest supporter. Now, for the first time, he sided with my mother and Betty, and urged me to pack it in before my luck ran out too.

We returned home really chastened, because Jochen's Lotus 72 had just re-written the performance standards, something we had never believed it could do so quickly. The French Grand Prix was at Clermont–Ferrand, where I had never raced. I visited a couple of weeks beforehand on behalf of the Grand Prix Drivers' Association, and walked a lap with the organisers to advise on safety. That was another mistake. To see all the roadside precipices and rock faces, where from the cockpit you'd never imagine such things, was a real eye-opener. It then took me two days of practice to set a competitive time—fifth fastest, alongside Jochen.

I then made a terrible start—what had normally been one of my driving strengths seemed to have deserted me that year. I had to dip the clutch and try again, and I was engulfed. Clermont was narrow, and twisty, and again I found the V12 Matras particularly wide, perhaps since Henri Pescarolo and Beltoise were on home soil. I then joined forces with Denny's McLaren and we tried really hard to pull back the leaders. They were so far ahead I felt disheartened, and although I drew away from Denny and set fastest lap, towards the end I feared my fuel was running out so eased off. Jochen won again, from Chris Amon second, and I was third.

I felt better analysing the race afterwards, because if I had made an adequate start I should have been wheel-to-wheel with Jochen for the lead. I felt more philosophical then, and the British GP was run again at Brands Hatch, ths was one of my favourite circuits...until that year that is!

BELOW
A quiet moment with my father in our transporter at Zandvoort during the 1970 Dutch Grand Prix meeting. It was there, after the death of Bruce McLaren in testing, and of Piers Courage in this race, that Dad urged me to not to reconsider retirement but give up now—the risks were no longer tenable. Coming from my staunchest supporter—the figure who had always unfailingly encouraged me in face of our womenfolk—this moment was decisive…but looking back I feel I could have had at least another three to four years in my tank.

Jochen had now won three consecutive Grands Prix and to stand a realistic Championship chance I had to win at Brands. He made fastest practice time on Thursday which I equaled on Friday morning. As the race began, Jacky Ickx's increasingly effective flat-12 Ferrari took an immediate lead, from myself and Jochen. There wasn't much we could do about it until the Ferrari's transmission failed. I slowed to avoid it, and Jochen shot alongside, to my right, and I found myself wheel-to-wheel with him, for the lead of the British Grand Prix, around the outside on Paddock Hill.

I sat him out, but at the top of the following hill, into the right-handed Druids Hairpin, he had the decisive line. I then had to follow him faithfully for the next 60 laps! His car was quicker along the straight but I could hold him everywhere else. I tried to pressure him into a mistake and eventually he missed a gear leaving Bottom Bend and I outbraked him into the next left-hander at South Bank. My manouevre put us both off-line, so we both lost impetus, but I was able to out-drag him down the next straight and then drew away. Jochen had had enough. He resigned himself to finishing second. As he put it, "The old man was going to win for sure…".

Entering the final lap I held a 13-second lead. It was a bit shattering for everybody in our team, but especially for me, when I entered Stirling's Bend, with only Clearways to go before the finishing straight, and my engine died.

We'd run out of fuel. Ever since the start I'd been concerned about a hesitancy on initial pick-up whenever I opened the throttle. It was symptomatic of the engine running rich, using more fuel than it ideally required. In fact it had run very rich and had used about a pint too much. Certainly, there should have been two gallons left. I remember it was topped-up on the line.

As I went swishing along, engine dead, under the bridge, and out into the main crowd and grandstands' view at Clearways, everybody just went wild. I could hear Jochen's Lotus coming, and then he went by me, his head turning from side to side, heading for the chequered flag. As I coasted past the pits, tucked up under the right-side barrier, I just felt sick and empty. I crossed the line, and coasted to a halt on the grass at the top of Paddock Hill. And as I was coasting to rest, I spotted in my mirrors our mechanic Ron Dennis sprinting out of the pit lane, along the track behind me. I suddenly thought, "I bet I know what's happened, the silly buggers left the injection set on 'Full Rich'..."—the setting used to start the engine from cold, and it had been really cold that morning. I shrugged off my belts and leapt out of the cockpit, determined to be first to check the metering unit setting. I got there just before Ron—and sure enough—it was on "Full Rich". I didn't say anything, just looked at him...and pointed.

It was just like Monaco all over again—only worse. This time not my fault. For the following 30 years I'd blame Ron Dennis for having failed to correct that fuel setting before the race, but at dinner with another of our team mechanics, Nick Goozee, in 2002, he said, "Remember Brands Hatch in '70, when we set the injection onto full-rich to start the engine cold that morning, and forgot to re-set it for the race? Well, that wasn't Ron—it was me...". So now we know. I promised I wouldn't tell...

Actually, I felt like giving up there and then. I thought we really deserved to win that day. Jochen had already resigned himself to second place, he said he didn't like winning that way, and I believe he meant it.

Running out of fuel on the last lap was always a danger, and one to which I was certainly no stranger. But it had certainly wrecked any dream I might still have cherished about retiring from driving in a blaze of glory—as four-time World Champion.

The German Grand Prix followed, for the first time, at Hockenheim, where in practice the car seemed pretty competitive until the crucial last day of practice when it wouldn't stay in gear, nor handle properly. After practice we investigated the gearbox, but everything inside looked perfect. Then one of the boys discovered that an engine-mounting bolt had broken, so the engine—with the gearbox attached behind—was actually shifting relative to the chassis, and pulling the transmission out of gear.

We then changed the engine in the pretty unfavourable conditions of the Hockenheim paddock, and next day—just before the race—we found the clutch playing up. The car went onto the grid obviously still not right and after the warm-up lap I deliberately moved onto the starting grid as late as I dared, wanting to arrive just as they dropped the flag. But, as I stopped, the clutch started dragging—taking up drive on its own—and I was standing on the brakes trying to avoid jumping the start, while also trying to keep the engine running against the clutch. Just momentarily before the flag fell—my engine juddered and stalled. All my driver chums rushed off, leaving me wreathed in drifting smoke. I complained bitterly to them afterwards—not one had waited for me.

We had a struggle to restart and I still had to get it in gear somehow and dash after them. It crunched into gear, clutchless and I shot round that opening lap in a blind fury, which got worse as an oil pipe union disturbed in the engine change came apart. I retired in disgust after just

ABOVE AND BELOW
This still makes me spit—1970 British GP at Brands Hatch—the third race that year I was poised to win, but the BT33 has run out of fuel while leading on the final lap. I'm coasting to the flag, and there behind my visor is the "1,000-mile stare" of a bloke seething. Ron's disappointed too (right), while Alan Brinton politely asks, "What happened?".

one lap, and went straight home. Rolf Stommelen, finished fifth, while Jochen won his fifth Grand Prix of the year.

Back home I faced intense family pressure to retire immediately. Even my father had been on at me repeatedly to give it up while still able. That really shook me, but I appreciated their viewpoint. They all knew it was my last year and couldn't see the sense of my continuing to run risks when all hope of that final title was now lost. But to quit with races remaining was not an acceptable alternative. I still really enjoyed driving, and Ron certainly wanted to continue. Then there were our contractual obligations—most notably to Goodyear and Esso. So we pressed on—although home was certainly not a quiet and peaceful place for the remaining few months of my frontline career.

In Austria on the wonderful new Österreichring circuit Ferrari fielded three flat-12s, driven by Ickx, Regazzoni, and Ignazio Giunti. They simply flew. I made another indifferent start, and was passed—amongst others—by Francois Cevert in the second of Ken Tyrrell's dark blue March cars. I slipstreamed him along the back straight and was right on his gearbox...when his engine exploded. My vision was totally masked as hot oil covered my visor. With my car sliding I was trying to steer with one hand while clutching at my visor rip-off with the other. I managed to clear my sightline just in time to avoid leaving the road, but only one side of the visor film had pulled free, and the airstream then blew it back over my eyes while I was sliding through the middle of the next braking area. By the time I'd sorted out this little fracas the leading group were well away...and I was beginning to think, "What the hell can go wrong next?"

Jochen's engine blew up and I caught Giunti's fourth-placed Ferrari. That flat-12 was incredibly fast along the straight, but passing the pits Giunti put two wheels onto the inside verge, and fired a stone straight through my radiator! A fountain of hot water and steam gushed out of the top ducts just ahead of me, and I dived into the pits where a fresh radiator was fitted complete. I finally finished thirteenth.

We thought our last Italian Grand Prix could only be better. But then Jochen was killed when his Lotus 72 crashed in practice, and I was perhaps more shocked than most of his rival drivers apart from his genuinely close friend and neighbour, Jackie Stewart.

Our car again lacked straightline speed. I ran with less wing incidence in the race even than we had tried in practice, and became embroiled in the usual slip streaming pack. It didn't matter if you were first or tenth during the opening laps at Monza, because the race would almost always be decided only in the last few crucial minutes.

My car's water temperature was climbing, so I ran out of the slipstream as much as possible without getting dropped by the bunch. Then my engine started to misfire under acceleration—particularly out of the *Parabolica* past the pits, and before long I lost the tow. Now at least the water temperature stabilized and the engine cleaned-up so I made a big push to regain contact.

When I got back into their slipstream, I felt as if I could tow past them all, but after only a couple of laps my water temperature soared and the misfire returned. Then my engine quit abruptly on the exit from the *Parabolica* which flung me broadside—I corrected but used up the remaining road width so I clattered into retirement against the guardrail. My last Italian GP had ended in a minor accident. And there was another funeral to attend —if only I could have talked Jochen into returning to us that year.

Only the Canadian, United States, and Mexican GPs remained. Canada's Ste Jovite circuit was terribly rough. In practice I tried Rolf's car, and on the first lap the steering stiffened and a front suspension wishbone had broken right on the joint. I did my best to stop, but the car wouldn't turn right, which was a pity, because the next corner was a right-hander, so I slithered off the road into the bank, and knocked the offending wheel right off.

My own car wouldn't handle, so I started from the back of the grid, and eventually retired with vibrations, convinced its rear end was about to drop off. I'd really begun to lose interest by that time. Watkins Glen was little better. It had never been "a Goodyear circuit", perhaps because of the temperatures, and again we could not compete. I qualified on row eight...beyond a joke.

In the race Jackie Stewart's new Tyrrell lapped me which left me completely demoralized—not just because he lapped me, but by the manner in which he did it, overtaking on the straight as if my car was anchored, looking round and giving me a little wave just to rub it in. His new Tyrrell broke before the end, enabling Lotus's new boy Emerson Fittipaldi to win his first Grand Prix, which secured the World title posthumously for Jochen—which I thought was fitting, on balance.

Back home we investigated our car's performance loss, and finally isolated the gremlin. After Brands Hatch, an engine breather line to the oil tank had been changed, creating tremendous back pressure which had caused oil to gather in the engine's bottom end. In effect we were wasting engine power in heating-up our own oil. That was why our car had been so slow from the British Grand Prix forward but now we had located the reason too late for it to matter.

At least we could compete with all the other Cosworth-Ford engined teams in the final race at Mexico City, even if none of us could match the flat-12 Ferraris which shone there. I was fifth fastest on Friday, but was livid—unable to talk to anyone because a press agency had ignored an embargo and leaked my retirement announcement! On the Saturday I was third fastest, headed only by Regazzoni and Stewart. This was to be my last Grand Prix, but I felt we were at last competitive again which greatly cheered me up!

My last start was not particularly good, but I recovered to run third behind the Ferraris of Ickx and Regazzoni. It felt good to be sawing through a race field one last time in earnest. I was resigned to the fact that third place was the best I could expect unless the Ferrari twins broke down. But suddenly it was my engine which cut. A casting split inside the engine lost all oil pressure, and it seized solid. With 13 laps from the end—after 23 long and hectic years —the disappointing end to my career as a full-time professional racing driver. But I had to look on the bright side. I had survived.

BELOW
Final curtain—1970 Mexican Grand Prix. My BT33 leading Graham Hill in Rob Walker's latest Lotus 72—a sister car to the one in which Jochen Rindt had been killed at Monza—and the McLarens of Denny Hulme and Peter Gethin. The crowd was huge and they lined the trackside like this all the way round. For me in my last frontline race this was like déjà vu—though the wild and woolly tracks on which I'd raced in the 1950s were probably better policed!

Margaret and me—my former secretary, who simply grew on me…we married in 1996.

CHAPTER 18

REFLECTIONS AND LATER LIFE

Time to look back on the old, to celebrate the new, to come over "all historic", and to enjoy the achievements of a new Brabham racing dynasty

When I retired from racing at the end of 1970, Ford organised a fantastic send-off dinner in my honour. Graham Hill had the entire room in stitches telling lies about me—every line raising terrific laughter. I got my own back, recalling how on my arrival in Britain, people like Cooper and Salvadori asked whether Aussies actually used knives and forks, with the usual "convict" references. Well, my first recollection of Britain was that plenty of criminals had yet to be caught—and I'd spent 16 years racing with most of them.

Betty wanted us to return to Australia, in particular to insulate the boys from racing. Ron took sole control of Motor Racing Developments into 1971, before selling to Bernie Ecclestone. His designer, Gordon Murray, then performed brilliantly, and the Brabham marque would achieve two more World titles, in 1981 and 1983, for Nelson Piquet.

Flying had paralleled my racing, and now assumed extra importance. I'd always revelled in its excitements and how, like racing, it can highlight character. For example I recall John Cooper pranging his single-engined Piper Tri-Pacer which nosed-over on landing at Fairoaks Aerodrome. Colin Chapman was with him. As they hopped out unhurt and saw the damage and leaking fuel his instant reaction was, "Quick John set fire to it—claim the insurance!"—at which John obediently grabbed for his lighter, before hesitating and mumbling, "Umm, I'm not sure if Dad has paid the premium...". Then the crash crew arrived, and John's fleeting chance had passed. That was the difference between Chapman and Cooper.

Once, while my own aircraft was being serviced, I chartered a De Havilland Dove to fly to the Albi Formula 2 race. On the return during pre-flight check I confirmed the fuel tanks had been refilled, but couldn't check the oil level in one engine because the cap was too tight to undo. I studied the bill for fuel and oil, saw both had been added, so signed it and took off.

Typically we were overloaded, with my parents, mechanics, and I think a racing engine. Just abreast of Le Mans I saw the oil pressure dip on the engine with the jammed filler cap, then recover. I watched intently. It dipped again, and again. So I shut down the engine and radioed a nearby military airfield for permission to land. I noticed my mother gazing intently at the feathered engine. "No Mum", I said, pointing out the other side, "that's the engine to watch, the only one that's keeping us

Knighted by the Governor-General—1979—proud owner outside the Bankstown Ford dealership which Austin Tauranac ran for me in the early 1970s—memories, I've had a few—with Lord March, at his fantastic annual Goodwood Festival of Speed in Britain—so many enthusiastic owners preserve our cars these days, here are the BT24, Indy BT12, and the unique BT19.

A proud moment for me, carrying the Olympic flame towards the games, in Sydney 2000.

BELOW
Looking back, barely avoiding trees, while trying to land my first Cessna in Charlie Cooper's recommended field behind his Cornish cottage at Restronguet. After several attempts I gave up! A '60s holiday in Corsica with Gary and David. Frank Gardner taught me to dive, and got me into trouble in small boats, teaching me to sail a catamaran. A series of "twins" like this Cessna 310 carried me, the family, our team for literally thousands of happy, productive hours.

up here!". I'm not convinced that my comment made my mother feel any better.

But experience counts. Recalling Wing Commander Crombie's death in the Beaufighter in 1944 when he'd dropped the shut-down engine, I requested a reverse-direction circuit before landing, so I could keep our dead engine high throughout the turn. We landed safely.

Weather could always be the private flyer's enemy—like the time I found myself blanketed in a snowstorm over the Chiltern Hills near Amersham. Fortuitously a hole opened in the cloud base through which I made an emergency landing in a farm field, already under thin snow. I taxied towards farmhouse lights in the gathering gloom. Suddenly the farmer sprinted into view, looking first furious, then stunned, then happy. Hearing my engine he'd thought somebody was stealing his tractor!

Meanwhile, in the late 1960s, I'd bought Kingsford-Smith Aviation's hangar and business at Bankstown Airport, Sydney, and installed Roy Coburn there to run it for me. Roy had maintained my aircraft in Britain, and in 1968 I had sold my Queenair twin to Bib Stillwell back home. Roy prepared it with long-range tanks and we flew it Britain-Australia.

A 1,000 miles (1,600 kilometres) out over the Indian Ocean, with about another 1,000 to run before landfall—we were just sitting there, with the Queenair on auto-pilot, sun beating in through the cockpit windows—when one engine suddenly starved and died. Almost instantly the other engine followed. Roy and I snapped fully alert! We realised instantly what had happened, and dived for the fuel tank change-over cock between our seats. We were running on the rear ferry tank and had calculated it should have given us another half-hour. But as we dived for the tap, our heads cracked together!

That accident knocked us both almost senseless before flicking the cock. Meantime the autopilot had sensed our

REFLECTIONS AND LATER LIFE | 251

speed-loss, so fought to maintain our pre-set altitude, 14,000 feet (4,270 metres) by pulling up the nose. This bled more speed so when Roy and I looked up, still dazed, the Queenair was nose high, set to stall.

I recovered it, then fought to restart. The engines' fuel injection lines had sucked-in air, which had to be purged before fuel could get through again. We just had enough speed for the engines to windmill, all the time the Queenair descending like a silent lift, seawards. We lost over 7,000 feet (4,270 metres) before first one engine, then the other, struck up. Thank goodness we hadn't been cruising at 7,000 feet. We'd just have become another mystery: triple-World Champion Driver missing without trace over Indian Ocean.

Roy ran our aviation company for the next 10 years. Betty persuaded me to buy a farm, where she hoped the boys could grow into a future away from racing. Frank Hallam, the Repco engineer, found us a place outside Melbourne, on the Howqua River, 350-acres, tiny by Australian standards, which we kept for three or four years before up-grading to what eventually became a 4,300-acre spread at Galore, between Wagga-Wagga and Narandra, with a 5-mile (8-kilometre) frontage on the Murrumbidgee River. There the boys grew up, having a ball in the open-air. Betty's ambition to wean them away from motor racing would be foiled as through the 1970s they went racing anyway, with great success. But unfortunately Betty and I had grown apart, and things only got worse. Perhaps enforced life on a farm I never really wanted didn't help. And I very quickly came to regard my retirement from racing as premature, and still do. For us, early retirement wasn't a comfortable period.

I'd initially retained my British garages at Chessington, Worcester Park, and Ewell. In 1970 I opened a Ford dealership in Bankstown, Sydney, run by Ron Tauranac's brother, Austin. I sold it in 1973, while keeping the

BELOW

In 1966 I won in Alan Brown's big V8 Ford Mustang against the nimble Lotus-Cortinas and "in retirement" have raced saloon cars including two Bathurst 1,000s. Getting together with old friends is always fun; with Ron and Roy Billington, and our former 1966 F2 season mechanic Nobuhiko Kawamoto during his latter-day Presidency of Honda. Two blokes who were so instrumental in my career, John Cooper (left) and Dean Delamont (right). Racing a *Lowline* again, in the wet Goodwood Revival, 1999.

ABOVE
From the family album—my parents with their grandsons, Geoffrey, Gary, and David. Into 2004 I'm now watching my own grandchildren beginning to race.

FAR RIGHT (TOP)
Now son, this is a racing car, and your mother doesn't want you to drive 'em..."—Geoffrey, Gary, and David all grew up to drive racing cars most successfully. David began racing karts in 1983, won the Australian Gold Star in Formula Pacific 1987, became British Formula 3 Champion 1989, drove in Formula 3000 and Formula 1, won the Bathurst 1,000 sharing a BMW with Geoffrey in 1997, and developed into one of the world's leading sports car drivers, starring in American Le Mans series racing. He took 2nd at Le Mans for Bentley in 2003 and raced on into 2004.

aviation business until 1979–1980. It didn't make much money, but it made sense of flying my own aircraft between the business and the farm, where we had a modest grass runway. Initially just mown pasture, one day I saw some road works nearby using a sizeable grader—a word with the road crew, and they did a lovely job grading my airstrip.

In 1973 I'd bought a brand-new twin-engined Beech Baron which doubled on occasional charter and hire until 1975, when we collected its replacement new from Beech in Wichita, Kansas. Austin and I flew it to Las Vegas, where we spent a couple of diverting nights, then on to San Francisco. Navigational aids weren't as good then, and I didn't fancy finding Hawaii, so a proper ferry pilot then delivered it to Bankstown.

And one day in 1979 I received a letter from someone called Malcolm Frazer at the Prime Minister's office in Canberra. It asked, "If you were offered a Knighthood would you be prepared to accept it?". I wasn't just surprised, I was completely shocked. But I wasn't about to refuse. I'd always been a very proud Australian, and really respected the traditions which shaped us. And so I was knighted for services to motor sport—quite something to see my name paralleled with Sir Henry Segrave and Sir Malcolm Campbell. Mine was the first postwar motor sporting knighthood, and it was years before I would be joined by Sir Frank Williams, Sir Stirling Moss, and Sir Jackie Stewart. The knighthood really helps when you're trying to book a decent table in Californian restaurants but it doesn't come with any money.

Meanwhile I'd begun to accept occasional invitations to race for fun, starting with an Australian Race of Champions at Calder, in Formula Ford single-seaters. I squeezed into the car we were running under our Ford dealership colours for Bob Beasley, and won.

I'd do the same again subsequently in America, and I was teamed with Stirling Moss in a Holden in the 1976 Bathurst 1,000 saloon car classic. During practice, entering the right-angle corner onto the pit straight at the end of the 150mph (240km/h) downhill Con-Rod Straight I was right behind Frank Gardner when I found that I had no brakes.

As he turned into the corner I managed to smash-in second gear—which locked-up the rear wheels—and just (and I mean just) missed his tail and whizzed up the escape road. An all-nighter replaced the car's engine and gearbox, but on the starting grid I could not find a gear and got stuffed up the tail. In 1977 I co-drove there with my son Geoffrey and lost third place only when the engine blew.

Historic "Retro" events followed worldwide. I was able to drive my old cars again—the 1961 Kimberly-Cooper at Laguna Seca, a *Lowline* and other cars at Lord March's stupendous Goodwood Festival and Revival events. Then South Australians Dean Rainsford and Dave Edwards founded the Adelaide Classic Rally, and asked me to become its patron, plus Retro Formula 1 races on the Adelaide Grand Prix circuit.

The Goodwood Revival of 1999 was flooded, but wet weather racing had never bothered me, and Stirling in a loaned Maserati 250F and myself in Noddy Coombs's *Lowline* both shone that day, like old times. Unfortunately, I came unstuck there in 2000 in the McCaw collection's '67 McLaren-BRM. I was tagged from behind and spun backwards into the bank. I'm told it looked terrible but I was unconcious at the time, after cracking my head against the roll-over bar. For the first time ever, a racing accident put me in hospital overnight. I was concussed, had cracked ribs and bruised lungs. It only really hurt when I laughed. Every visitor made it hurt. Then, you wouldn't believe it, in the Adelaide Classic a jay-walking tree hit my loaned Aston Martin DB4GT.

In to 2004 I am still driving whenever I get the chance: in Galaxies and Cobras at Goodwood's Festival of Speed and Revival Meeting. I really enjoy demonstrating our old Brabhams whenever asked.

Along the way, Roy Coburn had introduced a lady named Margaret Taylor. She became my Ford dealership secretary in 1970, and later joined the aviation business. They say Australians are not romantic people. I dispute such Pommie allegations. Margaret has never really forgiven me, but I did tell her one day, "You know, Margaret, you've really grown on me...like a wart".

Betty and I were divorced in 1994. Margaret and I then married in November 1995 and we are very happy together. Meanwhile, I had sold the Bankstown aviation business. Someone walked in the door and asked if I'd be interested in selling. I locked the doors so he couldn't get out and did the deal. I'd sold my Chessington garage in 1971–1972 to BP, then rented it back before finally passing it over to our manager, Brian Turner. I kept the Ewell garage longest, selling it only in 2002. I'd started Engine Developments Ltd with John Judd, our ex-Climax, ex-Repco engineer—who eventually took it over and has run it very successfully ever since.

Margaret and I lived in Sydney until 1998, then moved to Surfers' Paradise, Queensland. I stopped flying when I sold the farm as I had no further use for a private plane. Just like a racing car—unless you've got a use for an aeroplane, you'r better off without one. Margaret had two daughters and between us now we have 10 grandchildren. Geoffrey's boy Matthew is showing great promise racing karts, Gary has two boys (Lachlan and William), and David three (Jason, Sam, and Finn). Margaret's daughter Susan has two boys (Kurt and Clayton), and her daughter Carol has two girls (Belinda and Briony).

And after all these years of clean, restful living, never having put myself at any risk—simple food, no more than one glass of wine with a meal, and never having smoked a cigarette—plus the occasional slice of good luck, I really don't feel my age. But one day, I'm told, I might at last grow up.

I'll let you into one final secret, which some have said before but it's certainly true of me, I want to be a man who dies without an enemy in the world; I aim to outlive the bastards.

BELOW
Sun, sea, the lure of speed, and a satisfying life, apart from not having seen so many of my friends lose theirs, one could ask for little more.

INDEX

Figures in *italics* indicate captions.

AAR Eagle *218*
Abarth 51
Absalom, Hughie *204*
ACL 221
Adelaide Classic Rally *30*, 252
Adelaide GP 252
Agapiou brothers *236*
Aintree 13, *51*, *53*, *54*, 56, 65, 70-1, 85, 143, *149*, 154
Aintree "200" 81, 142, 151-2, 157, *158*, *170*, 171, *171*
Albert Park, Melbourne 7, 37, *102*, 103, 105
Albi 178, 213, 214, 249
Allison, Cliff 68, 71, 94-5, 126
Alta works *59*
Amilcar *28*, 30
Amon, Chris *163*, 189, 209, 219, *226*, 229, 240-43
Anderson, Bob 210
Andretti, Mario *221*
Anglo-America Racers Eagle *13*, *178*
Ardmore aerodrome circuit 37, 44, 49, *103*, 104, *104*, 105, *106*, 185
Argentine GP 36, 69, 79, 104, 111-2, *112*
Armstrong, Bill *24*, 27
Arundell, Peter 162, *162*, 175, *175*, 213
Ashby, Frank 37
Aspern aerodrome, Vienna 212-13
Aston Martin 7, 15, 55, *68*, 72, 76, 79, *88*, 200
  DB3S sports cars 51
  DB4GT 252
  DBR1 76
Atkins, Tommy 79, 108, *110*, 127, 145
Attwood, Richard 181, 213
Austin Tauranac 249
Austin-Healey 3000 sports car 140
Australian GP *34*, 37, 49, 57, *57*, 103, 156, 185, 187, *187*, 188
Australian Hill-Climb Championship 11
Australian National Formula Junior Championship 149
Australian Race of Champions 252
Austrian GP *144*, 162, 164, 177, *177*
Autocar Formula 2 Championship 214
AVUS track, Berlin 85, 87, *87*, 121

Baghetti, Giancarlo 142, *183*
Bahamas Speed Week 91, 126
Baldwin, Bert *200*
Ball, Ernie 35
Bandini, Lorenzo 162, 177, 178, 179, 182, 196, 201, 208
Barber, John 36
Barcelona *15*, 194, 230
Barlow, Vic 133, 143
Barney, Mike 93, 111, 116
Bathurst 107, 121, 129, *189*
Bathurst 1,000 race *204*, 252, *252*
Bathurst "100" 189
Bedding, Fred and Pete *50*
Behra, Jean 74, 82, 85, 87
Belgian GP *9*, *11*, 74, *116*, 117-8, *118*, 143, 153, 158, *174*, 175, 176, 178, 194-6, 208
Beltoise, Jean-Pierre 237, 240, 243
Bettenhausen, Tony 130
Billington, Roy 151, 152, *175*, 185, 186, 188, 193, *204*, 218, *251*
Binython, Kim 35
Bira, Prince (Birabongse Bhandubandh), 54
Blanch, David 7
Bonnier, Jo 75, 82, 84, 112, 121, 142, 163, *163*
Bowmaker Lowline 105
Bowmaker team 108, 185
Bowmaker-Yeoman *144*

Brabham
  BT23A 188
  BT25 222, *223*-5, 239
  BT30 239
  BT31 *189*
  BT33 *238*, 239, *243*, *245*, 247
Brabham, Betty (first wife) 14, *33*, 49, 55, 56, 57, *65*, 69, 88, 133, 140, 162, *217*, 231, 243, 249, 251, 253
Brabham, David 36, *204*, *207*, *217*, *250*, 252, 253
Brabham, Gary 36, 133, *207*, *217*, *250*, 252, 253
Brabham, Geoffrey 36, 49, 55, 56, 59, 69, 162, *204*, *207*, *211*, *217*, 252, 253
Brabham, Sir Jack (John Arthur), OBE
  background 11
  early life and education 19-21
  first "business venture" 21
  RAAF service 21, 22-4, *22*, *23*, 24
  midget racing 11, 26-7, *27*, *28*, 30-1, *30*, *31*, 33, 35
  first motor race 31, 33
  buys the *RedeX Special* 36
  sells the *RedeX Special* 49
  arrives in Britain 52
  turning point in his career 55
  starts to race full-time for Cooper 64
  World Champion Driver (1959) 10, *10*, 96-7, *96*, *97*, 106, 130, 211
  World Champion Driver (1960) *9*, 10, *10*, 106, 121, 122, 211
  Chessington garage business *138*, 149, 253
  MRD set up 14, 141, *165*
  leaves Cooper 142, 145, 149
  and first major "Brabham" victory 175, *175*
  World Champion Driver (1966) 15, *196*, *204*, 205
  wins French GP (1966) 197
  serious injury at Silverstone (1969) 227-8, 230, *235*
  father urges him to retire 243, *244*, 246
  his last Grand Prix 247
  aviation company 250, 251, 252, 253
  Ford dealership in Sydney 251
  knighthood 252
Brabham, Margaret (second wife) *248*, 253
Brabham, May (mother) 19, 243, 249-50
Brabham, Mr (father) 243, *244*, 246
Brabham, Tom 11
Brabham- Honda BT30 215
Brabham-BRM BT8 sports car *179*
Brabham-Climax *163*, 171, 177, 188, *188*, 194, 202, 210
  BT2 149
  BT3 *147*, *148*, 149, 151, *153*, 154, 156, 160, 161, 162, *163*, 164-7
  BT4 156, 185
  BT5 *156*, *157*
  BT7 156-7, *160*, 161, 162, 178
  BT8 162
  BT10 *176*, 213
  BT11 178, *180*, *182*
  BT17 193
Brabham-Cosworth BT26A *226*, 228, *231*, 232, *233*, 235
Brabham-Honda 15, 192-3, 194, 196, 199, 203, 214, *214*
  BT18 *196*, *212*, 214
  BT19 *197*, *199*, *249*
  BT21 214
  BT23C 215
Brabham-Offenhauser BT12 172
Brabham Formula Junior 145, 149, 151, 156, *158*
Brabham Racing Organisation team 14, *147*, *168*, *204*, *206*, 211, 219
Brands Hatch 15, 42, 56, 64, 69, 71, 75-6, 80, 88, 103, 108, *140*, 143, 145, 148, 151, 154, 156, 176, 181, 192, 197, 199, *199*, 200, 203,

207, 214-5, 220, 229, 237, 239, 243, 244-5, *245*, 247
BRDC International Trophy 49, 54, *80*, *81*, 114-5, *192*, 228
Brinton, Alan 59, 60, 141, *245*
Bristow, Chris 11, 118
British Autocar Championship 108
British Automobile Racing Club 52
British GP 9, 10, 13, 15, *50*, *51*, *53*, *54*, 56, 65, 75, *76*, 85, 85, 119, *119*, 120, *120*, 143, *149*, 154, 159-60, 176, 181, 197, 199, *199*, 220, 244-5, *245*, 247
British Racing Drivers' Club (BRDC) 54, 111
Broad, Patricia *106*
Brooks, Tony 65, 66, 67, *69*, 74, 75, 78, 80, 82, 84, 87, *87*, 89-90, 93-6, *94*, 96
Brown, Alan 169, 170, 181, *251*
Brown, David 79
Brussels GP 113, *113*, *114*, 145
Buckler, Derek 141
Buenos Aires 36, 69, 104, 111, *112*

Cabral, Mario 87
Calder 252
California "500" *240*
Campbell, Donald 185
Can-Am series 211, 214, 236, 237
Canadian GP 15, 155, 210, *216*, *227*, 230, 246
CanAm sports cars *14*
Catalina Park 149
Caversham aerodrome, near Perth 185
Centro Sud team 87
Cevert, François 215, 246
Chaparral sports car company 127
Chapman, Colin 15, 71, *76*, *88*, 112, 115, 127, 141, *150*, 151, 152, 157-8, 197, *221*, 239, 241, *244*
Charlton, Dave 191
Chase, Bob 54, 55
Christchurch 104-8, *106*, 186
Chrysler 77 20
Clark, Jim *110*, 120, 144, *144*, 151, 152, 153, 155-6, 158-63, *161*, *163*, 169, 170, *171*, *171*, *174*, 175-8, *176*, *179*, *184*, 187, 188, *188*, 193, 199-200, 202-3, *203*, 208-210, 212-15, *221*
Clermont-Ferrand 181, *181*, *182*, 213, 243
Cobden, Dick 17, 42, 44, 51
Coburn, Roy 250, 251, 253
College Station, Texas 237
Collins, Peter 54, 65, *75*, *75*, *76*, *76*, 79
Colotti, Valerio 80
Confederation of Australian Motor Sport (CAMS) 37, 44, *45*
Constructors' World Championship 10, 11, 77, 89, *90*, *99*, 121, 155, *188*, *206*, *207*, 211
Coombs, John (Noddy) 91, 125-6, 212, 214, 215, 239, 252
Cooper, Charles 13, *50*, *51*, 54, 58, 60, 69, 70, 77, 79, *79*, 80, 82, 89, *97*, 103, 104, 111, *111*, 113-6, *115*, 119, *119*, 139, 140, 142
Cooper, John 13, 36, 49, *50*, 51, 52, 54, 55, 57, *61*, 66, 67-8, 70, 71, 75, 79, *79*, 80, 82, 88-91, *88*, 93-7, *97*, 104, 107, 108, 111, 113, 114, 122, 124, *128*, 129-31, *131*, 133, 139, 140, 142, 144, 197, 249, *251*
Cooper *Monaco* 15, 91, 124, *125*, 126, *127*, 155, 185
Cooper Slimline 144, 149
Cooper-Alta 7, 13, *47*, *48*, 49, 51, 52, 54, 56, 81
Cooper-Bristol 13, 36, 39, *47*, 54
  Bobtail *50*, *51*, *53*, 54, *55*, 56, *57*, 58, *58*, 65, 103, 104, 108, 124
  RedeX Special 17, *34*, 36, *36*, 37, *38*, 39, *39*, *41*, 44, 45, 47, 49, 51
Cooper-Climax 7, 14, *14*, 15, 60-1, *62*, *63*, 69, 74, 75, 78, *91*, 96, *103*, 105, 108, 109, *113*,

128, *130*, *143*, 153
  Lowline *9*, *10*, 11, 108, *110*, 111, 113, 114, 115, *115*, *116*, 117, 118, *118*, *119*, 127, 129, 139-42, *144*, *145*, 200
  T51 98, *99*, *100*
  V8 143-4, *143*, 149, *149*, *152*, *153*, 160
Cooper-JAP 1000 *256*
Cooper-JAP 1100 11
Cooper-Maserati 87, 195, 196, 199, 201, *203*, 205, 209
Copenhagen GP *149*
Cosh, Les 51
Cosworth 196
Courage, Piers 215, 231, *231*, 241, 242, 243, *244*
Courage, Sally 243
Cousins, Ron 218-19, 221
Coventry Climax 13, 60, *61*, 77, 131, *139*, 159, 193
Crombac, "Jabby" 64
Crombie, Wing Commander 22, 23, 24, 250
Crouch, John 35, 36, *57*
Crystal Palace circuit 56, *56*, 64, 108, 194, 212, *212*
Cunningham, Briggs *126*

Danish Grand Prix *122*
Dark, Eddie 35
Davison, Lex 17, 44, 70, 104, 109, *169*, *184*, 187
Daytona 239
Daytona 24-Hours 237
Delamont, Dean 13, 44-5, 49, 57, *65*, 95, *251*
Dennis, Ron 228, 245
Dibley, Hugh 193
Driver's World Championship 10, *12*, 13, 15, 78, 79, 89, 91, *92*, 94, 95, *95*, 195
Dundrod *50*
Dunlop Tyre Company/tyres 13, 44, 105, 130, *132*, 133, 135, *135*, 136, 143, *165*, 169, 188
Dutch GP *9*, 15, 74, 82, 84, 116-17, 132-3, *147*, 152, 158-9, *159*, 173, 175, *182*, 199, *199*, *218*, 219, 231, 242-3, *244*
Dvoretsky, "Dev" *84*

Eagle cars 14, 194, *197*, 208, 209, 220
Eagle-Climax 199
Eaton, George 237
Ecclestone, Bernie 249
Ecurie Australia car *184*
Ecurie Ecosse team 126
Edwards, Dave 252
Ellsworth, Stan 151
Engine Developments Ltd 253
Enna, Sicily 161, 162, 213
ERSA 64
Essarts circuit, Les 65
Esso *4*, *45*, 52, 91, *102*, *204*, 246

Falkner, Dr Frank 93, *97*, 129, 130
Fangio, Juan 15, 65, 69, *75*, 91
Fengler, Harlan 130
Ferguson, Andrew 111
Ferguson, Harry 22
Ferrari
  Enzo 122
  Monza 104, *104*
  "Sharknose" 144, *145*
  SuperSqualo *103*, 104
FIA (Federation Internationale de l'Automobile) 69, 74, 108, 212, *233*
Firestone tyres 136, 188, 201
Fittipaldi, Emerson 246
Flockhart, Ron 65, *65*, 76, *83*, 89, *105*, 107
Ford
  Falcon 194
  G7A CanAm car 236-7, *236*
  Galaxie 169
  Mustang 181, 194, *251*

Zephyr 104
Zodiac 159
Foyt, A.J. *173*
Frankenheimer, John 199
Frazer, Malcolm 252
Freighter Trailers *18*
French GP *9*, *10*, 14-5, 65, 68, 74-5, *75*, 78, 84-5, 118-9, *119*, *142*, 143, 153, 159, *168*, *174*, 175, *175*, 176, 181, *181*, *182*, *183*, 190, 196, *196*, 209, *209*, 227, 243

Gardner, Frank 151, 152, 157, *158*, *184*, *188*, 211, 213, 215, *250*, 252
Gavin, Bill 213
Gaze, Tony 37, 44, 51
Gendebien, Olivier 77, 84, 119
German GP 14, 15, 65, 75, 76, 85, 87, *87*, *139*, 143-4, *144*, 152, 154, 161, 164, *166*, *182*, *200*, *203*, 206, 209-210, *210*, 220, *220*, 227, *227*, *231*, 232, *233*, 245-6
Gethin, Peter *247*
Gibbins, Bob 35
Gilmore Broadcasting Brabham BT32 *240*
Ginther, Richie 152, 162-3, *177*, 182, 183
Giunti, Ignazio 246
Glass, Arnold "Trinkets" *70*, 185
Glover Trophy 60, 70
Gnoo Blas circuit 36-7
Goddard, Geoffrey *117*
Goodwood 7, 13, *39*, *47*, 49, 52, 55, 60, 68, 70, 80, 81, 89, 90, 108, 125, 126, 141, *142*, 151, 154, *156*, 157, *157*, *158*, 164, 169-70, *169*, 179, *179*, 191, 193, 241
Goodwood Festival of Speed *249*, 252
Goodwood Revival *251*, 252
Goodyear 179, 187, 188, 189, 199, *200*, 201-2, 227, 242, 246
Goozee, Nick 245
Gould, Horace 39, 40
Grande Epreuves 11, 14
'Grands Prix de France' 15, 108
Grant, Gregor 56, 64
Greason, Reg 44
Gregory, Masten 79, *79*, 80, 81, 82, 84, 85, 87, 89, *89*, 90, 155, 172, *173*, 222
Grohmann, "Noddy" 82, *88*, *92*, 93, 111, 116, 129, 159, 187
Guards Trophy 203
Gulf-McLaren 237
Gurney, Dan 14, 89, 113, 120, 121, *123*, 142, *145*, 153, 155, 155, 156, 157, 159, *160*, *168*, *171*, *174*, 175, *175*, 176, 177, 178, *178*, 181, *182*, 183, 187, 194, 197, *197*, 208, 209, *209*, 218, *218*, 220

Hall, Jim 127
Hallam, Frank 251
Hameenlinna, Finland 215
Hassan, Wally 71, 81, 143, 154, 157-8
Hawkins, Paul *158*
Hawthorn, Mike 54, *54*, 65, *71*, 75, 76, *76*, 77, 79, 91
Herrmann, Hans 85, *87*
Hewland, Mike 158, 194
Heysel circuit *145*
Hill, Graham 70, 71, *76*, 88, *110*, 120, *120*, 126, 153, 156, 159, 162, 169, 171, 175-9, *175*, *179*, *180*, 182, 187, 188, 209-13, 215, *221*, 230, *247*, 249
Hill, Phil 77, *78*, 89, *90*, 118, 119, *124*, 144, 153, 187, 188
Hillard, Keith *45*
Hobbs, David *158*
Hockenheim 215, 245
Holbay company 141
Holbert, Bob 155
Holden 40, 43, 44, 44
Honda 170-1, 182, 183, 192, 213, 214, 215
Hulme, Denny 14, *14*, 15, 115, 156, 157, *158*, 159, 161, 164, *176*, 178, 179, 181, *181*, *183*, 186, 187, 188, *188*, 191, 193, 194, 195, 196, *196*, *197*, 199, *199*, 200, 202, 203, *204*, 205, *206*, 207, 208, *208*, 210, 211, 213, 214, 218, 231, 240, 243, *247*
Hunt, Reg 35, 57
Hurstville, near Sydney 19

HWM-Jaguar 44
Hyeres 55

Ian Walker Racing team 157, *157*
Ibsley aerodrome 13, *48*, 54
Ickx, Jacky 15, 194, 215, 221, 226, 227, *227*, 229-32, *231*, *233*, 240, 244, 246, 247
Ickx, Pascal 227
Imola 58, *58*
IMSA GTP title *204*, *207*
Indianapolis 15, 127-37, 168, 172, 172-3, *173*, 193, 222, *223*, 229, 240
Indy BT12 *249*
InterContinental Formula (ICF) races 145
Ireland, Innes 112, 115, 117, 122, *144*, *145*, 162, *163*, 169, 177
Irving, Phil 193
Irwin, Chris 214
Italian GP 15, 68, 77, 88-9, *90*, 121, 144, 161, 164, *182*, *183*, 200, 203-5, 210, 221, *221*, 227-8, 246

Jaguar E2A *126*
James, Bill 82, *84*
Jarama circuit, Madrid 211, 215, 218, *239*, 240
Jeffrey, Dick 13, 44, 45
Jenkinson, Denis 7, 10, 231
Jennings, Spike 35
Jensen, Ross 105
Jensen, Syd *103*
Jones, Alan 49, *169*
Jones, Parnelli *173*
Jones, Stan 44, 49, 57, 104, *169*
Judd, John 218, 221, 253

Kangaroo Stable 51, 55-6
Karlskoga, Sweden 126, *145*, 161, 164, 202, 213, 214
Katoomba circuit *36*
Kawamoto, Nobuhiko 214, *251*
Keimola 203
Kent Trophy 108
Kentish "100" 76, 88, 108
Kerr, Phil 79, 104, *140*, 141, 159, 162, *204*
Kilburn Speedway, Adelaide *30*
Kimberly, Jim 130-31, *133*, *135*, 136
Kimberly Cooper-Climax 131, *133*, 136, *136*, 252
Kingsford-Smith Aviation 250
Kyalami 207, 218, *226*, 227, *238*, 239

Lady Wigram Trophy 104, *105*, 106, *106*, 107, 185
Laguna Seca 126, 127, 155, 252
Lakeside, Brisbane *187*, *188*
Lambert, Chris 215
Lavant Cup Formula 2 race 108
Lawson Organisation 218
Le Mans 49, *50*, 65, *65*, 76-7, 209, 214, 239
Le Mans 24-Hour race 55, *126*, *204*, 237
Lee, Leonard 71, 77, 79, 98, 193
Levin circuit 105, 108, 185
Lewis-Evans, Stuart 69, *70*, 77
Light Car Club 35
Ligier, Guy 209, 210
Lister-Jaguar 82
Lola-Chevrolet 193, 214
Lola-Climax V8 153
London Trophy 64
Longford circuit, Tasmania *4*, 108, 109, 187-8, *187*, 192
Los Angeles Times GP *124*
Lotus
  49T 189
  Monte Carlo 127
  Type 18 112, 117-18, 119
  Type 19 127, 155
  Type 21 *144*, 151
  Type 23 155
  Type 24 149, 152, 154-5, 158, 162
  Type 25 *150*, 158, 159, 161, *163*
  Type 32 *176*
  Type 33 *170*, 171, *171*, 188
  Type 49 208, 209, 211, *221*, 229, 230, 240
  Type 72 242, 246

Lotus-Climax 188, *188*
  24 151, *162*
  V8 191
Lotus-Cortina 194, *251*
Loudon, Nick 214
Love, John 191, 209
Lukey, Len 106, *191*
Lycoming Special *105*
Lyons, Pete 236

McCaffrey, Christine *204*
Macdonald, Dave 172, *173*
MacDowel, Mike 64
McGrath, Charles 193
McKay, David 51, *169*, *184*, 185, 187, *187*, 202
McLaren 231, 236, 240
McLaren, Bruce *14*, 39, 44, 69, 75, 77, 79, *79*, 84, 85, 89, 90, *90*, 93-6, *96*, *97*, 104-8, *106*, *107*, *110*, 111-16, *112*, 118, 121, 122, *125*, 127, 129, *139*, *140*, 145, 153, 158, *161*, 175, *178*, 181, 185-8, *187*, 211, *236*, 237, 241-2, 243, *244*
McLaren, Leslie "Pop" 37, 39, 44, 104
McLaren M8B 236
Maddock, Owen *51*, 111, *111*, 113, 139
Maggs, Tony 212, 213
Mairesse, Willy 118, 152-3
Mallory Park 153, 212
Mann, Alan 237
Mansell, Johnny *105*
March, Lord *249*, 252
Maserati
  250F 13, 44, *49*, 55, 56, 57, *59*, 63, 104, 105, *105*
  Lightweight 65
Matich, Frank *169*, 186
Matra team 15, 237, *237*, 239
Matra-Ford 229, 230
Maybach Special 44, 49, 57
Mays, Raymond 111
Mediterranean GP 161
Mehl, Leo 227
Melbourne GP *102*, 105
Mercedes-Benz 51, 55
Mexican GP 15, 155-6, 163, 164, 178, 182-3, *182*, 205, 221, 237, 246, 247, *247*
Michigan Raceway 236
Mildren, Alec 104, *184*
Mille Miglia race *70*
Monaco GP 10, 13, *13*, 15, 60-61, *62-3*, 64, 74, 81, *81*, 82, *83*, *84*, 95, 98, 115, 124, 132, 143, 157, 158, *171*, 172, 179, *180*, 181, 208, *208*, 215, 218, 230, *231*, *233*, 240-41, *243*
Monsanto Park circuit, Lisbon 87, *88*
Montlhéry 64, 108, 152, 178, 213, 237
Monza 68, 77, 88, 89, *90*, 121, 144, 162, 178, 182, 205, 215, *216*, 221, *221*, 227, 230, 231, 239, *241*, 246, *247*
Moore, Denny 173
Moroccan GP 68-9, *69*, 77
Morrice, Peter 55
Moser, Silvio 220
Mosport Park 155, 210, 230, 231
Moss, Sir Stirling, OBE FIE *4*, *7*, 7, *11*, 54, 55, 56, 65, *66*, 69, 70-71, *71*, *72*, 75, 76, 77, 80, *80*, 81, 82, 84, 85, 87-91, *90*, *91*, 93-4, *94*, 95, 98, 104-8, *107*, *110*, 112, *114*, 115, 116, 117, 120, 121, 122, *123*, 126, 143, 144, 189, 200, 252
Motor Racing Developments Ltd (MRD) 14, *14*, 15, *140*, 141, 142, 145, 148, *148*, *157*, 165, 169, 178, *206*, 249
MRD 141-2
MRD-FJ 142
Mt Druitt circuit 36, 39, *42*, 57, 256
Muller, John *204*
Murray, David 126
Murray, Gordon 249
Musso, Luigi 75, 79

Nakamura, Yoshio 170, 193, 214
Nassau 126
Nassau Trophy 91
Neil, Merv 105
New South Wales Championship 11, 33, 37
New South Wales GP 37

New Zealand GP 7, 13, 37, 44, 49, 54, 57, 69, *69*, 103, *103*, 104-8, *104*, 106, *107*, *184*, 185, 186
Nürburgring 7, 14, 65, 72, 75, 76, *139*, 143, *143*, *144*, 152, 154, 161, 162, 177, 200, *200*, 201, *206*, 209, *210*, 220, 227

Oliver, Jackie 240
Oran Park 188
Orange 37, *40*, 57, 106
OSCA 58
Oulton Park 103, 178, 181, 192, 193
Oulton Park Gold Cup 68, 89, *91*, 108, *110*, 121, 125, 144, 155, 162, 164, *176*, 205, 207, 211, *211*, 213, *233*
Oulton Park Spring Cup 207
Oulton Park Tourist Trophy 193
Owen Racing Organisation 59

Palmer, Jim 184
Parkes, Mike 196, *196*, 197, *203*, 205, 207
Parnell, Reg 37, 44, *103*, 104
Parnell team *163*, 181
Parramatta Park Speedway, Sydney 11, 27, 31, 35
Pau 81, 113, *145*, 213, 215
Pau GP 151
Pearce, George 256
Pescara GP 66, *66*, 67
Pescarolo, Henri 243
Phil Irving HRD Supercharged Special 35
Philip Island 103
Piccolo Maserati *75*
Pierpoint, Roy 194
Piper, David *107*, 120
Piquet, Nelson 249
Pontiac GP car *124*, 127
Port Wakefield, South Australia 57, *57*
Portuguese GP 9, 87, *88*, 89, 108, 120-21
Prix de Paris 64

Queensland Road Racing Championship 36, 37

RAAF *21*, 22-3, 26
Raby, Ian 65
RAC Tourist Trophy *142*
Rainsford, Dean 252
Ralt racing specials 139
Ramsey, Aub 35
Rand GP 191
Ravell, Ray *28*, 33
RedeX 11, 13, 37, 40, *40*, 44, 104
RedeX Round-Australia Trial 40, 42-4, *44*
Rees, Alan *176*, 196, *212*, 213, 214
Regazzoni, Clay 215, 246, 247
Reid, John 141
Reims-Gueux *10*, 74, 75, *78*, 84, 118-19, *119*, 143, 153, 159, 196, *196*, *197*, 213
Repco *145*, 151, 186, 188, 189, 193, 207, 215, 216, 217, 221, 222, *224*, 219
Repco Brabham 14, 15, 149, 185-6, 187, *189*, 191, *192*, 197, 199, 205, 206, 221
  BT19 *4*, *13*, *190*, *191*, 194, 202, 203, 204, 208, *208*, 221
  BT20 199, 203, 204, 205, 207, 208, 209, 220, 221
  BT24 *14*, *206*, 208, 209, *209*, 210, 218, *218*, 220, 221, *249*
  BT25 229
  BT26 *216*, 218, *219*, 220, 229, *231*
  BT30 215
  BT31 189, 221
Reventlow, Lance *109*
Revson, Peter 222
Richardson, Gordon 155
Rindt, Jochen 15, *176*, 189, 195, 196, 199, *203*, 207, 211-6, *216*, 218, *218*, 219-22, *220*, 227, 229, 230-1, *231*, 239-47, *247*
Riverside Raceway 122, *124*, *125*, 126-7, *126*, *127*, 155, 179, 239
Rob Roy hill-climb 35, 37
Roche, "Toto" 68-9
Rodriguez, Pedro 207, 242
Rodriguez, Ricardo 152, 155
Rome GP 213
Roskilde, Denmark 126, *145*, 154-5
Rouen-les-Essarts 153, *168*, *174*, 175, *175*, 214, 215, 220

Royal Automobile Club 13, 44
RRC Walker Racing Ltd 71, 74
Ruby, Lloyd *173*

Sachs, Eddie *133*, 172, *173*
Salvadori, Roy 54, 64-8, *69*, *70*, 74, 75, 79, *88*, 108-9, *110*, 126, 144, 249
Sandown Park, Melbourne 109, *109*, 187, *187*, 188, 189, 191
Scarab InterContinental 109
Schell, Harry 56, 59-60, *92*, 93, 114-15
Schlesser, Jo 152, *158*, *176*, 213
Schonberg, Johnny 11, *24*, 26, 27, *123*
Scott-Brown, Archie *70*
Scribante, Aldo 191
Scuderia Veloce *184*
Sebring, Florida 13, 89, 90, 91, *92*, 93-7, *112*, 122, 126, 129
Senior, Art *28*, 30
Sharp, Hap *125*, 127
Shelly, Tony 186
Shepheard, Reg 36, 37
Siffert, Jo 230
Silverstone 15, *49*, 54, 68, 75, *76*, *80*, 81-2, 98, 113, 114, *115*, 119, 120, *120*, 125, 131, *139*, 143, 152, 157-60, 164, 171-2, 179, *192*, 193-4, *194*, 207, 210, 226-30, *227*, *228*, 242
Smith, Clay 130
Snetterton *55*, 56, 89, 125, 151, 169, 213
Solitude GP *153*, 160, *162*, *163*, 176-7
South African GP 10, 15, 156, 164, 178, 185, 189, 191, *191*, 207, *226*, *238*, 239
Spa-Francorchamps 11, *116*, 117, 118, *118*, 153, 158, *174*, 175, 181, 194-5, 242
Spanish GP 15, 230, *239*, 240
Speedway Royale *26*, *28*, *31*, 33, *33*

Spence, Mike 183, 191
Spiers, Harry *61*, *148*
Stacey, Alan *11*, 118
Stewart, Sir Jackie 179, 182, 183, 188, *188*, 196, 202, 204, 213, 229, *231*, 239, *239*, 240, 241, 246, 252
Stillwell, Bib *70*, *169*, 185, 186, 188, 250
Stommelen, Rolf 242, 246
Sulman, Tommy 42, 51
Surtees, John 109, *110*, 120, 121, *121*, *144*, 153, 162, 176-9, 185, 194, 195, 196, 201, 202, *203*, 204, 205, 207, 210, 211, *218*, 230, 231
Surtees, Pat 109
Sutton, Ken 35
Sydney Royal Showground 11, 33, 35
Syracuse GP 59, 60, 113, 142, *183*, 193

Tasman Championship 103, 188, 189
Tauranac, Austin 11, 13, 35, 139, 251
Tauranac, Norma 139, 140
Tauranac, Ron 11, *14*, 15, *15*, 27, 35, *61*, 109, 139, 140-41, *140*, 145, 148, *150*, 151, *151*, *153*, 154, *154*, 156, *157*, 159, 162, 164, *165*, *178*, 186, *190*, 193, 199, *204*, *206*, 211, 213, 217, 222, *223*, 229, 232, *233*, 237, 238, 239, *245*, 251
Tavoni, Romolo 93
Taylor, Cary *204*
Taylor, Geoffrey 54, *59*
Taylor, Henry 119
Taylor, Mike *11*, 91, 118
Taylor, Sid 193, 214
Taylor, Simon 214
Taylor, Trev 160, 161, 162, *163*
Team Gunston 209, 218
Teretonga 105, 106, 185

Thompson, Mickey 172
Thompson, Reg 57, *102*, 191
Times GP 127
Tingle, Sam 218
Tojeiro-Jaguar sports car *105*
Tourist Trophy 50
Tresise, Rocky *187*
Trintignant, Maurice "Trint" 74, 75, *80*, *92*, 95, *96*, 114
Tulln-Langenlebarn, Austria 215
Turle, Bryan 52
Turner, Brian 253
Tyrrell, Ken *90*, 194, *238*, 239, 246

UDT-Laystall 155
United States Automobile Club (USAC) 130, *130*, 131, *131*, 135, 222, *223*
United States GP 13, 14, 89, *92*, 93-7, 121, 122, 126, 127, 144, *153*, 155, 162-3, 164, 182, *182*, 205, 210, 211, 221, *231*, 236, 246

Vallelunga 213
van Rooyen, Basil 218
Vanwall 56, 65, *66*, *69*, 74, 75, *75*, 77
von Trips, "Taffy" 75, 94, 95, *119*, 144

Walker, Pete 56
Walker, Rob 59, 60, *62*, 69, 89, 91, 104, 106, 108, 112, 115, *123*, 155, *163*, *247*
Walker Cooper 7, *7*, 60, 61, *62*, 68-71, 74, 76, 80, *80*, 81, 87, 88, *90*, *92*, 95, 105, 108, 113, 121, 163
Walker Cooper-Climax 82
Walker Lotus 107, 108, *110*, 115, 116, 117, 120, 121, 144

Wall, Tim 91, 93, *102*, 109, 111, *123*, *145*, 151, 159, 185
Ward, Rodger *128*, 129, 130
Warwick Farm "100" 108, 189
Warwick Farm, Sydney 107, 185-8, *188*
Watkins Glen 126, 144, *153*, 155, 162, 178, 182, 205, 210, 211, 221, 230, 231, 246
Watson-Offy *173*
Weiss, Sam *127*
West Coast Professional series 126
Wharton, Ken 37, 56, *103*, 104, *104*
Wheatcroft, Tom 232
Whitehead, Peter 37, *42*, *47*, 49, *49*, 52, 54, *103*, 104
Wiles, Geoff 104
Williams, Sir Frank 215, *231*, 241, 242, 252
Williams, Jonathan 215
Wilson, Norm 218
Windsor-Smith, Peter 154
Winkelmann Racing 213, 214, 215
Winkelmann, Roy 196, *212*, 213
Wisdom, Norman *138*
World Championship of Makes race 237

Yarbrough, Lee Roy *240*
Yeoman Credit Cooper *107*, 115, 118, 119, *119*, 121, 142
Youl, Gavin 141, *142*, 149

Zandvoort 74, 82, 116, 117, 132, 143, *147*, 152, 158, *159*, *161*, 173, 199, *199*, 200, *200*, 208, 215, 219, 227, 230, 242, *244*
Zeltweg aerodrome *144*, 145, 162, 177, *177*
Zink, John 169, 173, *173*
Zolder 194, 215

Acknowledgements

THE AUTHORS AND PUBLISHERS would like to thank all those who have contributed to this autobiography. Most particularly Lady Brabham, David and Geoffrey Brabham, Roy Salvadori, John "Noddy" Coombs, Sir Stirling Moss, Sir Jackie Stewart, John Surtees, Dick Cobden, and Nick Goozee have been especially generous in their support, input, and time.

The bulk of the photographs reproduced in these pages are from Sir Jack Brabham's personal collection—accumulated over many years—and from Mr Paul Vestey's GP Library Collection in Britain, encompassing the contemporary work of photographers Geoffrey Goddard, Franco Lini, and the later material of Nigel Snowden.

Particular thanks goes to Jim Brownett in Australia for his special photography of Sir Jack's trophies, driver wear, crash helmets, and other memorabilia, and to Neil Sutherland in Britain for his special photography of the four "landmark cars" from Sir Jack's career preserved for many years within the Donington Collection at Donington Park, Derby, Britain. This would not have been possible without the enthusiastic cooperation of Collection founder Mr Tom Wheatcroft and Mr Kevin Wheatcroft and their helpful staff at what is the World's largest single-seater racing car museum.

Whenever we were in difficulty finding particular images of Australian racing David Blanch of Autopics, Australia, came to the rescue with shots from his superb collection. Riverside sports-racing and Indianapolis photography was provided by Bob Tronolone in California while the CanAm photography is by the great Pete Lyons. Nick Loudon supplied the outstanding Formula 2 images used on pages 212-215. Great help with factual reference and cross-checking has been unstintingly provided by Barry Lake, Ray Bell, and John Midgley in Australia, and by Dave McKinney in the UK. The enduringly enthusiastic Nostalgia Forum membership of <atlasf1.com> has proved its breathtaking specialist racing knowledge many times in connection with production of this work. Special thanks also to Peter Higham and his helpful staff at LAT Photographic—repository in particular of the photo archives of *Autosport*, *Motor Sport*, *Motor*, and *Autocar* magazines. To any other contributor whose name has been omitted here we apologise, this error is entirely ours but all assistance has nonetheless been invaluable in making this work as comprehensive and attractive as it can be.

RIGHT
In the end, the beginning—I broke into road racing with my first Cooper—this second-hand Mark IV fitted with the 1000cc HRD engine from a second-hand motorcycle. At Mt Druitt in May 1953, Clive Turner's rare photo shows us we're ready (8) for a match race with George Pearce's Cooper-JAP 1,000 which I won.